YOUNG FOUCAULT

YOUNG FOUCAULT

THE LILLE MANUSCRIPTS ON PSYCHOPATHOLOGY, PHENOMENOLOGY, AND ANTHROPOLOGY, 1952–1955

ELISABETTA BASSO

TRANSLATED BY
MARIE SATYA MCDONOUGH

FOREWORD BY
BERNARD E. HARCOURT

Columbia University Press   *New York*

Columbia University Press
Publishers Since 1893
New York   Chichester, West Sussex
cup.columbia.edu

Copyright © 2022 Columbia University Press
All rights reserved

Library of Congress Cataloging-in-Publication Data
Names: Basso, Elisabetta, author.
Title: Young Foucault : the Lille manuscripts on psychopathology, phenomenology, and anthropology, 1952–1955 / Elisabetta Basso.
Description: New York : Columbia University Press, [2022] | Includes bibliographical references and index.
Identifiers: LCCN 2021058068 (print) | LCCN 2021058069 (ebook) | ISBN 9780231205849 (hardback) | ISBN 9780231205856 (trade paperback) | ISBN 9780231556194 (ebook)
Subjects: LCSH: Foucault, Michel, 1926–1984. | Foucault, Michel, 1926–1984—Archives. | Foucault, Michel, 1926–1984—Manuscripts. | Binswanger, Ludwig, 1881–1966—Influence. | Phenomenological psychology. | Psychology, Pathological. | Philosophical anthropology. | Psychology and philosophy. | Psychology—History—20th century. | Philosophy, French—20th century.
Classification: LCC B2430.F724 B385 2022 (print) | LCC B2430.F724 (ebook) | DDC 194—dc23/eng/20220316
LC record available at https://lccn.loc.gov/2021058068
LC ebook record available at https://lccn.loc.gov/2021058069

Cover image: Detail from the photograph of
Michel Foucault by Jean-François Miguel.
Cover design: Chang Jae Lee

To my men, Gualtiero and Ludovico

CONTENTS

A Genealogy of Archaeology by Bernard E. Harcourt ix

Introduction: New Avenues for Research 1
1 Archives and Intellectual Networks 15
2 The Binswanger Dossier 81
3 Archaeological Method 137
Conclusion 197

Acknowledgments 207
Notes 211
Bibliography 277
Index 309

A GENEALOGY OF ARCHAEOLOGY

BERNARD E. HARCOURT

The mark of true genius is to elaborate an approach to human inquiry that enters the public imagination and becomes so widespread, it turns invisible. So natural and common, so pervasive, so extensive, people absorb it into their ordinary lives and no longer even recognize that they are using it. Foucault's early method, what he called "archaeology," is just that. An approach to studying how people come to know and understand reality, and live and function within it, Foucault's archaeological method rests on the idea that our experience of reality is embedded in a deep conceptual and epistemological coherence that itself becomes invisible. The method has become so pervasive today that contemporary thinkers deploy a word cloud of expressions with family resemblances—*conditions of possibility, constitutive, organizing concepts, afterlives, styles of reasoning*—to communicate in everyday parlance the idea that Foucault developed under the more technical title of *épistémè*. The method has become so extensive, it now encompasses practically all aspects of human life, from the social and political to the deeply subjective to the outer limits of sexuality. In the political realm, Foucault's method has evolved to reveal the way in which people are embedded within relations of power they often do not even see, yet that shape how they act and, simultaneously, how they unwittingly reproduce those very relations. In the sexual realm, it has evolved to expose how we came of age in a time that took for granted the very notion of "sexuality"—a relatively modern invention, Foucault reminds us—that both shapes us and our conduct and that we reconstitute with our every sexual act.

Remarkably, Foucault's archaeological approach is in itself both a method to study our experience of the world and the very way that we live and experience reality. It is both an analytic technique and our way of being. In both contexts, it rests on a deeply aporetic insight: an impossible combination of inhabiting spaces at the same time that we are shaped and constituted by them and that we reproduce them. And as both the method and the way of being become invisible, the paradox is redoubled, almost like a double helix fading into infinity. Today we have so internalized this mystery, due to the wide proliferation of Foucauldian ideas and writings, that we are almost unable to understand the mystery even when it is unveiled to us. That is what happens when a method—and a way of being—becomes our truth.

In this brilliant book, *Young Foucault*, Elisabetta Basso meticulously disarticulates this aporia and genealogically traces the birth of Foucault's archaeological method back to his formative encounter with phenomenology and existential psychiatry in the early period of 1952–1955. It is at that time—while himself deeply immersed in reading Edmund Husserl and Martin Heidegger, teaching psychology at the University of Lille and the École normale supérieure in Paris, experimenting as a psychologist in an electroencephalography laboratory in a mental hospital and prison, and working through a Marxian form of materialism—that Foucault explores the method of "existential analysis," or what was called at the time in German *Daseinsanalyse*. Developed by the Swiss psychiatrist Ludwig Binswanger, existential analysis draws on the phenomenological writings of Husserl and Heidegger, in active conversation with Sigmund Freud and Carl Jung, to develop a new therapeutic practice beyond psychoanalysis. *Daseinsanalyse* represented for Foucault a methodological innovation that ultimately put him on the path of a historicized theorization of present experience that would ground his mature writings.

With exacting precision, Basso unpeels the layers of Foucault's methodological development, demonstrating how the core archaeological concept of the "historical *a priori*"—if ever there was a paradoxical term!—traces back in steps, first, to the phenomenological use of the notion of the *a priori*, and second, more directly, to the concept of "*a priori* structures" that grounded Binswanger's method of *Daseinsanalyse*. In this manner, Basso draws a through line from Foucault's earliest writings—including his introduction to Binswanger's *Dream and Existence* published in 1954 and his other manuscripts of the period on Binswanger, psychology, phenomenology, and the anthropological question (only now being published)—to his mature works of archaeology from the 1960s culminating in *The Order of Things: An Archaeology of the Human Sciences* and *The Archaeology of Knowledge*. Basso insists, rightfully, on the *methodological* dimension.

Deep into this erudite analysis of Foucault's early writings, Basso reminds the reader of the stunning Borgesian opening to *The Order of Things*. Foucault there recounts reading, with amusement as you will recall, the various labels of animals categorized in a "certain Chinese encyclopedia," which include those "(a) belonging to the Emperor, (b) embalmed, (c) tame, (d) sucking pigs, (e) sirens, (f) fabulous, (g) stray dogs, . . .

(k) drawn with a very fine camelhair brush, . . . (m) having just broken the water pitcher, (n) that from a long way off look like flies."[1] That amusement, that shock, is precisely the jarring experience of incoherence that reminds us of the internal coherence of our own understanding of reality. As Basso beautifully demonstrates, it is not the categories themselves that are so surprising as the fact that they could coexist with internal coherence in an understanding of the world that makes sense.[2] Foucault's archaeological method serves to expose the internal coherence that makes possible our ways of thinking and understanding, hidden to us, yet so formative to the present.

Basso meticulously unpacks the concept of the "historical *a priori*," first to clarify its meaning in the face of certain rebukes Foucault had received from critics and, second, to trace its lineage to the phenomenological approach in philosophy and to existential analysis in psychiatry. The term is so paradoxical and puzzling—though now so internalized and normal—because, as Basso writes, it "is always contemporary to the phenomena which it has the task of explaining."[3] It is first expressed in Foucault's notion of "an *a priori* of existence" in his first published monograph, *Maladie mentale et personnalité* (originally published in 1954 and never translated into English), which had a deep Marxian strand and two openly Marxist concluding chapters (later deleted, revised, and replaced with a synopsis of *The History of Madness* in the revised second edition of 1962 under the titled *Mental Illness and Psychology*).[4] It then evolves by means of Foucault's reading of Husserlian phenomenology—an approach to analyzing lived experience in which, as Foucault writes, "meaning only ever emerges in the land of meaning."[5] It then grows through Foucault's encounter with Binswanger's existential analysis into the notion of "*a priori* structures which determine the modalities according to which the patient's global experience or 'world-project' is constituted."[6] Existential analysis, Foucault maintains, begins from the patient's experiences and practices of reality in order to understand the inner coherence that makes them initially comprehensible as experiences.

The archaeological method blooms first in Foucault's earliest major work, *The History of Madness*, which explores historically the actual experience of madness, rather than the history of a particular diagnosis of mental illness. It then develops in Foucault's second major work, *Birth of the Clinic*, which contains, as originally formulated in the first edition in 1963, the proposition that "it is a structural study that attempts to decipher in the depth of the historical the conditions of history itself."[7] It is there that Foucault deploys the term: "the historical and concrete *a priori*."[8] It then comes to full bloom in *The Order of Things* and, of course, *The Archaeology of Knowledge*. Basso captures the genealogical trace of *Daseinsanalyse* beautifully:

> Following the trail of the "historical *a priori*," we see that it is at the level of methodology that the appeal and utility of existential analysis's theoretical device becomes visible and plays itself out for Foucault. It is precisely from this point of view that we will seek out the traces of this device, which we might deem the most precious tool that Foucault the archaeologist used in his digs.[9]

There can be no doubt. With the release of the new series of Foucault's lectures and manuscripts before the Collège de France, with the trove of Foucault archives newly deposited at the Bibliothèque nationale de France, and with the publication of Basso's important book, the significance of the "young Foucault" is indubitable.

In the English preface to the final volumes of the *History of Sexuality*, which Foucault penned shortly before his untimely death in 1984, Foucault explained that the mature historical method he developed in the final volumes of the *History of Sexuality* had been deeply influenced by his original encounter with *Daseinsanalyse*: "To study forms of experience in this way—in their history," Foucault wrote (referring to volumes 2 and 3 of his *History of Sexuality*), "is an idea that originated with an earlier project, in which I made use of the methods of existential analysis in the field of psychiatry and in the domain of 'mental illness.'"[10] In *Young Foucault*, Basso skillfully explicates this exact connection, putting the emphasis—the italics—on the word *method*.

In this early period and throughout his philosophical journey, Foucault was in search of a method—like other great philosophers at the time who were trying to discovery a new path to ground forms of materialism in the experience of existence. Foucault sought to resolve problematics not in a linear fashion but in a punctual way, responsive to the political, cultural, and historical conjunctures of the moment. In the process, Foucault crafted new concepts and approaches, sometimes discarded them, at other times returned to them, as the political and historical situation changed. Foucault developed a unique philosophical praxis.[11]

Philosophical methods and concepts—and philosophical encounters—are portals that can move our understanding of the present forward. Basso shows this magnificently in Foucault's encounter with existential psychiatry. Herself the foremost expert on Foucault's relationship to Binswanger, a member of the scientific research team now editing the new collection of Foucault's early lectures and manuscripts before the Collège de France, and an editor of the new revised edition of the Collège de France lectures, few are in an equal position to guide us through this early and formative period of Foucault's intellectual journey. Weaving in passages from Foucault's intellectual journals and preparatory manuscripts now held in the Foucault archives at the Bibliothèque nationale de France, from the newly published early lectures and manuscripts, from correspondence in Binswanger's archives and in the private archives of key interlocutors (such as Jacqueline Verdeaux, who translated Binswanger's work and with whom Foucault worked closely)—even from Foucault's handwritten annotations on his own copy of Binswanger's book from his own personal library still in the possession of his longtime companion, Daniel Defert—Basso opens the door to the new treasure trove of Foucauldian archives and serves as an expert guide.

At a very early date, Basso had an intuition that Binswanger was an important figure in Foucault's intellectual development. At the time, as a young graduate student, Basso had little to rely on other than her intuition. The only thing published at the time was Foucault's introduction to Biswanger's *Dream and Existence*—the rest of the manuscripts and the entire archive remained hidden, still undisclosed, in Daniel Defert's bank vaults. Despite warnings and guidance to avoid the topic, Basso stuck with that intuition and wrote her doctoral dissertation on the topic—a lengthy four-hundred-plus-page dissertation in Italian completed in 2007. Since that time, tens of thousands of pages of Foucault's manuscripts, reading notes, lectures, and intellectual journals have surfaced, are now open to the public at the Bibliothèque nationale de France, and are being digitally archived. Basso, the first to have made the Foucault-Binswanger relationship the subject of her scholarly research, now returns to the topic and guides us through it like no one else. This is a gift for which I—and I know other readers—will be eternally grateful.

March 25, 2022

YOUNG FOUCAULT

INTRODUCTION
New Avenues of Research

FOUCAULT BEFORE FOUCAULT

In 1979, the German psychiatrist Karl Peter Kisker (1926–1997), one of the founders of "social psychiatry" (*Sozialpsychiatrie*),[1] defended Foucault against the antipsychiatrists who wanted to use his *History of Madness* to argue that the diagnosis of mental illnesses amounted to an abusive pathologization of social deviance.[2] Among Kisker's polemical targets was the French psychiatrist Henri Ey (1900–1977). In his introduction to the debates at the "Journées annuelles de l'Évolution psychiatrique," an annual conference that in 1969 was devoted to *History of Madness*, Ey had critiqued Foucauldian archaeology's ideological and "psychiatricidic" position.[3] According to Ey, by calling into question the very concept of "mental illness," Foucault was ultimately challenging the raison d'être of the therapeutic function and by the same token the very legitimacy of psychiatry.[4] Yet curiously, according to Ey, this position was incompatible with Foucault's interest in the fundamental problems of psychopathology and psychoanalysis in his writings of the 1950s. Indeed, Ey had been among the first to praise the French translation of Ludwig Binswanger's (1881–1966) article "Traum und Existenz,"[5] to which Foucault had contributed an introduction in 1954, which Ey had deemed "magnificent and substantial" in *L'Évolution psychiatrique*.[6]

Ey was well placed to judge the young Foucault's engagement with existential psychopathology: a member of the *Évolution Psychiatrique* (Psychiatric Evolution) group since the 1930s and editor-in-chief of its eponymous journal after it was relaunched after World War II,[7] he was also the cofounder, with Jean Delay (1907–1987), of the World Psychiatric Association in 1950; he would later become its general secretary. Indeed, it was in Ey's book series *Bibliothèque neuro-psychiatrique de langue française* (French-Language Neuro-Psychiatric Library), launched with the publisher Desclée de Brouwer in 1948, that Foucault published his translation of the German physician, physiologist, and anthropologist Viktor von Weizsäcker's (1886–1957) masterwork *Der Gestaltkreis* (*Le cycle de la structure*); Ey had contributed a preface to the volume. Throughout the 1950s, the book series had introduced and developed German-language phenomenological psychopathology in France, by publishing the works of key figures, including Eugène Minkowski (1885–1972) and Françoise Minkowski (1882–1950), Roland Kuhn (1912–2005), Ludwig Binswanger, and Frederik J. J. Buytendijk (1887–1974).

In his defense of *History of Madness*, Kisker particularly praised the palpable influence of a phenomenological perspective in the work—the idea that madness must be understood as an extrascientific phenomenon, independent of any clinical classification. According to Kisker, Foucault was therefore a "historical-philosophical defense lawyer" for madness in the original sense of the term, before its appropriation by medical science.[8] For Foucault, indeed, the task was not to trace the history of a "truth" of mental illness that could finally be uncovered, but rather to follow "this degree zero of the history of madness, when it was undifferentiated experience,"[9] and which "still remains for us the mode of access to the natural truth of man."[10] Yet, within this perspective that considers madness in advance of any psychopathological conceptualization, there is no longer room for any kind of psychiatry, even in its anthropological-existential form. As Foucault announced in 1962 in the new edition of his first book, *Maladie mentale et personnalité* (Mental Illness and Personality),[11] reissued as *Mental Illness and Psychology*: "If carried back to its roots, the psychology of madness would appear to be not the mastery of mental illness and hence the possibility of its disappearance, but the destruction of psychology itself and the discovery of that essential, nonpsychological because nonmoralizable relation that is the relation between Reason and Unreason."[12]

These declarations seem undeniably to contradict the philosophical approach to psychopathology that Foucault had explored in his first publications, namely, the book *Maladie mentale et personnalité*, the introduction to Binswanger's essay "Traum und Existenz" (published in French as *Le rêve et l'existence*), and two articles on the history and epistemological status of psychology, "La psychologie de 1850 à 1950" (Psychology from 1850 to 1950) and "La recherche scientifique et la psychologie" (Scientific Research and Psychology).[13] Moreover, because Binswanger's name and the names of other psychopathologists linked to phenomenology disappear almost completely from Foucault's works of the 1960s, some scholars suspect that Foucault experienced something of a "false start."[14] A few of them have attributed this conceptual rupture to biographical and academic contingencies. The sociologist Luis Moreno Pestaña, for example, argues that the introduction to *Le rêve et l'existence* reflects a "situational response to the specific demands of the market":[15] in other words, we could see Foucault's choice to work on phenomenological anthropology at the beginning of the 1950s as an exercise in legitimation, allowing him to secure a professional future in the French philosophical context of the era—a context marked by the dominance of existential philosophy.

With a few exceptions,[16] Foucault's early writings have therefore been considered by most interpreters as juvenilia[17]—as immature in relationship to the real archaeological work he launched with *History of Madness*. Indeed, *Maladie mentale et personnalité* was not included in the two volumes of the philosopher's *Œuvres* recently published by the Bibliothèque de la Pléiade.[18] This reading of Foucauldian thought has found widespread success, especially in the English-speaking world, where no translation of *Maladie mentale et personnalité* exists; similarly, Foucault's study of Binswanger's phenomenological anthropology was only translated into English in the mid-1980s, for a special issue of the *Review of Existential Psychology and Psychiatry*. His two articles from 1957 have never been translated into English.

That being said, the availability of numerous documents and textual sources that researchers could not previously consult has made it considerably easier to analyze Foucault's works today. In 2012, Foucault's work archives were classified as "French national treasure" and, in 2013, they were deposited in the manuscripts department of the Bibliothèque nationale de France (BnF) in Paris.[19] If these new archives are extremely promising in terms of their ability to help us better understand the evolution of Foucault's thought and methodology over forty years, the period of his thought with the potential to be best illuminated by these "discoveries" is the 1950s. This is the decade often characterized as "Foucault before Foucault," from which has emerged a "body of writings that—although they were eventually published—seem difficult to reconcile with the public image of the author as it was later constituted: informal writings that we might consider as preparatory, or even as dead ends."[20] But this position becomes untenable in light of the archives of this period, which now allow us to acknowledge the discrepancy between the tremendous amount of work that Foucault produced and the very few writings that he actually published in the decade before the publication of his doctoral dissertation in 1961. Indeed, still unknown to the public are the lectures on philosophical anthropology given by Foucault between 1952 and 1955, when he was a lecturer at the University of Lille and at École normale supérieure (ENS), as well as an unpublished work on Ludwig Binswanger's existential analysis and a dense manuscript on phenomenology and psychology dating from the same period. Besides, further archival sources provide us with new information and details about the scientific context and intellectual network in which Foucault elaborated his first works on psychopathology, phenomenology, and anthropology, thereby letting us gain a new and deeper understanding of his intellectual biography.

With regard to these earliest writings, the materials deposited by Foucault's family at the BnF include, in addition to the folder containing Foucault's master's thesis, numerous work notes and lecture notes on the subject of psychology (methods, history, bibliography). This section of the archive also contains files related to Foucault's defense of his two doctoral theses in 1960—*History of Madness*, and the translation and introduction to Kant's *Anthropology*—as well as his correspondence with editors and some personal papers that will not be available until 2050 (university and administrative documents; correspondence, including with family members; personal writings from the late 1940s and early 1950s). Finally, it contains preparatory manuscripts for *Maladie mentale et personnalité*, the introduction to *Le rêve et l'existence*, and the two articles from 1957.

When we look at this period, Foucault's correspondence is particularly interesting. The letters currently available to scholars at the BnF can clarify Foucault's relationship with the editors who accepted or rejected his earliest writings; meanwhile, the Binswanger archives at the University of Tübingen (Germany) hold Foucault's correspondence with two of the psychiatrists who most drew his notice in the mid-1950s, Ludwig Binswanger and Roland Kuhn.[21] These communications were often mediated by Jacqueline Verdeaux (1920–2016), with whom Foucault worked on the translation of Binswanger's "Traum und Existenz." These letters have much to reveal about the context of Foucault's trips to Switzerland to visit the psychiatrists, in March and September 1954, respectively.[22] Other important documents on this topic may be found in the archives of the Canton of Thurgau, in Frauenfeld, Switzerland, which contain the archives of the Münsterlingen psychiatric clinic, as well as, since 2013, the Roland Kuhn archives. Also useful are the documents still held by the Kuhn family and the testimonials of Kuhn's former colleagues in Münsterlingen. Among other private archival objects, the documents that Foucault's family turned over to the BnF include copies of photos of a carnival held at the Münsterlingen clinic in 1954, which Foucault attended during his visit. We now know that Jacqueline Verdeaux took them, and the complete, original series of photographs—as well as a two-minute-and-twenty-second color film shot by Georges Verdeaux on the same occasion—is held in the Verdeaux family's private archives.[23] This archive also includes correspondence between Foucault and Jacqueline Verdeaux starting before Foucault's departure for Sweden in 1955 and covering part of his sojourn there, as well as editorial correspondence focusing on Verdeaux's translations from German throughout the 1950s. Indeed, beyond *Le rêve et l'existence*, Verdeaux also published translations of the Swiss psychiatrist Jakob Wyrsch's (1892–1980) *La personne du schizophrène* in 1956,[24] of Binswanger's clinical case study *Suzanne Urban* in 1957,[25] and of Roland Kuhn's study on interpretations of masks in the Rorschach Test: *Phénoménologie du masque: À travers le test de Rorschach*.[26]

All of these archives now allow us to argue that Foucault's interest in existential psychopathology was not merely incidental to his intellectual formation. In the first chapter of this book, I will refer to Foucault's reading notes from the 1950s to show that he had a profound understanding not only of the entirety of Binswanger's available works, but also, more generally, of the German psychopathology of the first half of the twentieth century—to the extent that he had planned to devote a volume to existential analysis, whose manuscript he preserved. Foucault's interest in existential psychopathology, for that matter, was not shared strictly by an academic network. Rather, it was inscribed in an intellectual milieu and research network pertaining to psychiatry, to which Foucault belonged during his Parisian years before his departure for Sweden.

In the first two chapters of this study, I reconstruct this network by analyzing Foucault's work archives and situating him in the French philosophical, psychological, and psychiatric contexts of this period. Within this framework, I analyze the posthumously published book dedicated to Binswanger and existential analysis; this book not only clarifies the stakes of the enigmatic introduction to *Le rêve et l'existence*, but also helps us to better understand how Foucault's attitude toward phenomenological psychology and psychopathology—and thereafter philosophical anthropology—evolved. Indeed, if, on the one hand, Foucault prolongs the interest in the anthropological side of German phenomenology that had been explored in France since the early 1940s by Sartre and Merleau-Ponty, on the other, he perceptively analyzes and criticizes its philosophical implications. In other words, rather than contributing to the project of founding a phenomenological anthropology—a project dating back to the first half of the twentieth century, especially in Germany and Switzerland, which found some of its most significant expressions in the fields of psychology and psychiatry[27]—Foucault explores its presuppositions and consequences. The strictly theoretical point of view from which he begins ends up extending first into an epistemological perspective, with the archaeology of knowledge in the 1960s, and then into a genealogical approach from the 1970s onward. Foucault's manuscripts of the 1950s thus constitute a significant history of phenomenology in Europe, not only with respect to the analysis of its transformations from the internal evolution of Husserl's thought, but also with respect to its potential in relation to other fields, first and foremost psychopathology.

By interweaving Foucault's biography with the new archival resources, we can expect to gain a more profound and original understanding of the first steps of the philosopher's intellectual itinerary. Moreover, a thorough analysis of his early writings will also lead us to better understand Foucault's writings of the early 1960s. The third chapter will demonstrate that the early "phenomenological" phase of Foucault's work is coherent, from a methodological point of view, with his development of the archaeological method.

This book therefore constitutes an analysis of the general epistemological shape of the "style"[28] and methodology of Foucault's intellectual project at the moment of its inception. In other words, rather than categorically supporting or rejecting the idea of Foucault's embrace of phenomenology,[29] I will ask whether it might be possible to identify, *through* Binswanger, a certain Foucauldian reading of or approach to phenomenology.

In particular, I will analyze the Binswangerian approach to the phenomenological notion of the *a priori* as an immanent law of reality; I will show that Foucault's *historical a priori* is an analogous theoretical mechanism. Having done so, I will interpret the Foucauldian concept of the *historical a priori* in light of Foucault's writings on Binswanger. By emphasizing how existential analysis meets the requirement that one make sense of experience by starting from experience itself, from its historical forms and internal laws, I argue, Foucault stresses the very characteristic that will form the basis of his own project: knowledge, practices, and experiences must be analyzed from the standpoint of their actual instantiation, of their function, rather than from the standpoint of an external explanatory principle.

Here I do not claim to identify a continuity or unity that Foucault himself would have disavowed in his own work. Yet this study aims to restore the richness of this trajectory—a trajectory that deserves to be investigated and complicated in order to raise new questions, in light of the new archives and new corpus that we now have at our disposal.

THE FONDS FOUCAULT AT BIBLIOTHÈQUE NATIONALE DE FRANCE

Foucault's archive at the BnF is made up of three parts, each of which has a unique form and acquisition history. Daniel Defert, Foucault's partner and heir, had already donated the first manuscript versions of *The Archaeology of Knowledge* (1969) and of two volumes of *The History of Sexuality* (*The Use of Pleasure* and *The Care of the Self*, both from 1984) to the BnF in 1994. Foucault's family deposited further personal documents covering the period from the end of the 1940s, when Foucault was still a student, until his departure for Sweden in 1955. These are fundamental texts for studying Foucault's earliest writings. The entire Fonds Michel Foucault consists of nearly forty thousand handwritten and typed sheets of paper, including reading notes, notes for lectures and conferences, some preparatory manuscripts for books, as well as several notebooks that constitute Foucault's intellectual journal.[30] All these documents make it possible to follow the evolution of Foucault's thought over a period of almost forty years: from his notes and his very early writings as a student, as well as his various dissertation projects, up to the gestation of the lectures at the Collège de France and the series of volumes about the *History of Sexuality*. This archival material immediately became an indispensable tool for scholars aiming to study Foucault's thought in depth, and it has inspired a range of new editorial projects.

The book series *Philosophie du present: Foucault inédit* was launched by Jean-François Braunstein, Arnold Davidson, and Daniele Lorenzini with the Parisian publisher Vrin in 2013; several volumes have already appeared, collecting various previously unpublished lectures and writings by Foucault.[31] In 2015, the prestigious Bibliothèque de la Pléiade series (Gallimard) brought out the edition of Foucault's *Œuvres* to which I referred earlier; that same year, the publication of all of Foucault's lectures at the Collège de France (published in Paris by Seuil/Gallimard/EHESS in the *Hautes Études* series) was completed.[32] In 2018, the fourth volume of *The History of Sexuality*, which was almost complete at the time of Foucault's death, was also published.[33] In 2016, the French publisher Seuil inaugurated a new series titled *Cours et travaux de Michel Foucault avant le Collège de France*, consisting of the unpublished manuscripts of Foucault's lectures and writings from the period before he obtained a chair at the Collège de France in 1970. Several volumes are planned up to

2026; more specifically, the series will include, from the 1950s, the lectures on philosophical anthropology (*La question anthropologique. Cours. 1954–1955*)[34] given by Foucault when he was lecturer at the University of Lille and at the ENS in Paris, an unpublished book on Ludwig Binswanger's existential analysis,[35] and a dense manuscript on phenomenology and psychology (*Phénoménologie et psychologie, 1953–1954*).[36] From the 1960s, the new series will include the Brazilian lectures on "The Order of Things" given in São Paulo before the publication of the book of the same title, the lectures on sexuality given at the universities of Clermont Ferrand (1964) and Vincennes (1969),[37] the lectures given at the University of Tunis in 1966–1968 on philosophical discourse and on Descartes, the lectures on Nietzsche given at the University of Vincennes (1969–1970), as well as two conference papers on Nietzsche delivered in the United States between 1970 and 1971.[38]

Many scholars have begun to examine Foucault's archives dating back to the time when he was a student at the ENS;[39] plans to publish his master's thesis from 1949, *La constitution d'un transcendantal dans la* Phénoménologie de l'esprit *de Hegel* (The Constitution of a Transcendental in Hegel's *Phenomenology of Spirit*),[40] are underway. Studying this text and Foucault's many student notes, which are also held by the BnF, has opened a new front in Foucault studies, such that the work of a very young Foucault is now destined to be considered an integral part of his intellectual trajectory.

The availability of these archives has also led to a further editorial project: the reissuing of the courses at the Collège de France as mass-market paperbacks, in the *Points. Essais* collection of the Éditions du Seuil. The goal of this new editorial project is not only to revise the transcriptions of the courses—whether made from recordings or manuscripts—in order to correct any errors, but also to enrich and standardize the editorial apparatus. Indeed, there are sometimes significant differences between the manuscripts and the lectures as they were delivered. In particular, during the period over which the thirteen courses at the Collège de France were published, the editors' use of Foucault's archives changed markedly; the critical apparatus of the more recently published courses is significantly more elaborate than that of those that were published earlier, since they take Foucault's notes into account.

To this long list of publications, whether recent or still on the horizon, we must add the numerous texts—manuscript fragments or unpublished interviews—that have been published in recent years in journals or edited volumes,[41] and that could form the basis of yet another volume of Foucault's *Dits et écrits*.

Beyond making new sources available and providing Foucault scholars with a new corpus, these new editorial projects open up new avenues of research that bear on our understanding not only of the content of Foucault's thought but also of his method, and, more broadly, on the use and modes of exploration of archives. The work on the Fonds Foucault, indeed, raises epistemological questions about how knowledge is recorded, created, and shared. One of the most interesting aspects of the Foucault archives is the opportunity to approach the philosopher's work through the lens of his reading, by analyzing his reading practices and the directions his thinking took, which are not always apparent if we limit ourselves to the published work. The thousands of reading notes and preparatory notes for books and courses written and preserved by Foucault especially make up a fundamental part of his archive. These documents allow us not only to reconstitute Foucault's "virtual library" by revealing which authors and bibliographical sources commanded his attention at each stage of his work, but also to test the theories about the materiality of discourse and of the archive laid out in his "archaeology of knowledge."[42]

It was precisely in order to highlight this material that, in 2017, the École normale supérieure de Lyon (Triangle Laboratory, UMR 5206) obtained an important grant from the French National Research Agency (ANR) for the project "Foucault Fiches de Lecture / Foucault Reading Notes" (FFL), in partnership with the BnF and the École normale supérieure in Paris (ENS-Paris Sciences et Lettres).[43] This project aimed foremost to explore and make available online, via the public platform FFL-Eman[44] and the digital library Gallica,[45] a large selection of Foucault's reading notes, which have been digitized for this purpose by the BnF.[46]

1

ARCHIVES AND INTELLECTUAL NETWORKS

"A PHILOSOPHER WHO TURNED TO PSYCHOLOGY"

On the dust jacket of the first edition of *History of Madness*, in 1961, Foucault presents his book as the work of someone who "was surprised," whose "author is by profession a philosopher who turned to psychology, and from psychology to history."[1] Even allowing for the rhetorical thrust of this statement, we must acknowledge the rich and varied nature of the young Foucault's intellectual trajectory. In 1952, Foucault obtained a diploma in psychopathology at the Institute of Psychology in Paris. The following year, he also earned a diploma in experimental psychology. Having earned his *agrégation* in philosophy in 1951, he became an assistant lecturer in psychology at the University of Lille in 1952; he remained in this position until the fall of 1955. From October 1951 to the spring of 1955, thanks to the support of Louis Althusser, he was also a lecturer in psychology at the ENS. The philosopher and historian of science Gérard Simon (1931–2009), who attended his courses in 1953–1954, preserved many notes on the sessions Foucault devoted to "causality in psychology": the arc he traces runs from Leibniz, La Mettrie, and

Cabanis, through Gestalt theory, Husserl, and Freud, to Binswanger and Merleau-Ponty.[2] In the fall of 1955, Foucault left France for Sweden, where he was appointed director of the Maison de France in Uppsala.[3]

At the very beginning of the 1950s, in addition, Foucault worked as a psychologist in Georges Verdeaux's (1915–2004) and André Ombredane's (1898–1958) Parisian laboratory,[4] created in 1947 at the Hôpital Sainte-Anne within Professor Jean Delay's department. Foucault assisted the neuropsychiatrist Georges Verdeaux and his wife Jacqueline[5] with their experiments on the clinical use of electroencephalograms (EEGs), performed on patients at the hospital. He also familiarized himself with the Rorschach psychodiagnostic test, which he found particularly intriguing. In Georges Verdeaux's archives, a report from 1952 about an experiment with polygraph techniques mentions a young "M. Foucault, holding an *agrégation* from the University, lecturer at the École normale supérieure, working on the development of a tachiscopic test 'targeting the mentally ill, delinquents, and normal subjects.'"[6] At the time, the Verdeaux directed the EEG unit at the Centre national d'orientation created by the administration of the Fresnes penitentiary. Foucault would accompany Jacqueline Verdeaux there every week in order to perform medico-psychological exams on prisoners.[7]

At the beginning of the 1950s, then, Foucault seems to have turned toward psychology, to the point that he aspired to create a psychology laboratory at ENS.[8] From his correspondence with André Ombredane, which is available in the BnF's archives,[9] we know that he expected to use this laboratory to lead a study "on the perception of forms from the perspective of information theory,"[10] and that this same lab would be supported by the work of a "seminar devoted to psychological research and study."[11] The archives indicate that Ombredane was the main instigator of the enterprise. The correspondence covers a period of two years, from 1953 to 1955; in a letter from March 1953 to the then deputy director of the ENS, Fernand Chapoutier (1899–1953), Ombredane outlined the project of such a seminar, whose research topics included, in particular:

"a. The study of personality ("Personology") by means of various techniques, especially projective techniques, with the fundamental concern of carrying out validations based on well-established experimental designs.
b. Study of certain behaviors (perception, conditioning, memory, learning, abstraction, problem solving, etc.) in terms of information theory—a new and promising perspective, in which I have begun to conduct research with my students in Brussels. It is in the same perspective that a book on Work Analysis will be published this year by my collaborator M. Faverge (who teaches at the University of Paris and the University of Brussels)."[12]

At the time, Foucault was even considering psychiatry; Daniel Lagache (1903–1972)—whom Foucault had known since finishing his *licence* (undergraduate studies) in psychology at the Sorbonne in 1949—dissuaded him from pursuing this path. Indeed, Foucault's interest in psychology was profoundly intertwined with his training in philosophy. Following in the steps of a French tradition going back to the nineteenth century, with Théodule-Armand Ribot (1839–1916), Georges Dumas (1866–1946), Pierre Janet (1859–1947), Paul Guillaume (1878–1962), Henri Piéron (1881–1964), or even Daniel Lagache, the most influential professors in the history of psychology have also been philosophers. The study of psychology formed an integral part of the undergraduate degree in philosophy; it was only at the end of the 1940s that psychology was institutionally recognized as its own discipline in France. The first diploma in psychology was created by Lagache at the Sorbonne in 1947, and it was as chair of child psychology that Merleau-Ponty, appointed to the Sorbonne in 1949, articulated his phenomenological project. In his article "La recherche scientifique et la psychologie" (Scientific Research and Psychology), which Foucault drafted in the early 1950s and which was published in 1957, he described precisely this paradoxical situation, in which "medical, scientific, or even philosophical training served as guarantors for the recruitment of researchers doing experimental psychology."[13]

At the time, in France, philosophers did not think highly of psychology. This situation was noted explicitly by Jean Piaget, who succeeded Maurice Merleau-Ponty at the Sorbonne from 1952 to 1963:

> French psychology has only been able to develop in the fringe of official institutions and in constant struggle with the powers that be of academic philosophy.... There is certainly a *licence* in psychology of recent date, ... but practically this *licence* leads to very little, for from the point of view of a teaching career it remains insufficient without the Diplomas of the Institute of Psychology, originating in the no-man's land between official chairs and not having the same official status of the Faculties.... Briefly, the implicit permanent principle of the French university authorities is that psychology is part of philosophy, that every philosopher is fit to teach psychology, but that the converse is not true.[14]

At the Sorbonne, moreover, Georges Canguilhem—who had offered a polemical answer to the question "What is psychology?" in his famous lecture of 1956 at the Collège Philosophique[15]—in 1960–1961 devoted a course to the history of scientific psychology.

He asserted that "instead of worrying about the existence of the 'human sciences,' philosophy must examine what is at stake in this psychology, what its titles are."[16]

At the very beginning of the 1950s, like most philosophy students interested in psychology, Foucault regularly attended Merleau-Ponty's lectures at the Sorbonne.[17] In his famous 1952 course, *Human Sciences and Phenomenology*, Merleau-Ponty presents psychology as more than simply an autonomous science. Rather, it is a mode of reflection that, beyond its explicit declarations,[18] is destined "to outrun itself through its own momentum"[19] toward phenomenology. The numerous reading notes preserved in the BnF's archives reveal that Foucault was well acquainted with the two works that Merleau-Ponty had published in the mid-1940s, *The Structure of Behavior* (1942) and *Phenomenology of Perception* (1945).[20] Among the documents that Foucault drafted as he prepared his courses at the beginning of the 1950s, there is a manuscript titled "The Psychological Themes in Husserl's and Merleau-Ponty's Phenomenology";[21] during this period, he also mentioned to Jean-Paul Aron that he was working on an article on Merleau-Ponty.[22] This article appears to correspond to a thirty-eight-page typed document conserved at the BnF, in which Foucault examines how Merleau-Ponty's philosophy simultaneously draws on and distances itself from Husserl's phenomenology.[23] The text is quite polemical in its analysis of Merleau-Ponty's thought, which is defined as bourgeois and ideological; this marks it as belonging, in all probability, to the brief period between 1950 and 1952 during which Foucault was a member of the French Communist Party. The archives also contain some of Foucault's notes on Merleau-Ponty's 1947–1948 course on Malebranche, Maine de Biran, and Bergson at ENS.[24] It is likely that it was this course that led Foucault to further study the post-Cartesians, especially

Malebranche and Bayle, while completing his diploma in psychopathology.

In 1951, with Georges Canguilhem's support, Foucault was admitted to the Fondation Thiers, a residential research foundation; the research topics he proposed ran the gamut from "the problem of human sciences in post-Cartesian philosophers" to "the notion of culture in contemporary psychology."[25] One of the first doctoral thesis projects considered by Foucault, who asked the Sorbonne's Henri Gouhier (1898–1994) to direct his secondary thesis on "Malebranche psychologue,"[26] dates back precisely to this period. When Raymond Polin (1910–2001), chair of the department of philosophy at the University of Lille, recruited Foucault to teach psychology—on Jules Vuillemin's (1920–2001) recommendation—he was looking for a philosopher, not a psychologist. At the time of their meeting in 1952, Foucault explained that he was writing a thesis on the "philosophy of psychology."[27] He was relatively free to choose the topics of his courses. In a letter to Jean-Paul Aron, while complaining about the medical doctors teaching psychology at the university, he stated that he intended to "organize a 'seminar' in theoretical psychoanalysis," since "no one else dared to risk such 'indecencies.'"[28] Indeed, many lecture notes in Foucault's archives at the BnF are focused on psychoanalysis; these are lectures he could have delivered either at Lille or at ENS. Their titles include "L'angoisse chez Freud" (Anxiety in Freud), "Maladie et personnalité chez Freud" (Illness and Personality in Freud), "Freud et la psychologie de la genèse" (Freud and the Psychology of Genesis), "La théorie psychanalytique" (Psychoanalytic Theory), "L'inconscient en psychanalyse" (The Unconscious in Psychoanalysis), "Un exemple de psychanalyse: l'homme aux loups. La notion de milieu psychanalytique" (An Example of Psychoanalysis: The Wolf Man. The Notion of a Psychoanalytic Milieu).[29]

Foucault's interest in Freudian theory during this period was always intertwined with a theoretical reflection on classic philosophical subjects, such as experience, signification, expression, and language. The very many reading notes and lecture notes that Foucault devoted to psychoanalysis are coeval with his equally rich and detailed notes on Husserl's phenomenology.[30] The archives also inform us that, in 1952, he drafted an essay titled "Remarks on the Teaching of Phenomenology."[31] His correspondence with editors reveals that he had submitted this essay to the *Revue de l'enseignement philosophique* (Journal of the Teaching of Philosophy), which had rejected it as "unsuited to the character of the journal."[32] In this article, Foucault laments the silence of philosophy programs with respect to the teaching of German phenomenology, and in particular of Husserl's thought, which he defines as "a philosophy whose vocabulary is arduous, whose development is circuitous, and which is only partially available to the francophone reader."[33] In light of the erudition and rigor of Husserl's works, Foucault argues, French programs prefer to present the "friendlier, more human side of phenomenology," filtering it through the existential interpretations of "psychologists who philosophize" such as Merleau-Ponty, Minkowski, or Buytendijk—to cite only Foucault's examples. While these figures "might be of great interest for research, they risk having disastrous pedagogical effects," Foucault observes; he concludes that "a work will one day have to be written about Husserl where exactitude and esotericism are no longer synonymous."[34]

We know from Foucault's correspondence with the German publisher Mohr (Paul Siebeck, Tübingen) that between 1952 and 1953 he intended to translate Husserl's article "Philosophy as Rigorous Science" into French.[35] A curriculum vitae appended to a letter addressed to Georges Dumézil (1898–1986) in October 1954, moreover, tells us that he was planning a thesis on the "notion of 'World' in phenomenology and its importance for the human sciences." His secondary thesis, on the other hand, bore the title "A Study of the Psychophysics of Signals and the Statistical Interpretation of Perception."[36] It is therefore clear that the theses and other writing projects Foucault had in the works during this period were as numerous as they were varied. A letter that Jacqueline Verdeaux sent to Ludwig Binswanger in 1954 suggests that, at the time, Foucault intended to prepare a "work on delusions."[37] This theme would retain his interest even beyond the 1950s; in the early 1960s, as he was working on *Death and the Labyrinth*, he wrote the following notes in his intellectual journal:

> The voice of the enemy
> Small study of persecutory delusions, of dialogic delusions of hallucinations.
>   Ex[ample] of persecutory delusions
>   Rousseau
> End of days
> Mystics and madmen of language.[38]

The archives from this period are extremely dense and show us a young Foucault active on many fronts: beyond psychology (social psychology, animal psychology, cybernetics, reflexology, etc.)[39] and phenomenology (many reading notes on Max Scheler, Paul Ricoeur, and Trân Duc Thao),[40] many reading notes are devoted to philosophical anthropology, cultural anthropology, and sociology.[41] Whereas Hegel had been omnipresent in Foucault's notes since the 1940s, in the 1950s Foucault began to read Heidegger and Nietzsche assiduously. His curiosity with regard to Heidegger is observable in his very rich notes on "The

Anaximander Fragment,"[42] on the *Letter on Humanism* (whose French translation by Roger Munier was published in 1953),[43] on some key concepts of *Sein und Zeit*, and on the study *Kant and the Problem of Metaphysics* (whose French translation by Alphonse de Waelhens and Walter Biemel was published by Gallimard in 1953).[44] Foucault's reading of Nietzsche, which he dated roughly to 1953,[45] might have been spurred by his reading of the German psychiatrist and philosopher Karl Jaspers.[46] This hypothesis seems to be confirmed by the archives from this period: they attest that Foucault was studying Jaspers's and Nietzsche's works at the same time.[47] Indeed, Jaspers's book on Nietzsche appeared in French translation at the very beginning of the 1950s.[48] Jules Vuillemin wrote one of its first reviews.[49] Foucault mentioned Jaspers's book in one of his courses at ENS—probably the course on anthropology—in a lecture devoted to Nietzsche.[50]

PSYCHOLOGY'S "NEW ORIENTATION"

Despite this bountiful philosophical panorama, the only work that Foucault published in the 1950s was devoted to mental illness. *Maladie mentale et personnalité* came out in 1954 as part of the Presses Universitaires de France's *Initiation philosophique* series, which was edited by Jean Lacroix (1900–1986) and whose editorial board included Gaston Bachelard, Georges Bastide, and Paul Ricœur. The work was solicited by Louis Althusser, whom Foucault had known since he was a student at ENS. In his correspondence with the young philosopher, Jean Lacroix explains that he wishes to publish "short volumes that are *simple*, clear, easy," whose goal would be to "examine in broad strokes the various questions covered by the program of the *baccalauréat* [high school leaving exam] and establish a basic classroom library."[51]

This is the task that Foucault executed: in his study, he presents and compares the principal psychological and psychiatric approaches to mental illness, from evolutionary psychology to psychoanalysis, from existential analysis to Pavlovian behaviorism.

Although Foucault had left the French Communist Party in October of 1952—he had become a member through Althusser—*Maladie mentale et personnalité* reveals his commitment to a materialist perspective that was associated, at the time, with the Marxist journal *La Raison: Cahiers de psychopathologie scientifique* (Reason: Journal of Scientific Psychopathology), which had been founded in 1951 by Henri Wallon, who remained its editor.[52] In the first section of this text, which tackles the "psychological dimensions of illness," Foucault surveys some of the recurrent themes in the contemporary critical landscape, such as the centrality of the problem of "signification" in psychology, and Freudian theory's ambiguity in relation to evolutionary theory, on the one hand, and the historicity of forms of experience, on the other. However, in the second section, which deals with the "real conditions of illness," he is clearly echoing the *Cahiers*'s main arguments. In this way, he asserts that a person with a mental illness is nothing but an extreme expression of the conflicts of bourgeois society. He explains that such a society mythologizes "mental alienation" while simultaneously pushing it to the outer limits of the city; this dynamic is but a translation of the scandal of an alienation whose true nature is social and historical. Also in keeping with the *Cahiers*'s perspective, Foucault writes about Pavlovian theory in glowing terms, describing it as the only viable perspective for "an experimental study of conflict."[53]

These positions elicited some gentle pushback from Lacroix, who wrote to the philosopher that he had "a single, slightly delicate question" about "the approach adopted in the last pages (stemming of course from the previous analyses)":

> I consider it eminently desirable that students' attention be drawn to the social problem of mental illness. . . . However, I do not believe that every psychic conflict has a solely social origin; in fact, I think that in any society men will experience conflicts. . . . I do not want to dispute your argument, which is wholly admissible. But considering the goal of the book series, I wonder whether some changes in presentation might be helpful.[54]

While the reference to Pavlov would disappear from Foucault's later works, other elements of this text would remain central to his thinking. Among them, we might observe the necessity of referring any definition of mental alienation back to the society characterizing it as such. His praise of the investigative report on the "wretchedness of psychiatry" led in 1952 by Albert Béguin (1901–1957) in the journal *Esprit*—where psychiatrists such as François Tosquelles (1912–1994), Henri Ey, Louis Le Guillant (1900–1968), Lucien Bonnafé (1912–2003), and Georges Daumézon (1912–1979) deplored the condition of the "madmen" in hospitals[55]—calls to mind the tone of *History of Madness*. It is also worth noting, on this subject, that Henri Ey's book series at Desclée de Brouwer, the *Bibliothèque neuro-psychiatrique de langue française*, had issued two edited volumes focused on these themes: Georges Daumézon and Lucien Bonnafé's *Le malade mental dans la société* (The Mentally Ill in Society, 1946), and Jean Lauzier and Lucien Bonnafé's *Au-delà de l'asile d'aliénés et de l'hôpital psychiatrique* (Beyond the Insane Asylum and the Psychiatric Hospital, 1951), both of which offered a strong critique of the asylum.[56]

Another theme that emerges from *Maladie mentale et personnalité* is a critique of an overly speculative approach to mental illness. This theme recurs throughout Foucault's handwritten notes from the mid-1950s. For example, in one manuscript from the Lille period, Foucault explains that, in refusing "any scientific and real analysis of human conduct," the anthropo-phenomenological approach had the result of discovering "an essence of man that uncovers itself only in the negative modality."[57] In a brief comment appended in pencil to the manuscript fragment, Foucault concludes: "Psychology, under the pretext of analyzing the concrete—phenomenology, under the pretext of returning to things—both converge toward the most abstract thing: toward an essence of man valid only in the realm of anthropological speculation."[58] Here, Foucault is explicitly referring to the school of "concrete psychology," established by the French philosopher and Marxist theoretician Georges Politzer (1903–1942) at the end of the 1920s, which had struck a chord with French philosophers—in particular Sartre and Merleau-Ponty—from the 1930s to the 1950s. In his *Critique of the Foundations of Psychology*,[59] as in the *Revue de psychologie concrète* (Journal of Concrete Psychology), which he had founded in 1929, Politzer proposed a "new orientation" to reform psychology. This orientation would reject both associationism and the "myth" of interior life. Instead, it would be guided by the principle of the "concrete": a practical understanding of human life, more closely aligned with wisdom than with the scientific knowledge derived from physiology. It might not be surprising, then, that in 1946 Emmanuel Mounier (1905–1950) went so far as to describe Politzer as "the John the Baptist of this Good News," who "denounces the systematic objectification of psychological life" by psychological approaches carried out "in the third person."[60]

The critique of associationism and the need to lay the foundations for a new "concrete method of psychological analysis"[61] are also at the root of the program that Jacques Lacan had devised for psychiatry in the 1930s, especially in his doctoral thesis from 1932 on paranoid psychosis. There he insists on the need for psychiatry to concentrate its attention on those specific anomalies of personality that can be defined not in reference to the "'the associative link' of the mental phenomenon," but rather in the form of "concrete facts of the subject's affective history."[62] This might explain this "new psychology's" privileged relationship with psychopathology and the clinic. It might also explain Lacan's important decision to forgo "adding, according to custom, a new morbid entity—whose autonomy we could not affirm—to existing frameworks"; instead, he would categorize cases on the basis of "a concrete description rather than a descriptive synthesis that, out of a need for generality, would strip away the specific traits of the case."[63]

In this context, even medicine began to be understood by French philosophers as a "technique (art) at the crossroads of many sciences," to cite Daniel Lagache, able to offer itself as an "introduction to concrete human problems."[64] It was precisely this "clinical art," understood as the study of complete and concrete living beings, that Lagache, in his review in 1946 of Canguilhem's book *The Normal and the Pathological*, presented as the condition of possibility for the psychological disciplines and their unified foundation.

The concept of "personality" as it is presented in *Maladie mentale et personnalité* corresponds precisely to the concern for the "concrete" that characterizes French psychological and psychiatric thinking during this period. We might cite the manner in which Lacan introduced the notion of personality in his doctoral thesis of 1932: he wanted to account for the facts of psychosis through a "more theoretically rigorous method" and a "more concrete description"[65] that would oppose, simultaneously, a purely psychological and a purely organic conception of mental illness. Henning Schmidgen suggests that Lacan's emphasis on the concept of personality at the beginning of the 1930s was influenced by Max Scheler, via Binswanger.[66] Foucault's analytical angle of attack reveals that he shares Lacan's concern, and the notion of personality—understood as "the element in which the illness develops, and the criterion which allows it to be evaluated"[67]—is also introduced in the context of problematizing the relationship between mental and organic medicine. Foucault's interest in existential psychiatry arose precisely from this context; while supporting here also the critique of the psychology of elementary reactions, Foucault now insists on the need for an approach guided by the idea of totality, the idea that "illness concerns the individual's global situation in the world": "instead of being a physiological *or* psychological essence, [illness] is a general reaction of the individual understood in his or her psychological *and* physiological totality."[68]

Here Foucault does not hesitate to critique the manner in which French philosophers confronted the problem of the "concrete" in the fields of psychology and medicine. He begins by noting that "We have seen in this priority of the notion of totality a return to concrete pathology and the possibility of understanding the fields of mental pathology and of organic medicine as a single domain."[69] Still, he adds, "Because of the unity it ensures and the problems it eliminates, this notion of totality is well disposed to create within pathology a climate of conceptual euphoria. It was from this climate that those who were inspired by Goldstein, whether directly or indirectly, sought to benefit. But unfortunately, euphoria has not turned out to be on the same side as rigor."[70] Indeed, in one of the preparatory typescripts of *Maladie mentale et personnalité*, Foucault mentions some of the French authors influenced by the German neurologist Kurt Goldstein (1878–1965). These include Merleau-Ponty, with *La*

Structure du comportement (1942), and Canguilhem, with *Essai sur quelques problèmes concernant le normal et le pathologique* (1943).[71]

During this period, Foucault was reading Minkowski, Jaspers, and especially Binswanger. The hundreds of reading notes he devoted to existential psychopathology in the first half of the 1950s range far beyond "Traum und Existenz." In the BnF's Foucault archives covering the first half of the 1950s, there are two boxes[72] containing approximately four hundred sheets of paper each; each box holds several hundred sets of reading notes gathered into various folders devoted to, respectively, the work of Binswanger (texts, clinical cases, concepts), Roland Kuhn, Paul Häberlin (1878–1960), Hans Kunz (1904–1982), Viktor Emil von Gebsattel (1883–1976), Alfred Storch (1888–1962), and Erwin Straus (1891–1975).

Paul Häberlin taught philosophy and pedagogy, first in Bern from 1914 to 1922, and then in Basel until 1947. He had an important influence on Binswanger, who always considered him one of the most impactful philosophers in his training. Together with Binswanger and Carl G. Jung, Häberlin was one of the first to join the Freudian Association (Freudsche Vereinigung), which was formed in Zurich in 1907 around Eugen Bleuler's group. However, he soon distanced himself from Freudian theory. A voluminous correspondence testifies to his personal and intellectual relationship with Binswanger, thereby allowing us to trace the evolution of *Daseinsanalyse* from its inception.[73] In his reading notes, Foucault refers to the following works by Häberlin: *Der Gegenstand der Psychologie: Eine Einführung in das Wesen der empirischen Wissenschaft* (The Object of Psychology: An Introduction to the Nature of Empirical Science, 1921)[74] and *Der Mensch: Eine philosophische Anthropologie* (Man: A Philosophical Anthropology, 1941).[75] Moreover, other reading notes concern the following articles: "Der Gegenstand der Psychiatrie" (The Object of Psychiatry, 1947)[76] and *Der Charakter* (1925).[77] Häberlin's anthropological studies, *Der Mensch* and *Der Charakter*, are also mentioned by Foucault in the manuscripts for the lectures on anthropology that he gave in Lille and at ENS in the early 1950s.[78]

Hans Kunz, after having undertaken studies in law at the universities of Basel and Heidelberg, was impressed by Jaspers's courses at Heidelberg and abandoned law for psychology and philosophy. In 1934, he defended a dissertation on the topic of "phenomenology and the analysis of expression" (*Zur Phänomenologie und Analyse des Ausdrucks*) under Paul Häberlin at the University of Basel. He worked for several years at the Lucerna foundation's Institute of Anthropology. After completing his professorial thesis on the anthropological significance of fantasy (*Die anthropologische Bedeutung der Phantasie*, 1946),[79] Kunz continued to teach at the University of Basel, despite the offer that he received in 1957 from Hans-Georg Gadamer and Karl Löwith to join them at the University of Heidelberg. In his reading notes, Foucault focuses especially on the following works by Kunz: "Die anthropologische Betrachtungsweise in der Psychopathologie" (The Anthropological Approach in Psychopathology, 1941);[80] "Idee, Wesen und Wirklichkeit des Menschen: Bemerkungen zu einem Grundproblem der philosophischen Anthropologie" (Idea, Essence and Reality of the Human Being: Remarks on a Fundamental Problem of Philosophical Anthropology, 1944).[81] He also cites "Die Psychoanalyse als Symptom einer Wandlung im Selbstverständnis des Menschen" (Psychoanalysis as a Symptom of a Change in the Self-Understanding of the Human Being, 1931).[82]

Viktor Emil von Gebsattel worked as assistant physician in Munich in Emil Kraepelin's psychiatric clinic between 1915 and 1920. He trained in psychoanalysis and opened a private practice in Berlin. After the fall of the Nazi regime, he worked as Head of Medicine in the Badenweiler sanatorium, in Baden-Württemberg, before obtaining a teaching position in medical psychology and psychotherapy at the University of Freiburg. In 1950, he was named interim professor and chair of psychiatry and neurology at the University of Würzburg, where he also taught courses in medical psychiatry. At Würzburg, he founded the Institut für Psychotherapie und Medizinische Psychologie, the first in Germany. Gebsattel is an important reference in Binswanger's work, and Foucault wrote reading notes on the following works: "Über Fetischismus" (1929);[83] "Zur Psychopathologie der Phobien. I. Teil: Die psychasthenische Phobie" (1935);[84] "Die Welt des Zwangskranken" (The World of the Obsessive-Compulsive Patient, 1938);[85] "Zur Frage der Depersonalisation: Ein Beitrag zur Theorie der Melancholie" (On the Question of Depersonalization: A Contribution to the Theory of Melancholia, 1937);[86] "Störungen des Werdens und des Zeiterlebens im Rahmen psychiatrischer Erkrankungen" (Disorders of Becoming and Experience of Time in the Context of Psychiatric Illnesses, 1939).[87]

Alfred Storch emigrated to Switzerland in 1934, after medical studies in Heidelberg and habilitation as *Privatdozent* in neurology and psychiatry. He worked as an intern at the Münsingen psychiatric hospital, in the canton of Bern. In 1950, he defended his professorial thesis in philosophy at the University of Bern. Very attentive both to the development of psychoanalysis and to Binswanger's *Daseinsanalyse*—he maintained a correspondence with Binswanger—he is one of the most influential representatives of the existential school in psychopathology, about which he wrote many works beginning in the 1930s. In his manuscripts and reading notes, Foucault focuses especially on the following texts by Storch: *Das archaisch-primitive Erleben und Denken der Schizophrenen. Entwicklungspsychologisch-klinische Untersuchungen zum Schizophrenieproblem* (The Archaic-Primitive Experience and Thought of the Schizophrenic: Developmental-Psychological and Clinical Studies on the Schizophrenia Problem, 1922);[88] "Die Welt der beginnenden Schizophrenie und die archaische Welt: Ein existential-analytischer Versuch" (The World of Incipient

Schizophrenia and the Archaic World: An Existential-Analytical Experiment, 1930);[89] "Die Daseinsfrage der Schizophrenen" (1947);[90] "Tod und Erneuerung in der schizophrenen Daseins-Umwandlung" (Death and Renewal in the Schizophrenic Transformation of Existence, 1948);[91] "Die Psychoanalyse und die menschlichen Existenzprobleme" (Psychoanalysis and the Human Problems of Existence, 1939);[92] "Zum Verständnis des Weltuntergangs der Schizophrenen" (On Understanding the End of the World of the Schizophrenic, with Caspar Kulenkampff, 1950);[93] "Existenzphilosophisch Richtungen in der modernen Psychopathologie: Erwiderung zu R. De Rosa" (Existential Philosophical Directions in Modern Psychopathology: Response to R. De Rosa, 1952).[94]

A neurologist and psychiatrist, Erwin Straus was a professor of psychiatry at the University of Berlin before being forced, as a Jew, to immigrate to the United States in 1938. In 1928, he was one of the founders of the journal *Der Nervenartz*. After having taught philosophy and psychology at Black Mountain College in North Carolina, in 1946 he received from Johns Hopkins University the authorization to work as a medical doctor in the United States, and he became a professor at the University of Kentucky, in Lexington. After the war, he resumed contact with his German and Swiss colleagues—notably Viktor Emil von Gebsattel, Eugène Minkowski, and Ludwig Binswanger—whom he regularly met in Europe. In the early 1950s, he was visiting professor at Frankfurt, and then at Würzburg in 1961–1962. Straus's thought is a constant point of reference in Binswanger's work, and more broadly in that of every author affiliated with the phenomenological approach to psychopathology. Foucault wrote numerous reading notes about his work in the 1950s. A folder titled "Erwin Straus," in particular, contains twenty-eight pages devoted to his most celebrated work: *Vom Sinn der Sinne: Ein Beitrag zur*

Grundlegung der Psychologie (From The Sense of the Senses: A Contribution to the Foundation of Psychology, 1935).[95] In other notes, Foucault tackles the problem of the pathology of time and space according to Straus's perspective; the works he cites are the following: "Das Zeiterlebnis in der endogenen Depression und in der psychopatischen Verstimmung" (The Experience of Time in Endogenous Depression and Psychopathic Resentment, 1928);[96] "Die Formen des Räumlichen: Ihre Bedeutung für die Motorik und die Wahrnehmung" (The Forms of the Spatial: Their Significance for Motor Skills and Perception, 1930);[97] *Geschehnis und Erlebnis: Zugleich eine historiologische Deuteung des psychischen Traumas und Renten-Neurose* (Event and Lived Experience: At the Same Time: A Historiological Interpretation of Psychological Trauma and Retirement Neurosis, 1930);[98] "Die aufrechte Haltung: Eine anthropologische Studie" (The Upright Posture: An Anthropological Study, 1949);[99] and "Ein Beitrag zur Pathologie der Zwangserscheinungen" (A Contribution to the Pathology of Obsessive-Compulsive Disorders, 1938).[100]

A large folder in Foucault's archive is dedicated to the work of Karl Jaspers, whose *General Psychopathology*[101] and whose philosophical work Foucault was well acquainted with.[102] If Foucault's earliest publications contain only partial references to all of these authors and works, they figure prominently in the manuscript *Binswanger et l'analyse existentielle*. The reading notes also provide valuable information about how Foucault worked: he let himself be guided by the authors he was reading, following the trails of their bibliographic references. While some of these references remain indirect sources in Foucault's notes, we can now see which texts most attracted his notice, which passages he underlined, which concepts he spent time thinking about.

The various bibliographic inventories drawn up by Foucault during these years suggest that he intended to write a doctoral thesis on existential psychiatry. When Jacqueline Verdeaux proposed, in 1953, that he help her with the translation of "Traum und Existenz," Foucault already had an advanced understanding of this field of research. His collaboration with both Verdeaux spouses at Sainte-Anne further reinforced the young philosopher's interest in existential analysis at a time when he was actively studying Husserl's and Heidegger's phenomenology.

In drawing upon phenomenology, the psychiatrists Foucault was reading during this period did not follow to the letter the imperatives of pure philosophy. Rather, they deployed it in the context of a practical orientation, which they acknowledged as the foundation of a new philosophical approach to psychology and psychiatry. Lacan emphasized this point in 1933, when he derived the "so-called phenomenological viewpoints of contemporary psychiatry" from the "intuitive genius befitting observation" of "a Kraepelin," and connected his own work on paranoid psychosis with Binswanger's.[103] For his part, Minkowski did not hesitate to juxtapose phenomenology's exhortation to "examine phenomena without bias"[104] with Politzer's appeal to psychology to conceive of psychic phenomena as irreducible experiences, without which "psychology does not and cannot ever allow us to know any beginning. It is not at the beginning, it is in the middle."[105]

Still, in *Maladie mentale et personnalité*, Foucault opted for the route of materialism in the form of Pavlovian reflexology. In his other essay of 1954, his introduction to *Le rêve et l'existence*, as in the manuscript on *Binswanger et l'analyse existentielle*, he delved deeper into the other side of this demand for the "concrete" experienced simultaneously by French philosophers, psychologists, and psychiatrists. He therefore explored phenomenological anthropology, in order to analyze "what foundations have been proposed for concrete reflection on man."[106] Yet on this subject we must note that, at the time, Politzer's positions influenced both the materialist and the various phenomenological approaches to psychology. In 1949, for example, in *L'Univers morbide de la faute* (The Morbid Universe of Fault), the psychoanalyst Angelo Hesnard (1886–1969) drew on Politzer as he addressed himself to phenomenology and materialism at the same time: they were "two sides of scientific observation."[107] This book, which featured a preface by Henri Wallon and an introductory note "to the reader" by Daniel Lagache, attracted Foucault's attention, and he devoted lengthy reading notes to it.[108]

During the 1980s, looking back at his earliest works, Foucault would admit to having succumbed to the then-dominant "dilemma of a philosophical anthropology and a social history,"[109] before he finally "understood that the subject would have to be defined in terms other than Marxism or phenomenology."[110] The meeting point of these two approaches—so radically opposite on their face—would be, for Foucault, history. This is why, while he acknowledged having been absorbed by existential philosophy and phenomenology, he also stressed that even at this time his "research was an attempt to discover the extent to which these could be defined in historical terms."[111]

EXISTENTIAL ANALYSIS IN FRANCE: BETWEEN PSYCHIATRY AND PHILOSOPHY

Among the "few dates in the history of psychiatry" that Foucault cites in his appendix to *Maladie mentale et personnalité*, Ludwig Binswanger's work is listed alongside classics by Philippe Pinel (1745–1826), Emil Kraepelin (1856–1926), Sigmund Freud (1856–1939), Ivan Petrovič Pavlov (1849–1936), and Eugen Bleuler

(1857–1939). This shows Binswanger's importance in Foucault's estimation, despite the latter's skepticism about existential analysis in this text.[112] Foucault was not alone, at the time, in deeming Binswanger's program as one of the most significant within the landscape of psychiatric research. At the time, the psychiatrist from Kreuzlingen was well known in the European psychiatric milieu. By the mid-1950s, he had published the majority of his work on *Daseinsanalyse*: the book *Über Ideenflucht* (On the Flight of Ideas), published in 1933[113] (which Foucault, like many French psychiatrists, particularly appreciated), a large number of articles that had been collected in the two volumes of *Ausgewählte Vorträge und Aufsätze* (Selected Lectures and Essays),[114] five major clinical case studies (Ilse, Ellen West, Jürg Zünd, Lola Voss, Suzanne Urban, which would be gathered in 1957 in the volume *Schizophrenie*),[115] the important work from 1942 *Grundformen und Erkenntnis menschlichen Daseins* (Basic Forms and Knowledge of Human Dasein),[116] and finally, a study of the Norwegian playwright Henrik Ibsen and the problem of self-realization in art in 1949.[117]

During the first World Congress of Psychiatry, held in Paris in 1950, the Dutch psychiatrist Henricus Cornelius Rümke (1893–1967) presented *Daseinsanalysis* as the "method that is all the rage";[118] in the treatise on psychiatry published in the same year by Paul Guiraud (1882–1974), the phenomenological school is analyzed alongside psychoanalysis, the Zurich school, and organo-dynamism.[119] In 1955, Henri F. Ellenberger (1905–1993), in his *Traité de psychiatrie* within the *Encyclopédie médico-chirurgicale*, edited by Henri Ey, described existential analysis as one of the "great innovations of modern psychiatry" and as "one of its most promising disciplines."[120]

French psychiatrists had access to Binswanger's ideas mostly because of the coverage he received in *L'Évolution psychiatrique*. The journal had been founded in 1925 around a group of psychiatrists and psychoanalysts that included René Allendy (1889–1942), Angelo Hesnard, René Laforgue (1894–1962), and Eugène Minkowski; its goal was to promote "a practical, new, fundamentally clinical psychology,"[121] using "the method created by Professor S. Freud and expanded by numerous foreign medical doctors and psychologists."[122] Binswanger's name appears in the very first issue of the journal, in a contribution by Minkowski on the subject of schizophrenia.[123] In 1938, one of Binswanger's articles on Freud and philosophical anthropology would launch a series of French translations of his work.[124] The translator was one of Minkowski's assistants, Hans Pollnow (1902–1943), a Jewish psychiatrist and philosopher who had fled Nazi Germany in 1933 and was giving courses on child psychology at the newly established Institute for the History of Science at the Sorbonne.[125]

Minkowski was very familiar with Binswanger's writings. They had both been students of Eugen Bleuler in Zurich, and they shared the project of using Husserl's phenomenological method to rethink psychopathology from the ground up. The two psychiatrists had met for the first time in 1922 in Zurich, during the sixty-third meeting of the Swiss Society of Psychiatry; Minkowski had presented a "Psychological Study and Philosophical Analysis of a Case of Melancholic Schizophrenia," in which he cited Binswanger's work as an example of the way in which "phenomenology quickly found a vast scope of application in every scientific domain."[126] At this same conference, Binswanger had given his famous lecture "On Phenomenology."[127] Minkowski recalled these events at the 1957 Zurich Congress, in a plenary session whose theme was phenomenology and existential analysis—Binswanger and Lammert van der Horst (1893–1978) were rapporteurs: "I have a vivid memory of this meeting. Our colleagues seemed bewildered. On their faces, I thought I could read: 'here are two colleagues who give the impression of being serious and likeable—how unfortunate that, by deserting the certain terrain of facts, they are stumbling around in the metaphysical darkness, so far from the bright, healthy clinic!'"[128] Binswanger remained a constant reference in Minkowski's writings; in turn, in 1928 Binswanger published a laudatory review of Minkowski's monograph *Schizophrenia* in the *Schweizer Archiv für Neurologie und Psychiatrie*.[129] Further, in the new edition of that work published in 1953 (the original had been published in 1927), Minkowski emphasized the value to be found in translating Binswanger's work and introducing *Daseinsanalyse* in more concrete terms to the French psychiatric scene.[130] In so doing, he was paving the way for *Le rêve et l'existence*.

If Binswanger principally owes his introduction in France in the early 1920s to Minkowski, we should not underestimate Jacques Lacan's influence. He discovered Binswanger's writings in the early 1930s, and at the end of the 1940s played an important role as a relay between Swiss psychiatrists and the French philosophers he had rubbed shoulders with as a young psychiatrist[131]—whether at Alexandre Kojève's Hegelian seminar at the École Pratique des Hautes Études (EPHE) or through the intermediary of the Évolution psychiatrique group and of the Société Psychanalytique de Paris. In 1953, when Roland Kuhn attempted (without success) to meet Merleau-Ponty in Paris, it was Lacan he asked for help. This missed opportunity would lead another enthusiast of *Daseinsanalyse*, the philosopher Henri Maldiney (1912–2013), to complain about French phenomenology's "intellectual protectionism."[132]

Among philosophers, Sartre and Merleau-Ponty were some of the first to take an interest in existential analysis, and in particular in Binswanger's writings. They did so in the context of a critique of the basic assumptions of empirical psychology and of the different "explanatory idols"—as Sartre put it in 1943—through which it had attempted, until then, to understand human reality.¹³³ For Sartre, this critique became materialized in the project of elaborating a "phenomenological ontology" that aimed to complete the path to the "concrete" opened by Politzer, a project and path to which the "existential psychoanalysis" he wished to elaborate, drawing on Binswanger, also seemed to lead.¹³⁴ In contrast, Merleau-Ponty used Binswanger's writings in the context of a reflection on Freudian theory and on the manner in which it restored to concrete existence relations and attitudes that had previously been understood as related to consciousness. According to Merleau-Ponty, philosophers reflecting on existence must turn their attention to the analysis of the "lived body" and the "sense-directions" running through it; one of the most striking examples of this model he cites is Binswanger's analysis of dreams.¹³⁵

Binswanger himself was aware of the French debate and deeply admired Merleau-Ponty's work in particular; he often cited it in his writings, surprised to see, as he wrote the Russian philosopher Simon Frank (1877–1950) in 1950, "how open the French have always been to phenomenology."¹³⁶ During his visit to Paris for the World Congress of Psychiatry in 1950, he had a long meeting with Jean Wahl,¹³⁷ and in his presentation at the Sorbonne—which also involved responding to remarks by Eugène Minkowski, Jakob Wyrsch, Medard Boss (1903–1990), and Henricus Cornelius Rümke¹³⁸—he stressed the distance between *Daseinsanalyse* and Sartre's positions. In his article "*Daseinsanalyse* in Psychiatry," published a year later in *L'Encéphale*,¹³⁹ he distanced himself from Sartre's positions in the following way:

> If any term is equivocal, certainly "existence" is; this is why I will reject it and replace it with the German term "*Dasein*"— "existential analysis" thereby becoming "Dasein-analysis" [*Daseins-Analyse*]. This word is almost untranslatable; we might

at the limit propose "phenomenological anthropological analysis," if we did not fear that this expression might land a bit heavily in French. . . . I have two special reasons for avoiding this term "existential." First, because it brings to mind the idea of "Existentialism" and specifically the existentialism of Mr. Sartre, who, in *Being and Nothingness*, reproaches Heidegger for taking *Dasein*, and not consciousness, as his point of departure. But it is precisely the idea of *Dasein*, not that of consciousness, that is important in psychiatry. . . . The second reason for avoiding the term "existential analysis" and privileging the term "*Daseinanalysis*" is that *Dasein* includes the soul and the body, the conscious and the unconscious, the voluntary and the involuntarily, thought and action, emotivity, affectivity, and instinct—and that an idea that embraces all of this can be nothing other than the Being itself, excluding any qualification.[140]

Merleau-Ponty had therefore been able to correctly interpret, in the *Phenomenology of Perception*, the stakes of Binswanger's theoretical project—a project that corresponded to his own research program, "which puts essences back into existence, and does not expect to arrive at an understanding of man and the world from any starting point other than that of their 'facticity.'"[141] This debate about the value to assign to facticity, this idea of a concrete existence that corresponds neither to the objectivity of a Being nor to an existence apprehended from the starting point of consciousness, would not escape Foucault and his reading of "Traum und Existenz." This is why, in the note to readers he drafted in 1954 for the French translation of the essay, he underscored that he had chosen, with Binswanger's approval, to render the German term *Dasein* as "presence"—a term, he writes, that simultaneously expresses "the facticity of an existence in situation (presence here) and, at the same time, its openness to a world (presence to the world)."[142] The question of "existence" and of its relation to facticity is therefore at the heart of Binswanger's reception in France, and as we will see, Foucault and Binswanger would exchange letters on this subject during the preparation of the translation of "Traum und Existenz."

In 1950, Jacqueline Verdeaux was in attendance when Binswanger presented at the Congress of Psychiatry at the Sorbonne. We know it from a letter she wrote to Foucault in the spring of 1954, in which she discusses the draft of the introduction to *Le rêve et l'existence* that Foucault had recently sent her. She remarks on the distance of this text from Sartre's positions:

> In the passage about "Pierre" that you first find in Sartre and then continue for yourself, when we move from Sartre to Foucault there is a palpable change of register, a wholly different intention. Sartre's Pierre, who appeared only as a *quisque*, becomes the Other, and finally you end up at the opposite of what he was saying. It seemed to me that I heard Binswanger say very similar things during the Congress of [19]50, if my memory is correct. It seems to me (maybe this is completely wrong) that you are coming within an inch of the major heresy of a *Weisheit* [wisdom] that I heard you strongly condemning with Kuhn. This is the cost of asking for critiques, too bad for you.[143]

The appeal of Sartre's and Merleau-Ponty's phenomenological models, and the simultaneous need to differentiate his own work from theirs, are pervasive in Foucault's writings of the 1950s. Indeed, Foucault sees these models as an "existentialist" deviation from phenomenology that obscures its lineage. In a manuscript from the mid-1950s titled *Phénoménologie et psychologie*, in particular, Foucault is very clear on this topic: existentialism is "not at all the legacy of phenomenology," but rather constitutes "the forgetting of this legacy and omission of what phenomenology is in its true sense."[144]

Foucault's dissatisfaction with existentialism was linked to his precocious interest in psychopathology. It is interesting to note that it was precisely because he was distancing himself from the French phenomenological model—in particular Merleau-Ponty's—that Georges Gusdorf (1912–2000), Althusser's predecessor at ENS, decided in 1946–1947 to open "the doors of the world of madness in its intrinsic reality" to the ENS's philosophy students.[145] Due to his friendship with Georges Daumézon,[146] he brought Foucault and his fellow students to the psychiatric hospital in Fleury-les-Aubrais, near Orléans, and to Sainte-Anne, where Paul Guiraud was organizing presentations of patients. The "lack of interest, among philosophers, in direct contact with human reality"[147] that Georges Gusdorf complained about also led Gaston Bachelard to turn to phenomenological psychopathology at this time. In 1948, he reflected in his book *La terre et les rêveries du repos* (Earth and Reveries of Repose) that "very often, pursuing our solitary work in books, we have envied psychiatrists to whom life offers new 'cases' each day."[148] In a letter he wrote to Binswanger a few years later, he added: "Oh! How I would love to have human beings under my gaze like you! If nothing else, how you help the philosopher of books that I am by bringing me these direct testimonies of human life in its multiplicity!"[149]

"A SCIENCE OF MADMEN AND OF GENIUS"

In the mid-1950s, Bachelard had already largely developed what he termed the "nocturnal side"[150] of his thinking in his works devoted to the poetic imagination. Phenomenology only began to replace the psychoanalysis of elements with *The Poetics of Space* (1957);[151] still, the Bachelardian approach to the problem of the imagination had already caught Binswanger's attention at the beginning of the 1940s, with the publication of *Water and Dreams* (1942)[152] and *Air and Dreams* (1943).[153] In one of his most famous clinical studies, *The Case of Ellen West* (1944–1945), Binswanger described Bachelard's *Water and Dreams* as "so important for existential analysis."[154] Moreover, in his essay "The Existential Analysis School of Thought" (1946), he devoted a long passage to the way in which Bachelard, in *Air and Dreams*, "impressively and beautifully demonstrates the existential-analytical significance of the fundamental metaphors *de la hauteur, de l'elevation, de la profondeur, de l'abaissement, de la chute*" (in French in the text).[155] Foucault knew this essay well and recalled it in his introduction to *Le rêve et l'existence*, observing about Binswanger's conception of dreams that "no one has better understood the dynamic work of the imagination and the incessantly vectorial nature of its movement."[156]

Binswanger was not alone in noticing a certain proximity between Bachelard's intuitions and the phenomenologico-existential approach to the human psyche. In 1960, while recalling her youth, Simone de Beauvoir observed that "in *L'eau et les rêves* Bachelard investigated the imaginative processes in terms of something very much like existential psychoanalysis; hitherto hardly anyone had risked exploring this particular field, and the book interested us as a result."[157]

Bachelard discovered Binswanger's and Kuhn's works after the war. In a letter he wrote to Kuhn in 1947, Bachelard expressed "growing enthusiasm" for the *Daseinsanalytic* "school," while lamenting the isolation into which France had fallen during the war.[158] From this correspondence we learn that the philosopher and the psychiatrist had met in Paris during one of Kuhn's visits to Georges and Jacqueline Verdeaux; it was thanks to Kuhn that Bachelard was later able to make contact with Binswanger.

Jacqueline Verdeaux played the role of intermediary: she organized the meetings, made note of German-language publications, and circulated them among French scholars.[159] Bachelard put Kuhn's and Verdeaux's suggestions to good use. For example, in a letter to Bachelard dated January 7, 1948, Kuhn suggests that he read Binswanger's book *Grundformen und Erkenntnis menschlichen Daseins* (1942)—a task that Bachelard proposes to undertake immediately. This "great and beautiful book," as the philosopher called it several months later in one of his letters to Binswanger, often came up in the correspondence between Binswanger and Bachelard, who mentioned that he "reread it constantly," "spoke about it to [his] students at the Sorbonne," and even intended to devote "a series of in-depth lectures" to it in the future.[160]

In addition, we learn from a letter that Bachelard sent to Binswanger on January 26, 1948, that he had received the first of the two volumes of *Ausgewahlte Vorträge und Aufsätze*, which the psychiatrist had just published. This volume included, among others, the essay on "The Existential Analysis School of Thought" (1946), in which a long passage is dedicated to the Bachelardian approach to the imagination. It was probably after having read this passage that Bachelard decided to "add a quick note" to *La terre et les rêveries du repos* "to refer to some of your pages."[161]

In his article, indeed, while praising Bachelard's approach to the "materiality" of the imagination, Binswanger added: "This *materialité* of the world-design, originating from the 'key' (*Gestimmtheit*) of the existence is by no means confined to the environment, to the world of things, or to the universe in general, but refers equally to the world of one's fellow men (*Mitwelt*) and to the self-world (*Eigenwelt*) (as demonstrated in the cases of Ellen West and Jürg Zünd)."[162] This is why—as we learn from the correspondence—Binswanger's shipping of the *Ausgewahlte Vorträge und Aufsätze* also included the two clinical case studies mentioned earlier. The quick note to which Bachelard refers in his letter corresponds in all likelihood to the passage that we find at the end of the second chapter of *La terre et les rêveries du repos*, in which he turns to "certain remarks that might indicate the orientation of [his] research" and concludes,

> If our efforts could be sustained, we might have the possibility of examining the universe of expression as an autonomous world. We would see that this universe of expression sometimes offers itself as a means of liberation in relation to the three worlds conceptualized in *Daseinsanalyse*: *Umwelt, Mitwelt, Eigenwelt*, the environing world, the interhuman world, and the personal world. At the very least, three worlds of expression, three kinds of poetry can be distinguished here.[163]

We could certainly ask whether the research outlined by Bachelard here corresponded to Binswanger's wishes. In any case, it is certain that Binswanger understood the essence of Bachelard's theoretical remarks when he underscored the philosophical significance of Bachelard's metaphors, which he connected to his own vision. For example, in his letter of February 12, 1948, Binswanger draws the philosopher's attention to the manner in which he developed the theme of *Dasein*'s vertical "sense-direction" (*Bedeutungsrichtung*) in "Traum und Existenz"—a theme that shows, he writes, how close their positions are. In this essay, indeed, Binswanger emphasizes that poetic expression is not merely "an analogy in the logical sense" or "a pictorial metaphor in the poetic sense": "The inner nature of poetic similes," he explains, "lies, in fact, *behind* that to which logic and theories of expression bring to light" [*sic*].[164]

This is a critical concept for *Daseinsanalyse*, one to which Binswanger often returned in his clinical case studies. In the Suzanne Urban case study (1952), for example, while discussing the metaphors patients use to express themselves, he declares that they are founded on a "harsh reality": "Before getting to work, we must clearly establish that metaphors are the modes of movement of transcendence, even more, say, than metaphors are the language of transcendence."[165] In other words, to cite a relatively famous passage in "Traum und Existenz": "When, in a bitter disappointment, 'we fall from the clouds,' then we *actually* do fall. Such falling is neither purely of the body nor something (analogically or metaphorically) derived from physical falling."[166]

We therefore understand why Binswanger particularly appreciated the "fundamental metaphors" that Bachelard described in his works of the early 1940s, his way of understanding the "ascensional life" as a real verticality rather than as a futile metaphor. This reality, from which images are constituted, must nevertheless not be confused with sensory or even mental experience. Still, while Bachelard delved more deeply into this perspective by asking about the nature of the creative imagination,[167] Binswanger followed the thread of an anthropological inquiry about the existential structures that define man's being in the world, which reveal themselves in the imagination and in dreams. This is why in his essay from 1946, while praising Bachelard's approach to the imagination, he critiques it for being entirely founded on the "*forces imaginantes de notre esprit* [imagining forces of our spirit]," which is to say, on psychology, and therefore lacking "an anthropological, and even more, an ontological, basis."[168] Maybe it was for this reason that, in a letter to Kuhn dated December 28, 1947, Bachelard asked to be educated "as much on your school of *Daseinsanalyse* as on the anthropological point of view," and to be advised as to which "essential works" might help him "concentrate [his] efforts in a book about a cosmology united to anthropology."[169]

The themes of the imagination and of the benefits that might be derived from inscribing it within anthropology are at the heart of Foucault's reading of Binswanger in the introduction to *Le rêve et l'existence*. Foucault's goal, as he explicitly announced to Binswanger in a letter dated April 1954, was precisely to "sketch out an anthropology of the imagination that appeared to subtend his text."[170] In his reading of Binswanger, and especially of his essay on dreams, Foucault therefore seems to be following in the footsteps of Bachelard, who, while appreciating existential analysis and using it for inspiration, eventually went beyond it. In his introduction from 1954, Foucault would continue the effort to examine the universe of expression while situating it in the context of a problematization of anthropology. He would take up the scholarly torch lit by the philosophers who came before him—Politzer, Sartre, Merleau-Ponty, Bachelard—with the goal of giving philosophy, using psychopathology, the "foreign matter"—as Canguilhem put it in 1943—it needed to feed its reflection.

THE RORSCHACH TEST AND *DASEINSANALYSE*

The relationship between Bachelard and the Swiss phenomenologist-psychiatrists is an important element in the picture I am sketching out, an element that speaks not only to the exchanges between French- and German-speaking psychiatrists and philosophers in the first half of the last century, but also to the place of Bachelard's thinking in European psychiatric phenomenology around the 1950s. A letter conserved in the Roland Kuhn archives in the canton of Thurgau in Frauenfeld is instructive in this regard. It tells us that, in 1952, a group of psychologists and psychiatrists at the University of Utrecht asked Bachelard to join the editorial board of a new journal, which would be devoted to phenomenological psychiatry and *Daseinsanalyse*.[171] The journal would be titled *Situation: Jahrbuch für phänomenologische Psychologie und Psychopathologie*; its editors in chief would be Frederik J. J. Buytendijk and Jan Hendrik van den Berg (1914–2012). Its first special issue would concern "familiar spaces" (*Die vertrauten Räume*). Bachelard's name is listed alongside those of Binswanger, Minkowski, Gebsattel, Kunz, Merleau-Ponty, Erwin Straus, Viktor von Weizsäcker, Helmut Plessner, Karl Löwith, Henri Maldiney, and Georges Gusdorf.

Bachelard's interest in phenomenological psychopathology is also important because it illuminates a further piece of the history of existential analysis in France: the Rorschach inkblot test.[172] The French reception of the psychodiagnostic test is at the crossroads of several intellectual networks and has important theoretical stakes not only for psychiatry and psychology, but also for philosophical research. This is why it is worthwhile to pause briefly on its history, in order to recognize the traces it left on Foucault's biography and intellectual trajectory. Among his manuscripts at the BnF, beyond test protocols drafted by Foucault himself, we find numerous reading notes regarding psychodiagnostic techniques, based on the secondary literature of the 1940s and 1950s in German and in English.[173] These notes are concurrent with those concerning the Swiss psychopathologists; this is not happenstance. I will therefore attempt to investigate the link that connected these two areas of interest for Foucault in the mid-1950s in order to show that the Rorschach psychodiagnostic test is one of the ways in which existential analysis penetrated France from the 1930s until its apogee in the mid-1950s.

In his praise for Bachelard's "ascensional psychology" in "The Existential Analysis School of Thought," Binswanger particularly insists on its "greatest importance" "for the understanding of Rorschach results."[174] As for Bachelard, in *La terre et les rêveries du repos*, he advocated for a "psychology of the imagination of matter" that made considerable use of the psychodiagnostic test based on the perception of shapes. He rued having discovered "the great work of Ludwig Binswanger and Roland Kuhn too late" and immediately associated "*Daseinsanalyse* and Rorschachian analysis."[175]

In his article from 1955 on existential analysis in the *Treatise on Psychiatry* of the *Encyclopédie médico-chirurgicale*, Ellenberger insists on the fact that this new approach to mental illness "in no way signals an intrusion of philosophy into psychiatric questions."[176] He adds that "the fact that this method draws its concepts from one of the systems of existentialist philosophy, or is inspired by them, does not change that fact that it constitutes in itself a scientific discipline."[177] As for its practical application, "the existential analyst, ... by all appearances, does little different from an ordinary psychoanalyst or psychiatrist. The crux lies in the vision of the world that he has assimilated."[178] Still, within the list of means used, Ellenberger mentions "psychological tests," and "particularly the Rorschach, which is revealing itself to be one of the most precious auxiliary instruments in this field."[179] As an example, he cites the use of this test in one of Binswanger's clinical case studies: the Jürg Zünd case, which Binswanger published between 1946 and 1947.[180] Foucault describes this case study at length in his manuscript *Binswanger et l'analyse existentielle*, as well as in his reading notes from the 1950s, specifically in relation to the Rorschach test.

When Foucault and the Verdeaux were using it, the Rorschach test was deployed in France in experimental psychology laboratories, especially in the context of psychometric testing applied to work psychology. It might seem curious and even paradoxical to observe that one of the ways in which the phenomenological current in psychopathology entered France was through experimental psychology. On this topic, we should note that the psychiatrists who were trying to introduce existential analysis in France at this time did not consider it to be any less scientific than experimental psychology. This position seems to be echoed by Foucault, in his manuscript *Binswanger et l'analyse existentielle*, when he asks whether and how Binswanger succeeded in "moving from a descriptive and even prescientific apprehension of the human being (*Menschsein*) to a rigorously scientific anthropology."[181]

The first article about the Rorschach inkblot test appeared in France in 1934, two years after the publication of the second Swiss edition of the *Psychodiagnostik*.[182] Its author was Marcel Monnier (1907–1996), a Swiss neurophysiologist and neurologist who played a central role in the development of electroencephalography in Switzerland.[183] The article appeared in the psychiatry journal *L'Encéphale* under the title "Le test psychologique de Rorschach"; its goal was "to draw the attention of French physicians and psychologists to a psychic diagnostic method used frequently in Switzerland, Germany, America, and England for over ten years."[184] After having considered the practical applications of the test in the fields of psychology, pedagogy, and psychometrics, as well as psychopathology and psychoanalysis, Monnier insists particularly on its value for character analysis, relating it to graphology. He also suggests that the test might be useful for genealogical and ethnological research, especially for studies of heredity, and cites Eugen Bleuler's studies on the administration of the test to members of the same family.[185] He concludes by lamenting that "Rorschach's work, which is currently so widely known and appreciated across numerous countries, is not yet translated into French," but adds that it is still quite probable that this lacuna will soon be addressed.[186] It would in fact take thirteen more years for such a translation to be published, in 1947.[187]

Indeed, it was only in the 1940s that the *Psychodiagnostik* truly made its mark in France. The decisive players were Daniel Lagache,[188] Françoise Minkowska[189] (whose works were collected by Eugène Minkowski in a posthumous volume in 1956),[190] and especially the scientific network of the Hôpital Sainte-Anne in Paris. Tracing the history of the *Psychodiagnostik*'s French reception opens two paths to us, which cross in a unique fashion and reveal the epistemologically complex[191]—others might also say "modest"[192]—nature of the Rorschach test. The first of these is that of experimental psychology and especially psychotechnics as a technique of work psychology;[193] the other is existential psychopathology. It is this second path that we will follow.

Georges and Jacqueline Verdeaux played a crucial role in this trajectory. They first met Roland Kuhn in 1947 at the Münsterlingen psychiatric hospital in the canton of Thurgau, on the Swiss shore of Lake Constance. It was Henri Ellenberger who brokered their contact with the psychiatrist. Ellenberger had left France and settled in Switzerland during the war, and at the time he held the position of Head of Medicine at the Breitenau mental hospital in Schaffhausen.[194] During this time, he played an important role in France as a relay for Swiss and German psychiatric culture. Kuhn was known as the great specialist of the *Psychodiagnostik*, whose technique he had refined from the time of his arrival at the Waldau psychiatric clinic in 1937, where he met two of Rorschach's disciples, Arnold Weber (1894–1976) and Hans Zulliger (1893–1965). It was because of his work on the Rorschach test that the Verdeaux spouses wanted to meet him; conversely, Kuhn took advantage of their visit to learn more about the EEG technique, which he had pioneered in Switzerland in the late 1930s.[195] Georges Verdeaux had studied in Lyon (his hometown), completed a psychiatric internship at the Maudsley Hospital in London, and trained in electroencephalography with Grey Walter (1910–1977). He participated in the first International EEG Congress in London in 1947. Most importantly, he was one of the five founding members of the French Society for Electroencephalography and Related Sciences in 1948, together with Alphonse Baudouin (1876–1957), Antoine Remond (1917–1998), Herman Fishgold (1899–1982), and Henri Gastaut (1915–1995). With the support of a private sponsor, Verdeaux bought an EEG machine directly from the United States, which he donated to Sainte-Anne in order to perform electroencephalography in psychiatry at the same time as Fishgold was beginning to use EEG in neurosurgery. Georges and Jacqueline Verdeaux developed the use of EEG in the domain of psychiatric pathology, especially with respect to the effects of psychotropic drugs. They disseminated this knowledge in *Électroencéphalographie Clinique* (Clinical Electroencephalography), published by Masson (Paris) in 1946. This famous volume was translated into several languages and republished many times, and has been used to train many generations of neurologists and psychiatrists in EEG.[196]

Foucault must have known this work: there is a double box in his personal archives dating from the second half of the 1940s, when Foucault was a psychology student, titled "Neurophysiologie, Lagache & EEG."[197] Indeed, as Foucault's notes show, psychology students were trained in EEG technique. Foucault's reading notes collected in a file titled "Electroencéphalogramme et psychologie" bear the following headings: "Monnier: L'organisation des fonctions psychiques à la lueur des données neurophysiologiques";[198] "Personality and the EEG"; "EEG, attention, and mental work"; "EEG and level of consciousness"; "Types of [α-wave] and psychological types";

"EEG and emotion."[199] At that same time, at the Institute of Psychology at the University of Paris, in the division of "pathological psychology," Jean Delay was giving courses on "electroencephalography in clinical psychiatry" and on "theoretical and practical aspects of psychosurgery."[200]

After several visits to the Verdeaux's laboratory at Sainte-Anne, Kuhn would set up an EEG unit at the Münsterlingen hospital. At Münsterlingen, Kuhn was therefore the heir of Hermann Rorschach (1884–1922), who had worked in this very clinic from 1909 to 1913.[201] Not only did he use his technique; more significantly, he also gave a larger meaning to this experiment. Indeed, he shared Rorschach's interest in visual art and his conviction that humans reveal, in artistic expression, their "personal world" or rather the "structure of [their] personality."[202] He devoted several publications to the Rorschach test in the early 1940s.[203] Like Rorschach, Kuhn also used drawing not only to interact with patients but also to uncover the various clinical forms of their behavior and of their lived experience. In his clinical practice, Kuhn used what he called "painting tests" alongside the Rorschach test. These were experiments carried out by observing patients' reactions to reproductions of artworks. He also studied his patients' drawings, analyzing them at length in his clinical case studies and conserving them in his patients' files.[204] In a letter he wrote to Henri Maldiney in 1986, Kuhn went so far as to assert that all of his thought and research had been decisively determined by the Rorschach test, and that, without it, he would never have arrived at "this kind of phenomenologico-Daseinsanalytical thinking."[205]

Foucault was fascinated both by Kuhn's analyses of his patients' drawings, which he described and commented on in his manuscript on existential analysis, and by Kuhn's examination of the results of these patients' Rorschach tests. In the archives, among Foucault's reading notes, we find a long note about Kuhn's essay from 1952 on the meaning of limits in delusion ("Über die Bedeutung vom Grenzen im Wahn"),[206] in which he analyzes the drawings of a schizophrenic patient.

Kuhn's collaboration with Ludwig Binswanger, which began in the late 1930s, allowed him to further refine his approach to the Rorschach test. It came about, in emblematic fashion, because of a discussion concerning the *Psychodiagnostik*. The two psychiatrists first met in 1939, when Binswanger asked his young colleague, who had just become Head of Medicine at Münsterlingen Hospital, to contribute an expert opinion on a patient by means of the Rorschach test. For many years, the two psychiatrists met every two weeks at the Bellevue, the sanatorium Binswanger directed in Kreuzlingen, a few kilometers away from Münsterlingen, to discuss cases on the basis of Rorschach test results. In his autobiography, Kuhn narrated this first meeting, in which Binswanger directly asked him: "Do you understand anything about the Rorschach test?"[207] Kuhn remembered going to meet physicians at the "Gartenhaus" (Garden house) villa: "There I was presented with the Rorschach test of a patient who was then hospitalized at the Bellevue clinic and asked to analyze this test and offer a blind diagnosis. Then, an assistant from the clinic would present the patient's history, which Mr. Binswanger would analyze in order to bridge the clinical approach and the Rorschach test."[208]

Binswanger had received Rorschach's book favorably when it was published in 1921, and had devoted a brief review essay to it, in which he argued that it expressed "a brilliant understanding of men achieved through life experience."[209] Indeed, the Rorschach test was not originally designed to establish a psychological theory, to offer interpretations of the contents of life experiences, or, in the case of psychopathology, to inquire about the causal or etiological links between the forms of experience it analyzed. This is why, for that matter, Rorschach did not share the psychoanalytic understanding of artistic experience. In the Freudian tendency to interpret such forms, he saw the risk of a "domestication of the *Unheimlich* [uncanny]," which would have ended up flattening the constitutive dynamism of the human spirit.[210] The goal of the inkblot test, to his eyes, was to observe the empirical regularity of perceptual experiences in order to determine their characteristic proportions, which Rorschach defined as *Erlebnistypen* (types of lived experience).

If, on the one hand, the *Psychodiagnostik*'s data collection method was founded on statistics, on the other, the knowledge that this method ostensibly produced was not characterized by scientific objectivity of an arithmetic nature. In other words, Rorschach did not claim that the knowledge produced by his method—that is, the types—had any objective value. He even asserted that the clinical picture of a set type, as it emerges from the results of the inkblot test, is what is expressed by ordinary language.

For this reason, Binswanger observed in his review essay of 1923 that Rorschach had succeeded in "understanding, where others limited themselves to calculation,"[211] since "in the field of psychology numbers mean something completely different than they do in physics."[212] We should specify on this topic, as do Peter Galison and Naamah Akavia,[213] that Hermann Rorschach reserved the German term "test" exclusively for the technical and material aspects of his procedure. He conceived of the procedure, considered in its totality, as an "experiment" or "trial" (in German, *Experiment, Versuch*)—terms that give it a much more indeterminate, open-ended character. Indeed, the "objectivity" that Binswanger identified in psychology consisted in the ability to "see" (*Anschauungsfähigkeit*) through experience and to offer an overall view (*Überblick*) of the individual on the basis of the test results. In other words, if knowledge in psychology has an empirical foundation, it can be found in humans' practical knowledge rather than in a knowledge whose validity would be founded on the objective data of experience.

This perspective happily corresponded with the trend in psychopathology research that had been developed in France since the 1930s by Minkowski, Lacan, Lagache, Ey, the Évolution psychiatrique group, and all of the psychiatrists and philosophers who—in the wake of the movement toward the concrete ushered in by Politzer—considered it necessary to rebuild the psychological sciences on the basis of a practical understanding of man. This would allow them to prioritize an orientation toward the clinic. As I will emphasize later in this book, we find this appreciation for existential analysis's clinical approach in the way Foucault conceptualizes it in his manuscript *Binswanger et l'analyse existentielle*; as we will see, most of this text consists of the description and analysis of case studies. It is only when *Daseinsanalyse* tries to become independent of the clinic that, in Foucault's eyes, paradoxically it loses its theoretical efficacy.

It was in this context that, in 1947, Ombredane took on the project of translating Rorschach's manual. He asked Georges and Jacqueline Verdeaux to put him in contact with Kuhn in order to send him his translation; it was published later that year. In the years that followed, until Ombredane's death in 1958, the two physicians exchanged numerous letters about their respective research on the test.[214] Ombredane also translated with Georges and Jacqueline Verdeaux in 1948 an essay by Ruth Bochner and Florence Halpern, *The Clinical Application of the Rorschach Test*, to which he appended a foreword explaining the terminology and symbols to use in French.[215] In 1950, with the encouragement of the International Association for the Rorschach, which had been founded in Zurich in 1948, Ombredane and both Verdeaux participated in the launching of the Groupement français du Rorschach, with Lagache as honorary president and, among its members, Henri Piéron, Henri Wallon, Paul Fraisse (1911–1996), and Merleau-Ponty.[216] The earliest members also included the Minkowski spouses, which reveals how closely related Rorschach's work and the phenomenologico-structural approach to psychopathology were in France from the start. The test's almost exclusive interest in the form of perceptions rather than in their contents, its focus on beginning by identifying the orientation, attitude, or disposition that determines the typology of the lived experience and its potentialities, neatly corresponds to the phenomenological analysis of the "sense-directions" that determine anthropological forms, or, to use Binswanger's words, the "possibilities and powers of being of human life in general."[217]

It was in this context that Jacqueline Verdeaux, in the early 1950s, undertook the project of translating into French a whole series of German-language works on the subject of *Daseinsanalyse*, including Kuhn's study of the interpretation of the mask in the Rorschach test, *Maskendeutungen im Rorschachschen Versuch* (Interpretations of Masks in the Rorschach Test). The French translation of Kuhn's book appeared in 1957, with a preface by Bachelard. This preface highlights both the value of the Rorschach-instrument for phenomenological analyses of the expressions of human behavior and its affinity with dream interpretation. Indeed, Kuhn's book aimed to go beyond psychopathology and instead pertain to, as Kuhn explained, the fields of folklore, anthropology, and "the philosophy and psychology of expression."[218] Psychopathology, he added, "has, until now, hardly considered the problem from the point of view we are adopting."[219] And indeed, with the exception of Binswanger, Erwin Straus, Jakob Wyrsch, and Viktor E. von Gebsattel, it was not psychiatrists but rather writers, historians, philosophers, and art historians that he took as landmarks in his text. By presenting the interpretation of masks in Rorschach's inkblots, Kuhn's goal was not to establish diagnoses that psychiatrists could use but rather to emphasize "forms of existence" or "images of the world": "Here we are taking on problems that transcend questions of health and illness and that are of a generally human scope."[220]

We also see this anthropological orientation in Kuhn's explicit refusal to formulate a psychological theory. What the perception of masks tells us about are the "modes of existence" or "well-defined modes of human relationship"[221] in which the various existential structures that form the basis of any relationship with the world and with others take shape. We can note that the French title chosen for Kuhn's book is *Phénoménologie du masque* (Phenomenology of the Mask)—a choice that does not reflect its original title, but rather that foregrounds the link between the Rorschach test and existential analysis.

Kuhn's methodology is illuminated by Bachelard, who explains, while associating the interpretation of masks with the interpretation of dreams, that "the virtual mask is a veritable schema for analysis."[222] The idea of the schema echoes quite precisely Rorschach's conception of "types" in the *Psychodiagnostik*, insofar as these do not represent ideal theoretical models, empty abstractions, or arbitrary constructions, but rather—as Binswanger was already insisting in the early 1920s in *Einführung in die Probleme der allgemeinen Psychologie* (Introduction to the Problems of General Psychology)—"concepts that can be meaningful in reality, against which we are not simply 'measuring' reality."[223] However, Bachelard does not dwell on this transcendental dimension of the *Daseinsanalytic* interpretation of the mask in his preface. Instead, he insists on the vital, innovative, even creative value of the interpretation of masks: "to interpret virtual masks is to penetrate into the very zone in which ideation and imaging are constantly exchanging their actions."[224] On this topic he cites Georges Buraud's *Les Masques* (1948), in which masks are likened to dreams, "ephemeral and moving, fluid masks that are born, play out their comedy or their drama, and die."[225] This aspect was underlined by Jean Starobinski in his review in 1958 of Kuhn's book in the journal *Critique*. While insisting on the methodological rigor of Kuhn's approach to the Rorschach test, Starobinski pauses on Bachelard's "remarkable preface" and concludes,

> Before the psychologist's will to *elucidate*, man retains a murky desire for obscurity and depth. And even when he has learned that the scientist contests the reality of that depth, he takes pleasure in it as he would an imaginary possession. Were it for nothing, he wishes to dispose of his appearances sovereignly, to organize the space of his presence or absence as he wishes, or even to lose sight of himself, as if an abyss lived inside him.[226]

In an offprint of this preface sent by Bachelard to Georges Canguilhem on June 29, 1957, we can read the following dedication: "To my friend Canguilhem in order to convince him that in a well-balanced 'duplicity,' on the side of the 'subject' as on the side of the 'object,' phenomenology is a science of madmen and of genius."[227]

ON THE "LAKESIDE" OF MÜNSTERLINGEN

In the Western imagination, wrote Foucault in 1963, "reason has for a long time belonged to solid ground (terra firma)," whereas madness, "in the old landscapes of our imagination," is

FIGURE 1.1 © CENTRE DOCUMENTAIRE DU CAPHÉS—UMS 3610, École normale supérieure-PSL, CALL NUMBER CAN 1080 ["*À l'ami Canguilhem, pour le convaincre que dans une 'duplicité' bien équilibrée, du côté du 'sujet' comme du côté de 'l'objet,' la Phénoménologie est une science de fous et de génie. Daté du lendemain d'un grand jour, 29 Juin 1957*"]

characterized by an "essential liquidity."[228] From the theory of humors in antiquity, passing through the myth of the *Narrenschiff* (ship of fools) in the fifteenth century, until the establishment of hydrotherapy by psychiatric medicine, water has been complicit with madness, albeit in an ambivalent way: at once the substance of unreason and a medium to counteract it, "for her—against her."[229]

Reading these passages, one is tempted to ask whether the visit that a young Foucault made to the Münsterlingen asylum in 1954 could have influenced his reflections on "water and madness" in some way. What is clear is that Foucault remembered this experience at the beginning of the 1960s. In the pages of his intellectual journal, while he was working on his book *Death and the Labyrinth*, he wrote the following notes:

Madmen, feasts
The tradition of the feast of madmen
Masks and blasphemy
The fool
The intoxication of language
A few examples of maniacal delusion.[230]

Since its founding in the middle of the nineteenth century,[231] the Münsterlingen psychiatric hospital, in the canton of Thurgau, has always been strongly marked by its proximity to the lake. Indeed, it has been identified by the region's inhabitants as on the *Seeseite*, or "lakeside," of the town to distinguish it from the rest of the hospital, situated on the railway side.[232] Many psychiatrists who are well known to historians, such as Ludwig Binswanger Senior (1820–1880), grandfather of the founder of existential psychiatry, and Hermann Rorschach, worked there; but throughout its long history Münsterlingen was also a site through which intellectuals, historians, and philosophers passed. The clinic rose to fame in the world of psychiatry primarily thanks to Roland Kuhn, who was its head of medicine starting in 1939 and became its director from 1970 to 1979. In the early 1950s he discovered Imipramine, the first antidepressant medication; it came to market in 1957 under the name Tofranil. In the asylum guestbook, in the 1950s, one can read the names of Henri Maldiney, Jacques Schotte (1928–2007),[233] Viktor Emil von Gebsattel, and Kurt Goldstein.[234]

This is the context in which, in March 1954, the young Foucault visited the canton of Thurgau, accompanied by Georges Verdeaux and his wife Jacqueline. At the time, Foucault and Jacqueline Verdeaux were very close to completing the translation of "Traum und Existenz," which they wished to discuss in person with Binswanger. Thanks to Kuhn's intervention, they met the psychiatrist at the Bellevue clinic in Kreuzlingen; Bellevue was the private sanatorium that the Binswanger family had directed for three generations. The visit to Münsterlingen took place during the "Mardi Gras holidays," as specified by Jacqueline Verdeaux in a letter to Binswanger dated January 14, 1954:

> I am happy to tell you how much pleasure it has given me to translate *Traum und Existenz*. I spend all my free time on it and hope to have finished at the beginning of March. We would very much like to take advantage of the Mardi Gras holidays (March 2) to visit you and revise the translation with you. I will try to send you the manuscript a few days in advance so that you can read it carefully and peacefully, and prepare your critiques. We could perhaps work with you on March 3 and 4, if these dates are convenient.[235]

Through Jacqueline Verdeaux and Ludwig Binswanger's 1954 correspondence, we learn that once the translation of "Traum and Existenz" was underway, it was often Binswanger who suggested and sent to Verdeaux certain of his writings. The initial translation project had included other texts, probably on the model of the first volume of the *Ausgewählte Vorträge und Aufsätze*, published in Bern in 1947. In a letter dated January 6, Binswanger reports that the French publisher contacted his publisher in Bern to explain that "only 2 or 3 of my lectures would appear in the first small volume. He would make some suggestions in addition to 'Traum und Existenz,' but has not yet done so. I think it would be better if the three of us, you, Foucauld [sic], and myself, made a decision."[236] In the same letter, Binswanger suggests—at Roland Kuhn's prompting— publishing his lecture on psychotherapy[237] and his text "Lebensfunktion und innere Lebensgeschichte" (Life function and inner life history).[238] He also wonders about the possibility of sending Verdeaux and Foucault his essay "Geschehnis und Erlebnis" (Event and Lived Experience).[239] In the end, only *Le rêve et l'existence* would be published, and a collection of Binswanger's essays would not appear in French until 1971.[240] This collection was spearheaded by Verdeaux and Kuhn, but Foucault was no longer part of the project.

On June 22, 1954, Jacqueline Verdeaux received from Binswanger the text of the lecture "Daseinsanalyse und Psychotherapie" that the psychiatrist gave in Zurich and published later that year. The text is joined to a letter asking her to translate it into French with Foucault's help: "I am enclosing an 'allocution' that I intend to give in July at the International Congress of Psychotherapists in Zurich. I would be very grateful to you and to Mr. Foucault if you had the kindness of translating it into French as soon as possible. It will certainly interest you and Mr. Foucault, also from the point of view of its contents."[241] J. Verdeaux sent him the translation only two days later, once she had "carefully revised it with Foucault," adding—referring to the carnival feast—that "*Walpurgisnacht* inspired us."[242]

Jacqueline Verdeaux played the role of intermediary between Binswanger and Foucault for a long time. It was she who conveyed information concerning ongoing translations, who organized meetings, and who transmitted messages and encouraged exchanges between the famous psychiatrist and the young philosopher.[243] She kept this role even after the two men had met and begun their correspondence, so much so that Binswanger often addressed questions about Foucault to her. In the letter of January 6, 1954, for example, Binswanger tells her that "the French publisher has written to the publisher in Bern that Prof. Foucauld [sic] would like to write a 100-page introduction" to "Traum und Existenz"; he adds, "I am thrilled about it, please let him know."[244]

In the fall of 1955, Foucault left France for Sweden, where he stayed three years. Jacqueline Verdeaux continued to oversee shared translation projects in the field of psychopathology and to maintain contact with French publishers. It was to her that Foucault wrote from Sweden on December 29, 1956, inquiring about the possibility that a publisher would accept the volume that he was in the midst of drafting, which would become *History of Madness*: "Do you think that the publisher would accept a book such as this one, at the end of which there will be twenty-five to thirty pages of scholarly notes. After all, unreason is serious."[245]

The correspondence between Binswanger and Foucault, in contrast, began on April 27, 1954. It consists of five letters that uncover several previously unknown elements surrounding the publication of the introduction to *Le rêve et l'existence* and its translation more generally. Indeed, we learn that the visit to Lake Constance in March 1954 was to be put to good use revising the translation of "Traum und Existenz" and part of Roland Kuhn's book on masks, which Jacqueline Verdeaux had also been working on. The correspondence between Roland Kuhn, Ludwig Binswanger, and Jacqueline Verdeaux gives us still more details. We learn that Verdeaux and Foucault went to Switzerland twice, in March and in September 1954. The work of translating "Traum und Existenz," which had begun at the end of 1953,[246] ended in February 1954, after Verdeaux had "revised it once with [her] friend Foucault," whom she esteemed to be "a precious reference from a philosophical point of view."[247] On February 3, she sent a first draft of the work to Binswanger so that he could read it and "prepare his critiques" before their meeting in Kreuzlingen. She added, on Foucault's behalf as well, that both of them were very pleased "to be able to hatch dreams for the future" with the texts that he would be willing to give them.[248]

According to Kuhn's recollections, after the visit to Münsterlingen, he met Foucault in Paris on other occasions during this period.[249] In any case, the second meeting between Foucault and Binswanger occurred midway through September 1954. This time, Foucault, still accompanied by Jacqueline Verdeaux, joined Binswanger in Brissago (canton of Ticino),[250] where the psychiatrist often spent his vacations and where he would meet with the Husserlian philosopher Wilhelm Szilasi (1889–1966), Heidegger's successor at the University of Freiburg. Binswanger's letter to Foucault dated May 6, 1954, informs us that it was with Szilasi that he shared his first reading of the draft introduction that Foucault had just sent him. During this second visit, Binswanger had already received the final version of the translation of "Traum und Existenz," as we learn from a letter that Binswanger wrote to J. Verdeaux on June 2, 1954, thanking her for the copy he had just received.

As for their joint projects, Binswanger also inquired in this letter about her progress on the translation of the Suzanne Urban case study, while indicating that he wanted to avoid "breathing down her neck."[251] In her response of June 24, she announced that the publication date for *Le rêve et l'existence* had been set for September 15. She would also like to send him the first half of *Suzanne Urban*, which "had given her a few additional grey hairs." But she was mostly pleased that he liked Foucault's introduction, which she was "personally thrilled by."[252] Binswanger's response stressed the extreme competence that he could discern in the text, but also its intelligence and "productive" aspect in relation to "Traum und Existenz."[253] Indeed, Foucault and Verdeaux, through their translation work, wanted to introduce something that was truly new to "French readers still so attached to old things."[254]

In a letter dated September 2, 1954, Jacqueline Verdeaux wrote to Binswanger: "Foucault and I have decided that *Suzanne Urban* should come out as a single volume, with an introduction, and that at the end of the translation we would like to add a kind of small dictionary of anthropo-phenomenological terms, and we need to discuss it with you."[255] Indeed, after the publication of *Le rêve et l'existence*, the correspondence between the Verdeaux, Binswanger, and Kuhn primarily concerned the translation of *Suzanne Urban*. Several letters between Roland Kuhn and Georges Verdeaux,[256] as well as between Kuhn and Binswanger, show that it was through Kuhn's intervention that Binswanger agreed to write a preface for the French translation of the work. He concludes this preface by expressing his gratitude first to Jacqueline Verdeaux for her "excellent translation," but also to "his friends Roland Kuhn and Michel Foucault, whose opinions were precious."[257]

While Binswanger and Jacqueline Verdeaux's correspondence becomes increasingly friendly as time goes by, the letters between Binswanger and Foucault maintain a more formal tone and address only theoretical matters. In his letter of May 10, 1954,

Binswanger decides to open up a more detailed discussion of some of the principal concepts of *Daseinsanalyse* on the basis of Foucault's readings of them. Of chief concern is the relationship between ontology and anthropology—a theme that in the early 1950s was absolutely critical for Foucault. To Binswanger, who accuses him of having claimed, in his introduction, that "the human being is only the concrete and effective content of what ontology terms facticity," Foucault replies by correcting his own assertions.

Issues of the relationship between dreams, dreams of dying, and suicide also arise. On one of the rare occasions in which Binswanger offers criticisms to Foucault, he reproaches him for having "somewhat exaggerated" his formulations.[258] In general, though, the psychiatrist declares himself very satisfied with Foucault's text and thanks him for the "great scientific honors" he has bestowed upon him:

> In my opinion, you have done an excellent job, especially as concerns the main point, which is to say, the movement of the *imagination* [in French] [and] its relationship to the *image* [in French] etc. Another important contribution is your capacity to treat the *imagination* [in French] such that it is applicable both to the waking imagination and to the imagination of dreams. Another major merit lies in your new bibliographic references concerning dreams and the imagination. You are enriching my bibliography, just as I enriched Freud's.[259] But whereas Freud was saddened by it,[260] I can only be thrilled by this progress; I always feel like simply another link in the chain of the "spiritual movement" that we all hold dear.[261]

On his side, Foucault wanted to tackle the problem of the basis of anthropological knowledge, but by looking at it especially through the lens of the concept of "facticity." This is a Heideggerian notion that was bound up with the concern for the "concrete" at the heart of French psychology and philosophy in the first half of the twentieth century, as Foucault writes to Binswanger in his letter of May 21, 1954:

> Since Sartre we have been too inclined, in France, to make facticity the root, in a way, of all existentials. I readily acknowledge that this is not at all the perspective of *Daseinsanalyse*, and that it would be incompatible with your conception of love. I will therefore correct this sentence in my text. But I would be very happy if, one day when I once again have the great pleasure of meeting you, you allowed me to ask you a few questions on this problem of facticity, transcendence, and love.[262]

As we will see in our analysis of the manuscript *Binswanger et l'analyse existentielle*, these are fundamental concepts in two ways: first, Binswanger develops them in a way that clearly differentiates his thinking from Heidegger's existential analysis. Moreover, they are at the heart of the harsh critique that Foucault will ultimately direct toward *Daseinsanalyse*.

Unfortunately, we do not have any documents that can inform us about the second meeting between Foucault and Binswanger. By the beginning of the 1950s, Binswanger had begun to distance himself from the anthropological approach borrowed from the Heideggerian analytic. He turned his attention to the theme that had preoccupied him at the beginning of his scholarly career: the examination of the structural principles of consciousness that would undergird the transcendental constitution of experience. In 1954, *Daseinsanalyse* had already made its choice—a choice that did not correspond, as we will now see, to the alternative suggestion advocated by the young Parisian philosopher.

FIGURE 1.2 Photo taken by Georges Verdeaux in 1954. On the left Roland Kuhn, at the center Michel Foucault, on the right Jacqueline Verdeaux (© Éditions EHESS)

LIST OF READING NOTES CONCERNING PHENOMENOLOGICAL PSYCHOPATHOLOGY(BNF, FONDS MICHEL FOUCAULT, CALL NUMBER NAF 28730)[263]

BOX 33 A (FOLDER o)

- Binswanger, Häberlin etc. [folder cover]
- *Wege der Weltorientierung*
- Le *Verfallen*
- Préface à la 1ère édition des *Grundformen*
- La spatialité
- Anthropologie et phénoménologie husserlienne

- Ontologie et anthropologie
- La temporalité
- L'instant
- La transcendance
- Histoire et rationalité selon Jaspers
- E. Küppers, "Psychologische Analyse im Dienste der Neurologie," *Nervenarzt* 1953

BOX 38 (FOLDER 1)

- [Ludwig] Binswanger (articles) [folder cover]
- Binswanger, "Wahnsinn als lebensgeschichtliches Phänomen und als Geisteskrankheit," *Monatsschrift für Psychiatrie und Neurologie*, vol. 110, n. 3/4, 1945, p. 129
- "Über Psychotherapie," *Der Nervenarzt*, [vol. 8], 1935[: 113–121, 180–189]
- *Die Auffassung und Deutung des Traumes von den Griechen bis zur Gegenwart*, Berlin[: Springer], 1928
- Jaspers et la Psychiatrie ["Karl Jaspers und die Psychiatrie"], *Schweizer Archiv für Neurologie und Psychiatrie*, 1943, vol. 51, fasc. 1, 1–13
- Binswanger, *Grundformen und Erkenntnis menschlichen Daseins* [Zürich: Niehans, 1942]
- Cas d'analyse existentielle
- "Conception de l'homme chez Freud à la lumière de l'anthropologie philosophique" [(1936), trad. par Hans Pollnow, *L'Évolution psychiatrique*, vol. 10, no. 1, 1938: 3–34.]
- Transformation de l'idée d'homo natura en théorie biologique de la nature, et sa signification pour la psychologie médicale
- "Traum und Existenz"

- "Über Phänomenologie" 1922 (Communication à la Soc. suisse de Psychiatrie)
- "Lebensfunktion und innere Lebensgeschichte," *Monatsschrift für Psychiatrie und Neurologie*, vol. 68, 1928[: 52–79]
- ["Lebensfunktion und innere Lebensgeschichte"] Histoire de ces deux notions
- "Über die daseinsanalytische Forschungsrichtung in der Psychiatrie," *Schweizer Archiv für Psychiatrie und Neurologie*, [vol. 57,] 1946, [209–235]
- "Daseinsanalytik und Psychiatrie," *Nervenarzt*, [vol. 22, 1951: 1–10]

BOX 42 B (FOLDER 1)

- [Karl] Jaspers [folder cover]
- Les trois modes du *Transzendieren*
- L'être et la transcendance
- *Weltorientierung*
- Le *Selbstwerden*
- L'élucidation de l'existence
- *Dasein und Transzendieren*
- La transcendance et la philosophie
- La transcendance
- Le chiffre de la Transcendance
- La *Daseinsanalyse*
- *Formale Seinsbegriffe*
- Philosophie et situation
- La situation
- *Erscheinung*
- *Daseinsanalyse und Existenzerhellung*
- *Philosophieren*

- L'existence
- [untitled]
- [K. Jaspers] "Eifersuchtswahn: Ein Beitrag zur Frage: Entwicklung einer Persönlichkeit oder Prozess?," *Zeitschrift für die gesamte Neurologie und Psychiatrie*, vol. 1 (1910), 567–637
- L'amour selon Jaspers
- La compréhension
- Le concept de normal en médecine organique / Psychopathologie
- L'expression
- Phénomènes primaires et phénomènes secondaires
- La compréhension génétique
- La méthode phénoménologique
- Critique de la psychanalyse
- La notion de phénoménologie
- La vie psychologique non interpénétrable / Psychopathologie
- L'inconscient
- La maladie psychique / Psychopathologie
- Jaspers, *Psychopathologie*
- [Jaspers. Psychopathologie] V. Les ensembles de la vie psychologique
- *Psychologie der Weltanschauungen*, [Berlin: Julius Springer], 1919
- *Bewältigung der Transzendenz als Aufgabe*
- [Eugen Fink,] "Vergegenwärtigung und Bild," *Beiträge zur Phänomenologie der Unwirklichkeit*, [vol. 11 (1930): 239–309]
- Binswanger et autour. [top folder cover]
- [Hans] Kunz [folder cover]
- Interprétation anthropologique de l'imagination
- La signification anthropologique de l'imagination
- "Idee, Wesen und Wirklichkeit des Menschen. [Bemerkungen zu einem Grundproblem der philosophischen Anthropologie," *Studia Philosophica*, vol. 4, no 147 (1944): 147–169]. Hans Kunz

- [Viktor Emil von] Gebsattel [folder cover]
- Gebsattel, "Über Fetischismus," [*Der Nervenarzt*, vol. 2, no. 1 (1929): 8–20]
- Le temps d'après Gebsattel
- La phobie psychasténique selon Gebsattel
- Gebsattel, "Die Welt des Zwangskranken," *Monatsschrift für Psychiatrie und Neurologie*, vol. 99 (1938): [10–74]
- Gebsattel, "Zur Frage der Depersonalisation. (Ein Beitrag zur Theorie der Melancholie)," [Der Nervenarzt, vol. 10, no. 4 (1937): 169–178; vol. 10, no. 5 (1937): 248–257]
- [Gebsattel, "Zur Frage der Depersonalisation"] Interprétation
- [Alfred] Storch [folder cover]
- Storch: "Tod und Erneuerung in der schizophrenen Daseins-Umwandlung," *Archiv für Psychiatrie und Neurologie*, vol. 181 (1948): 275–293
- Storch. Die Psychoanalyse und die menschlichen Existenzprobleme. *Schweizer Archiv für Neurologie und Psychiatrie*, vol. 44 (1939): 102–118
- A. Storch. "Die Daseinsfrage der Schizophrenen," *Archiv für Neurologie, Neurochirurgie und Psychiatrie*, [vol. 59,] (1947): 330.
- [Storch, "Die Daseinsfrage der Schizophrenen"] Histoire du malade
- [Storch, "Die Daseinsfrage der Schizophrenen"] Daseinsanalyse.
- Erwin Straus [folder cover]
- La sensation considérée comme mode de communication
- La théorie de l'immanence des sensations
- Les synesthésies. Liberté vitale et conditionnement (*Verbundenheit*) vital
- Le rapport de la sensation et du mouvement
- [Le rapport de la sensation et du mouvement] La fausse classification du mouvement (*Verdinglichung*)

- [Le rapport de la sensation et du mouvement] La visée pré-scientifique et le point de vue de la science
- [Le rapport de la sensation et du mouvement] L'intérieur et l'extérieur
- [Le rapport de la sensation et du mouvement] Les rapports de totalité et les limites
- [Le rapport de la sensation et du mouvement] L'Ici et le maintenant
- [Le rapport de la sensation et du mouvement] g. *Sich-bewegen und Bewegungsvollzug*
- [Le rapport de la sensation et du mouvement] Les théories atomistiques du mouvement
- Critique de l'épiphénoménisme de la *Gestalt*
- E. La différence entre la sensation (*Empfinden*) et la connaissance (*Erkennen*)
- La différence de la sensation et de la perception
- Famille naturelle et famille humaine
- Le "*Faktische*" est le thème de la perception
- La psychologie traditionnelle de l'espace et du temps
- Le problème de l'espace
- Le problème du temps
- La certitude sensible
- Théorie des hallucinations
- Szilasi [folder cover]
- *Geist* et *Seins-Möglichkeit*
- *Suzanne Urban*
- [*Suzanne Urban*] Anamnèse
- [Suzanne Urban] B. Daseinsanalyse
- *Ideenflucht* [folder cover]
- Le nivellement dans l'*Ideenflucht*
- La méthode daseinsanalytique [*Ideenflucht*]
- La structure existential-anthropologique de l'*Ideenflucht*

- Anthropologie et clinique
- [Anthropologie et clinique] Vers une psychopathologie de l'*Ideenflucht*
- [Vers une psychopathologie de l'*Ideenflucht*] L'homme maniaco-dépressif
- *Lola Voss* [folder cover]
- *Lola Voss*

- Catamnèse [*Lola Voss*]
- Les cas précédents et celui de Lola Voss
- [Les cas précédents et celui de Lola Voss] 2. "Die Unheimlichkeit des Fürchterlichen"
- *Jürg Zünd* [folder cover]
- Comparaison des cas Ellen West, Nadia e Jürg Zünd
- Le cas Jürg Zünd [Observation]
- [Le cas Jürg Zünd] Observations dans le premier hôpital
- [Le cas Jürg Zünd] Selbstschilderungen
- [Le cas Jürg Zünd] Daseinsanalyse
- [Le cas Jürg Zünd: Génie et *Wahnsinn*] "Die Existenz oder der singuläre Modus"
- [Le cas Jürg Zünd] [Comparaison avec Ellen West]
- [Le cas Jürg Zünd] "Ergebnisse der Daseinsanalyse"
- [Le cas Jürg Zünd] L'angoisse
- [Le cas Jürg Zünd] La culpabilité
- [Le cas Jürg Zünd] *Wahn*
- "Die leere Zeit des Autismus"
- *Ellen West*
- Cas Ellen West
- La cas Ellen West
- [Le cas Ellen West] Daseinsanalyse
- [Le cas Ellen West] Daseinsanalyse et psychanalyse
- [Le cas Ellen West] Analyse psychopathologique et clinique

- [Le cas Ellen West—Le cas Nadia] Le "*Schamphänomen*"
- R. Kuhn [folder cover]
- R. Kuhn. Compte rendu de Binswanger, *Grundformen*
- Interprétation daseinsanalytique de l'acte de Rudolf
- "Die Trauer" (R. Kuhn, "Mordversuch [eines depressiven Fetischisten und Sodomisten an einer Dirne," *Monatsschrift für Psychiatrie und Neurologie*, vol. 116, nos. 1-2-3 (1948): 66–151])
- R. Kuhn, Étude daseinsanalytique sur la signification des limites dans le délire ["Über die Bedeutung vom Grenzen im Wahn," *Monatsschrift für Psychiatrie und Neurologie*, vol. 124, nos. 4–6 (1952): 354–383]
- R. Kuhn, Daseinsanalyse d'un cas de schizophrénie ["Daseinsanalyse eines Falles von Schizophrenie"]. *Monatsschrift für Psychiatrie und Neurologie*, [vol. 112], nos. 5–6 (1946): [233–257]
- "Zur Daseinsanalyse der Anorexia mentalis. II. Studie." R. Kuhn. *Der Nervenarzt*, vol. 22, no. 1 (1951): 11[–13]
- R. Kuhn. "Daseinsanalyse im psychotherapeutischen Gespräch." *Schweizer Archiv für Neurologie*, vol. 67 (1951): 52–60
- R. Kuhn. "Zur Daseinsstruktur einer Neurose" [*Jahrbuch für Psychologie und Psychotherapie*, vol. 1, no. 2 (1953): 207–222]
- [R. Kuhn] Zur Daseinsanalyse der Anorexia mentalis. II. Studie (*Der Nervenarzt*, [vol. 24 (1953):] 191–198)
- Psychopathologie phénoménologique
- Contre la *Daseinsanalyse*
- Le rêve
- Sur la perception (normale et pathologique)
- [Bibliographical references]
- Pathologie de l'espace [Bibliographical references]
- L'espace [Bibliographical references]
- Phénoménologie et psychologie [Bibliographical references]
- Genèse et essence [Bibliographical references]

- Bibliographie
- [Caspar Kulenkampff] "Über Wahnwahrnehmungen. Ihre Interpretation als Störung der 'Wohnordnung,'" [*Der Nervenarzt*, vol. 24 (1953): 326–333]
- [Rudolf Bilz] "Die Metapher des Untergangs in der Schizophrenie," *Der Nervenartzt*, [vol. 20] 1949: 258–262
- [L. Binswanger], "Das Raumproblem in der Psychopathologie," *Zeitschrift für die gesamte Neurologie und Psychiatrie*, vol. 145 (1933): 598–647
- [Das Raumproblem in der Psychopathologie] 2. "Der gestimmte Raum"
- Sur la spatialité
- L'espace selon Straus
- Le temps selon Straus
- "Zeitstruktur und Schizophrenie" [*Zeitschrift für die Gesamte Neurologie und Psychiatrie*, vol. 121 (1929): 544–574], Franz Fischer
- Sur la spatialité
- La schizophrénie selon Wyrsch
- Hans Kunz, "Die anthropologische Betrachtungsweise in der Psychopathologie," [*Zeitschrift für die gesamte Neurologie und Psychiatrie*, vol. 172 (1941): 144–180]
- "Die Erfahrungsgrundlage der Daseinsanalyse Binswangers" [*Schweizer Archiv für Neurologie und Psychiatrie*, vol. 67, no. 1 (1951): 64–82]. [Wilhelm] Szilasi
- Jürg Zutt, "Über Daseinsordnungen. (Ihre Bedeutung für die Psychiatrie)," *Der Nervenarzt*, vol. 24, 20 Mai 1953
- Jürg Zutt. Interprétation du délire
- [Medard] Boss. [folder cover]
- M. Boss. *Sinn und Gehalt der sexuellen Perversionen.* [*Ein daseinsanalytischer Beitrag zur psychopathologie des Phänomens der Liebe*, Berne: Huber, 1947]

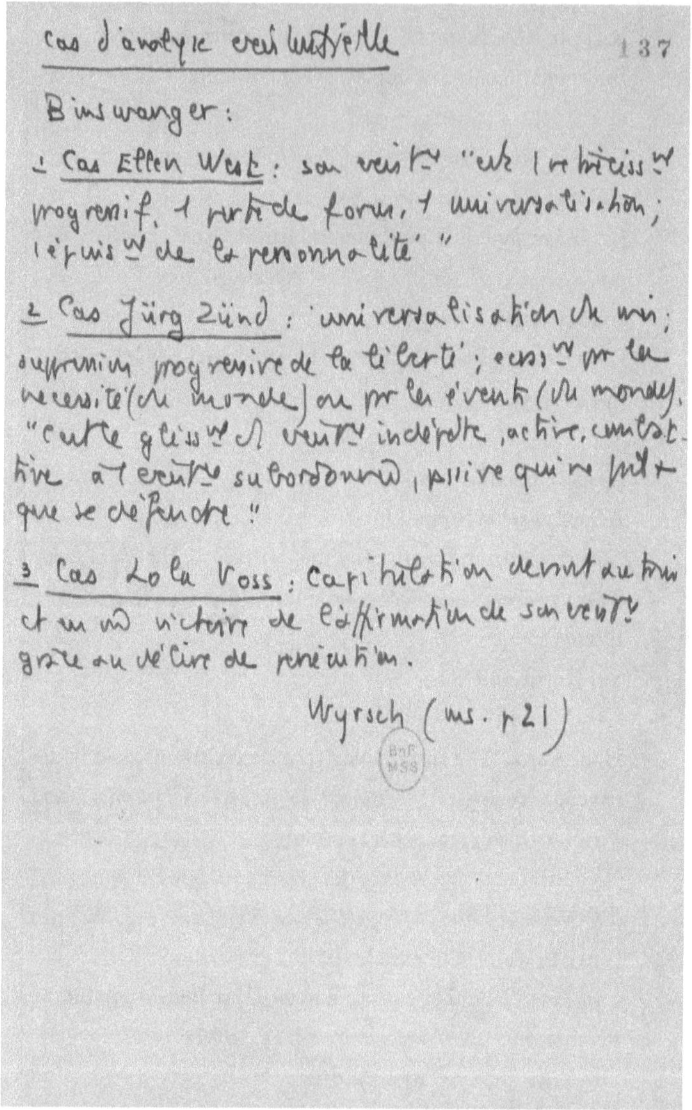
Cas d'analyse existentielle 137

Binswanger :

1. Cas Ellen West : son existence "est rétrécissement progressif, perte de forme, universalisation ; l'épuisement de la personnalité"

2. Cas Jürg Zünd : universalisation du moi ; suppression progressive de la liberté ; écrasement par la nécessité (du monde) ou par les événements (du monde). "cette glissement d'une existence indépendante, active, constitutive à l'existence subordonnée, passive qui ne peut plus que se défendre"

3. Cas Lola Voss : capitulation devant autrui et une victoire de l'affirmation de son existence grâce au délire de persécution.

Wyrsch (ms. p 21)

FIGURE 1.3 One of Foucault's reading notes (© BNF, Fonds Michel Foucault, box 38, folder 1, call number NAF 28730)

- 2. La théorie anthropologique
- La dialectique de l'amour et du monde et ses perturbations chez les pervers sexuels—A. Un fétichiste
- Une homosexuelle "constitutionnelle"

- [Paul] Häberlin. [folder cover]
- L'Anthropologie selon Häberlin (*Der Mensch.* [*Eine philosophische Anthropologie*, Zürich: Schweizer Spiegel, 1941]
- Anthropologie, biologie et psychologie
- Häberlin, *Der Gegenstand der Psychologie. Eine Einführung in das Wesen der empirischen Wissenschaft*, [Berlin: Springer], 1921

- [Eugène] Minkowski. [folder cover]
- L'espace vécu in *Le Temps vécu* [*Études phénoménologiques et psychopathologiques*, Paris: D'Artrey, 1933]
- 2. Problème des hallucinations et problème de l'espace
- Phénoménologie et psychopathologie selon Minkowski
- Observation. Analyse psychologique et phénoménologique

2

THE BINSWANGER DOSSIER

In light of the intellectual network and theoretical context that we have just presented, Foucault's introduction to *Le rêve et l'existence* no longer appears as the isolated, enigmatic text it seems to be if compared only to the rest of his published oeuvre. In the following pages, I will begin by retracing the theoretical context within which Foucault developed his arguments. In particular, I will examine Foucault's initial interest in phenomenology in the context of psychology, before he became disappointed by its inability to account for the complexity of pathological experience. At this point, he encountered existential analysis; at first, Foucault considered it to be the only approach capable of explaining pathological experience without presupposing a separation between the person and the illness. However, as had happened with psychoanalysis, Foucault eventually identified the weaknesses of Binswanger's theory—in particular, its vacillation between a clinical approach centered on the patient and his or her concrete history and a speculative approach without a clear grasp on the real person, which had taken on the character of a prescriptive, almost religious ethics. These positions brought Foucault to radically reconsider Binswanger's project of developing a phenomenological anthropology, and eventually to radically question the validity of any anthropological project in philosophy. This questioning would be at the heart of the archaeological project Foucault developed in the 1960s.

One avenue we might eventually want to pursue in order to better understand Foucault's interest in phenomenological psychopathology in the early 1950s is his critical attitude with respect to Freudian psychoanalysis. Indeed, this was a position he shared not only with Binswanger, but also with many French psychiatrists and philosophers who, during this period, embraced the phenomenological approach to psychology. In order to describe and to illuminate this point, in this chapter I will begin by examining how Foucault understands psychoanalysis in relation to phenomenology in his introduction to *Le rêve et l'existence*. Once again, I will do so by situating this text within the intellectual milieu of French psychiatry that surrounded the young Foucault. I will then turn my attention to two manuscripts from the Lille period: *Binswanger et l'analyse existentielle* and *La Question anthropologique*, the latter of which concerns issues in philosophical anthropology.

PSYCHOANALYSIS'S AMBIVALENCE

Binswanger manifests an ambivalent position with regard to Freudian doctrine throughout his writings. From the time of his university training at the Burghölzli Clinic in Zurich at the beginning of the twentieth century, under the supervision of Eugen Bleuler, he read Freud's writings attentively and forged relationships with some of the earliest and most important representatives of what was, up to that point, merely an intellectual movement. At Burghölzli, a young Binswanger met Karl Abraham (1875–1925), Franz Riklin (1878–1938), Max Eitingon

(1881–1943), Herman Nunberg (1884–1970), and especially Carl Gustav Jung, who directed his master's thesis on the psychogalvanic reflex in experiments dealing with associations. In 1907, Jung brought his student and collaborator to Vienna to meet Freud. From that moment on, Binswanger would establish a continuous dialogue with psychoanalysis, which would materialize in several meetings with Freud and his circle and find its expression in several studies that are explicitly dedicated to him.[1]

The young psychiatrist's interest in psychoanalysis was always of a critical and methodological nature; it never took the form of a zealous theoretical adhesion to the master's teachings. The comparison between psychoanalysis and clinical psychiatry, a constant theme across Binswanger's oeuvre, always had as its principal goal rethinking and reinventing the epistemological foundations of psychiatry. Binswanger particularly appreciated the anamnestico-hermeneutic side of the psychoanalytic approach, which is to say, the possibility it opened up for conceptual thinking, to grasp the patient's personality as an individual. However, he could not accept the "physics of the psyche" that formed its basis; in his eyes, it "transformed the person into a reservoir of forces," with regard to which "the psychic sphere always and only has a representative, metaphorical value."[2] For Binswanger, psychological phenomena were "dramatic" realities, and he saw the value of phenomenology for psychology in its ability to uncover the "intentional world" included in these phenomena and their relationships.[3] Psychology, then, had to direct itself toward the "history of life," since it was only there that "[this essence of the human being] documents and manifests itself."[4] It was precisely on the basis of these considerations that Binswanger, retracing the historical development of psychology, credited psychoanalysis—a "hermeneutic method, in the sense that it explores, explicates, and reconstructs the interior history of life"—with rightfully belonging to the new psychology and thereby of doing justice to its own theory of dynamic, functional vital mechanisms.[5]

In the early 1930s, Lacan contributed to importing into France the phenomenological movement in German psychiatry. Like Binswanger, he saw the revolutionary potential of the Freudian method, specifically in its "attitude of submission to the real," to "human reality," and to the density of its history.[6] Foucault, also, did not fail to underscore in *Maladie mentale et personnalité* that Freud's true "stroke of genius" consisted in envisioning a "psychology of individual history" and, in this way, in opening our access to "the historical dimension of the human psyche."[7]

In a handwritten manuscript fragment among his lecture notes from the beginning of the 1950s, Foucault writes:

> Freud, while attempting to conform with the Darwinian model, liberated—in opposition certainly to his intention, and without always noticing it—a psychology with a naturalist epistemology. Instead of explanations that dispel contradictions, he offered explanations by means of contradiction; instead of the important notion of the conservation of life (or of adaptation—or of utility—or of interest) reigning over all of the life sciences, up to and including the science of man, he opposed a conflictual dialectic between Eros and Thanatos; instead of the evolutionary schemas that insist on the present succeeding the past, he offered a mode of analysis in which present and past culminate in an indissociable unity.[8]

This is an argument that Foucault lays out in almost all of his published writings of this period. In *Maladie mentale et personnalité*, for example, he identifies the Freudian concept of anxiety as the point of transition from a "psychology of evolution" to a "psychology of genesis."[9] In "La psychologie de 1850 à 1950," he places the Freudian system at the origin of a "great overthrowing of psychology" from which "causal analysis transformed itself into a genesis of significations."[10] In addition, in his introduction to *Le rêve et l'existence*, Foucault sees Freud's *Interpretation of Dreams* and Husserl's *Logical Investigations* as a "twofold attempt by man to recapture his meanings and to recapture himself in his significance."[11] Similarly, in a manuscript on psychoanalysis from the 1950s, Foucault observes:

> The adventure of psychoanalysis, and the risk it took with regard to traditional pathology, certainly consist in its having moved beyond a biologically oriented analysis of illness toward an understanding of its psychological signification. This transformation did not, however, take the form of a rupture; and the psychoanalytic "revolution" has the character more of a progressive, slow turn, from a psychology of evolution to a historical psychology of genesis. Moreover, the progressive point of view was never abandoned, and up until the most recent forms of the psychoanalytic approach to neurosis, the evolutionary horizon—the first homeland of Freudian thought—remains present, more real than a backdrop, truer than a myth, a veritable landscape in which the characters of the Freudian drama can move about.[12]

This ambivalent appreciation of the Freudian enterprise is also evident in Merleau-Ponty's *Phenomenology of Perception* when he discusses the problem of sexuality from the vantage point of the incarnate subject's relation to his world, while retracing Binswanger's analysis of one of his clinical cases. If existential analysis shows that "the body expresses existence at every moment," in the same way, psychoanalysis shows how to grasp the "existential significance" of sexuality, in order to identify in "sexual drama" this "incarnate significance" or "primary process of signification" through which "the body expresses total existence":[13] "Whatever the theoretical declarations of Freud have been ... the significance of psychoanalysis is less to make psychology biological than to discover a dialectical process in functions thought of as 'purely bodily,' and to reintegrate sexuality into the human being."[14]

The notion of "drama" was at the heart of the critique of psychoanalysis developed in the late 1920s by Georges Politzer, an author who was at this time very important to Lacan, Merleau-Ponty, and Foucault. While critiquing Freudian doctrine, Politzer's reflection also acknowledged its fundamental intuition, the polemical principle that threatened to blow up the edifice of traditional psychology. Specifically in its effort to understand psychological facts as they pertained to the subject in his or her individuality, "in the first person," psychoanalysis appeared to Politzer as the incarnation of the fundamental aspiration of authentic psychology. Indeed, for him the practice of interpretation entailed recognizing that the psyche has an eminently "dramatic" character, deriving from the intentional dialectic that translates the individual's concrete, historically embedded life.

And yet, while acknowledging for this reason the importance of "doing justice to Freud,"[15] Politzer showed how—despite its most authentic inspiration—Freudian doctrine ended up falling into the dogma and the "mythology" of traditional psychology. The "abstraction" and "realism" that distinguished the latter could be also found in Freud's theoretical-doctrinal approach. Already in *The Interpretation of Dreams*, and specifically in the chapter titled "The Psychology of the Processes of Dreams," Freud does not stop with his intuition that dreams are forms of wish fulfillment (a concrete and dramatic approach). He continues to build on this foundation—specifically on the observation of the difference, in dreams, between manifest and latent content—a hypothesis about the general structure and organization of the psychic apparatus. In following this route, Politzer argued, Freud deforms the individual concrete drama and replaces it with an "impersonal drama" that ultimately reflects the functional formalism of classic psychology.

At the time, this ambivalence with regard to psychoanalysis was common among French authors. Even Lacan, who, as early as his doctoral thesis on paranoid psychosis, had acknowledged the methodological potential of psychoanalytic technique for the new psychology, did not hesitate to critique its metapsychological doctrine. He did so in 1946, in the same terms as Politzer; indeed, Politzer was certainly in Lacan's intellectual orbit throughout the 1930s and 1940s.[16] Although he highlighted the "concrete" character of Freudian concepts such as "the complex," "drama," and "conflict," which he acknowledged as Freud's major "phenomenologically acquired knowledge," Lacan could not accept the notion of the libido, through which "Freudian psychology, propelling its induction with an audacity that verges on recklessness, claims to move from interpersonal relations . . . to the biological function that is taken to be their substratum."[17] Already in his doctoral thesis, Lacan had commended psychoanalytical technique for expressing itself in a "semantics of behavior" drawing its value from the immediate data of the cathartic experience to which it is integrated; but by the same token he critiqued the symbolism mobilized in its interpretation of this data as "too complex and distant."[18] He thus concluded: "Our method, founded on the *relations of understanding* immediately graspable in phenomena, abstains in principle from using these symbolic relations."[19] For Lacan, the symbols generated in psychosis have a "value of reality" that is "in no way diminished by the genesis that excludes them from the mental community of reason," and therefore delusions "need no interpretation to express by their very themes—and marvelously so—the instinctive and social complexes that psychoanalysis had difficulty in bringing to light among neurotics."[20]

These ideas were broadly shared at the time. Minkowski, too, opposed during the 1940s and 1950s concepts such as conflict, the "novel," drama, and the complex to the notion of libido, through which "Freud, guided by the principle of causality, ... had built the energetic image of the evolution of human life, and in so doing, through an excess of 'scientism,' had drifted away from the human being as he is given to us in an immediate way, before anything else."[21] And Minkowski also emphasized the "great wretchedness of psychoanalysis, despite the critically important facts that it was able to bring to light."[22]

We can hear the echo of these remarks in Foucault's judgment of Freud's work in his writings of the 1950s. Just as Politzer had seen in the "dramatic" method and the "first-person approach" of psychoanalysis, despite its theoretical constructs, the polemical principle capable of blowing up the edifice of classical psychology, Foucault credits Freud with having operated this "overthrowing of psychology" that finally gave it for an object a person with "an actual history."[23] The justice Foucault seeks for psychoanalysis is in every respect that which Politzer had claimed earlier, as we can see when he asserts that "the history of psychoanalysis had itself done justice to its retrograde elements."[24] And just as Politzer saw in the history of psychology not the history of an organization, but the dissolution of a mythology, Foucault acknowledged the movement of psychological research as that of "a truth that is unraveling, of an object destroying itself, of a science that only seeks to demystify."[25]

AGAINST THE "METAPHYSICS OF THE IMAGE"

It is interesting to observe that Foucault, like Politzer, Minkowski, Lacan, and Merleau-Ponty before him, introduced his analysis of Freudian discourse with a problematization of the notions of "signification," "expression," and "symbolism." As we have seen, Politzer's major critique of psychoanalysis focused on the doctrinal approach through which Freud had explained his process for interpreting dreams. The Freudian distinction between manifest and latent content in dreams, as well as the theory of the unconscious derived from it, reproduced in his eyes the "realist" approach of classic psychology in that it flattened the subject's signifying drama by bringing it back to a psychic entity. In this way, instead of analyzing the concrete, real present of the dream as an expression of a first-person, individual dialectic, an ontological—and thereby even mythological—doublet was imposed on the dream, thus denying any autonomy to expression in its own right.[26]

We can observe the traces of this critical outlook in Foucault's introduction to *Le rêve et l'existence*, when Foucault remarks that the "theoretical mythology" through which Freud explains the link between image and meaning in dream experience allowed him to "rediscover the themes that had been excluded in the hermeneutic stage of his interpretation of dreams."[27] What Freud overlooked, for Foucault, was precisely what Merleau-Ponty called the "primary process of signification in which the thing expressed does not exist apart from the expression and in which the signs themselves induce their significance externally."[28] As Merleau-Ponty had emphasized in his 1951–1952 course *Les Sciences de l'homme et la phénoménologie* [The Human Sciences and Phenomenology], what matters in the operation of signification is not the induction of an objective meaning so much as the action of signifying. It is not the symbol that must be at the center of analysis, but rather the symbolic realization.[29] And this is what Foucault meant when he stated, in somewhat enigmatic fashion, that "to have an image is therefore to leave off imagination," or that "the image constitutes a ruse of consciousness in order to cease imagining."[30]

Foucault's argument continues along the same lines as Binswanger's and Minkowski's analyses. Throughout the 1930s, they had highlighted the difference between "expression," in the sense of a meaning that is conveyed, and the action of "expressing."[31] But we must also mention Lacan, who had already, in his earliest writings about paranoia, approached psychosis with the intention of conceptualizing the lived experience of illness and the conception of the world it yields in syntactic, rather than semantic, terms.[32] In turn, Foucault distinguished the image from expression or the poetic imagination; he asserted that the latter would find its true dimension not "where it finds the greatest number of substitutes for reality, where it invents the most duplications and metaphors, but, on the contrary, where it best restores presence to itself—where the proliferation of analogies well up, and where the metaphors, by neutralizing each other, restore the depth to immediacy."[33]

The way in which Foucault thinks of metaphor as a "metaphysics of the image"[34] thereby reflects the critiques that Binswanger, Minkowski, Lacan, and also Merleau-Ponty had directed toward any hermeneutic approach to expression that sought to discover its hidden meaning. Like Binswanger, Merleau-Ponty understands the notions of "expression" and "meaning" as the "direction" or the "embodied sense" according to which existence realizes itself as an irreducible whole of body and world. He presents this argument by offering as an example one of Binswanger's clinical cases, that of a young girl who had lost the use of speech. According to Merleau-Ponty, what characterizes the phenomenological-existential approach is its attitude toward the phenomenon, in this case the symptom: instead of looking for the hidden cause (internal or external) or its meaning, the phenomenologist explains it by a "return to existence" that consists in dwelling upon its "modalities" or "forms." Now, according to the phenomenologist these forms actually *are* already the phenomenon's explication, so the loss of the speech *is* the refusal of intersubjectivity. In other words, the expression is already what it signifies; the sign "does not convey its significance, it is filled with it."[35]

The existential character of metaphor had been at the basis of Binswanger's approach to dreams since "Traum und Existenz." In 1952, in the Suzanne Urban case study, Binswanger explained that, in the metaphors used by his patients, "we will see not only a metaphor in the psychological and poetic sense, an evocative image, but especially an immediate verbal expression of the self's mode of being-in-the-world."[36] In turn, Minkowski explicitly stated that "when it comes to the concept of the symbol, as with metaphor, it disjoins too much what symbolizes and what is symbolized, and does violence in this way to the immediate data that we have before us."[37]

These are significant remarks insofar as it was precisely this approach to metaphor—which went hand in hand with the approach to symbolism—that formed the basis of Foucault's critique of psychoanalysis. In the mid-1950s, then, what attracted Foucault's attention to existential analysis was not only its "basic opposition to any science of human facts of the order of positive knowledge, experimental analysis, and naturalistic reflection,"[38] but especially its distance from the theory of signification on which Freudian hermeneutics was founded. For Foucault, "an inadequate elaboration of the notion of symbol" was at the root of its shortcomings: "Freud takes the symbol as merely the tangential point where, for an instant, the limpid meaning joins with the material of the image taken as a transformed and transformable residue of perception. The symbol is that surface of contact, that film, which separates, as it joins, an inner world and an external world."[39] Psychoanalysis, then, had reduced the image to meaning; but for Foucault, "the imaginary world has its own laws, its specific structures"—structures that are not only verbal but those of language, a "language that exists in rigorous syntactic rules and in the solid impress of morphological shapes."[40] Psychoanalysis had not succeeded in "finding a connection between these two orders of analysis," which is to say, between a psychology of language and a psychology of the image—whence the thesis of Foucault's introduction, which consists in arguing that "psychoanalysis has never succeeded in making images speak."[41]

In this regard, Foucault's criticism of Husserl's phenomenology is more muted. According to Foucault, while Freud's analysis sees only an artificial connection—the symbol—between meaning and expression, "phenomenology, on the contrary, enables one to recapture the meaning in the context of the expressive act that founds it,"[42] thereby "reinstat[ing] acts of expression in their fullness."[43] Thus, phenomenology would show the possibility of developing itself toward a "theory of expression." Nevertheless, even though phenomenology is able to reinstate the act of meaning in its expressive dimension, "it cuts [it] off from any form of objective indication. No external context can restore it in its truth," so there is no possibility of a "real encounter" with time, space, and others.[44] This is why, Foucault concludes, expression cannot be understood along the lines of pure phenomenology.

Reading these remarks alongside "Traum und Existenz," we can better understand why Binswanger responded to Foucault's announcement, in his cover letter for his introduction in 1954, that he had shown "how [Binswanger's] conception of the dream entails a complete reworking of analyses of the imagination"[45] by declaring that he had "completed and grounded" his work.[46] Binswanger proved quite indulgent with the young philosopher who had remitted an introduction twice as long as his own text. In truth, the intention to found an anthropology of the imagination was not at the heart of Binswanger's essay. He was far more interested in laying the foundations for a new method of analysis aiming to detect the transcendental structures or "sense-directions" (*Bedeutungsrichtungen*) of experience, using the phenomenon of dreams as a starting point for his reflection.

It was through the Heideggerian concept of *Dasein* or "being-in-the-world" that Binswanger became invested in studying the "forms" according to which the "world-projects" of the mentally ill are structured. If, on the one hand, this research orientation referred in a programmatic way to the approach elaborated in the Heideggerian analytic, on the other, it renounced its strictly ontological ambitions; instead, it elaborated a "practical existential analysis" that sought to examine a concrete human *Dasein* that "must be positively characterized, which is to say, on the basis of exclusive life in the space of *action*."[47]

Foucault decided not to pursue this question of the relationship between ontology and anthropology any further in his introduction. On this topic, he merely noted the fact that "Binswanger avoids any *a priori* distinction between ontology and anthropology" and relocates this distinction "at the terminus of an inquiry whose point of departure is characterized not by a line of division, but by an encounter with concrete existence."[48] Of course, he adds, these are topics that "pose problems"; but he prefers to "leave that issue to another time" and show instead "that one can enter straightway into the analysis of Binswanger."[49]

If neither Foucault's published works nor his correspondence with Binswanger allow us to understand the reasons for this choice, in contrast, the manuscripts available in the archives offer critical information on this topic. Indeed, one of the manuscripts that Foucault drafted while he was teaching in Lille—on Binswanger and existential analysis—concludes with a discussion of the analysis of expression. It is therefore in light of this manuscript that we can better understand not only the stakes of the introduction from 1954, but also the evolution of Foucault's attitude toward phenomenological psychopathology. From this perspective, this manuscript on existential analysis appears as a kind of missing link between the introduction to *Le rêve et l'existence* and *History of Madness*. By analyzing this posthumous text, I will demonstrate that Foucault's movement beyond existential analysis did not take the form of a sudden rupture, as we might suspect if we looked only at his published works. Examining this "theoretical and general introduction to *Daseinsanalyse*" shows us that the introduction to *Le rêve et l'existence*, far from representing a committed stance in favor of existential analysis in psychopathology, actually presented a critique of it and a route away from this approach to mental illness. We will therefore examine the thematic structure of the manuscript to see how Foucault introduces existential analysis and how, finally, he leaves it behind.

BINSWANGER ET L'ANALYSE EXISTENTIELLE

Foucault drafted the manuscript that we are calling *Binswanger et l'analyse existentielle* in the first half of the 1950s, in the period when he was teaching in the Faculty of Letters at the University of Lille. In the archives, this manuscript is classified alongside two other handwritten manuscripts about, respectively,

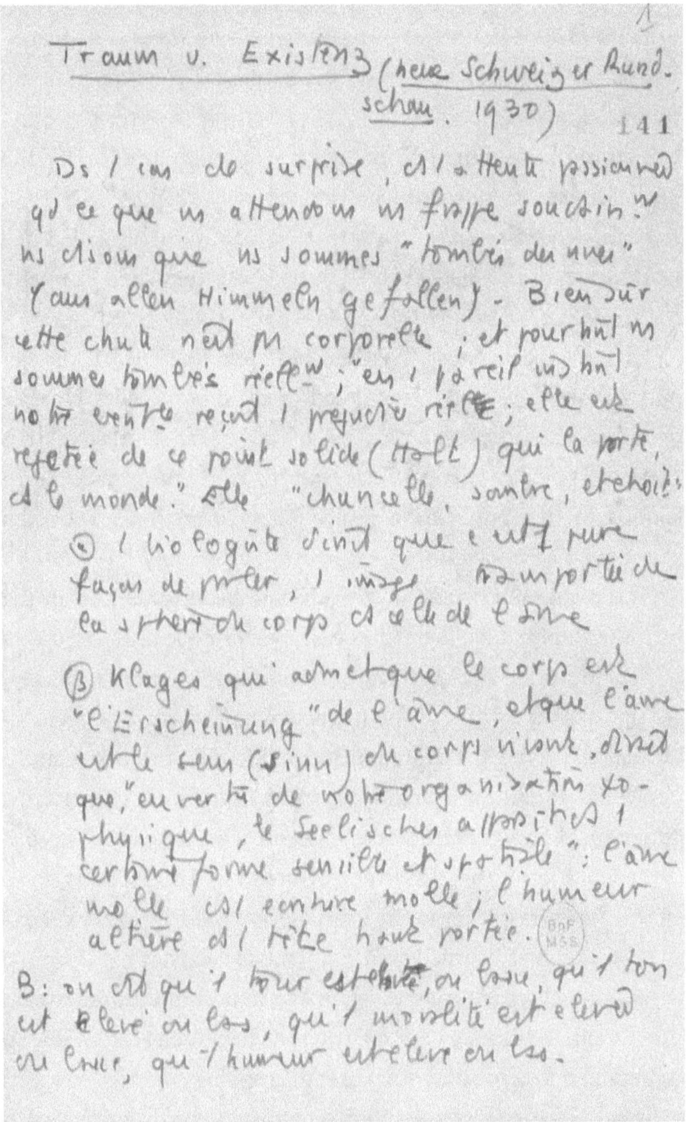

FIGURE 2.1 Excerpt from reading notes on *Traum und Existenz* (© BNF, Fonds Michel Foucault, box 38, folder 1, call number NAF 28730)

anthropology, and phenomenology and psychology.[50] It is difficult to make a definitive pronouncement on these documents. While *La Question anthropologique* reproduces the typical structure of notes for lectures he was preparing to give, the other two appear to be more polished texts. Although in all likelihood Foucault used all of these manuscripts for teaching, *Binswanger et l'analyse existentielle*, in particular, seems to be a finished work. Indeed, in a list of works in progress published in 1953 in the *Annales de l'Université de Lille*, we see a book titled *Psychiatrie et analyse existentielle*. Foucault indicates that this is his secondary thesis, which is "completed" and "in press" with Desclée de Brouwer.[51] However, this book was never published. It is therefore possible that *Binswanger et l'analyse existentielle* corresponds to this publication project, first announced and then abandoned by Foucault.

The work on existential analysis was also announced in the introduction to *Le rêve et l'existence*, where Foucault stated that he would undertake the task of "situat[ing] existential analysis" in "another work."[52] The manuscript *Binswanger et l'analyse existentielle* could therefore be this publication project. Finally, Foucault's intention to publish a study that would constitute a "theoretical and general introduction to *Daseinsanalyse*" is confirmed by a letter that he wrote to Binswanger on April 27, 1954. In this letter, referring to the introduction to *Le rêve et l'existence* that he had just finished writing, he asserted that for the time being he had sought only to "show the importance of the dream in existential analysis." As for the rest, he added, he "intended to pursue it in a broader study of anthropology and ontology."[53]

It is difficult to establish with certainty the order in which Foucault drafted his two works on Binswanger. In any case, *Binswanger et l'analyse existentielle* concludes precisely on the topic that forms the focus of the introduction to *Le rêve et l'existence*: the problem of expression. Indeed, in his introduction, Foucault seems to want to redeem *Daseinsanalyse* from the speculative drift he accuses it of in his manuscript. Through his analysis of the experience of dreaming, he offers *Daseinsanalyse* the path of analyzing the "objective forms of expression."[54] In any case, Foucault's judgment of existential analysis in his introduction is favorable. In response to the problems that he is willing to acknowledge, he states, "*we leave that issue to another time.*"[55] Could this be an allusion to *Binswanger et l'analyse existentielle*?

The manuscript comprises an introduction and five chapters. The introduction, which is very dense, seeks to pave the way for the presentation of *Daseinsanalyse* by analyzing the limitations and weaknesses of both Freudian psychoanalysis and Husserlian phenomenology. The originality of Binswanger's perspective is introduced, in rather emblematic fashion, though the analysis of a clinical case study—the Ellen West case—which Foucault retells, following Binswanger's narration quite closely, including Binswanger's comparison of the Ellen West case to Pierre Janet's famous case, the Nadia case. Foucault then retraces the psychoanalytic interpretation of Ellen West, still following Binswanger's narration, in order to bring out the specificity of existential analysis. Indeed, the latter is focused not on the symbolism and interpretation of unconscious affective complexes, but rather, in a more global and transparent way, on the "being-in-the-world" of the patient, on her "style of existence." Chapters 2, 3, and 4 are dedicated to the analysis of concepts that form the basis of Binswanger's clinical-diagnostic method: space, time, and intersubjectivity. These appear as *a priori* structures that determine the modalities according to which the patient's global experience or "world-project" is constituted. Finally, in the concluding chapter of the manuscript, Foucault turns a critical eye to the more or less explicit consequences of

Binswanger's existential anthropology, focusing in particular on its therapeutic vocation.

As in the introduction to *Le rêve et l'existence*, in this manuscript, Foucault's analysis of Binswanger's epistemological project to reform psychiatry is contextualized by a broader discussion of the relationship between phenomenology and psychology. Foucault raises this problem—which was actually the topic of another of his Lille courses—using the critique of Freudian theory's evolutionary foundation as a starting point. Once again, he sees a fundamental ambivalence in psychoanalysis between, on the one hand, Freud's need to justify his doctrine in accordance with the model of the natural sciences and, on the other, the descriptive style through which he understands lived experience in its historical dimension, using the concept of psychogenesis.

The evolutionary perspective within psychology and psychopathology is prominent in Foucault's work notes from this period. Numerous passages in these notes are devoted, in particular, to a critical discussion of the "neo-Jacksonian" model developed in France by Henri Ey and Julien Rouart (1901–1994).[56] In a footnote in the second chapter of the first half of *Maladie mentale et personnalité*, Foucault critiques neo-Jacksonism for having made of regression the "principle" of illness, which is to say, for having wanted both to exhaust its totality and to locate its cause in regression.[57] This note, in which Foucault explicitly names Henri Ey, was later eliminated from *Maladie mentale et psychologie*. Among the handwritten notes produced during the drafting of *Maladie mentale et personnalité*, there is a document titled "Maladie et personnalité dans le néo-jacksonisme" (Illness and Personality in Neo-Jacksonism), in which Foucault states that neo-Jacksonism highlighted "all of the personality's reactions to dissolution. The positive aspect of illness is not so much its residue as the reorganization of that residue in the form of a new personality that can mask the illness's deficits." He adds, "this idea of the reorganization of the personality following a dissolution leads to a new way of defining a symptom and an illness." Finally, he concludes: "There is nothing surprising in the aptitude for Jackson's and Ey's work to cohere so easily with that of Goldstein, Jaspers, and phenomenological psychology, since in all of these the subject is always constitutive in relation to illness."[58] As we will see later, the link between Kurt Goldstein's thought and phenomenological psychopathology is something that Foucault also insists on in his manuscript *Binswanger et l'analyse existentielle*.

The chapter of *Maladie mentale et personnalité* devoted to "Illness and Evolution" concludes on the need "to push analysis farther," to "complete this evolutionary, potential, and structural dimension of illness" with the "dimension that makes it necessary, significant, and historical": the patient's personal history.[59] However, in the manuscript on Binswanger, Foucault stresses that the move beyond evolutionism that was meant to take into account the historical, intersubjective genesis of signification might be the meeting-point of Freud's theory and Husserl's phenomenology: "The reflection of the positivist physician, trained by reading Darwin, converged with that of a logician, fed by neo-Kantian idealism. Without knowing about one another, together they fixed a decisive moment in the history of the human sciences: they pried them away from their naturalist context and gave them the primary task of returning to lived experience."[60] In a manuscript fragment from the same period, moreover, Foucault writes:

> 1. Phenomenology and naturalist evolutionary psychology have both led to a perspective on genesis in which they converged, yet which seemed as distant from an eidetic of consciousness that

would have presented itself as the equivalent of mathematics to the natural sciences as from a psychological naturalism that would have borrowed its principal concepts and modes of description from the sciences. From the need for an ideal foundation for the facts of consciousness, Husserl arrived at the idea of an ideal genesis of signification; from the need for a naturalist explanation of psychological evolution, Freud arrived at the description of a genesis of behaviors, and an elucidation of their meanings. 2. The significance of this convergence goes beyond corroboration. What the appearance of this genesis as an essential dimension of the description of consciousness points to is a radical transformation of the foundations of psychology.[61]

It is easy to recognize, in this bringing together of Freud and Husserl, one of the themes that Foucault's introduction to *Le rêve et l'existence* opens onto, as Foucault acknowledges in the two authors' approaches a "twofold attempt by man to recapture his meaning and to recapture himself in his significance."[62] However, in *Binswanger et l'analyse existentielle*, this analysis is followed by a clarification of the methodology of phenomenological psychology. This passage allows Foucault to emphasize the radical distance that separates the eidetic approach to lived experience, not only from a recourse to the immediate data of consciousness,[63] but also from any process of abstract generalization. If phenomenological psychology is capable of doing justice to the "plenitude of a concrete experience," Foucault comments, it is because the phenomenological grasp of essence is a "task of purification," "a movement of the spirit that, in the deployment of the possible, recognizes from experience the necessity that inhabits it."[64] In other words, it is from within life experiences, rather than from a theory of life above and beyond man himself,[65] that this psychology perceives "this structure that bestows the unity of meaning to lived experiences whose foggy unity is immediately given under diverse figures."[66]

At this point, Foucault raises the question of the relationship between eidetic psychology and the next step of Husserl's reflection, which is to say, transcendental phenomenology—the analysis of the constitutive activity of consciousness. However, in this manuscript, he does not delve more deeply into this problem, although he addresses it in many of his work notes from this period. In particular, in the notes that in all likelihood accompanied the manuscript titled *Phénoménologie et psychologie*, Foucault interrogates the legitimacy of transcendental phenomenology, again using the comparison between Freud and Husserl as a starting point. For him, as we have seen, it was specifically the genetic perspective that Freudian theory and phenomenology had in common. Yet, if on the one hand this genetic perspective brought Freud to "liberate psychology from a naturalist epistemology,"[67] on the other, it led Husserl to see "logical forms emerging from a pre-predicative field that always founds them and never presupposes them (*Erfahrung und Urteil*)."[68]

This was the point that Foucault insisted on in the manuscript on Binswanger, where the question of transcendental phenomenology allowed him to introduce the problem at the heart of the text: that of pathological experience. Indeed, Foucault observes, in Husserlian phenomenological description, from the static description of lived experience—which is to say, the grasping of essence—to transcendental constitution, "each genetic movement rests on the immediate presence of a world."[69] The "lifeworld" (*Lebenswelt*) is pregiven; it is an immediate evidence, anterior to any act of knowledge, "anterior to any genesis."[70] This signifies, according to Foucault, that "as Husserlian description unfolds, meaning only ever emerges in the land of meaning."[71] While is true that phenomenology succeeded in restoring the "concrete plenitude" of the lifeworld, this world whose metamorphoses it returns to us, this *Lebenswelt*, still "is never anything more than the flourishing of the world that is already there. . . . However the significations that we encounter in pathological experience are not deployed from the vantage point of a world that is already there; or rather, if they bring with them the presupposition of a world, it is that of another world that is a nonworld."[72]

From this point of view, to pose the problem of pathological experience "is to pose the problem of the absolute origin, of the jump, of the appearance from nothing, of the dimension to cross in one leap."[73] This is the problem, Foucault observes, that Jaspers found himself facing. All of Jaspers's work on psychopathology would therefore consist in an effort to free the field of phenomenology from this enigma of absolute origin. In the Jaspersian distinction between the intelligible and the unintelligible, Foucault sees an attempt to fix "limits between what pertains to a comprehension, an intuitive grasp in the manner of phenomenology, and what remains irreducible to any of these forms of recognition."[74] Yet, Foucault stresses, where the understanding cannot reach is precisely the realm of natural causation: the limits of phenomenological comprehension in its two components, "static" and "genetic,"[75] are thus measured by nature, such that explanations by recourse to nature—even if negative—end up becoming once again, in Jaspersian phenomenology, the criteria of the pathological. Once again, the alienated man is separated from his alienation and illness is considered outside of the sick person.

For Foucault, this is "the decisive moment in the analysis of mental illness; it is also the decisive moment for the radical surpassing of phenomenological analysis—in its effort to develop a genesis of constitutions and an understanding of meaning."[76] Here "another style of analysis" proves necessary.[77] And it is precisely at this moment that Foucault introduces the anthropological enrichment of phenomenology in the form of Binswanger's *Daseinsanalyse*.

"THE NIGHT OF TRUTH": PHENOMENOLOGY FACE TO FACE WITH PSYCHOPATHOLOGY

The critique of phenomenology in relation to the limit or obstacle presented by pathological experience is a central element in many of Foucault's work notes from this period. In his published work, we find this critique in particular in the article "La recherche scientifique et la psychologie." In this article, Foucault identifies the point of origin of scientific research precisely in these "obstacles on the path of human practice"[78] that call into question the principles and conditions of existence of a science. In the case of psychology, these are "the negative experiences that man has of himself,"[79] which constitute simultaneously the conditions of possibility and the positivity of psychological science. But Foucault's argument rests specifically on a critique with regard to the phenomenological approach: "it is from the point of view of the unconscious that a psychology of consciousness that is not purely transcendental reflection is possible;... it is from the point of view of sleep, of automatism, and of the involuntary that we can create a psychology of the alert man perceiving the world that avoids confining itself to pure phenomenological description."[80] In one of the preparatory manuscripts for this article, Foucault's critique of the phenomenological perspective is even more explicit and incisive:

> Phenomenology, in its critique of psychologism, ... remained ... haunted by the problem of knowing how truth could emerge in knowledge, and the accusation of naturalism leveled against psychological objectivities, the requirement of an analysis of the constitutive sphere, [and] the transcendental subjectivity's recourse to the ground of experience resolutely maintain philosophical interrogation in a clarified space from which the shadows of not-knowing, the night of truth, and the decay of man have been swept away. It is therefore not surprising, this adventure of phenomenology, that after having gotten rid of psychologism finds in psychology or in a reflection on psychology the starting point for its radical deepening.[81]

This is why, Foucault concludes, "Husserl has certainly deserved his Merleau-Pontys and his Binswangers."[82]

In the Lille manuscript, *Daseinsanalyse*'s anthropological project is introduced by way of a reflection on mental illness as an experience of decay. It is interesting to note that in the text, Foucault does not attempt to introduce and present Binswanger's psychiatric project from a purely philosophical point of view. He says very clearly that he does not intend to make a judgment about the "concern for orthodoxy" or "the abrupt rupture" that might exist between existential analysis and the philosophical models it is inspired by, especially Heidegger's existential analytic. Binswanger is presented here as more than an interpreter of Husserl and Heidegger. He is the heir of those psychiatrists who "seek to resituate the understanding of illness within the totality of the sick person,"[83] and of those clinicians who in a more general manner, as Roland Kuhn would put it, conceived of medicine as a science that had to give itself the task of understanding "not only the sick man, but the human being in general"[84] and who for this very reason believed that psychiatry must be reformed in accordance with the principles of a "global medicine" (*Ganzheitsmedizin*).[85]

Foucault was therefore interested first in Binswanger the psychiatrist and clinician, not Binswanger the philosopher, in the context of a reflection on the problem of the pathological. Indeed, a very large portion of the manuscript is devoted to the analysis of clinical case studies published by Binswanger (Ellen West, Lola Voss, Jürg Zünd),[86] Roland Kuhn (Franz Weber, Georg, Lina),[87] and Medard Boss (the Konrad Schwing case).[88] The entire first chapter of the text is turned over to the Ellen West case. In a letter from 1954 to Binswanger accompanying the draft of his introduction, Foucault wrote that the goal of the French translation of "Traum und Existenz" was to make his thought accessible to French readers.[89] Yet it is certain that the publication of this manuscript would have contributed much more efficiently to introducing *Daseinsanalyse* in France than did the introduction to *Le rêve et l'existence*.

If, on the one hand, existential analysis represents the anthropological surpassing of phenomenology that Foucault considered inevitable, on the other, it also allows him to delve more deeply into the flaws of the Freudian approach to pathology. From this point of view, the analysis of dreams is a paradigmatic example. As he also did in his introduction to *Le rêve et l'existence*, Foucault insists on critiquing psychoanalytic symbolism here: "The major error of psychoanalysis is to break the unity in which the patient expresses himself, and to divide it up on either side of a line that separates the symbol and the symbolized, the conscious and the unconscious, manifest expression and the instinctive drives that subtend it."[90] Conversely, for Binswanger, "the task is to locate the unity that forms the basis of all the dimensions of [man's] presence in the world, the root of his being."[91] Foucault affirms that man "is not a hierarchy of structures that fit into each other, . . . but a radical unity of all of the empirical forms of his existence."[92]

BINSWANGER'S "SURPRISING REVOLUTION"

What methodological approach allowed Binswanger to recognize and explicate pathological experience without presupposing a separation between man and his illness? The point of departure is the concept of *Dasein* or "being-in-the-world." This is where the unity of man must be found: at the level of his existence. According to Binswanger, the "being-in-the-world" is defined by *a priori* structural directions that determine the modalities according to which experience is constituted. These *a priori* structures are spatiality, temporality, and intersubjectivity, and they figure as the condition of possibility for what Binswanger calls the patient's "world-project" (*Weltentwurf*). It is precisely by analyzing these structures that the psychiatrist can uncover the "common signification," the "identity of meaning" or "unity of style"[93] of this world. In this way, pathological experience ceases to be pushed outside of the patient and can be acknowledged, instead, as his own "project":

> It is not a matter of knowing which alterations of his universe now denounce him as schizophrenic, but only in which universe this man, whom the psychiatrist designates as schizophrenic, lives. This is not to say only that the analyst has to bracket any distinction between the normal and the pathological, . . . it is not to say only that the space or time of a patient, instead of being a narrowed space and an altered time, is another time and another space; it is to say, very simply—but this is the capital point—that

the world of this schizophrenic person that we call Ellen West is nothing other than her world, with its time, its space, its human entourage. It is to refuse to ask the patient to give an account of this universe in order to find its basis in the patient himself: and not insofar as he is sick, but insofar only as he is a man, he is existence, he is free. The world of a sick man is not the process of the illness; it is the man's project.[94]

This is why Foucault often used the concepts of "destiny" or of "truth" to refer to illness. Undoubtedly also inspired by Sartre's work on Baudelaire (1947) and Genet (1952),[95] as well as by Jaspers's study on Nietzsche,[96] Foucault insisted on showing that illness, in an existential perspective, comes neither from nature nor—to quote Sartre—from the "obscure chemical changes which the psycho-analysts relegate to the unconscious."[97]

In a handwritten manuscript from the 1950s titled "L'agressivité, l'angoisse et la magie" (Aggressiveness, Anxiety, and Magic), Foucault cites precisely Sartre's book on Baudelaire: "Contemporary existentialism—Sartre in his *Baudelaire*—played the same game [as Husserl and Scheler] with freedom: by protecting pure freedom from any objective determination, it can assert it in the most concrete existence, and call on the psychoanalyst, or the psychopathologist, to discover freedom and its project in advance of any psychological constitution."[98]

The theme of destiny is crucial in this regard in the introduction to *Le rêve et l'existence*. Indeed, in order to illuminate the distance between *Daseinsanalyse* and the Freudian approach, in this essay Foucault insists on the fact that "the essential point of the dream lies not so much in what it revives of the past as in what it declares about the future."[99] If the dream cannot be reduced to the repetition of a traumatic past, it is because it "anticipates," it is "a prefiguring of history."[100] But if the dream is "prophetic," it is not so by virtue of a sort of magical power, but rather because it is the means by which existence "appears to itself,"[101] revealing a destiny that is nothing other than its structure, its form understood as an immanent condition of possibility.

For having in this way placed "psychopathology entirely [back] in the perspective of freedom and truth,"[102] Foucault recognizes that Binswanger accomplished a "surprising revolution"[103] in the field of psychopathology. While starting from the traditional horizon of psychiatry, he was able to operate "a radical transformation in the norms for understanding mental illness."[104] Why, then, did Foucault end up abandoning this model?

After having listed the fundamental aspects that separate *Daseinsanalyse* from traditional psychopathology, Foucault raises the questions that will occupy him until the conclusion of his manuscript. He asks,

> Does thinking mental illness in terms of freedom and of truth not entail returning psychiatry to a metaphysical point of view that organizes man's concrete reality in relation to transcendental abstractions? Does it not mean, in some way, trying to stifle the metaphysical scandal that has always existed in a sick way of thinking, a demented reason, a nonsensical behavior, to try to place them back into the calm universe of a freedom asserting itself and a constituted truth? By wanting to restore to the patient what is most essentially human in the human being, does Binswanger not bind himself to a quasi-theological detour to a freedom and a truth whose content transcends human existence, and whose origin precedes it?[105]

Once again, as in Foucault's critique of Husserl's phenomenological perspective, the "scandal" of illness is the obstacle that creates a crisis in psychopathological discourse. That said, Foucault's first response tends to support Binswanger. Up to this point, Foucault has addressed himself to Binswanger as a psychiatrist. It is from this perspective that he underscores that *Daseinsanalyse*, "insofar as it is a reflection on the sick man, can only ever concern man's ways of being and not his being as a human reality in a more general manner."[106] We can also recall that Foucault opposes an ontological approach to forms of existence in *Maladie mentale et psychologie*:

> To be sure, mental illness may be situated in relation to human genesis, in relation to individual psychological genesis, in relation to the forms of existence. But, if one is to avoid resorting to such mythical explanations as the evolution of psychological structures, the theory of instincts, or an existential anthropology, one must not regard these various aspects of mental illness as ontological forms.[107]

From this point of view, Foucault's analysis in *Binswanger et l'analyse existentielle* is quite similar to what he presents in his introduction to *Le rêve et l'existence*. In the introduction, he cautions us that "detouring through a more or less Heideggerian philosophy is not some initiatory rite that might open a door to the esotericism of the *Daseinsanalyse*";[108] similarly, in the Lille manuscript he stresses that, for Binswanger, "an ontological reflection in the manner of Heidegger can only ever be referential":[109] "The recourse to a Heideggerian conception of existence does not lead to exiling man to an ethereal universe of metaphysical reflection, but rather to taking up any reflection on man at the basic level of what man is himself in his existence.[110]

Yet in the introduction from 1954, Foucault also acknowledges that the manner in which Binswanger thinks through "the encounter and, no less surely, the status that is finally to be assigned to the ontological conditions pose problems."[111] Still, he adds, "*we leave that issue to another time.*"[112] These are precisely the questions that the final section of *Binswanger et l'analyse existentielle* addresses.

EXISTENTIAL ANALYSIS'S AMBIVALENCE

According to Foucault, problems arise precisely when Binswanger leaves behind the lens of clinical reflection—the "practical" existential approach he has deployed in his case analyses—and gives his approach an ontological foundation. This is where, Foucault writes, *Daseinsanalyse* reaches a "metaphysical impasse."[113] Binswanger first made this move beyond clinical reflection and toward speculation in his theoretical text *Grundformen und Erkenntnis menschlichen Daseins* (1942). In this book, he defines intersubjectivity as the structure of "love" and identifies it as "the origin of all significations and the foundation of all structures."[114] This book is often cited by Foucault in his published writings of the 1950s and in his reading notes from the same period. In a note titled "Binswanger, *Grundformen und Erkenntnis menschlichen Daseins*,"[115] in particular, he refers to the text through the lens of Henri Ellenberger's analysis of it in a series of articles he published on "Swiss Psychiatry" in *L'Évolution psychiatrique*.[116] Another reading note concerns a review essay Roland Kuhn wrote about the *Grundformen* in 1951.[117] Foucault remarks,

> In the *Grundformen*, Binswanger wishes to grasp man in his *Dasein* as a whole. Beyond the "*Zu sich selber Sein*" [being beside oneself], there are the *mit-menschlichen* relationships

(the *duale* and *plurale Daseinsmodus*). One is fulfilled in love; the other, in the *"Nehmen des Andern bei etwas"* [taking the other as something]. In the me-you relationship, Binswanger sees the *"Ürphänomen des Menschseins"* [originary phenomenon of Being-human]: it is fundamental with regard to the *Daseinsweisen räumlichen* [spatial ways of being] and temporal ways of being as well. Binswanger writes: We see that [in] the loving *Miteinandersein* [being with one another], love holds itself *"frierend"* [frozen] outside the door of this project of being" (on the subject of Heidegger). Binswanger is not trying to constitute a philosophical ontology like Heidegger, "he is not writing about the *Dasein* in itself but rather about the human *Dasein*. He seeks to make an anthropology, in the phenomenological sense of the term."[118]

In Foucault's eyes, it is true that *"Daseinsanalyse*, by elucidating the interhuman horizon of any existence, thereby uncovers the foundations on which therapeutic action can and must proceed";[119] yet in conceiving of this horizon as the ontological existential condition that pathological experience is deprived of, it ends up committing a double error. First, it replaces the concrete relationship between a doctor and a patient with a "ontological *we*,"[120] which condemns it to bypass the patient in his unique reality. Second, it ends up adopting the very attitude that Binswanger condemns in the doctor, which is to say, "taking the other 'by his weak point.'"[121]

This is an important idea to which Foucault returns a little bit later in the manuscript. In a discussion of Kurt Goldstein's conception of the therapeutic approach and of the doctor-patient relationship, he observes that Binswanger's position is quite similar:

> It is no longer a question of eliminating illness, as one would fill a gap, by allowing for the return of the functions that the illness

suppressed, but rather of opening new possibilities: it is no longer a question of erasing the past as much as of preparing the future.... Goldstein's idea that a piecemeal disruption, such as the suppression of a reflex, can be meaningful only within a totality that allows it to appear less like a disposition than like a positive mode of response has a practical consequence: the doctor-patient situation cannot have as its principal goal to bring to light and abstract from one's overall conduct the series of specific deficits. Instead, it must show which new style of behavior emerges through the illness, which original norms it obeys, which kinds of "realization" (*Leistung*) it remains susceptible to.... Goldstein, on the contrary, and Binswanger credit this positive signification of illness, and even if they base it on different points of reference (the normativity of the organism for Goldstein, the ontological meaning of existence for Binswanger), both of them come to the conclusion that a radical transformation of the doctor-patient relationship and a reinvention of the manner in which the patient is considered are necessary.[122]

And yet, for Foucault, *Daseinsanalyse* ends up

Looking for that which makes him [the patient] "not like the others," emphasizing disruptions that are designated as such in relationship to an ideal structured as a norm, exhausting the essence of the illness in the sum of the patient's deficits: a negative conception of illness that resembles a *cordon sanitaire* erected by the doctor around the patient, the security measure that he deploys to separate, in a radical manner, the normal from the pathological.[123]

In recognizing in this manner in illness "not an existential possibility that opens itself up, but an existential obligation that imposes itself," *Daseinsanalyse* ends up "superimposing an ethical reflection on its ontological and anthropological reflection. [These are] as many themes," he adds, "as are rejected in Heideggerian thought, and that might express the bad religious conscience of a school of thought that does not have the courage of its own thinking."[124]

These are harsh critiques with regard to existential analysis, which Foucault was not alone in articulating at the time. Indeed, among his reading notes we find thought-provoking references to other authors who had critiqued Binswanger between the 1930s and the 1950s for an excessively speculative approach to mental illness. In the bibliographic file dedicated to phenomenological psychopathology especially, there is a note titled "Contre la *Daseinsanalyse*" (Against *Daseinsanalyse*).[125] It contains references to two essays by psychiatrists who had critiqued Binswanger's project: Karl Friedrich Scheid's "Existenziale Analytik und Psychopathologie" (Existential Analytic and Psychopathology, 1932)[126] and Renato De Rosa's "Existenzphilosophische Richtungen in der modernen Psychopathologie" (Existential-Philosophical Directions in Modern Psychopathology, 1957).[127] With regard to the former, Foucault writes: "*Daseinsanalyse* misunderstands the boundary between a philosophical *Seinslehre* [doctrine of Being (*l'être*)] (ontology) and a psychological science of a being [*l'étant*]." About De Rosa's essay, Foucault notes: "Critique from a Jaspersian point of view: impossibility of taking the totality and the *Ursprung* [origin] of the *Menschsein* as a *Gegenstand* [object]."

A powerful critique had also been leveled at Binswanger's "doctrine" by the Dutch psychiatrist Henricus Cornelius Rümke during the first International Congress of Psychiatry in Paris in 1950, an event in which Binswanger had participated. Indeed, in a talk given during a session dedicated to the psychopathology of delusions, Rümke had stated that, in his opinion, "much of what Binswanger says should be stripped of its philosophical baggage, and that many things of great value would remain."[128] Psychiatry's need to choose between metaphysical speculation and objective reflection had also been illuminated in the early 1950s by the journal *La Raison*. After the Congress in 1950, an editorial in the journal had stressed the "crisis of contemporary psychiatry"; at the same time, it had reproached Jean Delay's inaugural address as president of the Congress for having given equal weight to "the modern forms of speculative metaphysics," represented by "phenomenology and existential analysis," and to "the most objective experimental scientific methods."[129]

Foucault therefore suggests that, in order to break out of its ambivalence between its methodological-clinical approach and its speculative foundation, *Daseinsanalyse* must focus its efforts on the clinical dimension of its theory: the relationship between doctor and patient. Since this relationship is founded on language, it is toward "a rigorous analysis of the phenomenon of expression"[130] that existential elucidation must turn, in order to map these structures or "sense-directions" that constitute the immanent condition of possibility of any form of experience.

Delving more deeply into the problem of expression is precisely what Foucault proposes in the introduction to *Le rêve et l'existence*, which is devoted to the topic with which the manuscript on *Binswanger et l'analyse existentielle* concludes. Through his examination of the experience of dreaming, Foucault offers it the path of an analysis of the "objective forms of expression and of the historical contents that it encloses."[131] Conversely, in the Lille manuscript he develops his critique of Binswanger's project by digging into the problems related to the ontological conditions of existence that the introduction had consigned to "another time." These are problems that the philosopher also mentions in his correspondence with Binswanger in 1954, after having met him in Kreuzlingen. Unfortunately, we do not have any documents to tell us about Foucault's second meeting with Binswanger.

In the face of its own ambivalence, Foucault writes, *Daseinsanalyse* finds itself in the position of having to choose between "a return to the problem of expression, the analysis of language, . . . and a metaphysical recourse to the classic theme of love, understood as the fundamental possibility of weaving between existences a connection that roots itself in them but that also transcends them."[132] In other words, for *Daseinsanalyse*, "It is a matter of choosing between history and eternity, between the concrete communication of men and the metaphysical communion of existences; between immanence and transcendence; in short, between a philosophy of love and an analysis of expression, between metaphysical speculation and objective reflection."[133]

Yet, in his manuscript, Foucault observes quite lucidly that "it is obvious that such considerations would break open the framework of existential analysis."[134] Pursuing the project of examining the universe of expression—as Foucault does in the introduction to *Le rêve et l'existence*—means going beyond the project of *Daseinsanalyse*. This also explains the precautions Foucault took when he presented this text to Binswanger: in the letter to the psychiatrist that accompanied the draft introduction, he wrote that he hoped that Binswanger would be able to "recognize [himself] in these few pages."[135]

ANTHROPOLOGICAL SPECULATION AND THE HUMAN SCIENCES

It is therefore evident that the fact that Foucault devoted a book manuscript to existential analysis does not entail a committed stance in favor of this theoretical perspective. In the introduction to *Le rêve et l'existence*, he tentatively adopts the approach that he is proposing to Binswanger for reformulating his psychiatric project; in doing so, he shows that he has already abandoned *Daseinsanalyse*.

This seems to be confirmed by other handwritten notes from the 1950s, in which Foucault expands on his critique of the phenomenological perspective that undergirds existential anthropology. In reality, he observes, if *Daseinsanalyse* has succeeded in making psychology and phenomenology converge in an anthropology, it is because this is the destiny of phenomenology. Indeed, if, on the one hand, man's "decay," represented by the experience of illness, leads phenomenologists toward a reflection on psychology, on the other, this reflection must take an anthropological direction: "The evolution of Husserl's thought from the idealist rationalism of the *Logische Untersuchungen* to the descriptive and genetic idealism of the writings on History or the genealogy of logic is nothing but the progressive discovery of the ever-more pressing necessity of an anthropology. Husserl's successors did not err: anthropology in Scheler, in Heidegger, in Sartre."[136] Yet this anthropology, if it is the condition of possibility for the very psychology that brought it into being, contests psychology's pretension to constitute itself as a scientific understanding of man:

> Indeed, in defining anthropology as the kind of analysis of human existence that inscribes the real conditions of this existence at the level of its ideal essence, we see that anthropology cannot be anything but the radical contestation of any scientific or dialectic analysis of the relationship of man to his environment. What anthropology denies psychology is its scientific ambitions. From this perspective, we can understand that psychologists are not

openly claiming anthropology, and that anthropology is not rushing to take up the contents of psychology.[137]

From this point of view, it is easier to understand the manner in which Foucault describes *Daseinsanalyse* in the opening of his introduction to *Le rêve et l'existence*, namely, as "a form of analysis that does not aim at being a philosophy, and whose end is not to be a psychology; a form of analysis that is fundamental in relation to all concrete, objective, and experimental knowledge."[138] He continues, "the working dimensions of anthropology can thereby be circumscribed. It is an undertaking that opposes anthropology to any type of psychological positivism."[139]

Now, in the manuscript from which I have been quoting, Foucault expands precisely on this "passage from a psychology to an anthropology that it perpetually calls upon and requires, but that also perpetually contests it and always refuses it any definitive guarantee or validation."[140] In this respect, he mentions the work of Merleau-Ponty, which he deems to be the "most lucid and measured reflection on this passage,"[141] and schematically describes "His book [*The Phenomenology of Perception*] as tackling the theme: phenomenological reduction takes place within psychology, such that psychology is called into question by the reflection on man that it has itself sparked[;] this book is in this way simultaneously the most lucid and the most naïve."[142]

Why would Merleau-Ponty's phenomenological project be naïve? The answer to this question is crucial for understanding the way in which Foucault ends up abandoning *Daseinsanalyse*, through this critique of what he sees as phenomenology's inevitable turn toward anthropology. It is important to note, on this topic, that Binswanger's existential anthropology occupies a central place in *The Phenomenology of Perception*. This is why Foucault, as noted earlier, associates Merleau-Ponty and

Binswanger when he examines the necessary alliance between phenomenology and psychology. The anthropological elaboration of phenomenology is naïve not only because it ends up calling into question the discipline—psychology—that gave rise to it, but also and foremost because anthropology, thus constituted, ends up postulating a human essence. And this is an essence that cannot be accessed, since in this anthropological perspective "objectivity no longer has any status, or rationality any meaning."[143]

Foucault also develops this theme in a manuscript that we have previously mentioned, dating from the same period as the Lille texts, titled "L'agressivité, l'angoisse et la magie." According to Foucault, these three phenomena incite psychology to turn toward anthropology precisely insofar as they "denounce the moment where a scientific and real analysis of human conduct is no longer possible."[144] If, on the one hand, these experiences enable the appearance of a human essence that can only be negatively defined,[145] on the other, Foucault remarks,

> This essence and its impossible content manifest themselves in a privileged manner in the human sciences. And even though they emerge clearly only at the level of philosophical reflection, the intermediary path of discovery, proof, or verification (the idea of a phenomenological psychology, of a phenomenological sociology, of a phenomenological aesthetics) always passes through the human sciences. This is to say that it is the human sciences that are charged with saying that the essence of man cannot be fully captured by an objective analysis; their mission is to show, in man, something other than his own conditions, something other than his own manifestations, something other than his own companions in humanity; in short, that it is incorrect to say that "man is the very root of man." Under the pretext of showing

man in his totality, contemporary sciences seek to show that man is something other than man.[146]

In a brief note penciled in at the end of the manuscript, Foucault summarizes the position he has developed in the following way: "Psychology, under the pretext of analyzing the concrete—phenomenology, under the pretext of returning to things—both converge toward the most abstract thing: toward an essence of man valid only in the realm of an anthropological speculation."[147] In another manuscript from this period, Foucault interprets this operation as a kind of reinvestment of the "idealist capital" that had previously been attached to theology:

> The meaning of phenomenology is to ensure a reutilization of this idealist capital. Anthropology is the vicar of theology, as the Pope is to Christ. Yet the paradox of this story is that psychology, which had previously played the antitheological role of a reduction to a determinism of affections, a theory of knowledge, of value, and of liberty, has made itself complicit in this theological maneuver. It allows itself to be led into error by the *here and now* claimed by anthropology, against the *there and then* of theology, and sees in this refusal of any beyond the guarantee of its positivity. We thereby see the movement of a psychology that purports to find its guarantee in an anthropology that recuperates the fundamental concepts of a theology through which the validity of psychology is contested. . . . Man has become the natural site of theology—and its point of application. And its scope. Whence the allure of the human sciences.[148]

Faced with a psychology that ends up "basing itself on an anthropology that evades objectivity"[149]—a trap to which *Daseinsanalyse* also falls victim—Foucault invites *Daseinsanalyse* to return to "objective reflection." However, in relation to the arguments made in *Maladie mentale et personnalité*, the "materialist approach" that Foucault claims for psychology becomes more complicated in his manuscript on Binswanger: "Materialism must be methodological in the human sciences. Loosening phenomenology's grasp on psychology is the only means of returning its materialist approach to psychology."[150]

In *Binswanger et l'analyse existentielle*, this "methodological" materialism toward which Foucault attempts to push *Daseinsanalyse* takes the form of "men's concrete communication" and of the "analysis of phenomena of expression"; these formulae bear witness to Foucault's attempt to give content to this notion of the "concrete" that had been deployed so insistently by French philosophers, psychologists, and psychiatrists since the late 1920s.

From the correspondence between Ludwig Binswanger and Jacqueline Verdeaux, we learn that in the fall of 1955, she planned to collaborate with Foucault—whose departure for Sweden was fast approaching—on a "kind of dictionary of *daseinsanalytical* terms" to accompany her translation of the Suzanne Urban clinical case study.[151] This text, however, would appear in 1957 without Foucault's name or any appended dictionary. In Uppsala, Foucault worked simultaneously on a translation of Viktor von Weizsäcker's *Der Gestaltkreis*[152] and on one of the volumes he had under contract with the publisher Les éditions de la Table ronde. The contract, which bears the provisional title *Histoire de la folie*, was signed by Michel Foucault and Jacqueline Verdeaux.[153] This book would become Foucault's principal thesis, defended at the Sorbonne in 1961 under the direction of Georges Canguilhem. As for Jacqueline Verdeaux, she continued to explore *Daseinsanalyse*. In 1955, she translated Jakob Wyrsch's *Die Person des Schizophrenen* and worked on the French version of Roland Kuhn's book on the interpretation of masks in the Rorschach test. Foucault agreed to read the proofs of her translations, which he asked her to send to Uppsala. But he asked himself, "am I still competent?"[154] In a letter he wrote to his friend Jean-Paul Aron at the end of 1954, Foucault mentioned the thesis that he was drafting on the notion of "world" in phenomenology. Declaring himself surprised by the turn around Husserl that what he called a *livre-champignon* (mushroom-book) had taken, Foucault asked "how [he was] able to play psychologist for many years."[155]

THE POSSIBILITY AND THE PERIL OF A PHILOSOPHICAL ANTHROPOLOGY

Any reader of Foucault knows the sharp critiques that he addressed, starting in the early 1960s, to any theoretical program stemming from anthropology—or rather from the "anthropological slumber in which philosophy and the human sciences were enchanted as it were, and put to sleep by one another."[156] People will have to awake from this slumber, he adds, "just as in the past people awoke from the dogmatic slumber."[157] Even in the mid-1980s, in his preface to the American edition of *The History of Sexuality*, Foucault stressed that his project of thinking about the historicity of forms of experience entailed, from the start, a "negative" task consisting in "a 'nominalist' reduction of philosophical anthropology and the notions that could rest upon it."[158]

These are crucial lines for understanding the shared stakes of Foucauldian archaeology and genealogy, and they have attracted the attention of several generations of scholars. If the text that Foucault wrote between 1959 and 1960 to introduce his translation of Kant's *Anthropology* has, since 2008, become part of his published corpus, many archival documents remain that merit further exploration. They need to be studied and put into relation with one another in order to better illuminate Foucault's positions with regard to philosophical anthropology. On this topic, it is useful to remember that throughout the first half of the 1950s, while he was teaching at the University of Lille and at ENS in Paris, Foucault gave lectures on anthropology; this discipline was at the heart of several of the young philosopher's publication projects. The edition of Foucault's translation of Kant's *Anthropology* published in 1964 was accompanied by a "Notice historique" to which Foucault appended a final note mentioning "a later work" concerning "the relationship between critical thought and anthropological reflection"[159]—a direct announcement of *The Order of Things*. But other, earlier declarations by Foucault point us to works that remain unpublished. Among them, we might especially cite Foucault's reference, in his introduction to *Le rêve et l'existence* from 1954, to "another work" in which he "shall try to situate existential analysis within the development of contemporary reflection on man."[160] A similar allusion can be found in a letter Foucault sent to Binswanger during this period, when he had just completed his introduction: as I have discussed, he specifies that he intends to work on a much larger study of anthropology and ontology.

As I have shown, this study corresponds in all likelihood to the manuscript *Binswanger et l'analyse existentielle*, in which Foucault presents and critically analyzes Binswanger's phenomenological anthropology in relation to classic psychopathology, Freudian psychoanalysis, and Husserlian phenomenology. This interest in *Daseinsanalyse* can therefore be situated in the context of a larger examination of the legitimacy of philosophical anthropology, an examination that takes up a large part of the Foucauldian archives of the 1950s and that seeks to show, as

Foucault explains in his introduction to *Le rêve et l'existence*, "by observing the inflection of phenomenology toward anthropology, what foundations have been proposed for concrete reflection on man."[161] In addition to the notes that accompany the manuscript for Foucault's secondary thesis on Kant's *Anthropology*,[162] most of Foucault's reading notes at this time concern the various kinds of phenomenological anthropology developed within the field of Germanophone psychopathology. Although Binswanger is the author who most attracts Foucault's attention, a very large number of notes concern the works of German and Swiss psychiatrists and psychologists who, starting in the early 1930s, had drawn on phenomenology to reform their disciplines in the direction of anthropology. Foucault's files from this period clearly demonstrate the common threads among his interests. A bibliographical reading note drafted in the course of reading Hans Kunz's writings, in particular, informs us about the works that Foucault might have consulted or wanted to consult during this period:[163]

> Erich Volland, *Die Stellung des Menschen in der naturwissenschaftlichen und in der philosophischen Anthropologie der Gegenwart* (Halle: Klinz, 1936);
> Paul Ludwig Landsberg, *Einführung in die philosophische Anthropologie* (Frankfurt: Klostermann, 1934);
> Otto Friedrich Bollnow, "Existenzerhellung und philosophische Anthropologie: Versuch einer Auseinandersetzung mit Karl Jaspers," *Blätter für Deutsche Philosophie* 12 (1938): 133–174;
> Dolf Sternberger, *Der verstandene Tod: eine Untersuchung zu Martin Heideggers Existenzialontologie* (Leipzig: Hirzel, 1934);
> Otto Friedrich Bollnow, "Existenzphilosophie," in *Systematische Philosophie*, 2nd ed., ed. Nicolai Hartmann (Stuttgart: Kohlhammer, 1942);

Matthias Thiel, "Was ist der Mensch?," *Divus Thomas* 20 (1942): 3–34;

Helmuth Plessner, *Macht und menschliche Natur: ein Versuch zur Anthropologie der geschichtlichen Weltansicht* (Berlin: Junker und Dünnhaupt, 1931);

Max Horkheimer, "Bemerkungen zur philosophischen Anthropologie," *Zeitschrift für Sozialforschung* 4, no. 1 (1935): 1–25;

Joachim Ritter, *Über den Sinn und die Grenze der Lehre vom Menschen* (Potsdam: Protte, 1933);

Theodor Litt, *Die Selbsterkenntnis des Menschen* (Leipzig: Meiner, 1938);

Franz Josef Brecht, *Der Mensch und die Philosophie* (Halle: Niemeyer, 1932).

If we add to this partial list the copious notes that Foucault dedicated to, among others, Max Scheler, Paul Häberlin, and Wilhelm Keller (1909–1987),[164] we might have reason to believe that this was material assembled in preparation for drafting the volume announced in 1954. Foucault was particularly attentive to Max Scheler's work, to which he devoted numerous reading notes.[165] The Schelerian conception of anthropology is also central in the lectures on anthropology that Foucault gave at the University of Lille and the ENS in the early 1950s.[166] It is interesting to observe, on this subject, that Scheler is a constant reference across Binswanger's oeuvre; we might therefore see this oeuvre as a channel through which Foucault familiarized himself with Scheler.[167] At the same time, during the period when Foucault was drafting these notes, many of Scheler's writings already existed in French translation.[168] At the start of an approximately fifty-page file on Scheler, Foucault draws up the following summary: *Sens de la souffrance*; "Amour et connaissance"; "Repentir et Renaissance"; *L'Homme du ressentiment*;

Saint, Génie, Héros; *Nature et Formes de la sympathie*; *Situation de l'homme dans le monde*; *La Pudeur*; *Phänomenologie und Erkenntnistheorie*."[169]

Yet, *Maladie mentale et personnalité* aside, the only two published works that emerged from this decade that Foucault devoted to psychology, phenomenology, and anthropology are quite polemical with regard to these three disciplines. Indeed, *History of Madness* and *The Order of Things*, like the work on Kant's *Anthropology*, lay the foundations for a radical critique of the human sciences that will remain, until the 1980s, the distinctive trait of Foucault's intellectual project. In the following pages, I therefore propose to analyze the manner in which Foucault tackles the question of anthropology—especially phenomenological anthropology—at the beginning of a philosophical trajectory in which phenomenology and anthropology play pivotal roles. Beyond the manuscript *Binswanger et l'analyse existentielle*, which I have just analyzed, I will focus on the notes for a series of lectures about anthropology.[170] This course, which Foucault gave either at Lille or at ENS roughly between 1953 and 1955, concerns the development of philosophical anthropology at the end of the eighteenth century. I will also refer to various lecture fragments and reading notes from the same period that take up the relationship between phenomenology and anthropology.

The hypothesis I will test is that Foucault's interest in anthropology was motivated, from the start, by a dissatisfaction with Husserlian phenomenology, and in particular with the way in which it excluded from its descriptions those "obstacles on the path of human practice"[171] represented by pathological lived experiences. This would be why Foucault found the various forms of phenomenological psychopathology and especially Binswanger's *Daseinsanalyse*—which he described as a "decisive moment for the radical surpassing of phenomenological analysis,"[172] which would finally offer a philosophical account of the contradictions of the human being—so appealing. I will conclude by showing that it was the route of Kantian "pragmatic" anthropology that ultimately led Foucault to lose faith in the approach to analyzing the human that had first been suggested to him by phenomenological anthropology.

THE ELUCIDATION OF THE ANTHROPOLOGICAL THEME AND PHENOMENOLOGY

According to the theoretical reconstruction that Foucault lays out in his course *La Question anthropologique*, the major obstacle that classical philosophy presented to the constitution of anthropology as an autonomous discipline was the former's erasure of the theme of the world in favor of nature. With the mathematization of philosophy wrought by Galileo and Descartes, the being of the world in its Greek sense, as originary totality and homeland of the being of man, disappeared from philosophical discourse in order to make space for a "questioning of the sense of being [i.e., of the meaning or signification] of truth."[173] In the horizon of classical metaphysics, Foucault explains, man was deprived of his truth to the benefit of nature, "either to the benefit of a semantics that confers only a purely symbolic value to the figures of the world, thereby preventing man from deciphering his own truth in the world, or to the benefit of a perfection where man does not need to fulfill himself, but only to fulfill God's truth, thereby erasing the truth of his own finitude."[174]

It is by posing the problem of the relationship between nature and the world that Kant's critique made a reflection on man possible. By substituting, for the classical opposition between the world and nature, the distinction between the universe and the domain of experience, "where nature and its truth receive their original meaning from the world as it is given to a finite intuition,"[175] critique made possible an anthropology, understood as the necessity of interrogating man at the level of his world. Anthropology as a subject in its own right, therefore, arose when man's experience of his own finitude—through sense-experience, thereby necessitating an aesthetics—was taken seriously, and when the myth of an infinite understanding was exorcised, thereby necessitating an analytic of reason.[176]

The keystone of anthropology is therefore finitude. It is through experience, through the imagination, that nature transforms itself into a world. This is why, Foucault writes, the problem that now poses itself is that "of the movement of truth, examination of the manner in which truth announces itself to man and founds any access he may have to it in his errors, his limitations and his finitude."[177] If "the world is not nature," it is "because it is originally *my* nature, *my* dream and *my* passion."[178] For this reason,

> The fourth question: what is man[?] (philosophical anthropology) does not mean: what is the truth of the human being, but rather, how can the human being be on the same level as the truth? Not what is this truth that inhabits man, but rather, how can man inhabit the truth?"[179]

We see adumbrated here the position that Foucault would adopt with regard to philosophical anthropology in the early 1960s, when he would explicitly argue that not only the possibility but also the "peril of an anthropology" could be found in

Kantian philosophy: "Starting with Kant, there is a reversal: the problem of man will be raised as a kind of cast shadow, but this will not be in terms of the infinite or the truth. Since Kant, the infinite is no longer given, there is no longer anything but finitude; and it's in that sense that the Kantian critique carried the possibility—or the peril—of an anthropology."[180] If anthropology presents a danger, it is because throughout the nineteenth century—through Hegel, Feuerbach, Marx, Dilthey—it developed itself not only as the culmination but also as a suppression of critique. It represents its culmination because, in keeping with the Kantian model, it examines man "in the world," a world that, as Foucault explains in his Lille manuscript about anthropology, "is our world, in which we have our home."[181] But it also represents its suppression insofar as anthropology, as we see most prominently in Dilthey's theorization of the *Leben* (understood as a region in which man's essence is deployed), gives rise to the project of assigning a region that is "anterior to all of the spiritual objectivations defined by the sciences of the spirit, more fundamental than the objective *Geist*" but that, at the same time, "will have to give an account of the forms of objectivity of the *Geist*."[182]

Phenomenological reflection, which raises the problem of a "return to origins that is at the same time a foundation of objectivity and a purification of essence,"[183] also develops in this space, according to Foucault. It is there that phenomenology's paradoxical destiny manifests itself: while presenting itself as anti-anthropological, it ends up "giving anthropology a new lease on life."[184] This destiny is determined first by the theoretical confusion provoked by phenomenology's thematization of the figure of the "originary," which is produced between the two levels of the empirical and the transcendental. Foucault develops this point initially in his introduction to Kant's *Anthropology* and then in *The Order of Things*.[185] It is also determined by

Husserlian phenomenology's inability to provide an account of the many human phenomena, such as pathological experiences, that do not enter into the "clarified space" to which it confines philosophical investigation. This is why, according to Foucault, phenomenology cannot avoid finding the point of departure for its radical rethinking in its reflection on psychology. This is the level at which Binswanger's existential anthropology finds its place. In *Binswanger et l'analyse existentielle*, indeed, Foucault presents it as the critical moment in which phenomenological analysis is surpassed "in its effort to develop a genesis of constitutions and an understanding of meaning."[186]

THE RISK OF ANTHROPOLOGY

In *Binswanger et l'analyse existentielle*, the idea of the world, even if it is approached from a more explicitly Heideggerian direction, appears once again as the pivotal point for Foucault's analysis. Binswanger's theoretical program is introduced with a critique of phenomenology that focuses, in particular, on the Husserlian idea of the "lifeworld" (*Lebenswelt*). If on the one hand Husserl had been able to restore the "concrete plenitude"[187] of the *Lebenswelt*—the pregiven world, anterior to any act of knowledge—on the other, as I have shown, this world whose phenomenological description restores its metamorphoses to us "is nothing but the flourishing of the world that is already there."[188] Yet pathological experiences "do not deploy themselves within a world that is already there."[189] These experiences have to do with the *particular* manner in which "human reality is present to the world":[190] this is why it is necessary to decipher, in morbid experience, the alteration of "the essence and structural elements (*Wesenstruktur*) of Being-in-the-world insofar as it is transcendental."[191] Binswanger's phenomenological project presents itself precisely as the analysis of the general forms this alteration takes.

In the manuscript of *La Question anthropologique* this project is presented as one of the ways in which the idea of anthropology was developed at the beginning of the twentieth century. Foucault describes this idea as "an interrogation of the style in which lived experiences gain coherence, of the general structures according to which presence-in-the-world articulates itself, and finally of man as the original foundation and significant source of everything that bears, for him, the face of the world."[192] In contrast, in the manuscript on existential analysis, Foucault illustrates the structures that determine the unity of style of various forms of existence. In this way, pathological experience ceases to be understood as a simple physical process exterior to the patient and becomes, instead, "the world of the patient," which is to say, the "project" of his existence.[193]

It is important to underline that, according to Foucault, it was analyzing these structures in a clinical context that allowed Binswanger to avoid reducing his anthropological discourse to a speculation on the essence of man. In other words, in Binswanger's clinical case studies, there is no question of "analyzing 'the fundamental structures of human existence,'" but rather an effort to analyze "the existential possibilities that *Dasein* has in fact chosen."[194] The transcendental character of the existential structures identified and analyzed by Binswanger cannot be separated from a concrete existence, one that is unfolding; while they are defined as *a priori*, these structures manifest themselves and can be recognized only from the vantage point of the phenomena through which they express themselves.

This is what Foucault underscores when, for example, he talks about "an *a priori* of existence"[195] in *Maladie mentale et personnalité*. In this expression, the concept of existence means nothing more than the presence in the world "of this very existence that bears such and such a name and has traversed such and such a history,"[196] as he puts it in the introduction to *Le rêve et l'existence*.

This *a priori* is somewhat paradoxical, since it is always contemporary to the phenomena that it has the task of explaining. This is why Foucault, in his introduction to *Le rêve et l'existence*, can present Binswanger's anthropology as a "science of facts," since it develops "in a rigorous fashion the existential content of presence-to-the-world."[197] He adds, "To reject such an inquiry at first glance because it is neither philosophy nor psychology, because one cannot define it as either science or speculation, because it neither looks like positive knowledge nor provides the content of a priori cognition, is to ignore the basic meaning of the project."[198]

When Foucault asserts, in *Binswanger et l'analyse existentielle*, that for existential analysis ontological reflection in the manner of Heidegger can only ever be referential, he means to emphasize that Binswanger appropriates the Heideggerian concept of *Dasein* or "being-in-the-world" not in order to base his reflection on a speculative foundation, but rather in order to "take up any reflection on man at the level of that foundation that is man himself in his existence,"[199] in conformity with the conviction that "man, in his forms of existence," is "the only means of getting to man."[200] If Foucault was at first enthusiastic about Binswanger's phenomenological anthropology, if this approach seemed to him to follow the "royal road" in contemporary anthropology,[201] it was precisely because it seemed to him to avoid, as he noted via Hans Kunz in a reading note from this period, "the peril inherent in anthropology, which is to build [its theories] in thin air and outside of any contact with psychopathological experience."[202]

Yet, the final part of the manuscript shows that, in Foucault's eyes, even existential analysis ends up falling victim to this "peril" stalking anthropology, insofar as the latter pushes it to abandon the path of experience in favor of the embrace of speculation. According to Foucault, as I have shown earlier, Binswanger crossed that threshold at the moment when he attempted to give an ontological foundation to his approach—when, in *Grundformen und Erkenntnis menschlichen Daseins*, he located in the existential structure of "love" the foundation of all structures. This "metaphysical recourse to the classic theme of love"[203] is precisely what forecloses the possibility of truly reaching real man.

THE PRAGMATIC POINT OF VIEW

I have shown that in a fragment dating from the same period as the Lille manuscripts, Foucault asserted that phenomenology ends up converging "toward an essence of man valid only in the realm of anthropological speculation."[204] He then adds,

> We can sum up phenomenology's stroke of genius by saying that it updated the theological concepts that were most opposed to any knowledge of man and restored them in such a way that the human sciences, not recognizing their theological roots, and subscribing to them because they believed that these theological concepts represented a concrete approach to man, signed, without knowing it, their own death warrant.[205]

The identification of man with an "original" essence that simultaneously founds and exceeds him ends up detaching him from any link to the real conditions that define his existence. In other handwritten notes from this period, Foucault attacks this model of anthropology explicitly. He describes it, along with scientific psychology or "anthropometry," as one of the "two ways of dominating the 'scandal' of psychology": "Anthropology, where man is trapped in forms of existence anterior to his life, to the morning of his world, in a dawn that is not yet compromised in any real world. But when the real world comes to manifest itself, it is declared that he is experiencing it in a fantastic mode wherein he alienates himself, and from that moment on, the world becomes alienated."[206]

Different from the program Foucault imagined through the clinical aspect of Binswanger's anthropology—which entailed elucidating how man's being-in-the-world, rather than his nature, is structured—this anthropology presupposes a man who can be purified of any mark of the real. It results in arguing that "it is incorrect to say that 'man is the very root of man.'"[207] Foucault observes,

> Contemporary thought protects itself against the danger of an effective science of man by caricaturing man in God's image. Through anthropology man has paradoxically become the natural site of theology, its point of application. If it was true during Feuerbach's time that man had made God in his own image, we can say that in contemporary anthropology, it is God who has made man in his own caricature.[208]

It is for this reason that, in *La Question anthropologique* as in his introduction to Kant's *Anthropology*, Foucault recognizes in the Nietzschean figure of the *Übermensch*—and thus of the death of man—the other face of the death of God.

If the question "*Was ist der Mensch?*" is "insidious,"[209] if it led post-Kantian thought into a slumber that has made us unable "to undertake a veritable *critique* of the anthropological illusion,"[210] if this is therefore the peril that lies in wait for any anthropological discourse, is it possible to do anthropology differently? In his two texts on anthropology, and especially in his Lille manuscript, Foucault concludes his examination of the vicissitudes of philosophical anthropology with an illustration from Nietzschean critique, which he defines as a "psychology, in its philosophical sense," or a "psychology of psychology," which leads to the dissolution of human essence. Indeed, it presents itself, he notes, as an "Analysis not of the soul, but of the movement through which man gives himself a soul; not of consciousness, but of the forgetting that allows man to presume to see himself reflected in his consciousness alone; not of the will, but of the superstition that allows man to believe that his will is transparent in the actions in which he diversifies himself."[211]

In other words, if Nietzsche's philosophy "gives a wholly new meaning to critique,"[212] it is because it "brings man back to his origins,"[213] and, in so doing, liberates him from his essence. But once this illusion has been unmasked—once the philosopher has awakened from the "anthropological slumber" that the human sciences pushed him into—does any space remain for anthropological reflection? What about the possibility that Kant opened up for anthropology, before successive philosophical movements adulterated its meaning? As we have shown, according to Foucault, Kant's anthropological question "What is man?" is not a question about the truth of the human being. Rather, it means asking, as Foucault does in the Lille manuscript on anthropology, "how can the human being be on the same level as the truth?"—or, in other words, how does his manner of inhabiting the world define itself?[214]

This task is simultaneously more difficult and more modest: it represents the "pragmatic" nature of an anthropological analysis that, without coinciding with a merely empirical analysis, does not burden itself with the "dead weight of the a priori"[215] and maintains its a posteriori character. Despite its a posteriori character—which is to say, based on observation—the anthropological gaze is capable of elaborating a systematic discourse on the human being on the basis of the phenomena that express that being, including its singular manifestations and its deviations. In other words, far from conflating the two levels of analysis, empirical and transcendental—as do, according to Foucault, post-Kantian philosophical movements—a Kantian anthropological observation gives itself the means of achieving an intermediary position, simultaneously *a priori* and *a posteriori*.

The Kantian anthropological gaze would in this way have the ability to make good use of a "concrete *a priori*," based on the regularity of phenomena. This is perhaps not so far from the scope of Binswanger's clinical anthropology, which Foucault describes at the beginning of his introduction to *Le rêve et l'existence* as a knowledge that "neither looks like positive knowledge nor provides the content of a priori cognition."[216] This kind of knowledge appears, to Foucault, as a possible avenue toward a method that is true to the object it studies: man in his world, in all his manifestations. Nevertheless, and at the same time, it is precisely Kantian anthropology that revealed to Foucault the peril concealed in any anthropological project that abandons the "originary" level of man in his real, temporal, even individual world in order to address a purified, ideal, and atemporal origin.

3

ARCHAEOLOGICAL METHOD

A METHODOLOGICAL INVESTIGATION

In the first edition of *History of Madness*, Foucault presented himself as "a philosopher who turned to psychology, and from psychology to history." This "history without dates or chronology," as he described it during his thesis defense on May 20, 1961,[1] has raised numerous questions among historians;[2] nonetheless, it was precisely the need to historicize the experience of mental illness that pushed Foucault to abandon existential psychiatry. In 1984, in the preface he drafted for the American edition of *The History of Sexuality*, Foucault returned to his interest in existential analysis, specifying that it ultimately left him dissatisfied because of "its theoretical weakness in elaborating the notion of experience, and its ambiguous link with a psychiatric practice, which it simultaneously ignored and took for granted."[3] In other words, Foucault could no longer be satisfied with the absence of a critical historical perspective in Binswanger's anthropological approach, which was limited to individual life history. In the face of concrete historical psychiatric practices, existential anthropology now appeared to Foucault to be something like a "mythical explanation."[4] This is why in the second edition of *Maladie mentale et personnalité* (*Mental Illness and Psychology*, 1962), the final chapters are no longer concerned with the "existential forms of illness" but rather with their "historical conditions." Foucault goes so far as to conclude that "it is only in history that one can discover the sole concrete *a priori* from which mental illness draws, with the empty opening up of its possibility, its necessary figures."[5] Foucault concludes the first part of *Mental Illness and Psychology* by arguing, "if this subjectivity of the insane is both a call to and an abandonment of the world, is it not of the world itself that we should ask the secret of its enigmatic status?"[6] The reference to the concept of "world" is quite ironic here, since this concept is central in Binswanger's existential psychiatry, whose aim was precisely to inquire into the patient's "world-project." Moreover, Foucault can no longer support the project of building a phenomenological anthropology, a project whose philosophical limits he has sketched out.

That said, the phenomenological approach still profoundly marks the next step in Foucault's trajectory, *History of Madness*. While opening onto a movement beyond existential psychiatry, this book owes a lot to its approach to mental illness. Foucault's project of thinking a history not of psychiatry but rather of madness, before any psychopathological conceptualization, is not far from that of the psychiatrist-phenomenologists who attempted to approach mental illness first as an extra-scientific phenomenon, independent of any clinical classification.[7] Indeed, for Foucault, the task was not to retrace the history of a truth of mental illness that could eventually be accessed, but rather to identify the "degree zero of the history of madness, when it was undifferentiated experience,"[8] which "still remains, for us, the mode of access to the natural truth of man."[9]

It is precisely for this reason that, if on the one hand, as Georges Canguilhem observed in the report he drafted in 1960 about Foucault's thesis, *History of Madness* has the merit of "reviv[ing] a fruitful dialogue between psychology and philosophy at a time when many psychologists are willing to separate their techniques from an interrogation of the origins and meanings of these techniques,"[10] on the other this philosophical reflection entails some difficulties. As Pierre Macherey insightfully puts it, "by moving beyond the idea of a psychological truth of mental illness toward that of an ontological truth of madness," the historical "rectification" toward which Foucault oriented his research at the very beginning of the 1960s ended up "leaving intact the presupposition of a human nature"[11] for which Foucault had critiqued philosophical anthropology throughout the 1950s. Once again, the question of man and of anthropology remained central to Foucault's preoccupations. It was precisely this question that he worked to refine and deepen in the 1960s with the development of his "archaeological" program, and especially of the critique of philosophical anthropology, which was at the heart of the archaeology of the human sciences developed in *The Order of Things*.

Should we therefore consider the "Binswanger dossier" to have been definitively closed by the early 1960s? In the following pages, I will examine the theoretical kernel of Foucault's archaeological project in the light of his writings on *Daseinsanalyse*, in order to explore whether it is possible to recognize points of convergence or continuity between Foucault's interest in Binswanger's thought and the archaeological project. My argument is that Foucault's relationship to Binswanger must be understood not as an evaluation of the possibility of elaborating a phenomenological anthropology, but rather as a confrontation whose nature was principally methodological. The critical unease that immediately appears as the fundamental characteristic of Foucault's thought would have initially found in Binswanger's theoretico-clinical approach not an anthropological model to adopt to the letter, but rather a methodological reference point: the example of a reflection that was structurally immanent to the practices, conceptual elaborations, attitudes, and behaviors that it had the goal of questioning and analyzing. For this reason, I believe that it would be reductive to stop at the surface of Foucault's statements, starting in the 1950s and continuing throughout the 1960s, denouncing the failure of any anthropological approach to philosophy. It would be too simple, in sum, to throw out Foucault's earliest writings on the basis of the archaeological diagnosis of anthropology's inherent philosophical error, independent of the diagnostic method he used in order to arrive at his conclusions.

Indeed, we must not forget that in all of these texts Foucault's critical attitude toward anthropology stems from an interrogation. Let us make no mistake: before the question "*Was ist der Mensch?*," Foucault asks, "what is anthropology?" Examined on these terms, in the context of an archaeologico-structural analysis, anthropology appears as a particular form or "structure" that determines a certain knowledge in its positivity. Foucault makes this explicit in his writing on Kant's *Anthropology*, when he remarks that "whatever its empirical content, then, anthropology has an epistemological structure of its very own."[12] Again, in 1965, he states that "By 'anthropology' I mean the strictly philosophical structure responsible for the fact that the problems of philosophy are now all lodged within the domain that can be called that of human finitude."[13]

Anthropology therefore appears as an epistemological configuration or "historical *a priori*" on the basis of which, as Foucault remarks in *The Order of Things*, "ideas could appear, sciences be established, experience be reflected in philosophies, rationalities be formed."[14] It is an *a priori* that, as I will now show, has an essentially operational value—a "transcendental" that does not precede the practices through which it can be "diagnosed," but that instead emerges from them and then "returns" to them in order to clarify their structure. Following the trail of the "historical *a priori*," we see that it is at the level of methodology that the appeal and utility of existential analysis's theoretical device become visible and play themselves out for Foucault. It is precisely from this point of view that we will seek out the traces of this device, which we might deem the most precious tool that Foucault the archaeologist used in his digs.

The compatibility between the existential approach in psychiatry and Foucault's archaeology has been highlighted by a French psychiatrist who played an important role in developing the phenomenological approach in France: Georges Lantéri-Laura (1930–2004). Lantéri-Laura begins by asking about the school of antipsychiatry, which since its origins in the 1960s has linked the existential tradition of psychiatry with Foucault's archaeological analysis. He maintains that phenomenology lent its tools and guiding questions to antipsychiatry, insofar as it did not present itself as a doctrine but rather as an "attitude" able to "bracket any preliminary theoretical position" toward any established (reductive) system of knowledge.[15] It would probably be an exaggeration to affirm—as did the French philosopher Henri Maldiney—that "if the phenomenological attitude had prevailed in psychiatry, antipsychiatry would not have been born."[16] Yet, one should admit that existential psychiatry played a central role in the works of such "antipsychiatrists" as Ronald D. Laing (1927–1989) and David Cooper (1931–1986), who refer explicitly to the projects of, respectively, Karl Jaspers, Eugène Minkowski, and Ludwig Binswanger.[17]

From this point of view, *History of Madness* shares with Binswanger's existential analysis the phenomenological attitude, insofar as it refuses to conceive of forms of existence and of their expression from the perspective of a science "of the order of positive knowledge."[18] Via Binswanger, Foucault clearly endorses the phenomenological project of overcoming both "science" and "speculation" in order to let phenomena appear, rather than tracing them back to a given order of meanings or categories. As Foucault himself made clear in 1980, if "reading what has been defined [as] 'existential analysis' or 'phenomenological psychiatry' certainly was important for [him] at a period when [he] was working in psychiatric hospitals," it is because this field showed him "something different to counterbalance the traditional grids of the medical gaze."[19] Thus, the very archaeology that ended up critiquing phenomenological psychiatry traces the grids shaping the different ways of experiencing reality.

In the preface to the American edition of *The History of Sexuality, Volume II*, one of his final writings, Foucault returns to his early interest in Binswanger and explicitly asserts that "To study forms of experience in this way—in their history—is an idea that originated with an earlier project, in which I made use of the *methods* of existential analysis in the field of psychiatry and in the domain of 'mental illness.'"[20]

This manner of emphasizing the methodological significance of phenomenological psychiatry, at the early stages of the archeological period, offers an orientation for our inquiry into Foucault's archaeology. In what follows I will first dwell on Binswanger's methodology, and in particular on his approach to the phenomenological concept of the *"a priori."* I will then try to show that Binswanger's own approach to this concept, which he understood as the immanent condition of possibility of experience, is compatible from a methodological point of view with Foucault's archaeological project of uncovering, within a given system of knowledge, the "conditions which define, *together with its historical possibility*, the domain of its experience and the structure of its rationality."[21]

BINSWANGER'S PHENOMENOLOGICAL APPROACH

The main question at stake in Binswanger's commitment to phenomenology is a methodological one. At the heart of Binswanger's psychiatric project is the problem of how to reconcile the living singularity of the "case" with the universality of scientific knowledge. This is the question that Binswanger put to psychiatry and tried to answer throughout his theoretical work: How might it be possible to explain the singular?

This was also the question that, at the same time, Karl Jaspers tried to answer by elaborating an *"understanding* psychology" (*verstehende Psychologie*); however, this project concluded by acknowledging the powerlessness of psychiatry to cope with illness precisely because of the chasm of the boundless mutability and incommunicability of the singular.[22] While Jaspers argued that it was impossible to formulate any laws in the field of psychology, Binswanger objected that, on the contrary, such a formulation of scientific laws was possible for psychology: it was a matter of finding laws that would be adequate to the particular "object" of psychological inquiry.[23] In this regard, for the young Binswanger, Freud's psychoanalysis was the perfect example of the possibility of systematically collecting the material of experience—namely, the "real lived experience of real and individual persons"[24]—"under rational themes and sense connections" (*Sinnzusammenhänge*).[25] It was precisely such a quest for the "structural connections and principles,"[26] or for the "rational and *a priori* laws"[27] that govern the organization and functioning of the psyche, that would lead Binswanger toward Husserl's phenomenology. For Binswanger, the great common intuition of Freud's methodology and Husserl's phenomenology was the idea that

> the experience [*Erleben*] of something and the knowledge about such an experience cannot be understood on the basis of a "cause" that would not be this same lived experience.... [They] are an originary phenomenon that is not further derivable; the science of "life" can be conceived on the basis of such a phenomenon, but inversely, this phenomenon cannot be explained by such a science.[28]

Such a conception, however, together with a closer adherence to Husserl's principle according to which the phenomenon must be grasped "in a more original and full way," apart from "any indirect hypostatization,"[29] would lead Binswanger to distance himself from Freud's theory of instincts during the 1920s; he saw in the latter the mark of a positivistic and reductionist view of the psyche. In this regard, the impact of Heidegger's *Being and Time* (1927) marks a further turning point in Binswanger's speculation, since the Heideggerian "analytic of *Dasein*," in Binswanger's opinion, enabled phenomenology to make use of its theoretical instruments to analyze existential and biographical actuality. According to Binswanger's reading of Heidegger, both psychoanalytic and phenomenological notions should address an anthropological research project oriented to the study of *Dasein*, namely, the being of man "in the world." Binswanger's essay that opens this new speculative phase is *Traum und Existenz* (1930). The theme of the dream plays an important role in Binswanger's reflection, since it leads Binswanger to conduct research in the fields of literary history and history of the "spirit."[30] This research, in turn, takes him toward that practical knowledge of the human being (*praktisches Menschenkenntnis*) which defines his reception of Heidegger's philosophical approach as essentially anthropological.

Thus, what appeals to Binswanger in Husserl's approach and, later, in Heidegger's analytic is the possibility of grasping phenomena on the basis of the phenomena themselves, apart from "any indirect hypostatization," as Binswanger writes in his founding text "Über Phänomenologie" (On Phenomenology)—that is, independently of any material or purely etiological theory or explanation.[31] In sum, it is a matter of an intuitive authority that seems to correspond well to the need for the rational and invariable evidence that Binswanger opposes to the merely empiricist or factual authority by which academic psychiatry tried to reach the status of the medical sciences. According to the phenomenological approach applied in psychopathology, in fact, the psychologist has to go beyond singular and contingent psychopathological expressions in order to "look for the *principle* that rules the formation of the series."[32] Thus, Binswanger identifies the phenomenological concept of "essence" with the "norm" or the "structure" of the psychic fact. Most importantly, such a norm or reason for the phenomenon, according to phenomenology, is immanent to the phenomenon itself. That means that the explanation for the phenomenon is always immanent to the phenomenon's description. Now, according to Binswanger, the norm or explanation for the phenomenon coincides with the self-normativity that governs what he calls the "world-project" of the patient. More precisely, such a normativity or world-project is a certain configuration of the psyche that is detectable on the basis of the "relationships of meaning" that govern behavior, which make possible or determine its different expressions *a priori*. These relationships of meaning do not exist independently of the singular experience;

yet they cannot be reduced to the singularity of experience, since they constitute its ordering scheme or structure.

In this vein, Binswanger emphasizes that the concept of *Dasein*—a concept that in Heidegger consists in an ontological thesis[33]—can also be used in a "practical existential-analytical investigation" as a methodological "systematic clue" in order to recognize the forms according to which individual "world-projects" are structured.[34] Indeed, Binswanger emphasizes that the *Dasein* reveals itself through a functioning that is "ordered according to a norm," a norm that "should be characterized positively."[35] As he maintains in 1946,

> If, for example, we can speak of a manic form of life, or, rather, of existence, it means that we could establish a norm that embraces and governs all modes of expression and behavior designated as "manic" by us. It is this *norm* that we call the "world" of the manic. . . . For we know well enough that that-which-is as such never becomes accessible to man, except in and through a certain world-design.[36]

Binswanger emphasizes this position through the first half of the 1950s. In his book *Drei Formen missglückten Daseins* (Three Forms of Failed Existence), for example, he refers back to Husserl's concept of "essence": "Fact should be grasped from its 'essence,' which works—according to Husserl—as the 'insurmountable norm' of a fact."[37] "But, differently from Husserl, for us the facticity of the 'natural world' or the 'natural experience' never disappears."[38]

Indeed, it is worth observing here that Binswanger always employs phenomenological concepts in the context of his reflections on "facticity." When he dwells upon the normative nature of being-in-the-world, he always considers this normativity to be the distinctive feature of the living being. In particular, he emphasizes the idea that it is the immanent structure of the living being that should lead to understanding life's forms. The theories of Kurt Goldstein and Viktor von Weizsäcker on this subject, in particular, drew Binswanger's attention. In his essay of 1932–1933 "On the Flight of Ideas," for instance, Binswanger mentions Goldstein in the following terms:

> Kurt Goldstein was the first neurologist to see . . . that a "pathological" behavior could be grasped only on the basis of a "new being in the world." . . . Jackson, v. Monakow, Head had recognized that the damaging of the function, for example, in aphasia, does not occur without a rule, but rather seems to develop according to a certain norm. . . . Thus, the concept of the pathological . . . was no longer the expression of something purely negative, . . . but it could be also conceived positively, on the basis of a norm. We owe Goldstein, in particular, the insight that this positive corresponds to a "new being in the world" (that is, a being ordered according to a norm, a sense, a structure) that one should characterize positively.[39]

From this idea, Binswanger develops the view that psychopathological experiences are not merely defective modes of health, but new forms of being in the world. It follows that the relationship between the scientific point of view of psychiatry and the singularity of the ill person is characterized by a respect for individual differences with regard to psychiatric classifications.

Along these same lines, Viktor von Weizsäcker appears as another fundamental point of reference for Binswanger. The way in which the German physiologist is presented in Binswanger's article "The Existential Analysis School of Thought" is particularly important in order to grasp the meaning and function that the phenomenological concept of *Dasein* or "*a priori* structure of existence" has for existential analysis. Indeed, in his most famous work, *Der Gestaltkreis* (1940), Weizsäcker had strongly criticized reflexology in order to lay the foundation for a medical anthropology according to which biological acts should be conceived not merely as fixed responses to environmental stimuli, but rather as the creation of some original forms of behavior. According to Weizsäcker, these forms would serve as the changeable norm, the variable "dispositions" or "conditions of possibility" of other future forms. In his reference to Weizsäcker's theory of the normative structure of behavior, Binswanger emphasizes the fact that such a norm or "fundamental condition cannot be recognized explicitly because it cannot in itself become the object," as it is rather "the 'court of highest appeal,' a power that can be experienced either as unconscious dependency or as freedom."[40]

It is precisely this fundamental condition which cannot become the object that Binswanger translates in terms of Heidegger's "being-in-the-world" or "*a priori* structure of *Dasein*." Thus, the "phenomenization" of Heidegger's ontological analytic worked out by Binswanger's analysis of *Dasein* would consist in such a concept of "structure" or "immanent normativity" of behavior borrowed from the fields of neurology and physiology. In other words, it is not the "ontological" as such that Binswanger takes from Heidegger, but rather the gap that Heidegger had established between, respectively, the level of "facticity" and the "existential" level, a level that the German philosopher identified with ontology, whereas Binswanger identifies it with the "*a priori* structure" of the patient's "world-project." In this way, Heidegger's existential analytic is translated by Binswanger into the analysis of the "*a priori* structure" of behavior that corresponds to the norm that, at one and the same time, makes the forms of existence possible and explains them, rather than reducing them to the categories derived from the classic psychiatric classifications.

In this respect, it is worth remarking that Binswanger, at the beginning of the 1930s (namely, at the time of his engagement with Heidegger's philosophy), emphasizes the methodological coherence between the natural and human sciences. As he states in his essay "On the Flight of Ideas" (1933),

> For the harmony that is brewing nowadays between the methods, respectively, of the natural sciences and of the human sciences, it is a good sign that the philosopher reaches the same methodical consequences not only as the psychiatrist who investigates the existential structure of psychosis, but also as the biologist and the neurologist, who think the "biological" in the full sense of the word.[41]

It might thus be worthwhile to examine Binswanger's scientific references between the end of the 1920s and the beginning of the 1930s, which is to say, when he turned to Heidegger's phenomenology. In a review published in 1928 of Eugène Minkowski's work *Schizophrenia*, for instance, Binswanger observes that the phenomenological direction taken by Minkowski by means of his reference to Husserl is part of a broader scientific movement aimed at "conceiving of the *form*" of experience (*Gestaltauffassung*)—a movement that would similarly include "psychology (Wertheimer, Köhler, Koffka, Michotte, etc.), biology (Buytendjik, Plessner, etc.), and psychopathology (Goldstein, Gelb, Schilder, Eliasberg and Feuchtwanger, Bouman and Grünbaum, etc.)."[42]

Foucault gives a clear example of the *Daseinsanalytical* concept of "*a priori* structure" in *Maladie mentale et personnalité*, where he presents the existential analysis of the structure of anxiety, a structure that Binswanger analyzes in particular in the Suzanne Urban clinical case study. Foucault describes this structure in terms of an "*a priori* of existence,"[43] meaning that it is a form of experience that, being anchored to its individual and historical manifestations, cannot be thought *before* them, yet that also goes *beyond* them, in that it organizes them, since it constitutes their norm. Thus, the "existential *a priori*" is historical in that it is inseparable from the phenomenon in which it manifests itself by providing it (the phenomenon) with its form. This is why Binswanger attaches a special importance to the phenomenon of the dream, insofar as it presents itself as the dramatization of this "*a priori* of existence" that Binswanger also calls the "sense-direction" (*Bedeutungsrichtung*) or the "spiritual trend" (*geistigen Tendenz*) of existence.[44]

In this regard, Foucault mentions a dream analyzed by Binswanger "well before the time of 'Dream and Existence,'"[45] in a collection of lectures published in 1928 on the subject of the "changes in the conception and interpretation of dreams from the Greeks to the present" (*Wandlungen in der Auffassung und Deutung des Traumes: Von den Griechen bis zur Gegengenwart*). Foucault concludes in the following manner; it is worth citing the passage in its entirety:

> The essential point of the dream lies not so much in what it revives of the past as in what it declares about the future. It anticipates and announces that moment in which the patient will finally deliver to the analyst that secret which she does not yet know and which is nonetheless the heaviest burden of her present. The dream points to this secret *already*, down to its content, with the precision of a detailed image. The dream anticipates the moment of liberation.... But as the subject of dream cannot be the quasi-objectified subject of that past history, its constituting moment

can only be that existence which makes itself through time, that existence in its movement toward the future. *The dream is already the future making itself,* the first moment of freedom freeing itself, the still secret jarring of an existence that is taking hold of itself again in the whole of its becoming. The dream means repetition only to the extent that the repetition is precisely the experience of a temporality that opens upon the future and constitutes itself as freedom.[46]

That is to say, in the "future anterior"[47] represented by the dream, the *a prioris* of existence present themselves as *actual* conditions of possibility of history. Thus, Binswanger does not conceive of dreams as phenomena to be "interpreted," but as "leading-categories" (*leitenden Kategorie*)[48] that can be used to disentangle the "basic, *a priori* structures" of pathological experiences.

Foucault wrote a reading note about this study of dreams; it is conserved inside an annotated copy of Binswanger's work that belonged to his personal library. In it he remarks, "The dream is an anticipation of a situation that has not yet occurred: the patient has not yet found the primary trauma. Therefore, the dream is not always a repetition of the past, as Freud had it, but also an anticipation of an expected discourse."[49] Now, in Binswanger's definition of the concept of *a priori* structure, the reference to the medical anthropologies of K. Goldstein and V. von Weizsäcker, respectively, is again of the utmost importance, in that for them, too, the biological concept of the *a priori* structure of behavior can be used to explain the forms of the living being from the perspective of the future. Indeed, even though these structures are *"a priori"*—they are "directions" of existence, leading-categories, so they are not yet actual—they emerge from the living being's history and cannot be conceived separately from this history: that is to say, they are "empirical *a priori.*" This is precisely the model that Binswanger has in mind when he turns to Heidegger's concept of *Dasein*.

It was therefore no accident that Foucault focused his attention on von Weizsäcker's chief work, *Der Gestaltkreis*, at the same time that he was studying Binswanger. Phenomenology, in this context, was received by Foucault—through Binswanger—less in a doctrinal sense and more as a methodological direction that asks philosophy to study the forms of experience in their history, in their concrete expression. In this context, we can better understand the meaning of Foucault's repeated warning, in his introduction to *Le rêve et l'existence*, that detouring through Heidegger's philosophy does not open a door to the "esotericism of the analysis of *Dasein*."[50] This is also why he explicitly maintains that existential analysis—even though it seeks out the "*a prioris* of existence"—does not refer to some *a priori* form of philosophical speculation.[51]

Thus, Heidegger's methodological intuition that "the question of existence never gets straightened out except through existing itself"[52] is discounted by Binswanger in the field of psychological research, and *Dasein* becomes the theoretical tool with which the psychiatrist uncovers, *in their history*, the *a priori* structures or conditions of possibility of existence in its various expressions. This is why, during this period, the French psychiatrist Henri Ey defined Heidegger's phenomenology in terms of "structural psychology" in his *Études psychiatriques*.[53]

A "BIOLOGICAL PHILOSOPHY"

This methodological approach to existence—one that starts with existence's concrete historical forms in order to explain these forms themselves—is exactly what drew French philosophers' attention to Binswanger at a time when Canguilhem, referring to Kurt Goldstein, held that "the thought of the living must take from the living the idea of the living."[54] That is to say, the phenomenon of living can only be explained from the inside, from the living itself.

One should consider, in this respect, that in France, the phenomenological criterion of immanence in the first half of the twentieth century became the theoretical core not only of a certain part of psychiatry, but also of a biology that approached life not via an extrinsic rationality, but rather from the immanent normativity of life itself. It is worth observing, for instance, that in 1946 the French psychiatrist Daniel Lagache considered Canguilhem's doctoral dissertation *The Normal and the Pathological* to be an "anthropological phenomenology," and he concluded by urging both psychology and biology to become aware of the potential implications of considering the "position of man in the world."[55] Canguilhem himself, in a paper written in 1947 on "biological philosophy," conceives of biology not just as "the universe of science, objectivity, and *hors de soi*" as opposed to the "universe of consciousness, subjectivity, value, and meaning,"[56] but as research that would be able to grasp all of these concepts as emerging from the intrinsic determinations of the organism. It is precisely the immanence of philosophical concepts to the living being to which Canguilhem lays claim in his harangue against rationalism, which he characterizes as "a philosophy of *après coup*."[57] And this is also the sense of his almost Heideggerian argument according to which man distinguishes himself from plants and animals to the extent that he "inhabits the world."[58]

Foucault would effectively describe the central concern of this philosophical biology in 1978, in his introduction to Canguilhem's *The Normal and the Pathological*, when he acknowledges the specificity of the biologist's knowledge in that it examines "a type of object to which he himself belongs, since he lives and since he . . . develops this nature of the living in an activity of knowledge."[59] It is exactly this concurrence of the philosophical investigation with its "objects" that Merleau-Ponty emphasized in 1947, in the same issue of the *Revue de Métaphysique et de Morale* in which Canguilhem published his "Note" on philosophical biology. Merleau-Ponty writes: "The universality of knowledge is no longer guaranteed in each of us by that stronghold of absolute (*a priori*) consciousness"; neither is it guaranteed by "the evidence of the object."[60] "The germ of universality" is to be found "in the thing where our perception places us."[61] This means that the "universality" for which philosophical research looks is always embodied and situated in a historical existence; it is to be found in existence as experiencing, living, being in the world, or, to quote Foucault's essay on Binswanger, "existence which is living itself and is experiencing itself, which recognizes itself or loses itself, in a world that is at once the plenitude of its own project and the 'element' of its situation."[62] Hence, Merleau-Ponty concludes, the only *a priori* the philosopher can turn to in his or her analysis of experience is something like an "*a priori of the species*," an *a priori* that coincides with the concrete, historical normative structure of being in the world. This is an *a priori* whose model Merleau-Ponty borrows from Gestalt theory, and "of which [man] forms no distinct concept but which he puts together as an experienced pianist deciphers an unknown piece of music: without himself grasping the motives of each gesture or each operation, without being able to bring to the surface of consciousness all the sediment of knowledge which he is using at that moment."[63] Here, Merleau-Ponty's point is that the "facts" of behavior correspond to a structure or norm, and that this norm is "inscribed in the facts themselves."[64] That means that this "internal rule" which lets these facts appear "is not the external unfolding of a pre-existing reason," but coincides with this same appearance—"it is the very appearance of the world and not the condition of its possibility; it is the birth of a norm and is not realized according to a norm."[65]

Now, such a concrete *a priori*, conceived as the norm of the phenomena and used to uncover in the experience itself the principle of its own justification, forms the methodological core of Binswanger's phenomenological approach. This is why Binswanger emphasizes the common methodological thread between the phenomenological attitude toward phenomena and a biology that inquires into the living being from the starting point of its immanent normativity. I believe that this reference to biology is crucial in order to understand the methodological meaning that French philosophers gave to phenomenology when they received and reworked it during the first half of the twentieth century. Indeed, this was the scientific and philosophical context in which the young Foucault, in 1958, translated into French von Weizsäcker's most important work, *Der Gestaltkreis*, which simultaneously claimed its alignment with the phenomenological attitude toward existence and put the idea of the "inner normativity" of life at the heart of the study of the living being and the structure of its being-in-the-world.[66] This work, together with Kurt Goldstein's *Der Aufbau des Organismus* (1934),[67] had already been the subject of Merleau-Ponty's research in the 1940s; it was published in the same collection as Binswanger's French translations (*Le rêve et l'existence* and the *Suzanne Urban* clinical case study). To this same collection—"Textes et études anthropologiques"—also belonged the French translation of one of the principal works by the Dutch physiologist Frederik J. J. Buytendijk, *Attitudes et mouvements: étude fonctionnelle du mouvement humain*,[68] with a preface by Minkowski, as well as Roland

Kuhn's book on the Rorschach test. The theme of normativity, developed in reference to Weizsäcker, played an especially important role in Buytendijk's writings: for him, questions about corporeal structure and behavior ought to be posed in the context of an anthropology. It is worth emphasizing, on this point, that Buytendijk was very close to Binswanger, to whom he devoted a course at Utrecht University in the 1950s.[69]

The French reception of German phenomenology in the first half of the twentieth century is characterized by a blurring of the boundaries between the "phenomenal field" and the "transcendental field" in an epistemologico-methodological sense that goes beyond the traditional philosophical domains of gnoseology and ontology. In the context of the reflection on biology, psychology, and psychiatry, phenomenology became not only an instrument to test the validity of the positive sciences; it was also used by these same sciences as a methodological tool allowing them to define and grasp their own objects. Merleau-Ponty's case is paradigmatic in this regard. We must underscore that Binswanger is mentioned by Merleau-Ponty precisely in this context, and that the authors to whom he refers in his phenomenological account of perception as "experience of the world"—notably, Goldstein and Weizsäcker—are also the principal references for Binswanger's inquiry into mental illness as a "world-project." When Minkowski writes, in the new edition of his study on schizophrenia in 1953, that Binswanger's existential analysis finally made the "specific world" of patients accessible to the psychiatrist by showing him "its form and its laws,"[70] this use of the concept of "law" is not only metaphorical. Indeed, it refers to a whole school of biology and of medical knowledge that had made normativity into the basis for the study of the living being and of the structure of its "being in the world."[71]

All this is very important for grasping the meaning of Binswanger's adoption of a phenomenological approach. In particular, we must observe that Binswanger insisted on the harmony between the methods of the human sciences and those of the natural sciences at the start of the 1930s—exactly when he was most committed to Heidegger's philosophy. For that matter, he was not the only one, during this period, to try to test Heidegger's intuitions against "concrete life." Indeed, Heidegger looms large in Weizsäcker's work as well as in that of the German psychiatrist Erwin Straus, whose trace we can glimpse in Merleau-Ponty's works of the 1940s, as well as in Foucault's writings and reading notes of the 1950s. While sharing with Heidegger's existential analytic the requirement that the problem of "existence" be tackled separately from a reflection on pure consciousness, these physician-philosophers distanced themselves from Heidegger's idea according to which the knowledge of the living should be limited to pure "biological life."[72] In the second edition of his major work, *Vom Sinn der Sinne* (1956), Straus actually referred to Binswanger in order to critique Heidegger; indeed, Binswanger had been very critical of the way in which Heidegger had discredited the biological and anthropological perspectives on existence.[73]

We can thereby better understand Foucault's repeated warnings, in his two texts on Binswanger, that "nothing could be more mistaken than to see in Binswanger's analysis an 'application' of the concepts and methods of the philosophy of existence to the "data" of clinical experience,"[74] or when he asserts that for *Daseinsanalyse*, "ontological reflection in the Heideggerian manner can only ever be referential."[75] Foucault intends to tease out "philosophical problems" from Binswanger's existential anthropology, instead of retracing it by deciphering it via exegesis.[76]

Like Binswanger's essay on dreams that Foucault chooses to analyze, then, Foucault's reading also "brings us even more than it says."[77] By situating Foucault's thought against the backdrop of these different relationships and theoretical contexts, we can see that it is not a strictly philosophical phenomenology to which we must address ourselves in order to detect the traces left by Foucault's encounter with Binswanger. To cite Merleau-Ponty, it is not by "covering a doctrine" or giving ourselves over to a "purely linguistic examination of the texts"[78] that we will find these traces.

FOUCAULT'S "HISTORICAL *A PRIORI*"

The analysis of this theoretical context is fundamental not only in order to understand Foucault's own reading of Binswanger's project during the 1950s, but also in order to better understand the core concept of Foucault's archaeology, namely, that of a "historical *a priori*." What Foucault discovered in Binswanger's clinical thought is the idea of a paradoxical *a priori*, a "structural" *a priori* that emerges from concrete, historical experience, before being theorized. This paradoxical transcendental presents itself at one and the same time as a tool *for diagnosing* a particular existential configuration and as the principle of configuration *to be diagnosed*. The emphasis that Foucault places on the future in his presentation of Binswanger's analysis of dreams—in order to illuminate the *a priori* structures of existence—has the precise function of pointing out this simultaneity of reality and of its conditions of possibility. As I have already mentioned, "the dream is *already* this *future* making itself," it "is not a later edition of a previous form," "it *manifests* itself as the *coming-to-be*."[79] In other words, the conditions of possibility of a form of existence coincide with this existence itself, an "existence which makes itself through time, that existence in its movement toward the future."[80]

It is therefore this methodological approach to the notion of the *a priori* as an immanent law of reality that attracted Foucault's attention in the early 1950s. In this perspective, I will not retrace the critical scholarship that rebukes Foucault for the theoretical imprecision of his concept of the historical *a priori* while analyzing it solely in the light either of the Kantian *a priori* or of Husserl's historical *a priori*[81]—and which then concludes, from this vantage point, that archaeology is doomed to fail from a methodological point of view.[82] For example, Béatrice Han-Pile describes Foucault as attempting to "'deanthropologize' the *a priori* while keeping open the need for a foundation."[83] In reality, it is precisely by giving up on the necessity of "founding" knowledge that Foucault uses the notion of the historical *a priori*. The stakes of archaeology are not gnoseological in character, and Foucault is not working at the level of the theory of knowledge,[84] but rather at a more expansive epistemological level that examines the transformations of historically given configurations of knowledge.

I will therefore examine the Foucauldian concept of the historical *a priori* by following the trail of existential psychiatry. Indeed, Foucault emphasizes that existential analysis succeeded in meeting the requirement of starting from experience—from its forms and internal laws—in order to understand this same experience. In so doing, he describes the characteristic that will also constitute the methodological principle of archaeology, which is to say, this same requirement that knowledges, practices, and experiences be analyzed "in their history," on the basis of their effective existence and of their functioning rather than on that of an extrinsic explanatory principle.[85] Foucault's historical *a priori*, indeed, is always defined by a "space," a "field," a "ground"; yet it is always this same *a priori* that paradoxically traces the contours of this ground or horizon as its condition of possibility. As he explains in *The Archaeology of Knowledge*, if "this *a priori* does not elude historicity," it is because it defines itself as a set of "rules [that] are not imposed from the outside on the elements that they relate together; they are caught up in the very things that they connect."[86] It is for this reason that Foucault does not further theorize this concept, even though it undergirds his works of the 1960s, but rather always presents it in action: as an organization, structure, disposition, or articulation of the discourses and therefore of the knowledges that it has the goal of explaining. And it is therefore for this reason that the concept of the historical *a priori* can meet the requirement that Foucault forcefully articulates in the preface to *The Birth of the Clinic*—which we might see as a programmatic manifesto for archaeology—when he underscores the need to "disentangle the conditions of its history from the density of discourse."[87]

What the young Foucault found appealing in Binswanger—at a time when he was looking for something different from the alternatives of pure phenomenology and Marxism's material causality[88]—was precisely the manner in which existential analysis was able to explain experience immanently, by means of experience itself. Thus, even though it functions in a different context and has different goals from clinical psychopathology, Foucault's archaeological concept of "historical *a priori*," from a theoretical point of view, has a methodological affinity with the "structural *a priori*" outlined by Binswanger's *Daseinsanalyse*. Therefore, it is at the level of methodology that one should consider the compatibility between Foucault's early interest in Binswanger and the development of archaeology. The "history" to which Binswanger and Foucault each refer is certainly not the same: while the psychiatrist is concerned with the patient's individual life history, the archaeologist aims to unravel the epistemological transformations and developments of knowledge. Yet, the ways in which the two approaches inquire into phenomena—by means of a historicized *a priori*—appear to me to be related. Just as Binswanger's "*a priori* of existence" is the actual form, or the normative, structural condition of possibility of the phenomenon, so Foucault's historical *a priori* is "a condition of reality for statements," "the specific form of their mode of being," "the *a priori* of a history that is given."[89]

Such a simultaneity between the conditions of reality and reality itself is the reason why Foucault, in *The Archaeology of Knowledge*, gives a theoretical account of the concept of historical *a priori* only after having already used it in *The Order of Things*. Indeed, in this latter work, Foucault presents it as the "organization," the "articulation," the "arrangement," or the "mode of being of the objects," the "structure" that "provides man's everyday perception with theoretical powers, and defines the conditions in which he can sustain a discourse about things that is recognized *to be true*."[90]

In this passage from *The Order of Things*, the concept of historical *a priori* seems to overlap with what Canguilhem, during this period, recognized as the epistemological distinction between "true saying" (*dire vrai*) and being "in the true" (*dans le vrai*)."[91] In this regard, it is interesting to observe that Foucault first deployed the notion of "historical *a priori*" in his 1950s essay "La recherche scientifique et la psychologie." In this essay, Foucault argued that the main feature of psychology is that it can choose whether or not to be scientific. Different from sciences like physics or chemistry, which "emerge as possible fields of research within an already scientific objectivity" (which is to say that they work in the frame of the "*dire vrai*"), psychology "does not articulate itself within the horizon of a science," "in the space of a science," "under the constellation of objectivity."[92] Therefore psychology must make a decision about its own status. It is a necessary choice, insofar as psychology can become "true psychology"[93] only to the extent that it opts for science. The contours of this horizon within which the "status of truth" of a science like psychology can be defined are precisely the historical *a priori*. And yet, this *a priori is* the same horizon whose conditions of possibility it maps out. In other words, the historical *a priori* is contemporaneous with the reality that it describes; it emerges and expresses itself only in its functioning. That is why it should be considered an operational concept, a methodological or diagnostic tool. This tool is finally able to meet Foucault's archeological demand for immanence, insofar as—as Foucault writes in *The Order of Things*—"the history of knowledge can be written only on the basis of what was contemporaneous with it."[94]

Hence, the historical *a priori* presents itself as an explanation of the phenomenon that is always contained within its description. This is why I maintain that the historical *a priori* responds to at least two of the main methodological concerns of phenomenology: first, the "principle of immanence,"[95] according to which philosophical research should respect phenomena and start from them in order to locate their rationality; and second, the idea that phenomena are normative—that they organize themselves according to a normative structure. But, departing from pure phenomenology, Foucault expands these concerns beyond the theory of knowledge (*connaissance*)—a theory working at the level of "*dire vrai*"—in order to study the historical emergence of knowledge as "*savoir*" ("*être dans le vrai*"). As Foucault explains in *The Birth of the Clinic*, archaeology presents itself as an epistemology that "defines not the *mode of knowledge*, but the *world of objects to be known*."[96]

Interestingly, in this same passage from *The Birth of the Clinic* Foucault deploys a metaphor taken from the field of psychology. With a critical reference to Gaston Bachelard's *The Formation of the Scientific Mind* (1938),[97] he asserts that what occurred to medical perception toward the end of the eighteenth century "was not a 'psychoanalysis' of medical knowledge." He goes on to state that "'positive' medicine is not a medicine that has made an 'objectal' choice in favor of objectivity itself,"[98] but rather a medicine that operates in another "world of objects." Archaeology is interested precisely in such a world, that is, the "articulation of medical language and its object"[99]—an articulation that defines, "with its historical possibility, the domain of its experience."[100] Foucault emphasizes that, between the articulation of the medical language and its object, "there can be no priority":[101] they are contemporaneous. There is no primary and ultimate truth-origin, any objective evidence at "the heart of things"; rather, there is a "penetrating, profound historicity."[102]

In this way, Foucault differentiates the gnoseological approach to knowledge (*connaissance*) from his own archaeological account of knowledge understood as "*savoir*," that is, as a broader epistemological configuration defining the conditions of possibility of the contents of *connaissance*. It seems to me that such a differentiation reflects in some ways the manner in which Foucault, in the 1950s, distinguished the theory of the objective meanings outlined by the psychoanalytical approach from Binswanger's manner of attending to the particular world or "world-project" within which meanings *can* mean what they mean and *actually* mean what they mean. What emerges from Foucault's position is a holistic approach that aims to grasp the configuration of the "world" within which meanings are inscribed—the global structure that rules the historical meanings of meanings, thereby furnishing them with their conditions of possibility.

Hence Foucault's epistemology is historical in that it does not seek to penetrate the objective meanings of discourses, but rather "our own world of discourse."[103] Such a "historical epistemology" maintains a strong methodological link to the phenomenological approach to psychopathology that the young Foucault had explored during the 1950s. In this regard, it is worth emphasizing the metaphor of the "diagnosis" that Foucault deploys to describe his epistemological method. In his *Archaeology of Knowledge*, for example, Foucault revisits the paradoxical character of the notion of the historical *a priori*, affirming that its analysis "*can define its possibilities only in the moment of their realization.*"[104] He defines the task of archaeological description specifically in terms of a diagnosis, as a form of research that can find its own "justification" or that can "elucidate that which makes it possible" only by "approach[ing] as close as possible to the positivity that governs it."[105] Foucault associates this medical metaphor—which in most instances he borrows from Nietzsche[106]—to the concept of "world" that is at the heart of the diagnostic exam developed by existential analysis. Indeed, as Foucault warns us, Nietzsche's excavation of the foundations of our present has as its goal to detect "How this world of thought, of discourse, of culture that was his world had been formed before him."[107] It is the contours of a world that archaeology has for its task to identify; it must diagnose how this specific structure of culture defines the manner in which we live our present, which is to say, our "modes of being."

THE GEOGRAPHIC METAPHOR OF ORDER

It is very interesting, on this topic, to pause on Foucault's geographic metaphors in his archaeological texts. *The Order of Things* is particularly enlightening in this respect. The extravagant taxonomy from Borges that opens the volume has precisely the goal of introducing the question of order or of "configuration" at the basis of our thought—an order that will emerge as the fundamental theme of this book. We might reread the very first lines of the preface:

> This book first arose out of a passage in Borges, out of the laughter that shattered, as I read the passage, all the familiar landmarks of my thought—*our* thought, the thought that bears the stamp of our age and our geography—breaking up all the ordered surfaces and all the planes with which we are accustomed to tame the wild profusion of existing things, and continuing long afterwards to disturb and threaten with collapse our age-old distinction between the Same and the Other.[108]

If I have cited this well-known passage from Foucault's volume, it is in order to emphasize certain points that seem very important for the analysis that I am proposing. What Foucault compares to Borges's "atlas" is precisely those "familiar landmarks" of thought that phenomenology would define as making up our "lifeworld." It is this familiarity, this "mute ground,"[109] that must be made to speak in order to show that there is no universal, "solid and self-evident"[110] "common ground"[111] that we always already inhabit. The fascination provoked by Borges's taxonomy, which Foucault fittingly describes as "exotic,"[112] has the goal precisely of showing us, through "astonishment," "laughter," and "uneasiness," that "the earth we inhabit"[113] is not universal and self-evident, but has defined limits, historically demarcated confines.

Foucault's geographic metaphors, then, first aim to return us—albeit with ironic distance—to the "belonging to the world" that phenomenology had identified as a fundamental self-evidence. However, once the doubt has set in that this "age-old distinction between the Same and the Other" might in fact have an "age" and a "geography," Foucault continues by showing that the borders of this "other" world that is Borgesian China are the same that also define the limits of our thought. Indeed, the impossibility of the Chinese atlas lies not so much in "the oddity of unusual juxtapositions"[114] that it presents, but rather in the impossibility of thinking the "common ground" of these meetings. The relativity of the concept of "world" is thus situated at a much more radical level than that of cultural relativism. By showing that the monstrousness of Borges's enumeration lies not so much in the possibility that these beings actually exist as in the impossibility that they should coexist—the impossibility of thinking "the mute ground upon which it is possible for entities to be juxtaposed"[115]—Foucault questions precisely the self-evidence of this ground that one might want to be originary, "since the beginning of time."[116] The challenge to phenomenology is quite explicit in the following passage: "In fact, there is no similitude and no distinction, even for the wholly untrained perception, that is not the result of a precise operation and of the application of a preliminary criterion."[117] Yet this order—this coherence that is given "preliminarily" in things—is not "determined by an *a priori* and necessary concatenation".[118] the only *a priori* that can be located in this process is coeval with this very order; its conditions of possibility consist in its "inner law."[119] These conditions are precisely, Foucault observes, the "*internal* conditions of possibility"[120] that coincide with the "mode of being" of the order itself. It is precisely to this "hidden network,"[121] to this "configuration of positivities,"[122] that archaeology addresses itself. Its task is to find the traces or rather the borders of this ground on which the basis of our system of knowledge has been erected.

The geographic metaphors though which Foucault develops his conception of order appear to confirm my hypothesis according to which there is a methodological affinity between the theoretical core of archaeology and the clinical device put into place by existential psychiatry. Indeed, Borges's Chinese taxonomy shows us the "alterity" of a world different from ours, different from "the earth we inhabit" and the familiarity with which we believe we have been operating "since the beginning of time": "There would appear to be, then, at the other extremity of the Earth we inhabit, a culture entirely devoted to the ordering of space, but one that does not distribute the multiplicity of existing things into any of the categories that make it possible for us to name, speak, and think."[123]

It is interesting to note on this topic that the "profound distress"[124] we might experience in the face of the impossibility of moving within the Borgesian space is the same that we will feel later in Foucault's text, when we attempt to put ourselves in Don Quixote's shoes. It is this distress that pushes us to define this "sign wandering through a world that did not recognize him,"[125] at the borders of the world of resemblance, as a madman—which is to say, as a man who lives in a different world, outside of the common world. This is a space that Binswanger would define as an *"eigene Welt,"* an "individual world." If we were to treat this character as a clinical case, it would not be difficult to see in Foucault's analysis the same principles that subtend existential psychopathology's structural perspective. Indeed, his attention is directed precisely toward the architecture of this world that determines and defines the modes of being, the "fundamental modes"[126] that constitute for the Foucauldian archaeologist the specific configuration of each era's *episteme*. From a methodological point of view, this approach is analogous to that which Binswanger develops in his study of mannerism, in which he conceives of the "schizophrenic transformation of existence" as a "change of era" in which certain configurations of the consciousness (*Bewusstseinsgestalten*) or "spiritual configurations" disappear.[127]

It is therefore not happenstance that, in order to discuss the "thought without space"[128] that arises from Borges's Chinese encyclopedia, Foucault uses a clinical case as an example: that of the aphasiac. Here too his analysis deploys the characteristic modalities of the structural analysis specific to existential psychiatry. He shows that the difficulty specific to this patient is that of someone "whose language has been destroyed: loss of what is 'common' to place and name"[129]—of someone who, deprived of language, is deprived of this order that would allow him to "orient" himself among the "differently colored skeins of wool"[130] placed before him. On this topic, it is quite interesting to note that there are many reading notes concerning aphasia in Foucault's archives from the 1950s. Foucault used Kurt Goldstein's writings as a starting point to study this problem;[131] it is from Goldstein that he borrows the example of the multicolored skeins of wool. Another of his interlocutors is André Ombredane, who had devoted his doctoral dissertation in medicine, in 1947, to the problem of *L'Aphasie et l'élaboration de la pensée explicite* (Aphasia and the Development of Explicit Thought).[132]

At this moment, we encounter another element of Foucault's discourse that bears further attention. It emerges from the difference that Foucault acknowledges between the uneasiness elicited by Borges's text and the distress of the aphasiac. In fact, the "impossible space" generated by the Chinese encyclopedia corresponds to the alterity of a determinate place, China—which is to say, to an "order" that, while remaining "other" in relation to our own order, retains the prerogative of "distributing" the proliferation of beings, of organizing it, of establishing it in a place. Although oneiric, the space evoked by Borges deploys itself inside an encyclopedia, in the order of a taxonomy; this explains our malaise, which ultimately culminates in an exotic fascination. Conversely, the aphasiac's malaise pushes him to "the brink of anxiety":[133] its cause is not the strangeness of an encounter with fantastic beings, but rather the absence of a space in which these beings might find a place. As Foucault demonstrates, atopia and aphasia go hand in hand. The anxiety of the aphasiac is the anxiety of someone who has lost a world in which he can orient himself; it reveals this "failed form of human presence," to cite the title of one of Binswanger's works, which consists of the infinite instability of an ill person whose mind "continues to infinity, creating groups then dispersing them again, heaping up diverse similarities, destroying those that seem clearest, splitting up things that are identical, superimposing different criteria, frenziedly beginning all over again, becoming more and more disturbed."[134]

We might also pause for a moment on the adjectives that Foucault uses to characterize the "ground," this space on which beings can be juxtaposed. He defines it as "mute," "obscure," "hidden," "silent." Similarly, Foucault had defined as "silent" the configuration "in which language finds support: the relation of situation and attitude to what is speaking and what is spoken about"[135] in *The Birth of the Clinic*. In this work, this configuration is recognized precisely as that which defines "the world of objects to be known."[136] We thereby see a concept of "world" emerge that—in opposition, but for this very reason also in relation, to its phenomenological equivalent—opens for Foucault the possibility of formulating the alternative to materialism and to phenomenology that is at the root of his research on the "historicity of forms of experience." These adjectives oppose to phenomenological self-evidence the reality of a less visible, but no less "fundamental,"[137] organization, understood as the "basis" or "horizon" within which "ideas could appear, sciences be established, experience be reflected in philosophies, rationalities be formed."[138]

In the end, the "transcendence" of this world investigated by archaeology reveals itself to be the *historical a priori* of "our world"; it can be summed up by the "there is" of an order that simultaneously makes possible and necessarily determines the forms of experience of those who inhabit it. This "world of objects to be known," understood as the order or epistemological configuration of an era, is no longer taken as constitutive of the fundamental structures of *Dasein*—as Heidegger wished[139]—but is seen instead as a "system" whose functioning is the only thing we can describe. It is for this reason that in 1970, in his inaugural lecture at the Collège de France, Foucault asserts—in a kind of crowning of the archaeological parabola—that "the world is not the accomplice of our knowledge."[140] Archaeology opposes the reality "of things actually said,"[141] a space understood as "a field of coordination and subordination of statements in which concepts appear, and are defined, applied and transformed,"[142] to a thought aiming to locate and elucidate the originary experience of "being-in-the-world" as the condition of any experience. While remaining *a priori*, this "world" described by archaeology is no longer conceived of as a "pre-established horizon":[143] this world's *a priori* character coincides with its historicity, with the putting into order (*mise en ordre*)[144] of these words and these things whose relationships it defines. In so doing, also defines the experience that we have of them: "This *a priori* is what, in a given period, delimits in the totality of experience a field of knowledge, defines the mode of being of the objects that appear in that field."[145]

Now distanced from the meaning given to it by phenomenology, the concept of the *a priori* draws nearer to that school of thought which, while distancing itself from the pure conceptuality of phenomenology, had also been inspired by it: existential psychopathology. Indeed, the latter characterized itself as a structural approach that deployed the phenomenological concept of the world in a methodological sense, in the clinical field, in order to examine existence from the point of view of its forms, of its modes of being. It is only through these, only by identifying the "structure of the universe" specific to a patient, that it would be possible—in the eyes of the psychiatrist-phenomenologist—to reach the kernel, the conditions of possibility of this universe. In this way, much as existential psychiatry, in its clinical approach, conceives of the notion of "world" only insofar as it is correlated to those real experiences through which it appears, in the archaeological "analytic" the concept of "world" takes on an essentially instrumental value. While retaining—as a "background," "ground," or "horizon" of concepts and of practices—a phenomenological inspiration, the geographic metaphor through which Foucault recovers the concept of "world" reveals itself, in the final analysis, to be a methodological fulcrum from which it becomes possible to distinguish and to study our thought and our system of knowledge, their possibility, and at the same time their necessity.

What is to be identified in this system is no longer its foundation but rather the intrinsic normativity that simultaneously defines its "conditions of emergence" and its "mode of being." It is precisely in this way that archaeological analysis overlaps methodologically with existential analysis. These forms of experience, these modes of being that for the psychiatrist are manifestations of the pathological behaviors, henceforth become for Foucault forms of knowledge (*savoirs*), and what the psychiatrist describes as the patient's "own world" becomes for archaeology the epistemological configuration within which conceptual constructions can emerge and develop. The systems of knowledge examined by the archaeologist, furthermore, must be understood as veritable "forms of experience"; Foucault announces this explicitly in an interview from 1966, when he specifies that the task of the archaeologist is to "show that our thought, our life, our manner of being, including our most ordinary manner of being, belong to the same systematic organization and therefore fall under the *same* categories as the scientific and technical world."[146]

This is precisely what Foucault is asserting when he opposes his archaeology to the history of ideas or the "psychoanalysis of knowledge," when he underscores the difference between the "scientific" positivity of knowledge and positivity conceived as historical *a priori*. In the same way as phenomenological psychiatry distinguishes between the "ideo-affective" and "structural" levels in the psychopathological experience, then, archaeology seeks to isolate this more fundamental "positivity" of knowledge that is not at the level of discoveries and theories, but rather at the level of the epistemological configuration that makes these discoveries and theories possible.[147] And just as, for existential psychiatry, the structural level of psychopathology consists in the architecture of the patient's "own world," epistemic positivity is seen by Foucault "in its archaeological depth, and not at the more visible level of discoveries, discussion, theories, or philosophical options."[148]

In this regard, it is interesting to observe the manner in which Foucault uses the term *disposition*[149] to characterize what determines the structure of knowledge in depth. This term appears quite often in *The Order of Things*, in the form of two-part expressions such as "fundamental disposition,"[150] "epistemological disposition,"[151] or "disposition of knowledge."[152] This term once again reveals the affinity between archaeology and the reflection on psychopathology that was at the heart of the young Foucault's interests. It is therefore worthwhile to recall the meaning of the notion of "disposition" in the context of the phenomenologico-structural school of psychopathology.

In light of the underlying structure that is the relationship between the sick person and his world, existential analysis opposes to the biological determinism that traditional psychiatry sees as the basis of pathological behaviors their essentially *possible* character. Minkowski stressed this point in his seminal work of 1927, *La schizophrénie*, in which he retraced psychopathology's trajectory and its culmination in its phenomenologico-structural school. It was precisely because of the notion of "disposition," explained Minkowski, that psychopathology was able to take the first step in crossing the boundary between the normal and the pathological; it became capable of approaching mental illness as a possibility, as a "form of existence," as a particular manner of "being in the world."[153]

Minkowski's intention was to show that structural psychopathology could move beyond a perspective seeking to make sense of the relationship between "human life" and its milieu through the notion of adaptation. Instead, it would propose an approach that could give an account of the creative or normative character of this relationship.[154] The French psychiatrist's thinking was therefore quite similar to that of the school of biology that wanted to replace the causal determinism then dominant in reflexology with the operational and self-determining character of the biological act. As I have shown in the previous pages, according to von Weizsäcker especially, the law that might be recognizable in a biological act does not derive from a causal relationship; rather, it should be considered from the point of view of the intrinsic normativity characterizing the relationship between the living being and its world. It is for this reason that the school of psychopathology that turned to biology to rethink the structural and normative link between man and the world embraced an analysis of the "own world" of the patient, a world that has its own laws and that can only be "interpreted" on the basis of these laws. The psychiatric "hermeneutics" that emerges from this approach does not aim to seek out the hidden contents that would determine the genesis of the illness. Instead, it turns its attention to the "disposition" of the patient in the face of reality, which, from the "origin," both *determines* and *is determined by* the structure of his "specific world." In the same way, archaeology aims to illuminate a "fundamental disposition of knowledge" which is "deep" not because it comes from a hidden origin, but rather because it coincides with the very normative system that defines "our own world of discourse."[155] Canguilhem was therefore right when, in his review of *The Order of Things* in 1967, he concluded that in this work it was "no longer a question of nature and things, but of an adventure that creates its own norms."[156]

POSSIBILITY AND NECESSITY OF EXPERIENCE

Normativity is therefore at the heart of archaeology, which is defined by Foucault as a diagnostic inquiry whose goal is to identify the "specific regularities,"[157] to "formulate [the] laws"[158] or the "own normativity"[159] that define "the system of functioning,"[160] which allows the various series of statements (*énoncés*) to appear. Foucault stresses this in the last chapter of *Archaeology of Knowledge*, when—after he has demonstrated the difference in level between the specific "scientificity" of some disciplines and the general epistemological system within which they are inscribed—he shows "*how a science* functions *in the element of knowledge.*"[161]

The manner in which Foucault uses the concept of normativity as that concrete transcendental in the light of which it is possible to glimpse the structure, the deep organization of knowledge (*savoir*), is once again very close to the manner in which existential analysis adopts the philosophical concept of the norm. As we have demonstrated earlier, this is a concept of normativity that existential psychopathology reelaborated, using the reflection on the biological notion of the organism as a starting point. Obvious traces of this affinity between archaeology and *Daseinsanalyse* can be seen especially in Foucault's frequent recourse to the concept of "functioning." Foucault deploys this concept to oppose, to anthropological humanism, a structural thought that can illuminate the mechanisms in accordance with which "the human species" functions;[162] he also adopts its prerogatives to theoretically clarify the use that archaeology makes of the transcendental. When he was asked about the significance of *The Order of Things*, he answered that he simply limited himself "to locat[ing] the rules that formed a certain number of concepts and theoretical relationships in their [Buffon's or Marx's] works. . . . I wanted to determine—a much more modest task—the functioning conditions [*conditions de fonctionnement*] of specific discursive practices."[163] When asked about his position vis-à-vis the notion of the transcendental subject, he responded, "Well, I am not Kantian or Cartesian, precisely because I refuse an equation on the transcendental level between subject and thinking 'I.' I am convinced that there exist, if not exactly *structures*, then at least *rules* for the *functioning* of knowledge which have arisen in the course of history and within which can be located the various subjects."[164]

The Order of Things seeks to "rediscover how that structure [*ensemble*] was able to function."[165] Archaeology addresses itself precisely to this effective functioning of knowledge (*savoir*), in order to lay bare a structure that reveals itself to be order: the system of regularity that determines in a *necessary* manner— through its laws—its *possibility*. It is this particular form of normativity that ultimately reveals itself as the historical *a priori* of knowledge (*savoir*). Such an *a priori*, because it does not establish a universally valid legality, must be described in its simultaneously contingent and necessary functioning—hence its historical character: "this *a priori* does not elude historicity: it does not constitute, above events, and in an unmoving heaven, an atemporal structure; it is defined as the group of rules that characterize a discursive practice: but these rules are not imposed from the outside on the elements that they relate together; they are caught up in the very things that they connect."[166] In other words, the very conditions that, in the form of norms and of regularities, determine the exercise of discursive practices are also those that define their existence: "regularity does not characterize a certain central position between the ends of a statistical curve—it is not valid therefore as an index of frequency or probability; it specifies an effective field of appearance."[167] In this way, the historical *a priori* is the "condition of reality" of statements and "the law of their coexistence," the principle that determines how they subsist, transform themselves, and also disappear.[168] This is a normative principle which can be neither applied from the outside nor deduced.

Once again, it is worthwhile to compare this theoretical device with that put in place by structural psychopathology. On the subject of the normative character of the pathological, Minkowski wrote that the pathological "therefore does not refer itself directly to a preestablished norm; this norm is one that it imposes itself, but it does so from that moment on in its own way."[169] Moreover, the principal object of Binswanger's existential analysis was to grasp the normative system presiding over the structuring of the relationship between the patient and his or her world. It was for this reason that the psychiatrist insisted on the distance separating *Daseinsanalyse* from traditional clinical psychiatry, which looked to external causes to explain pathological manifestations. In his study *Über Ideenflucht* (1933) in particular, Binswanger argued that explanations for the mode of being characterizing a determinate pathological manifestation must be sought in the manifestation itself: its description would reveal the architecture of the world in which it took its meaning. The following passage clarifies this theoretical approach:

> The concepts of "external occasion" and of "affect," of "event" being in and for itself, of "lived experience" being in and for itself, are not concepts that point to something that is concretely effective, something that manifests itself effectively "in life"; they owe their formation to an extremely unilateral, purely theoretico-constructive, and therefore extremely abstract manner of seeing things! "The same" event, "the same occasion" owe their sameness to an extremely complex abstraction. In the end their sameness "exists" in general only by virtue of this abstraction; yet, "in reality" each event *is* never an event producing itself univocally in an identical manner. . . . The anthropological problem is therefore not to know why the patient is irritated or complains about an event that has no importance to us, but rather to know in which world she truly lives (which always means knowing how the world, in general, constitutes itself for her such that she *must* react in this manner [aspect of necessity] or *can* decide about her life history in this manner [aspect of freedom]). The answer to this question leads us to take an

important step further inside the structure of the world of the person suffering from the flight of ideas, which always means the structure of the being-man from which the *possibility* of something like the flight of ideas becomes comprehensible.[170]

Foucault clearly understood the significance of this approach when he wrote about the Ellen West case, in *Binswanger et l'analyse existentielle*, that "The truth of psychosis is precisely where it expresses itself and nowhere else. Illness must not be situated in the back-world [*l'arrière-monde*] of the sick man; it is entirely in his world."[171] Indeed, the transcendental that guides Binswanger's methodological approach must be understood as the very structure, the norm presiding over the functioning of an existence. The condition of possibility of a certain manner of being or behavior, this condition that—once described—will guide the psychiatrist toward understanding the behavior, in this way coincides with the behavior as it effectively manifests itself. This occurs because causality, as an external explanatory principle, has been replaced by a description that reflects the general architecture of the "world" within which a certain mode of being *can* and *must* take the form specific to it.

The passage I have just cited from Binswanger's *Über Ideenflucht* clarifies the dynamic correlation of possibility and necessity that also seems, to my mind, to guide the Foucauldian concept of historical *a priori*. I will therefore compare this passage to the perspective developed by Foucault in *The Order of Things*:

> There can be no doubt, certainly, that the historical emergence of each one of the human sciences was occasioned by a problem, a requirement, an obstacle of a theoretical or practical order. . . . But though these references may well explain why it was in fact in

such and such a determined set of circumstances and in answer to such and such a precise question that these sciences were articulated, nevertheless, their *intrinsic possibility*, the simple fact that man, whether in isolation or as a group, and for the first time since human beings have existed and have lived together in societies, should have become the object of science—that cannot be considered or treated as a phenomenon of opinion: it is an event in the order of knowledge.[172]

Here, too, a distinction is made between the external, contingent occasion of an event and its intrinsic possibility. The latter is henceforth identified in relation to the order of knowledge (*savoir*) within which it emerges. Moreover, in rejecting contingency as the causal principle that explains the emergence of a science, Foucault establishes that the possibility of this science is also its necessity. Once again, he asserts this explicitly in *The Order of Things*:

> And just as it is not possible to understand the theory of verb and noun, the analysis of the language of action, and that of roots and their development, without referring, through the study of general grammar, to the archaeological network that makes those things *possible and necessary*; just as one cannot understand, without exploring the domain of natural history, what Classical description, characterization, and taxonomy were, any more than the opposition between system and method, or "fixism" and "evolution"; so, in the same way, it would not be possible to discover the link of necessity that connects the analysis of money, prices, value, and trade if one did not first clarify this domain of wealth which is the locus of their simultaneity.... In any given culture and at any given moment, there is always only one *episteme* that defines the conditions of *possibility* of all knowledge.... And it

is these fundamental *necessities* of knowledge that we must give voice to.[173]

For archaeology as for existential analysis, then, two principles that are at the heart of the phenomenological attitude, beyond its various fields and schools, are thus valid: the principle of experience[174] and the principle of immanence. The first emphasizes the priority of phenomena; it entails the conviction that philosophical research should root itself in experience in the manner in which it appears, beginning by describing it. It is a position that refuses the idea that the reason for or "essence" of phenomena is external to them, in what founds, determines, or causes them. This means—and this is the second principle—that the essence or *a priori* of experience is immanent to the experience itself. In other words, the conditions of possibility of the phenomena must be found in the phenomena themselves, in the way they give themselves.

"TAKING UP MADNESS AT THE LEVEL OF ITS LANGUAGE"

Even if the methodological principles of existential analysis seem to have left a deep—and as yet unthought—trace at the center of the archaeological method, Foucault's critique of *Daseinsanalyse* was already explicit in the 1950s. In the second chapter of this book, I showed that one of the reasons for this critique was the implication of Binswanger's thought in an anthropology giving into the temptation of speculative thinking. The pages that follow analyze Foucauldian archaeology by inquiring about the reasons why Foucault explicitly distanced himself from existential analysis.

Foucault's interest in psychoanalysis is at the heart of his writings of the 1960s, just as it was in those of the 1950s. If in the 1950s the critique of Freudian psychoanalysis was one of the engines driving Foucault to embrace existential analysis, at the beginning of the 1960s one of the factors that led Foucault to lose confidence in the Binswangerian "revolution" was the Lacanian psychoanalytic approach. Here I propose to analyze the role that the Lacanian approach to psychoses—such as it was formulated starting in the mid-1950s and especially in Séminaire 3 of 1955–1956—might have played in this new phase of Foucault's thought. In particular, I focus my attention on Foucault's first writings of the 1960s in order to examine, through Lacan, the role that psychiatry and psychoanalysis played in the constitution of the archaeological program. My aim is to show that the psychiatric knowledge with and against which Foucault constructed his project of the critique of reason has an operational value within Foucauldian epistemological discourse. In other words, if it is true that psychiatry, for Foucault, would end up exercising more than any other form of knowledge the function of a "discipline," it nonetheless played a truly philosophical role at the beginning of Foucault's reflection on knowledge. Indeed, some of the fundamental philosophical themes of this reflection were not derived from the domain of pure philosophy, but rather from problems and approaches inspired by and sometimes borrowed from concrete forms of knowledge.

As I have partly shown in the previous chapters, Foucault shared with the philosophical milieu active at the time he published his first works a disposition to acknowledge the philosophical value of psychiatry. On this topic, it is worth insisting on the importance accorded to psychopathology during Foucault's time as a student at ENS. The *caïman* (head lecturer) in philosophy in 1946–1947 was Georges Gusdorf, who organized for his students an introduction to psychopathology, which included presentations of patients at the Hôpital Sainte-Anne and a lecture series that featured psychiatrists such as Georges Daumézon, Julian de Ajuriaguerra (1911–1993), and Jacques Lacan. Althusser followed Gusdorf's example, and with him too, Foucault continued to visit Sainte-Anne, where he also took Henri Ey's courses.[175] We might also cite Jean Hyppolite's great interest in psychiatry, especially in the problem of alienation, when he became the director of ENS in 1954. Indeed, during this period Hyppolite was attending Lacan's seminars at Sainte-Anne; he was in dialogue with Foucault about the book he had just published, *Maladie mentale et personnalité*; and he had just organized at ENS a study group that included philosophers and psychologists.[176] In a lecture from 1955, "Pathologie mentale et organization" (Mental Pathology and Organization), Hyppolite explained his interest in psychiatry in the following terms:

> I was confirmed in the idea that the study of madness—alienation in the profound sense of the term—was at the center of an anthropology, of a study of man. The asylum is the refuge of those who can no longer be made to live in our interhuman milieu. It is therefore a means of understanding this milieu, and the problems it incessantly poses to the normal man, indirectly.[177]

In this context, the fact that psychiatry and psychopathology became integral to Foucault's philosophical reflection should not surprise us. Nevertheless, the specificity of his discourse such as it developed in this period cannot be attributed merely to the fact that its objects are psychology, psychoanalysis, and especially psychopathology. Above all, psychopathological reflection informed Foucault's discourse from within by lending it some of its questions and methodological instruments. From this point of view, Lacan's reflection seems to have played a critical role in the development of Foucault's thought. Lacan had taken German phenomenological psychiatry as a key point of reference from the early 1930s until at least his "Presentation on Psychical Causality" (1946), although in the mid-1950s he left the phenomenological method behind and instead used psychoanalysis to focus on the analysis of language.[178] It is precisely this articulation between psychiatry, psychoanalysis, and archaeology that my analysis will now take up.

In the second chapter, I showed that Foucault, in his introduction to *Le rêve et l'existence*, critiqued Freudian doctrine for its inability to give an account of the imaginary world, of its internal laws and specific structures: to connect a psychology of language with a psychology of the image, whence the argument that psychoanalysis had never been able "to make images speak."[179] But is it really possible to "make speak" images that do not belong to the order of speech? How can the "internal laws," the "specific structures" of an imaginary world that can be reduced neither to logic nor to a theory of signification be grasped? This was the problem Foucault grappled with in his thesis *History of Madness* (1961)—a work that, as I have demonstrated, owes much to the existential psychiatry that had galvanized Foucault in the 1950s and that, at the same time, partly opens onto its surpassing.

It was precisely in this context—the abandonment of a faith in an anthropological psychiatry capable of understanding the existential expressions of madness—that Lacan's thought might have played a critical role in the development of Foucault's thought. This connection can be observed when we examine the manner in which Foucault, in *History of Madness*, inverts the thesis on psychoanalysis that he had advanced in the introduction to *Le rêve et l'existence*.

At a more superficial level, the context in which Foucault introduces Freud's work in *History of Madness* is no longer that of the relationship between expression and signification, but rather that of the relationship between the psychoanalytic and psychiatric approach to madness. Foucault's most explicit argument is that if it is true that Freud "silenced the instances of condemnation" typical of the asylum structure, he also "exploited the structure that enveloped the medical character"[180] and for this very reason was not able to free the patient from the essential aspects of this structure. Thus, Foucault concludes, psychoanalysis "cannot and will never be able to hear the voices of unreason nor decipher on their own terms the signs of the insane."[181] This is the thesis that Foucault would develop throughout the 1970s, especially in his course "Psychiatric Power." Yet I do not propose to stop there. It is not in the light of Foucault's 1970s arguments that I intend to reread *History of Madness*'s passages on psychoanalysis, but rather in the light of the perspective laid out in the introduction to *Le rêve et l'existence*—a perspective that, as we have seen, concerns the relationship between psychoanalytic hermeneutics and language.

Foucault's formula at the end of the fourth chapter of *History of Madness* is quite famous: "we must do justice to Freud," insofar as Freud "restored the possibility of a dialogue with unreason"[182] after the silence imposed upon it by positivist psychiatry. Yet if this restitution of the possibility of a dialogue with madness was possible, it was because Freud—Foucault tells us—"took up madness at the level of its *language*."[183] This is a critical passage that must be interpreted beyond its most obvious meaning. Taking up madness at the level of its language, indeed, does not simply mean that Freud finally listened to the voices of unreason previously stifled by positivist psychiatry. Foucault's assertion rather presents itself as a response to the difficulty that he himself raised in his introduction to *Le rêve et l'existence*, when he reproached psychoanalysis for not having succeeded in "making images speak."

What Foucault now tells us is that if psychoanalysis did not succeed in making images speak, it is because it cannot do so—and it is precisely the fact that it recognized the essential impossibility of reducing madness to "meaning" that paradoxically opened to it the possibility of a dialogue with unreason. This dialogue is completely paradoxical because it does not play out at the level of semantic comprehension, but rather in its inverse: the acknowledgment of the radical alterity of the words of unreason. Recognizing the language that is proper to madness thus entails renouncing the possibility of understanding it; dialoguing with madness now means letting it express itself by means of incomprehensible words and images. The justice that Foucault claims for psychoanalysis therefore needs to be connected to the critique that he himself addressed to psychoanalysis in 1954 when he reproached it for not having succeeded in relating a psychology of language to a psychology of the image.

Now, I believe that this reading of Freud in *History of Madness* owes much to the way in which Lacan sketches out his approach to the problem of psychosis in the mid-1950s. This does not necessarily mean that the psychoanalysis that Foucault had in mind as he was writing his thesis was Lacanian psychoanalysis. By mentioning Lacan, I am much more interested in following Jacques Derrida's suggestion from 1992 to consider *History of Madness* "*a parte subjecti*, that is, from the side where it is written or inscribed and not from the side of what it describes."[184] On the side where it was written—which is to say, the period in which Foucault was working on his thesis—there was a certain state of French psychiatry, and this state was profoundly marked by Lacan's teaching. One of the principal features of this teaching, starting in the 1950s, consists in the abandonment of the phenomenological approach that had characterized Lacan's clinical and theoretical thought throughout the 1930s and for part of the 1940s. At that time, Lacan praised this approach for offering him a "more theoretically rigorous method leading to a more concrete description and at the same time to a more satisfactory conception of the facts of psychosis"[185]—a conception that thereby allowed "modern anthropology" to avoid reducing itself to a "positivist science of personality."[186] However, starting in the 1950s his attitude took another direction. Lacan could no longer accept positions, such as those of Jaspers or of Minkowski, that misunderstood psychoanalysis and its principal precept, the idea that any psychic phenomenon has a meaning that "can be explained," which is to say, a meaning that, "as illusory as it may be, ... is not without a law."[187] What is more, having acquired the theoretical tools he derived from his reading of structural linguistics and from surveying the laws of the symbolic order, Lacan inflicted another blow on Jaspers, whom he henceforth designated as the "spiritual advisor" among the principal figures responsible for the development of post-Freudian ego psychology.[188]

The crucial importance of the 1955–1956 seminar on psychoses can be understood at this level of analysis, insofar as Lacan's return to the subject of his *Thesis* from an anti-Jaspersian perspective allows us to measure the distance he had traveled through his commitment to psychoanalysis and his "return to Freud." In this seminar, not only can we distinguish the very explicit critique of Jaspers's opposition of *Erklären* to *Verstehen*—a critique that at the time Lacan incisively summed up in the formula "Don't try to understand!"[189]—but we also discover that the reasons for this critique have evolved. Psychic causality is no longer the only target of Lacan's critique of understanding; he also underlines the fact that it is no longer possible to approach the unconscious from the starting point of the laws of speech, and within the framework of the intersubjective relationship. This seminar marks a point of rupture in Lacan's teaching: the unconscious is henceforth presented as structured according to the laws of language, in accordance with the articulation of its significations. Psychosis therefore no longer simply coincides with the exclusion of an Other understood as the foundation of the intersubjective relation, but rather with a more radical "rejection" of the Other understood as the very order of signification. It is therefore why, Lacan writes, it is useless to "extol understanding"[190] of this unconscious. As he constantly specifies throughout the second half of his seminar, to say "that everything that belongs to analytic communication has the structure of language, this precisely does not mean that the unconscious is expressed in discourse."[191] Everything in the order of the unconscious is marked by the absence that essentially constitutes the signifier, which, "as such, signifies nothing."[192]

As I see it, this was the theoretical context within which Foucault was reflecting on the problem of madness and of psychoanalysis as he was writing his thesis. His earliest writings make it clear that he was reading Lacan during this period and was aware of his teaching, although we cannot know with any certainty which of Lacan's seminars at Sainte-Anne he audited.[193] The fact remains that the Lacanian critique of the psychiatric approach consisting in "understanding the meaning" of psychic phenomena, as well as the shift from speech to language that Lacan operated in his reading of psychoses, appears as a very pertinent avenue if we are to understand how Foucault, in the early 1960s, revised his position on Freud in relation to the critique he had leveled against him in 1954. Foucault's new emphasis on the link between madness and language, and the privileged relationship that he now seems to institute between madness and psychoanalysis, clearly point us in this direction.

There are three texts by Foucault that should always be read in parallel to *History of Madness* if we are to better understand its stakes. These are his volume *Death and the Labyrinth* (1963), his paper "Madness, the Absence of Work" ("La folie, l'absence d'œuvre," 1964), and his essay "The Thought of the Outside" ("La pensée du dehors," 1966). In these texts, the problem of psychoanalysis always emerges from a reflection on language. We could also cite the argument that Foucault makes in this same period in *The Birth of the Clinic*, according to which illness appears to the classical clinician as a text that must be deciphered.[194] It is equally interesting to note the manner in which Foucault once again does justice to Freud in 1964:

> One day we ought to do the justice to Freud of acknowledging that he did not make a madness *speak* that had been for centuries precisely a language (excluded language, babbling inanity, speech circulating indeterminately outside the pondered silence of reason); to the contrary, he exhausted its meaningless logos; it dried it out; he returned its words to their source—to that blank region of self-implication where *nothing is said*.[195]

Let us remember the problem raised in the introduction from 1954: Foucault critiqued psychoanalytic hermeneutics for its insufficient development of the notion of the symbol, insofar as, by reducing the symbol to meaning, this development was incapable of connecting the symbol to the specific laws of language. The argument's conclusions are now, as it were, inverted by Foucault. He now acknowledges the merits of psychoanalysis, which—precisely because it has not been able to draw this connection between language and meaning—renounced the project of discovering the "lost identity of a meaning" in order to "carve out—on the contrary—the disruptive image of a signifier."[196] And this is a signifier that must not be conceived, as Foucault states, as "the ruse of a hidden signification," but much more like "a figure that retains and suspends meaning, laying out an emptiness."[197]

In *Death and the Labyrinth* as in "The Thought of the Outside," psychoanalysis is not directly in question; neither is Lacan mentioned by Foucault. However, the philosophical problem of the radical experience of a language freed of any relationship to a meaning-giving subject—an experience that Foucault gives an account of by using expressions such as "*béance*"[198] or "the anguish of the signifier"[199]—is at the heart of his analysis. The reference to Lacanian psychoanalysis is for that matter rather obvious when Foucault asserts, in "The Thought of the Outside," that

> The breakthrough to a language from which the subject is excluded, the bringing to light of a perhaps irremediable incompatibility between the appearing of language in its being and consciousness of the self in its identity, is an experience now being heralded at diverse points in culture: in the simple gesture of writing as in attempts to formalize language; in the study of myths as in psychoanalysis.[200]

The question this imposes, then, is the following, which I raise by drawing once again on Derrida's formulation: "Would Foucault's project have been possible without psychoanalysis,"—and psychopathology, I would add—"with which it is contemporary?"[201] In other words, would the philosophical (and notably anti-phenomenological) project of examining the emptiness of an experience without a subject, the project that as early as *History of Madness* purported to renounce the comfort of any truth and of any knowledge of madness in order to trace unreason to its source, have been possible without psychopathology? The manner in which Lacan raises the problem of psychoses, indeed, speaks to the philosophical centrality of French psychopathology in the 1950s, and I truly believe that this approach became in some way operational within Foucault's discourse. Of course, there is no question of superimposing Foucault's and Lacan's respective discourses, and I would not push my analysis so far as to posit Lacanian foreclosure at the origin of Raymond Roussel's meaningless speech. Yet Lacan's analysis of the psychotic's relationship to language, in conjunction with his approach to the problems of "signification" and of "understanding," seems to have played an important role in the manner in which Foucault now shifts his attention to the idea of a language that dooms any hermeneutic enterprise to failure. This conception is at the heart of archaeology's epistemological project and in particular of its refusal of the figure of the meaning-giving subject.

In any case, Foucault seems to substantiate these claims when, in the final chapter of *Death and the Labyrinth*, he describes Roussel's unreason as his "illness."[202] If it is true that Roussel is "the inventor of a language which only speaks about itself,"[203] a language with which we touch "what is closest to us in our language"[204]—which is to say, the pure language that, in *The Order of Things*, should finally unmask the epistemological configuration of our time—it is no less true that it is a question pertaining to the domain of psychopathology that seems to motivate the initial epistemological development of Foucault's thought. Foucault's analysis of Roussel's language is indeed very close to Lacan's approach to the problem of psychotic delirium, starting with the analysis of "that special form of discordance with common language known as a neologism."[205] Just as Lacan describes as an "inconsistent mirage" any "relation of understanding"[206] concerning the words of a psychotic person, concerning "a meaning that essentially refers to nothing but itself,"[207] Foucault insists on a language "rhyming with itself,"[208] "extending its reign to find again the identical but never the identical meaning."[209] In fact, strictly speaking Roussel's words are not words, because these words have nothing to communicate. They "display what they show but do not disclose what is in them";[210] they refer to an image that is "perceived but not decipherable."[211] It is, in short, a language that one would struggle in vain to understand, because it is "before discourse and before words.... Before and after that which is articulated"[212]—a language in which the words have spoken "beyond memory."[213]

Faced with the phenomenon of this language that is pure auto-implication, Foucault's polemical targets are the same as those Lacan critiqued in his seminar of 1955–56: the phenomenologico-existential perspective and a certain naive vision of the Freudian approach, which consists in believing that, if psychoanalysis "restor[ed] meaning to the chain of phenomena," this "sense in question is what we understand."[214] On the one hand, Lacan reproached existential analysis for its faith in this "myth of immediate experience,"[215] which might lead to confusing, within the phenomenon, the domain of significance and that of signification. On the other hand, he also reproached a naive conception of psychoanalysis for attaching itself only to the meaning of phenomena, which is to say, to the simplistic formula according to which a dream "tells us" something. On the contrary, he specified, "the only thing that interests Freud is the elaboration through which the dream says this something"[216]—which means that the deciphering in question in *The Interpretation of Dreams* is the recovery not of a meaning but rather of the modalities of a language. This is what Lacan understood when he declared, paradoxically, that "the great secret of psychoanalysis is that there is no psychogenesis."[217]

In Foucault's writings of the 1960s, we see these same two polemical targets. On the one hand, the critique of existential psychiatry goes hand in hand with the explicitly anti-phenomenological position that characterized archaeology's refusal of any philosophical position relying on the figure of a meaning-giving subject. We can also recognize a critique specifically addressed to the phenomenologico-existential approach in psychiatry in the book on Roussel, when Foucault analyzes the pure language of unreason by remarking that the images that this language draws are of "calm, *worldless* landscapes."[218] The link between subject and world is indeed at the basis of existential psychiatry, especially in its Binswangerian form, which understands psychopathological forms of existence precisely in terms of the patients' "world-projects." And these worlds, while being specific, are nevertheless comprehensible insofar as they have a particular normativity. In other words, for Binswanger, "there is never a dissolution into pure subjectivity, rigorously considered, as long as man is man."[219] Even if the patient's "strongly subjective personalism" "puts into question the patient's foothold in the objective and impersonal,"[220] this personalism does not compromise what characterizes any kind of "presence," namely, "being in a common world." As Minkowski specified in his book on schizophrenia, this is a world that "becomes accessible to us insofar as we are able to respect its form and its laws."[221]

For Foucault, who analyzes it from the vantage point of the language of psychosis, the world of the patient no longer corresponds to any law, no longer has any form. There is only a "positive world"[222] that is deprived of any transcendence, a "world, placed out of reach by the verbal ritual that begins it,"[223] and that it would be useless to call on any ritual to analyze. Along the same lines, there is no longer any principle or foundation that can define the style of experience characteristic of a pathological form, that can give it the unity or "structure" to which existential psychiatry assimilates the various manifestations of an illness. Faced with Roussel's language, this unitary structure of illness or "*a priori* of existence" is no longer anything but a "timid psychological formulation."[224]

In contrast, the critique of the hermeneutic conception of psychoanalysis emerges at the moment when Foucault observes that the "contorted shapes" and "numerous mechanisms doing nothing" in the pure language exemplified in Roussel's oeuvre would naturally give "rise to the idea of an enigma, a cypher, a secret."[225] Yet in reality "no great effort is needed to make them reveal their secret,"[226] since this language that refers only to itself does not hide any "psychological background of the work."[227] As Lacan had it, there is no psychogenesis. Instead, there is a language "which comes before language"[228] and which must therefore not be interpreted, but rather "deciphered." For Freud, Foucault notes, "the unconscious has a languagelike structure," which is why "his problem, finally, is not a problem of linguistics, it is a problem of decipherment."[229] What allows Freud to avoid reducing this language to meaning, Foucault continues, is that psychoanalytic decipherment functions on the order of decryption: "Freud in effect decodes, which is to say, he recognizes that there is a message there. He doesn't know what that message means; he doesn't know the laws according to which the signs can mean what they mean. So he has to discover at one go both what the message means and what the laws are by which the message means what it means."[230] This is a perspective that Lacan's seminar on psychoses makes very explicit, when Lacan observes that Freud's "true stroke of genius . . . owes nothing to any intuitive insight—it's the genius of the linguist who sees the same sign appear several times in a text, begins from the idea that this must mean something, and manages to stand all the signs of this language right side up again."[231] And indeed, it is not by accident that Foucault specifically names psychosis as the privileged site in which the psychoanalytic decryption of this pure language, which carries the key to what it enunciates, might take place: "Madness must be treated as a message that would have its own key within itself. That is what Freud does when he's faced with a hysterical symptom; that is what is done by people who are now trying to address the problem of psychosis."[232]

But what does it mean to state that madness is a message that contains its own key? Foucault explained himself more clearly on this subject at the 1964 Royaumont colloquium, in the paper "Nietzsche, Freud, Marx." He returns to the theme of gaping (*béance*), which would characterize the radical experience of language emphasized by psychoanalysis, and observes that interpretation, as Freud understands it, does not consist in referring signs to a homogeneous space of signification, but rather is an "irreducible gaping [*béance*] and openness," inexhaustible, "always incomplete."[233] Now, if interpretation is "structurally gaping [*béante*],"[234] Foucault notes, it is because in the end "there is nothing to interpret," and if there is nothing to interpret, it is because "after all everything is already interpretation, each sign is in itself not the thing that offers itself to interpretation but an interpretation of other signs."[235] The emphasis is therefore clearly placed on significance rather than signification, and this is why from this moment on—as Lacan indicated in his seminar—nothing would be more false than to imagine that the meaning at stake in the language of the psychotic is what can be understood: "to understand patients . . . is a pure mirage."[236]

Foucault's paper of 1964 is striking because it does not present itself as a study of the psychoanalytic approach to psychopathology, but seems to prefigure one of the central theses of *The Order of Things*—the idea that "the reappearance of language in the enigma of its unity and its being"[237] marks the end of the epistemological configuration that characterized the era of the human sciences. Once again, the Lacanian psychoanalytic approach to language forms the core of Foucault's argument, and the argument returns once again to the subject of psychosis. If psychoanalysis does not belong to the order of the human sciences, Foucault observes, it is because it constitutes instead the "critical function" that crosses through them, by setting itself "the task of making the discourse of the unconscious speak."[238] And this is the crucial point, insofar as making the unconscious speak does not entail giving meaning or interpreting words, but quite the opposite: moving "towards the moment . . . at which the contents of consciousness articulate themselves, or rather stand gaping [*béants*]."[239] Now how does this gaping manifest itself? Precisely in the reappearance of language "in the enigma of its unity and its being." This is a unity, Foucault remarks, "that we ought to think but cannot as yet,"[240] because this language has freed itself from its content: it no longer has any place in the order of words and things; it no longer has either an object or a subject. This is why it does not belong to the epistemological order of the human sciences, and this is why psychoanalysis thereby becomes a "counter-science." Foucault concludes, almost paradoxically: "So psychoanalysis 'recognizes itself' when it is confronted with those very psychoses which nevertheless (or rather, for that very reason) it has scarcely any means of reaching: as if the psychosis were displaying in a savage illumination, and offering in a mode not too distant but just too close, that towards which analysis must make its laborious way."[241]

Even if for reasons different from those of his earliest writings, for Foucault in the 1960s "madness" seems to have continued to function as a royal road toward the demystification of the purported truths of anthropology and the human sciences. And yet, it is precisely an issue emerging from the domain and the discourse of psychopathology—the problem of psychoses as it had been understood in Lacan's psychoanalytic approach—that presented itself as the occasion and the fulcrum for Foucault's epistemological discourse. This is why, in the 1980s, at the end of his intellectual trajectory, Foucault would return to Lacan several times to credit him for finally freeing madness from its false liberators—psychiatrists since Philippe Pinel. And it is precisely in Lacan, then, that we might be able to recognize the theoretical site where the Foucauldian "hermeneutics of the subject" theorized in the 1980s overlaps with archaeology: a Lacan who "wanted for the obscurity of his *Écrits* to be the very complexity of the subject, and for the work necessary to understand it to be a work to carry out on the self."[242]

Even if Foucault never explicitly thematized it, then, Lacan's psychoanalytic theory constituted a fundamental element for understanding how Foucault distanced himself from existential analysis at the turn of the 1960s. The fact remains that, as I have shown in the preceding pages, the structural method that its clinical analyses had exemplified would continue to silently undergird the diagnostic approach at the heart of archaeological discourse.

CONCLUSION

About twenty years ago, when as a young graduate student I was first making my way in the world of research, I had proposed, as a subject for my doctoral dissertation, the relationship between Foucault's thought and existential psychiatry. I was not very surprised when a chorus of voices told me that I would not find much to say, insofar as the totality of the subject was contained within the 120 pages of Foucault's introduction to *Le rêve et l'existence*. The meeting between the philosopher and Binswanger, moreover, was nothing but a negligible biographical contingency in Foucault's intellectual trajectory. Why should I not instead focus on Foucault's relationship with the philosophy of Heidegger, Husserl, or Kant? I nevertheless persisted in my choice, in which I glimpsed elements that were original and might be of interest to scholars; in 2007, I was therefore able to publish a four hundred-page work in Italian.[1] I did not at the time have access to Foucault's work archives; nor did I suspect the existence of the manuscript *Binswanger et l'analyse existentielle*—or of Foucault's approximately eight hundred pages of reading notes on phenomenological psychiatry. Imagine my surprise, then, when in 2013 I discovered all of this material at the BnF!

I therefore had to return to my previous work, to test my intuitions and hypotheses, correct them, and compare them to and complete them with the new documents. This is what I have attempted to do in this book. Some of my hypotheses have been confirmed, while others I have had to discard. The possibility of finally confirming my intuitions about the texts and authors that Foucault knew, those who had most attracted his attention, was a fundamental aspect of my research. What has not changed, in any case, is my methodological approach. From my earliest readings of Foucault as a philosophy student, I had been very struck by a passage in *The Order of Things* in which Foucault provocatively asserts that he "learned more from Cuvier, Bopp, and Ricardo than from Kant or Hegel."[2] What if we were to add Binswanger to this list of nonphilosophers who shaped his intellectual project from the inside? This is the hypothesis I formulated in this book.

Until now, research on archaeology has privileged a purely philosophical approach to the problems and concepts that stem from Foucault's published work. With regard to Foucault's first writings, scholars have drawn on key concepts in the history of philosophy to attempt to identify continuities between Foucault's attitude toward existential analysis and the epistemological analysis of knowledge he developed starting in the 1960s. The concepts of the "transcendental" and of the "empirical" have to this point garnered the greatest scholarly attention.

Among the most recent publications, Béatrice Han-Pile's essay "Phenomenology and Anthropology in Foucault's Introduction to Binswanger's *Dream and Existence*" shows that the manner in which Foucault takes up Binswanger's concept of *Menschsein* (the "being of man")—which is neither the transcendental subject nor an empirical being—represents "the possibility of a relation between the empirical and the transcendental that goes beyond the Kantian critical project while avoiding the pitfall of the analytic of finitude."[3] Han-Pile concludes that from this point of view, the introduction to *Le rêve et l'existence* "sets the theoretical agenda for at least the next ten years"; set against the context of this early work, the key concept of archaeology—the historical *a priori*—reveals itself to be "the methodological successor to existential anthropology."[4] This is undoubtedly an original and fruitful intuition, which certain researchers had already adumbrated in the late 1960s. In the introduction that accompanies his translation of *The Birth of the Clinic* into Italian, for example, Alessandro Fontana assigned to Foucault's introduction to *Le rêve et l'existence* an "emblematic value for the development of the questions on the basis of which 'archaeology' and its methods will be constructed"[5]—a set of questions at the heart of which is precisely the dialectic between the empirical and the transcendental. Moreover, the Italian philosopher Carlo Sini has seen in the theme of the dream and the imagination Foucault's first historical *a priori*: indeed, the space of the dream that Foucault analyzes in his introduction to Binswanger's essay could constitute the "transcendental terrain on which the empirical space of human experience arises."[6]

While attempting to identify a throughline or at least coherent elements across Foucault's published works, these readings limit themselves to analyzing these works in the light only of those authors and concepts belonging to the philosophical tradition. Furthermore, these readings and interpretations remain internal to Foucault's works and do not take into account the theoretical and intellectual context in which they were conceived. Yet I believe that this context is fundamental for understanding the manner in which Foucault develops the concepts that form the basis of his philosophical project. From this point of view, drawing a link between Foucault's earliest writings and the intellectual context of his formative years does not mean, as Han-Pile has it, "join[ing] the game of trying to identify biographical reasons, nor attempt[ing] to give external reasons meant to justify (or denounce) the changes in Foucault's assessment of the potential of anthropology."[7] On the contrary, this link allows us to avoid limiting our analysis to exegesis, or to probing, in a general manner, the theoretical strengths and weaknesses of Foucault's thought in relation to the philosophical tradition. Instead, we can follow its mutations from the vantage point of the specific questions and stakes that animate it.

In my book, I therefore tried to blur the boundaries between biography and theoretical research in order to retrace the transformations, the difficulties, and sometimes the contradictions that characterize the intellectual trajectory of a philosopher who, as Foucault himself put it, "turned to psychology, and from psychology to history." From this perspective, situating Foucault's thought at the moment of its "meeting" with Binswanger entailed not giving myself over to the study of the influence of one author on another, but rather examining the general epistemological problem of the methodology of Foucault's intellectual project at the moment of its formation. We could therefore characterize this analysis as a methodological inquiry, since for me it was a matter of giving something like an account of the "style" of Foucauldian epistemology—this interrogation of forms of knowledge (*savoirs*) that gives itself the task of analyzing them not in the mode of a "psychoanalysis of objective knowledge [*connaissance*]" but rather by describing the configuration of their "objectuality," through an examination of the conceptual tools that determined at one and the same time their form and their history.

With the aim of investigating and highlighting Foucault's first writings by asking about their relationship to the archaeological works of the 1960s, I therefore considered the possibility of analyzing the archaeological project by blurring the boundaries between forms of knowledge (*savoirs*) and disciplines, all the while seeking to identify the conceptual tools that Foucault used or that he himself forged in order to develop his critique of knowledge. For this reason, my investigation exceeded the strict bounds of the history of philosophy; instead it borrowed the epistemological approach that Foucault had demonstrated as early as his writings of the 1950s. My examination of the key concept of archaeology—the historical *a priori*—against the backdrop of the French intellectual context in which Foucault took his first steps at the beginning of the 1950s showed that his scholarly method in philosophy and the history of science entailed transfers of theoretical approaches and assumptions between different disciplines such as psychology, psychiatry, medicine, and biology. By adopting this approach, I followed Georges Canguilhem's axiom, in his introduction from 1943 to his dissertation, *The Normal and the Pathological*, that "philosophy is a reflection for which all foreign matter [*matière étrangère*] is good, and we would gladly say, for which all good matter must be foreign."[8] In other words, what if the method adopted by a psychiatrist in the context of his research on mental illness had provided theoretical inspiration for the epistemological approach of a philosopher interrogating the transformation of forms of knowledge (*savoirs*)?

From this perspective, the analysis of Foucault's intellectual biography was very precious. It showed first that Foucault's interest in Binswanger's existential anthropology was not merely an isolated and somewhat exotic curiosity in the French postwar landscape. Indeed, the phenomenologico-existential school of psychiatry played an important role in a philosophical debate in which psychopathology and anthropology were central issues. In addition, analyzing this context revealed that the problem of anthropology, at the time at which Foucault began to attend to it, was at the heart of a philosophical debate that was not limited to academic philosophy, but rather extended to other fields such as psychology, psychiatry, medicine, and biology.

Foucault's interest in Binswanger's "existential analysis" therefore appeared particularly significant to me. Undoubtedly, the young Foucault experienced a certain enthusiasm for and a certain fascination with this anthropological psychopathology that, differently from the natural determinism of academic psychiatry, allowed him to glimpse the possibility of touching something like the "truth" of the human being. There was also a philosophical and literary inclination to explore "limit experiences," as well as a more or less conscious effort to give back to the experience of madness the richness and revelatory power that had been broken by the exclusion operated by reason. This effort would remain constant throughout Foucault's trajectory, from his text on dreams, through *History of Madness* and *Death and the Labyrinth*, up until *The History of Sexuality*.[9]

Still, it seems to me that it would be reductive to treat Foucault's engagement with these issues as mere fascination. Indeed, analyzed in its intellectual context, Foucault's penchant for Binswanger's anthropological project corresponds to a real epistemological problematization of psychologico-psychiatric knowledge and of its methodology, which was widespread among French psychiatrists and philosophers during Foucault's formative years. In order to understand the "episode" of Foucault's encounter with the Swiss psychiatrist's theoretical project, it was therefore necessary to reread Foucault's writings on Binswanger in light of the scientific and philosophical context that fostered the reception of existential analysis in France. It was also necessary to examine the epistemological stakes undergirding both this reception and the adhesion of many psychiatrists and philosophers to the phenomenological program. It was this context to which Foucault himself alluded, for that matter, when he announced in his "Introduction" a study that would aim to "situate existential analysis within the development of contemporary reflection on man."[10]

The archives confirmed this orientation and, in the first two chapters of this book, I drew on Foucault's intellectual biography to show that his meeting with Binswanger could be situated within the context of existential analysis's philosophical reception. This reception did not limit itself to interrogating existential analysis's strictly theoretical foundations, but also questioned the validity of psychiatric knowledge and especially of its clinical method. The manuscript *Binswanger et l'analyse existentielle*, in particular, revealed that Foucault's profound interest in *Daseinsanalyse*—although it developed at a time when he was studying Husserl's and Heidegger's phenomenology in depth—primarily concerned its diagnostic method and its position with regard to the relationship between the normal and the pathological. The question of Binswanger's orthodoxy with regard to his inspirations—in particular Heidegger's ontological analytic—is less important. Indeed, in the second chapter, an analysis of Foucault's manuscript demonstrated that he distanced himself from existential analysis at the moment when Binswanger exceeded the bounds of clinical case analysis in order to engage in a philosophical speculation about human nature.

It is for this reason that I chose to pursue my analysis of the relationship between Foucauldian archaeology and *Daseinsanalyse* by following the path of an examination of method. And once again, I did not limit my investigation to a purely philosophical study. In the third chapter, indeed, after having analyzed Foucault's writings on Binswanger in light of the new manuscript sources that are now at our disposal, I focused on the methodology at the basis of existential analysis's approach to pathological forms of experience. It was the concept of normativity operating within the Binswangerian methodological *dispositif* that most attracted my attention. It seemed to me that the manner in which Binswanger characterizes the "norm" is very significant for understanding Foucault's reception of his project within the context of the philosophical and psychiatric thought of his period. The idea that behavioral "facts" might correspond to a structure or norm, and that this norm might be inscribed in the facts themselves; the idea that this "internal law" according to which they appear—as Merleau-Ponty has it—"is not the external unfolding of a pre-existing reason,"[11] but rather coincides with the appearance itself: these are very important for characterizing the manner in which Foucault not only assesses the principle of immanence proper to existential analysis, but also imagines his own project of the analysis and immanent critique of knowledges (*savoirs*) through the notion of the historical *a priori*.

Rather than categorically support or reject the idea of Foucault's adhesion to "phenomenology," I therefore tried to see whether it might not be possible to detect, precisely *through* Binswanger, a certain Foucauldian "style" in phenomenology. What I tried to show was that for Foucault, but also for the French philosophers and psychiatrists to whom I alluded, there occurred a methodological reception of the phenomenological approach. For this very reason, this reception could allow itself to refer to Heidegger and to the phenomenological concept of *Dasein* as a "structure" of the "being-in-the-world" while challenging the German philosopher's admonition that positive sciences such as biology, psychology, and anthropology could not ask or think the problem of existence. On his side, Binswanger, in taking up the structural character of the "being-in-the-world," compared it to the concept of the biological world, pausing especially on ethology and neurology.

I therefore drew on Binswanger's writings to identify the meaning of the "startling," "barbarous"[12] concept that is the historical *a priori*, which responds to Foucault's need to "disentangle the conditions of its history from the density of discourse," or, as Foucault would retrospectively affirm while referring to his essay on Binswanger, to study forms of experience *in their history*. I showed how Foucault emphasized that existential analysis was able to respond to the exigency of starting from experience, from its historical forms and internal laws, in order to understand that very experience. In so doing, I argued, he described the characteristic that would form the basis of his own project of analyzing knowledges, practices, and experiences from the starting point of their effective existence, of their functioning, rather than from the starting point of an extrinsic explanatory principle. What seemed particularly interesting to me was the way in which Foucault, in his introduction to *Le rêve et l'existence*, praised existential analysis specifically because it does not refer anthropology to an *a priori* form of philosophical speculation, but rather uses this very *a priori* to indicate the *historicity* of forms of experience.

Similar to the structural *a priori* detected by existential analysis, Foucault's historical *a priori* has a visibility that is foremost operational, insofar as it emerges and expresses itself only through its own use. It therefore does not present itself as an autonomous philosophical theme, but rather as a "diagnostic principle" or methodological instrument capable of meeting the requirement for immanence according to which "the history of knowledge can be written only on the basis of what was contemporaneous with it."

Maybe, then, in order to attempt to resolve the oft-debated, controversial problem of Foucault's relationship to "phenomenology," instead of seeking to uncover a heretofore-unthought "foundation," we might direct ourselves toward what has remained most constant and closely held across the different questions and contexts that have guided phenomenology: its method. We might thereby assert, in the words of a psychiatrist-phenomenologist, Georges Lantéri-Laura, that this method "finds its culmination not in its own orthodox identity with itself, but in the just discernment of the problems it succeeds in raising, without having acquired all of the means of responding to them."[13]

ACKNOWLEDGMENTS

Most of this book was written during the two years I worked at the École normale supérieure de Lyon on a parallel project, "Foucault's Manuscripts on Phenomenology (1950s) at the BnF Archive: A Digital Approach to the Edition." This project received funding from the European Union's Horizon 2020 Research and Innovation Programme under the Marie Skłodowska-Curie grant agreement No 836888—EDIFOU. I am deeply grateful to the European Commission for supporting my work, as well as to Professor Michel Senellart, who welcomed me to the Triangle laboratory in 2019 as part of the team working on the "Foucault Fiches de Lecture / Foucault Reading Notes" (FFL) project. Special thanks go to Vincent Ventresque and Marie-Laure Massot, who introduced me to the world of digital humanities, and to all the members of the FFL team.

With respect to the study of Foucault's archives, I heartily thank the late Alessandro Fontana, who first introduced me to the reading of Foucault's manuscripts. I also would like to thank all the members of the editorial board of the "Cours et travaux de Michel Foucault avant le Collège de France" series at

Éditions du Seuil. I especially wish to thank Daniel Defert, François Ewald, and Henri-Paul Fruchaud for their guidance and belief in my work.

For supporting my research on the young Foucault's manuscripts in 2016–2017, I thank the European Institutes for Advanced Study (EURIAS) Fellowship Programme and the director of the Collegium de Lyon, Hervé Joly. I also wish to thank the Alexander von Humboldt Foundation, which funded my research stay at the Technische Universität Berlin in 2018, at the Innovationszentrum Wissensforschung (IZW) / Center for Knowledge Research, led by Professor Günter Abel, a great philosopher who means a lot to me.

For allowing me access to Roland Kuhn's house and private library, I sincerely thank Regula Kuhn and Liselotte Rutishauser. For the documents and information they made available to me, I thank Bruno Verdeaux and the Ludwig Binswanger Archives at the University of Tübingen.

For supporting my research since 2008, I would like to thank the Centre d'Archives en Philosophie, Histoire et Édition des Sciences (CAPHÉS)—CNRS, École normale supérieure, PSL Research University; for the scientific support and friendship shown to me throughout the years following the defense of my doctoral thesis, I cannot thank Mireille Delbraccio enough; the same is true of Professor Claude Debru. I also warmly thank the CAPHÉS' current director Mathias Girel and all his team, in particular the head of the Documentary Centre, Nathalie Queyroux.

I thank Marie Satya McDonough for her excellent work in translating and revising the original manuscript of this book and Columbia University Press for accepting this monograph. I am deeply honored to be featured in its catalog.

Finally, I would like to thank those who have made all of this possible, right from the start: my parents, Michela and Ausilio, and my twin sister, Ingrid, as well as the persons who remind me every day that the work of research is both exciting and worthwhile, my husband, Gualtiero Lorini, and our son, Ludovico.

NOTES

A GENEALOGY OF ARCHAEOLOGY

1. Michel Foucault, *The Order of Things* (New York: Vintage, 1994), xv.
2. Elisabetta Basso, *Young Foucault*, [166].
3. Basso, [131].
4. Basso, [130], quoting Michel Foucault, *Maladie mentale et personnalité* (Paris: Presses Universitaires de France, 1954), 54.
5. Basso, [89], quoting Michel Foucault, *Binswanger et l'analyse existentielle* (Paris: EHESS/Gallimard/Seuil, 2021), 27.
6. Basso, [97].
7. Michel Foucault, *Naissance de la Clinique: Une archéologie du regard medical* (Paris: Presses universitaires de France, 1963), xv.
8. Foucault.
9. Basso, *Young Foucault*, 141.
10. Michel Foucault, "Preface to *The History of Sexuality, Volume II*," in Michel Foucault, *The Foucault Reader*, ed. Paul Rabinow (New York: Vintage, 2010), 334.
11. See, generally, "A Preface to Philosophical Praxis," in Michel Foucault, *Sexuality* (New York: Columbia University Press, 2021).

INTRODUCTION

1. Sozialpsychiatrie was a movement that emerged in the Federal Republic of Germany in response to the need to reform psychiatry, in the context of a social reflection on the causes of psychic

suffering and on the modalities of treatment and access to care. The "Deutsche Gesellschaft für Soziale Psychiatrie" (DGSP; German Society for Social Psychiatry) was founded in 1970, following the "inquiry on psychiatry" launched by the FRG's Parliament to assess the state of psychiatric care. Karl Peter Kisker was the founder, along with Erich Wulff (1926–2010), in Hanover, of the first Sozialpsychiatrie institute—the "Hannoversches Modell"—which he directed from 1974 to 1994.

2. Karl Peter Kisker, "Antipsychiatrie (AP)," in *Psychiatrie der Gegenwart: Forschung und Praxis*, vol. 1, pt. 1, *Grundlagen und Methoden der Psychiatrie*, ed. Karl Peter Kisker, Joachim-Ernst Meyer, Christian Müller, and Erik Strömgren (Berlin: Springer, 1979), pp. 811–825; §F, "Theorien," 2, "Philosophische Züflusse," p. 821.

3. The term he used in French is *psychiatricide*. Henri Ey, "Introduction aux débats," in "La conception idéologique de 'L'Histoire de la folie' de Michel Foucault," *Journées annuelles de l'Évolution psychiatrique*, December 6–7, 1969, *L'Évolution Psychiatrique* 36, no. 2 (1971): 225–226, p. 226.

4. Ey, p. 225.

5. Ludwig Binswanger, "Traum und Existenz," *Neue Schweizer Rundschau* 23 (1930): 673–685, 766–779; French translation by Jacqueline Verdeaux, *Le rêve et l'existence*, introduction and notes by Michel Foucault, Textes et études anthropologiques (Paris: Desclée de Brouwer, 1954); English translation by Jacob Needleman, "Dream and Existence," *Review of Existential Psychology and Psychiatry*, special issue, ed. Keith Hoeller, 19, no. 1 (1986): 81–105. Foucault's introduction was later reprinted in *Dits et écrits*, ed. Daniel Defert and François Ewald, with Jacques Lagrange, Bibliothèque des sciences humaines (Paris: Gallimard, 1994), vol. 1, no. 1, pp. 65–118; English translation by Forrest Williams, "Dream, Imagination and Existence," in *Dream and Existence*, by Michel Foucault and Ludwig Binswanger, special issue of *Review of Existential Psychology and Psychiatry*, ed. Keith Hoeller, 19, no. 1 (1985): 29–78.

6. Henri Ey, "*Rêve et existence* (En hommage à E. Minkowski. Réflexions sur une Étude de L. Binswanger)," *L'Évolution Psychiatrique* 21, no. 1 (1956): 109–118, p. 109.

7. On the subject of Henri Ey and his work with the Évolution psychiatrique group, see Emmanuel Delille, *Réseaux savants et enjeux*

INTRODUCTION ᛕ 213

classificatoires dans l'Encyclopédie médico-chirurgicale (1947–1977): L'exemple de la notion de psychose, PhD diss., Contemporary History, École des Hautes Études en Sciences Sociales (Paris), December 6, 2008.

8. Karl Peter Kisker, *Dialogik der Verrücktheit: Ein Versuch an den Grenzen der Anthropologie* (Den Haag: Martinus Nijhoff, 1970), p. 9.
9. Michel Foucault, "Préface," in *Folie et Déraison*, Civilisations d'hier et d'aujourd'hui (Paris: Plon, 1961); reprinted in *Dits et Écrits, 1954–1988*, ed. Daniel Defert, François Ewald, with Lagrange 1, no. 4, pp. 159–167, p. 159; English translation by Jonathan Murphy and Jean Khalfa, "Preface to the 1961 edition," in *History of Madness*, ed. Jean Khalfa (London: Routledge, 2006), pp. xxvii–xxxvi, p. xxvii.
10. Michel Foucault, *Maladie mentale et psychologie* (Paris: PUF, 1962), p. 88; English translation by Alan Sheridan, *Mental Illness and Psychology* (Berkeley: University of California Press, 1987), p. 74.
11. Michel Foucault, *Maladie mentale et personnalité*, Initiation philosophique 12 (Paris: PUF, 1954).
12. Foucault, *Mental Illness and Psychology*, p. 74.
13. Michel Foucault, "La psychologie de 1850 à 1950" (1957), in *Dits et écrits*, ed. Daniel Defert, François Ewald, with Lagrange vol. 1, no. 2, pp. 120–137; Foucault, "La recherche scientifique et la psychologie" (1957), in Defert, Ewald, and Lagrange, *Dits et écrits*, vol. 1, no. 3, pp. 137–158.
14. See Alan Sheridan, *Michel Foucault: The Will to Truth* (London: Tavistock, 1980), p. 194.
15. José Luis Moreno Pestaña, *En devenant Foucault: Sociogenèse d'un grand philosophe*, trans. Ph. Hunt, Collection Champ social (Broissieux: Éditions du Croquant, 2006), p. 56.
16. Among the most recent studies emphasizing the importance of Foucault's first writings for the rest of his work, see Philippe Sabot, "L'expérience, le savoir et l'histoire dans les premiers écrits de Michel Foucault," *Archives de Philosophie* 69, no. 2 (2006): 285–303; Giorgio Agamben, *Signatura rerum: Sul metodo* (Turin, Bollati Boringhieri, 2008); English translation by Luca D'Isanto with Kevin Attel, *The Signature of All Things* (New York: Zone, 2009), chap. 3, "Philosophical Archaeology," pp. 81–111; Bryan Smyth, "Foucault and Binswanger: Beyond the Dream," *Philosophy Today*, no. 55, suppl. (2011): 92–101; Jean-Claude Monod, "Présentation," *Les Études philosophiques* 106, no. 3

(2013): 311–315; Guillaume Le Blanc, "Se moquer de la phénoménologie, est-ce encore faire de la phénoménologie?," 106, no. 3 (2013): 373–381; Béatrice Han-Pile, "Phenomenology and Anthropology in Foucault's 'Introduction to Binswanger's *Dream And Existence*': A Mirror Image of *The Order Of Things*?," *History and Theory* 55, no. 4 (2016): 7–22; Line Joranger, "Individual Perception and Cultural Development: Foucault's 1954 Approach to Mental Illness and Its History," *History of Psychology* 19, no. 1 (2016): 40–51; Burkhart Brückner, Lukas Iwer, and Samuel Thoma, "Die Existenz, Abwesenheit und Macht des Wahnsinns: Eine kritische Übersicht zu Michel Foucaults Arbeiten zur Geschichte und Philosophie der Psychiatrie," *NMT Zeitschrift für Geschichte der Wissenschaften, Technik und Medizin* 25 (2017): 69–98; Stuart Elden, *The Early Foucault* (Cambridge: Polity, 2021). Unfortunately, this last had not been published yet when I completed the present study.

17. Pestaña, *En devenant Foucault*, p. 133.
18. Michel Foucault, *Œuvres*, ed. Frédéric Gros, Bibliothèque de la Pléiade (Paris: Gallimard, 2015).
19. The Fonds Michel Foucault is inventoried under the call numbers NAF 28284, NAF 28730 and NAF 28803. On the archival deposit in 2013, see Marie-Odile Germain, "Michel Foucault de retour à la BnF," *Chroniques de la Bibliothèque nationale de France*, no. 70 (2014): 26–27. Another group of archives concerning Michel Foucault's work was assembled in 1986 at the Bibliothèque du Saulchoir in Paris by the Centre Michel Foucault and, in 1997, was deposited at IMEC (Institut Mémoires de l'édition contemporaine) in Caen, Normandy. Beyond the recordings of the Foucault's lectures at the Collège de France, these archives contain seminars he gave in the United States, interviews, and radio programs, as well as the manuscripts of a few articles, some correspondence, and a dossier of criticism about Foucault's work.
20. Cf. Louis Pinto, "Foucault avant Foucault: psychologie et sciences de l'homme," in *Lire les sciences sociales*, ed. Gérard Mauger and Louis Pinto, vol. 3 (Paris: Hermès Sciences, 1994–1996), pp. 116–122.
21. "La correspondance entre Michel Foucault et Ludwig Binswanger, 1954–1956," (introduction and notes by Elisabetta Basso, French translation by René Wetzel) was published in Jean-François Bert and Elisabetta Basso, eds., *Foucault à Münsterlingen: À l'origine de l'Histoire de*

la folie, with photographs by Jacqueline Verdeaux, Représentations (Paris: Éditions de l'EHESS, 2015), pp. 175–195.

22. See Bert and Basso, *Foucault à Münsterlingen*.
23. Some of these archives had already been consulted by Didier Eribon as he was writing his biography of Foucault in 1994: *Michel Foucault: 1926–1984* (Paris: Flammarion, 1989), 3rd published in 2011 (Champs: biographie, 847); English translation by Betsy Wing, *Michel Foucault* (Cambridge: MA, Harvard University Press, 1991).
24. Jakob Wyrsch, *Die Person des Schizophrenen: Studien zur Klinik, Psychologie, Daseinsweise* (Bern: Haupt, 1949); French translation by Jacqueline Verdeaux, *La personne du schizophrène: Étude clinique, psychologique et anthropophénoménologique*, Bibliothèque de psychiatrie (Paris: PUF, 1956).
25. L. Binswanger, "Studien zum Schizophrenieproblem: Der Fall Suzanne Urban," *Schweizer Archiv für Neurologie und Psychiatrie* 69 (1952): 36–77; 70 (1952): 1–32; 71 (1952): 57–96; reprinted in *Schizophrenie* (Pfullingen: Neske, 1957), study no. 5, pp. 359–470; French translation by Jacqueline Verdeaux, *Le Cas Suzanne Urban: étude sur la schizophrénie* (Paris: Desclée de Brouwer).
26. Roland Kuhn, *Über Maskendeutungen im Rorschachschen Versuch* (Basel, Karger, 1944), 2nd edition published in 1954; French translation by Jacqueline Verdeaux, *Phénoménologie du masque: À travers le test de Rorschach* (Paris: Desclée de Brouwer, 1957); newly revised and corrected edition, 1992.
27. On this point, see the classical study of Herbert Spiegelberg, *Phenomenology in Psychology and Psychiatry: A Historical Introduction* (Evanston, IL: Northwestern University Press, 1972).
28. See on this subject Jean-François Braunstein, "Bachelard, Canguilhem, Foucault: Le 'style français' en épistémologie," in *Les philosophes et la science*, ed. Pierre Wagner, Folio: Essais 408 (Paris: Gallimard, 2002), pp. 920–963, which draws on the notion of "style of thought" developed by the Polish physician and epistemologist Ludwik Fleck.
29. In the more recent literature on this topic, see the special issue *Foucault et la phénoménologie*, ed. Jean-Claude Monod, *Les Études philosophiques* 106, no. 3 (2013); and John Rogove, "La phénoménologie manquée de Foucault: Husserl et le contre-modèle de l'anthropologisme kantien," *Philosophie* 123, no. 4 (2014): 58–67. See also the now-classic studies by

Hubert Dreyfus and Paul Rabinow, *Michel Foucault: Beyond Structuralism and Hermeneutics*, 2nd ed. (Chicago: University of Chicago Press, 1983); Gérard Lebrun, "Note sur la phénoménologie dans *Les Mots et les Choses*," in *Michel Foucault philosophe: Rencontre International, Paris 9–11 janvier 1988* (Paris: Éditions du Seuil, 1989), pp. 33–52; Béatrice Han-Pile, *Foucault's Critical Project: Between the Transcendental and the Historical* (Stanford: Stanford University Press, 2002).

30. Foucault began to write an intellectual journal in the early 1960s, in relation to his work on *The Birth of the Clinic* and on *Death and the Labyrinth* (BnF, Fonds Michel Foucault, Boxes 91 and 92, call number NAF 28730).

31. Michel Foucault, *L'origine de l'herméneutique de soi: Conférences prononcées à Dartmouth College, 1980*, ed. Henri-Paul Fruchaud and Daniele Lorenzini, introduction and critical apparatus by Laura Cremonesi, Arnold I. Davidson, Orazio Irrera, Daniele Lorenzini, and Martina Tazzioli (Paris: Vrin, 2013); English translation by Graham Burchell, *About the Beginning of the Hermeneutics of the Self: Lectures at Dartmouth College, 1980* (Chicago, University of Chicago Press, 2016); Foucault, *Qu'est-ce que la critique?*, with *La culture de soi*, ed. H.-P. Fruchaud and D. Lorenzini, introduction and critical apparatus by D. Lorenzini and Arnold I. Davidson (Paris: Vrin, 2015); Foucault, *Discours et vérité*, with *La parrêsia*, introduction and critical apparatus by H.-P. Fruchaud and D. Lorenzini; introduction by Frédéric Gros (Paris: Vrin, 2016); Foucault, *Dire vrai sur soi-même*, conferences at the University of Victoria in Toronto, 1982, ed., introduction and critical apparatus by H.-P. Fruchaud and D. Lorenzini (Paris: Vrin, 2017); Foucault, *Folie, langage, littérature*, ed. H.-P. Fruchaud, D. Lorenzini, and Judith Revel, introduction by Judith Revel (Paris: Vrin, 2019). Among the publications of Foucault's lectures and seminars, we might also highlight the volume containing Foucault's lecture series at the University of Louvain in 1981: *Mal faire, dire vrai: Fonction de l'aveu en justice*, ed. Fabienne Brion and Bernard E. Harcourt (Louvain: Presses universitaires de Louvain, 2012). For a further account of these new publications, see Jean-François Bert and Jérôme Lamy, "Michel Foucault 'inédit,'" *Cahiers d'histoire: Revue d'histoire critique*, no. 140 (2018): 149–164; and Stuart Elden, "Afterword: Afterlives," in *The Lives of Michel Foucault: A Biography*, by David Macey (London: Verso, 2019), pp. 481–491.

32. For the publication history of Foucault's courses at the Collège de France, see Christian Del Vento and Jean-Louis Fournel, "L'édition des cours et les 'pistes' de Michel Foucault," *Laboratoire italien*, no. 7 (2007), http://journals.openedition.org.inshs.bib.cnrs.fr/laboratoire italien/144. See also Daniel Defert, "'Je crois au temps. . . .': Daniel Defert légataire des manuscrits de Michel Foucault," interview with Guillaume Bellon, *Recto/Verso*, no 1 (2007): 1–7.

33. Michel Foucault, *Les aveux de la chair*, ed. Frédéric Gros (Paris: Gallimard, 2018); English translation by Robert Hurley, *Confessions of the Flesh* (London: Penguin Random House, 2021).

34. Michel Foucault, *La question anthropologique. Cours. 1954–1955*, ed. Arianna Sforzini, Cours et travaux de Michel Foucault avant le Collège de France, ed. François Ewald (Hautes Études) (Paris: Seuil/Gallimard/EHESS, 2022).

35. Michel Foucault, *Binswanger et l'analyse existentielle*, ed. Elisabetta Basso, Cours et travaux de Michel Foucault avant le Collège de France, ed. François Ewald (Hautes Études) (Paris: Seuil/Gallimard/EHESS, 2021).

36. Michel Foucault, *Phénoménologie et psychologie, 1953-1954*, ed. Philippe Sabot, Cours et travaux de Michel Foucault avant le Collège de France, ed. François Ewald (Hautes Études) (Paris: Seuil/Gallimard/EHESS, 2021).

37. Michel Foucault, *La sexualité: cours donné à l'Université de Clermont-Ferrand, 1964; suivi de Le discours de la sexualité: cours donné à l'Université de Vincennes, 1969*, ed. Claude-Olivier Doron, Cours et travaux de Michel Foucault avant le Collège de France, ed. François Ewald (Hautes Études) (Paris: Seuil/Gallimard/EHESS, 2018); English translation by Graham Burchell, *Sexuality: The 1964 Clermont-Ferrand and 1969 Vincennes Lectures*, foreword by Bernard E. Harcourt, Foucault's Early Lectures and Manuscripts (New York: Columbia University Press, 2021).

38. On this project, see the special issue "Foucault Before the Collège de France," *Theory, Culture and Society*, ed. Stuart Elden, Orazio Irrera, and Daniele Lorenzini (forthcoming).

39. On this subject, see the presentation of Foucault's reading notes of the period 1946–1953 that Gautier Dassonneville published on the public platform FFL-Eman: "Foucault auditeur: Les études de philosophie

et de psychologie à Paris, 1946–1953," http://eman-archives.org/Foucault-fiches/exhibits/show/foucault-auditeur-les-ann—es-.

40. BnF, Fonds Michel Foucault, Box 1, folder 1, call number NAF 28803.

41. Michel Foucault, "Considérations sur le marxisme, la phénoménologie et le pouvoir: Entretien avec Colin Gordon et Paul Patton," ed. Alain Beaulieu, *Cités* 52, no. 4 (2012): 101–126; Foucault, "Une histoire de la manière dont les choses font problème: Entretien de Michel Foucault avec André Berten (7 mai 1981)," *Culture et Conflits*, nos. 94, 95, 96 (2014): 99–109; "Pratiques de soi," in *La question morale: Une anthropologie critique*, ed. Didier Fassin and Samuel Lézé (Paris: PUF, 2014), pp. 65–73; "Introduction à *L'Archéologie du savoir*," ed. and introduction by Martin Rueff, *Les Études philosophiques* 153, no. 3 (2015): 327–352; "La littérature et la folie: Une conférence inédite de Michel Foucault," *Critique* 12, no. 835 (2016): 965–981; "La magie—le fait social total," ed. Jean-François Bert, *Zilsel* 2, no. 2 (2017): 305–326; "Un manuscrit de Michel Foucault sur la psychanalyse," ed. Elisabetta Basso, *Astérion*, no. 21 (2019), https://journals.openedition.org/asterion/4410. See also various previously unpublished texts that appeared in Philippe Artières, Jean-François Bert, Frédéric Gros, and Judith Revel, eds., *Michel Foucault*, Cahiers de l'Herne 95 (Paris: L'Herne, 2011).

42. See on this subject Philippe Artières, Jean-François Bert, Judith Revel, Mathieu Potte-Bonneville, and Pascal Michon, "Dans l'atelier Foucault," in *Les Lieux de savoir II: Les mains de l'intellect*, ed. Christian Jacob (Paris: Albin Michel, 2011), pp. 944–962.

43. This project was selected by the ANR within the rubric "Société de l'information et de la communication (DS07) 2017, CE38: La Révolution numérique: rapports aux savoirs et à la culture" (https://anr.fr/Project-ANR-17-CE38-0001).

44. http://eman-archives.org/Foucault-fiches. This is a publicly accessible website that allows anyone to consult the digitized reading notes and to carry out keyword searches (title keyword, author name, word associated with a bibliographic reference). For a general overview of the Foucault project, see Elisabetta Basso, Arianna Sforzini, Vincent Ventresque, and Carolina Verlengia, "Présentation du Fonds: présentation scientifique," http://eman-archives.org/Foucault-fiches/prsentation-du-fonds.

45. See Laurence Le Bras, "Les fiches de lecture de Michel Foucault," *Le Blog Gallica*, https://gallica.bnf.fr/blog/18112020/les-fiches-de-lecture-de-michel-foucault?mode=desktop.
46. For a general overview of the project, see Marie-Laure Massot, Arianna Sforzini, and Vincent Ventresque, "Transcribing Foucault's Handwriting with Transkribus," *Journal of Data Mining and Digital Humanities*, Episciences.org https://jdmdh.episciences.org/5218; Arianna Sforzini, "Michel Foucault numérique: Les archives à l'épreuve des nouvelles archéologies du savoir," *Implications philosophiques*, July 16, 2021, https://www.implications-philosophiques.org/michel-foucault-numerique/. See also the project presentation page: "Foucault Fiches de Lecture / Foucault Reading Notes" (FFL): https://ffl.hypotheses.org/presentation-du-projet.

1. ARCHIVES AND INTELLECTUAL NETWORKS

1. Michel Foucault, *Folie et déraison: Histoire de la folie à l'âge classique*, Civilisations d'hier et d'aujourd'hui (Paris: Plon, 1961).
2. These notes can be consulted in Gérard Simon's archives, which are conserved in the Centre d'archives de philosophie, d'histoire et d'édition des sciences (Caphés), at ENS, Paris (call number GS. 4.9).
3. For a detailed chronology of Foucault's formative years, see Daniel Defert, "Chronologie (1926–1967)," in *Œuvres*, vol. 1, by Michel Foucault, ed. F. Gros, Bibliothèque de la Pléiade (Paris: Gallimard, 2015).
4. André Ombredane had studied at the École normale supérieure, earned his *agrégation* in philosophy, and become a medical doctor. Between the wars he was Georges Dumas's (1866–1946) assistant as chair of experimental psychology at the Sorbonne and associate director of Henri Wallon's (1879–1962) laboratory in child psychology. In 1947, he also became the director of the Centre d'études et de recherches psychotechniques, which had just been created by the Ministry of Labor. In 1948, he was named professor of psychology at the Free University of Brussels. In his reading notes of the 1950s, Foucault mentions the doctoral dissertation that Ombredane defended in 1947 at the Sorbonne, *L'Aphasie et l'élaboration de la pensée explicite* (Aphasia and the Development of Explicit Thought), Bibliothèque de philosophie contemporaine (Paris: PUF, 1951) (BnF, Box 38, folder 2, call

number NAF 28730). Ombredane's research on speech disorders also appears in a series of notes by Foucault gathered in a folder titled "Intelligence et neurologie" (Intelligence and Neurology), and in particular in a reading note concerning the pathology of perception—"Pathologie de la perception"—in which Foucault mentions the first volume of the *Études de psychologie médicale*, published by Ombredane in 1944: *Perception et langage* (Rio de Janeiro: Atlantica Editora, 1944) (BnF, Box 44b, folder 1, call number NAF 28730).

5. Georges Verdeaux was a neuropsychiatrist trained in electroencephalography, while his wife Jacqueline, who had begun and then abandoned medical studies, worked with him as an assistant. See Bernard Gueguen, "Hommage à Georges Verdeaux," *Neurophysiologie clinique* 34, no. 6 (2004): 301–302; and Bruno Verdeaux, "'Nous étions un peu plus qu'un et un peu moins que deux': Jacqueline et Georges Verdeaux," in *Foucault à Münsterlingen: À l'origine de l'Histoire de la folie*, with photographs by Jacqueline Verdeaux, ed. Jean-François Bert and Elisabetta Basso, L'histoire et ses représentations 10 (Paris: Éditions de l'EHESS, 2015), pp. 270–272.

6. This document is currently in the Roland Kuhn archives (Archives d'État du Canton de Thurgovie, Frauenfeld, call number 9'40); Kuhn must have received it directly from Georges Verdeaux.

7. Cf. David Macey, *The Lives of Michel Foucault: A Biography* (London: Verso, 2019), pp. 58–59.

8. See on this topic excerpts of Foucault's correspondence with Jean-Paul Aron (1925–1988), reproduced in "Archives: Vivre et enseigner à Lille," in Bert and Basso, *Foucault à Münsterlingen*, pp. 121–123.

9. BnF, Fonds Michel Foucault, Box 5, folder 1, call number NAF 28803.

10. In Box 44b of Foucault's archives there is a long reading note titled "Perception and information," in which Foucault dwells especially on Walter Pitts and Warren S. McCulloch, "How We Know Universals: The Perception of Auditory and Visual Forms," *Bulletin of Mathematical Biophysics* 9 (1947): 127–147.

11. See on this subject the letter that Ombredane wrote to Jean Hyppolite (1907–1968), who was then the director of ENS, on February 22, 1955 (BnF, Fonds Michel Foucault, Box 5, folder 1, call number NAF 28803).

12. BnF, Fonds Michel Foucault, Box 5, folder 1, call number NAF 28803.

13. Foucault, "La recherche scientifique et la psychologie" (1957), in *Dits et écrits*, ed. Daniel Defert and François Ewald, with Jacques Lagrange,

1. ARCHIVES AND INTELLECTUAL NETWORKS ∾ 221

Bibliothèque des sciences humaines (Paris: Gallimard, 1994), vol. 1, no. 3, p. 147.
14. Jean Piaget, *Sagesse et illusions de la philosophie* (Paris: PUF, 1965); English translation by Wolfe Mays, *Insights and Illusions of Philosophy* (New York: World, 1971), pp. 25–27.
15. Georges Canguilhem, "Qu'est-ce que la psychologie?," *Revue de métaphysique et de morale* 63, no. 1 (1958): 12–25; reprinted in *Études d'histoire et philosophie des sciences, Problèmes et controverses* (1968), 7th ed. (Paris: Vrin, 1997), pp. 365–381; English translation by David M. Peña-Guzmán, "What Is Psychology?," *Foucault Studies*, no. 21 (2016): 200–213.
16. Georges Canguilhem, "Naissance de la psychologie scientifique" (1960–1961), lecture, Caphés, Fonds Georges Canguilhem; quoted by Jean-François Braunstein, "Foucault, Canguilhem et l'histoire des sciences humaines," *Archives de philosophie* 79, no. 1 (2016): 13–26, p. 17.
17. These lectures were published in the *Bulletin de psychologie* between 1949 and 1952, and by the Centre de documentation universitaire. See also Maurice Merleau-Ponty, *Merleau-Ponty à la Sorbonne: Résumé de cours, 1949–1952* (Grenoble: Cynara, 1988).
18. Maurice Merleau-Ponty, *Les Sciences de l'homme et la phénoménologie* (Paris: Tournier et Constans, 1953), p. 3. See also introduction and part 1, "Le Problème des sciences de l'homme selon Husserl."
19. Merleau-Ponty, *Phénoménologie de la perception*, Bibliothèque des idées (1945; Paris: Gallimard, 1976), p. 87; English translation by Colin Smith, *Phenomenology of Perception* (London: Routledge and Kegan Paul, 1962), p. 60.
20. BnF, Fonds Michel Foucault, Box 33a, folder 0 (call number: NAF 28730). We also find, in the same box, notes on Merleau-Ponty's seminar "L'enfant et autrui."
21. BnF, Fonds Michel Foucault, Box 46, folder 4. Under the same call number, in Box 33a, folder 0, there are notes for a lecture by Foucault called "Husserl et Merleau-Ponty (Psychologie et phénoménologie)," which seem to correspond to the manuscript fragment conserved in Box 46. These notes bear the date November 23, 1951, but it is impossible to identify the notetaker.
22. Letter from M. Foucault to J.-P. Aron dated November 17 [s.d.]. Cf. P. Sabot, "Archives. Vivre et enseigner à Lille," in Bert and Basso, *Foucault à Münsterlingen*, p. 122.

23. Fonds Michel Foucault, call number NAF 28803, Box 3, folder 7.
24. BnF, Fonds Michel Foucault, Box 33a, folder 0 (call number NAF 28730).
25. D. Eribon, *Michel Foucault: 1926–1984* (Paris: Flammarion, 1989), 3rd published in 2011 (Champs: biographie 847); English translation by Betsy Wing, *Michel Foucault* (Cambridge: MA, Harvard University Press, 1991), p. 40.
26. Eribon, *Michel Foucault et ses contemporains* (Paris: Fayard, 1994), p. 106.
27. Eribon, p. 106.
28. See P. Sabot, "Vivre et enseigner à Lille," in Bert and Basso, *Foucault à Münsterlingen*, p. 121.
29. BnF, Fonds Michel Foucault, Box 46, folder 4 (call number NAF 28730). One of these manuscripts was recently published in the special issue of the journal *Astérion*, no. 21 (2019), on the subject of "Foucault à l'épreuve de la psychiatrie et de la psychanalyse," ed. Laurent Dartigues and E. Basso: "Un manuscrit de Michel Foucault sur la psychanalyse," https://journals.openedition.org/asterion/4410
30. For the reading notes on Freud, see especially BnF, Fonds Michel Foucault, Box 39 (call number NAF 28730); for those on Husserl, see Box 42a, folder 3 (call number NAF 28730).
31. BnF, Fonds Michel Foucault, Box 3, folder 6 (call number NAF 28803).
32. BnF, Fonds Michel Foucault, Box 5, folder 3 (call number NAF 28803). The letter from the journal's editorial board is dated February 1, 1952 and signed by Louis-Marie Morfaux.
33. BnF, Fonds Michel Foucault, Box 3, folder 6 (call number NAF 28803). Foucault would confirm this position in an interview with Colin Gordon and Paul Patton in April 1978, where he observed—looking back on his formative years—that "France only knew Husserl via an angle which I am not sure was, or represented, the main line of phenomenology. Because in particular, the whole fundamental problem of phenomenology was ultimately a problem of logic: how to found logic. We were not so familiar with all that in France, we knew instead a Husserl who inscribed himself here, it seems to me, if not ingratiatingly, at least with a degree of dexterity, in the Cartesian tradition. In any case, that was the phenomenology that we were taught." ("Considérations sur le marxisme, la phénoménologie et le pouvoir: Entretien avec Colin Gordon et Paul Patton," ed. Alain Beaulieu,

1. ARCHIVES AND INTELLECTUAL NETWORKS ∞ 223

Cités 52, no. 4 (2012): 101–126, p. 108; English version "Considerations on Marxism, Phenomenology and Power: Interview with Michel Foucault," *Foucault Studies*, no. 14 (September 2012): 98–114, p. 101.
34. BnF, Fonds Michel Foucault, Box 3, folder 6 (call number NAF 28803).
35. BnF, Fonds Michel Foucault, Box 5, folder 1, call number NAF 28803.
36. Eribon, *Michel Foucault et ses contemporains*, p. 112.
37. Letter from J. Verdeaux to L. Binswanger of August 14, 1954 (Binswanger Archive, Archives of the University of Tübingen, call number 443/60).
38. *La voix de l'ennemi*

> Petite étude du délire de persécution, des délires dialogués, des hallucinations.
> Ex. de délire de persécution
> Rousseau
> La fin des temps
> Mystiques et fous du langage.
> BnF, Fonds Michel Foucault, Box 91, notebook no. 2 (mars 1961-août 1962) (call number NAF 28730).

39. See in particular the reading notes held in Box 44 of the Fonds Michel Foucault, as well as the folders available under call number NAF 28803.
40. BnF, Fonds Michel Foucault, Box 37, folder 2 (call number NAF 28730).
41. BnF, Fonds Michel Foucault, Boxes 37, 38 et 44 (call number NAF 28730).
42. M. Heidegger, "Der Spruch des Anaximander," in *Holzwege* (Frankfurt: Klostermann, 1950), pp. 296–343.
43. Heidegger, "Lettre sur l'humanisme" (1947), French translation by Roger Munier, *Cahiers du Sud*, no. 319 (1953): 385–406; and no. 320 (1953): 68–88; reprinted in *Lettre sur l'humanisme* (Paris: Éditions Montaigne, 1957).
44. Heidegger, *Kant und das Problem der Metaphysik* (1929; Frankfurt: Klostermann, 1951); introduction and French translation by Alphonse De Waelhens and Walter Biemel, *Kant et le problème de la métaphysique*, Bibliothèque de philosophie (Paris: Gallimard, 1953). See Foucault's reading notes held in Box 33a, folder 0 at the BnF (Fonds Michel Foucault, call number NAF 28730).

45. M. Foucault, "Le retour de la morale" (1984), in *Dits et Écrits*, ed. Daniel Defert and François Ewald, with Jacques Lagrange, Bibliothèque des sciences humaines (Paris: Gallimard, 1994), vol. 4, no. 354, pp. 698–708, here p. 703; English translation by John Johnston, "The Return of Morality," in *Foucault Live: Interviews 1961–1984* (New York: Semiotext[e], 1996), pp. 465–473. See also Maurice Pinguet's account, "Les années d'apprentissage," *Le Débat* 41, no. 4 (1986): 122–131.
46. See Eribon, *Michel Foucault et ses contemporains*, p. 319.
47. The folder concerning Jaspers can be found at the BnF, Fonds Michel Foucault, Box 42b, folder 1 (call number NAF 28730); as for Nietzsche, see Box 33a, folder 1 and Box 33b, folder 3 (call number NAF 28730).
48. K. Jaspers, *Nietzsche: Einführung in das Verstädnis seines Philosophierens* (Berlin: de Gruyter, 1936); French translation by Henri Niel, *Nietzsche: Introduction à sa philosophie*, letter-preface by Jean Wahl (Paris: Gallimard, 1950).
49. J. Vuillemin, "Nietzsche aujourd'hui," *Les Temps modernes* 6, no. 67 (1951): 1921–1954. Soon afterward also appeared a French translation of Jaspers's book from 1922, *Strindberg et Van Gogh, Swedenborg, Hölderlin: Étude psychiatrique comparative*, trans. Hélène Naef, preceded by a study by Maurice Blanchot (Paris: Minuit, 1953).
50. Cf. the notes made by Gérard Simon and conserved at the Caphés (call number GS. 4.9).
51. In a letter to Foucault dated February 25, 1953, Jean Lacroix describes his collection in the following terms: "Even a very elementary presentation is possible—in any case the most *accessible* possible." So much so that, once Foucault had sent him a first version of the text, Lacroix would offer, on October 1 of that year, "a few somewhat external remarks": "Would it be possible for you (especially in the first chapter) to avoid or explain terms that, we must acknowledge, will be completely unknown to students? Or maybe . . . a small glossary at the end, defining some common terms and offering at least dates and principal works for some of the key figures?" (BnF, Fonds Michel Foucault, Box 5, folder 1, call number NAF 28803; underlined in the original).
52. See Luca Paltrinieri, "De quelques sources de *Maladie mentale et personnalité*: Réflexologie pavlovienne et critique sociale," in Bert and Basso, *Foucault à Münsterlingen*, pp. 197–219.

I. ARCHIVES AND INTELLECTUAL NETWORKS 225

53. Michel Foucault, *Maladie mentale et personnalité*, Initiation philosophique 12 (Paris: PUF, 1954), p. 92.
54. BnF, Fonds Michel Foucault, Box 5, folder 1, call number NAF 28803.
55. Foucault, *Maladie mentale et personnalité*, p. 109n1. See the special issue edited by Albert Béguin, *Misère de la psychiatrie*, *Esprit* 197, no. 12 (1952).
56. See on this topic Jean-Christophe Coffin, "'Misery' and 'Revolution': The Organization of French Psychiatry, 1900–1980," in *Psychiatric Cultures Compared: Psychiatry and Mental Health Care in the Twentieth Century: Comparisons and Approaches*, ed. Marijke Gijswijt-Hofstra et al. (Amsterdam: Amsterdam University Press, 2006), pp. 225–247.
57. M. Foucault, "L'agressivité, l'angoisse et la magie," BnF, Fonds Michel Foucault, Box 46, folder 4, (call number NAF 28730).
58. Foucault, note 12.
59. G. Politzer, *Critique des fondements de la psychologie: La psychologie et la psychanalyse*, La collection de l'esprit 4 (Paris: Rieder, 1928); English translation by Maurice Apprey, *Critique of the Foundations of Psychology: The Psychology of Psychoanalysis* (Pittsburg, PA: Duquesne University Press, 1994).
60. Emmanuel Mounier, *Traité du caractère*, Collection Esprit (Paris: Les Éditions du Seuil, 1946) (new ed., Collection Esprit. La Condition humaine, 1955), pp. 44–45. On Georges Politzer's philosophical reception in France, see Giuseppe Bianco, ed., *Georges Politzer, le concret et sa signification: Psychologie, philosophie et politique*, Hermann philosophie (Paris: Hermann, 2016).
61. Jacques Lacan, *De la psychose paranoïaque dans ses rapports avec la personnalité*, Le Champ freudien (Paris: Le François, 1932; Éditions du Seuil, 1975), pp. 346–349.
62. Lacan, p. 347. Cf. also Jacques Lacan, "Au-delà du 'Principe de réalité,'" (1936), §1, "Critique de l'associationnisme," in *Écrits* (Paris: Éditions du Seuil, 1966, 1999), vol. 1; English translation by Bruce Fink, in collaboration with Heloïse Fink and Russel Grigg, "Beyond the 'Reality Principle,'" *Écrits: The First Complete Edition in English* (New York: Norton, 2006), pp. 58–74.
63. Lacan, *De la psychose paranoïaque*, p. 267.
64. Cf. Daniel Lagache, "Le normal et le pathologique d'après Georges Canguilhem," *Revue de Métaphysique et de Morale* 51, no. 4 (1946): 355–370, p. 355.

65. Lacan, *De la psychose paranoïaque*, p. 15.
66. Henning Schmidgen, "'Fortunes diverses': L'œuvre de jeunesse de Jacques Lacan et la phénoménologie," *Psychanalyse à l'université* 19, no. 76 (1994): 111–134. The project of founding psychology on the basis of a "science of the person" was central in particular to Binswanger's book *Einführung in die Probleme der allgemeine Psychologie* (Berlin: Springer, 1922).
67. Foucault, *Maladie mentale et personnalité*, p. 10.
68. Foucault, p. 11.
69. Foucault, p. 10.
70. Foucault, pp. 11–12.
71. Canguilhem, *Essai sur quelques problèmes concernant le normal et le pathologique* (1943; Paris: Les Belles Lettres, 1950).
72. BnF, Fonds Michel Foucault, Box 38, folder 1, and Box 42b, folder 1 (call number NAF 28730). See also Box 33a (folder 0). See the list of reading notes appended to this chapter.
73. Paul Häberlin, *Briefwechsel: 1908–1960*, ed. Jeannine Luczak (Basel: Schwabe, 1997).
74. Berlin: Springer, 1921.
75. Zurich, Schweizer Spiegel (BnF, Box 33a, folder 0).
76. *Schweizer Archiv für Neurologie und Psychiatrie* 60, nos. 1–2: 132–144.
77. Basel: Kober.
78. See BnF, Box 46, folder 1.
79. Basel, Verlag für Recht und Gesellschaft.
80. *Zeitschrift für die gesamte Neurologie und Psychiatrie* 172: 145–180.
81. *Studia Philosophica* 4, no. 147: 147–169.
82. *Zentralblatt für Psychotherapie und ihre Grenzgebiete* 4: 280–302.
83. *Der Nervenarzt* 2, no. 1: 8–20.
84. *Der Nervenarzt* 8, no. 7: 337–346; no. 8: 398–408.
85. *Monatsschrift für Psychiatrie und Neurologie* 99: 10–74.
86. *Der Nervenarzt* 10, no. 4 (1937): 169–178; 10, no. 5 (1937): 248–257.
87. In *Gegenwartsprobleme der psychiatrisch-neurologischen Forschung: Vorträge auf dem Internationalen Fortbildungskurs*, ed. Christel Heinrich Roggenbau (Stuttgart: Enke), pp. 54–71.
88. Berlin: Springer.
89. *Zeitschrift für die gesamte Neurologie und Psychiatrie* 127, no. 1: 799–810.

1. ARCHIVES AND INTELLECTUAL NETWORKS ☙ 227

90. *Schweizer Archiv für Neurologie und Psychiatrie* 59, no. 1: 330–385.
91. *Archiv für Psychiatrie und Neurologie* 181: 275–293.
92. *Schweizer Archiv für Neurologie und Psychiatrie* 44: 102–118.
93. *Der Nervenartz* 21, no. 3: 102–108.
94. *Der Nervenarzt* 23: 421–423.
95. *Vom Sinn der Sinne: Ein Beitrag zur Grundlegung der Psychologie*, 2nd ed. (Berlin: Springer, 1956 [1935]).
96. *Monatsschrift für Psychiatrie und Neurologie* 68: 126–140.
97. *Der Nervenarzt* 3, no. 11: 633–656.
98. *Geschehnis und Erlebnis: Zugleich eine historiologische Deutung des psychischen Traumas und Renten-Neurose* (Berlin: Springer, 1930).
99. *Monatsschrift für Psychiatrie und Neurologie* 117, nos. 4–6: 367–379.
100. *Monatsschrift für Psychiatrie und Neurologie* 98, no. 2 (1938): 61–81.
101. Karl Jaspers, *Allgemeine Psychopathologie: Für Studierende, Ärzte und Psychologen*, 3rd ed. (1913; Berlin-Heidelberg: Springer, 1923); French translation by Alfred Kastler and Jean Mendousse, *Psychopathologie générale* (Paris: Félix Alcan, 1933).
102. BnF, Fonds Michel Foucault, Box 42B, folder 1, call number NAF 28730.
103. Cf. Jacques Lacan, "Le problème du style et la conception psychiatrique des formes paranoïaques de l'expérience," in *De la psychose paranoïaque dans ses rapports avec la personnalité*, Le Champ freudien (Paris: Le François, 1932; Seuil 1975), p. 385; English translation by Jon Anderson, "The Problem of Style and the Psychiatric Conception of Paranoiac Forms of Experience," *Critical Texts* 5, no. 3 (1988): "The phenomenologically inspired work on these mental states (for example the most recent work of a Ludwig Binswanger on the state called 'flight of ideas' that one observes in manic-depressive psychosis, or my own work on *Paranoiac Psychosis in Relation to Personality*) does not detach the local reaction, which is most often noticeable only through some pragmatic discordance, specifiable as mental disorder, from the totality of the patient's lived experience, which such work tries to define in its originality. This experience . . . can be validly described as the coherent structure of an immediate noumenal apprehension of oneself and of the world" (translation modified). Lacan also refers to "Binswanger's great study on *Ideenflucht*" in 1935 in his review

of Minkowski's *Le temps vécu*, in *Recherches Philosophiques*, no. 5 (1935–1936): 424–431, p. 428.

104. Eugène Minkowski, "À la recherche de la norme en psychopathologie," *L'Évolution Psychiatrique* 9, no. 1 (1938): 67–91, p. 89.
105. Georges Politzer, "Où va la psychologie concrète?," *Revue de Psychologie Concrète*, no. 2 (1929): 199; *Écrits*, 2:137–188.
106. M. Foucault, "Dream, Imagination and Existence: An Introduction to Ludwig Binswanger's 'Dream and Existence,'" in *Dream and Existence*, by Michel Foucault and Ludwig Binswanger, special issue of *Review of Existential Psychology and Psychiatry*, ed. Keith Hoeller, vol. 19, no. 1 (1985): 29–78, p. 31.
107. A. Hesnard, *L'Univers morbide de la faute*, Bibliothèque de psychanalyse et de psychologie Clinique (Paris: PUF, 1949), p. 461.
108. BnF, Fonds Michel Foucault, Box 42a, folder 3 (call number NAF 28730); see also Box 33a, folder 0 (call number NAF 28730).
109. M. Foucault, "Préface à l'*Histoire de la sexualité*" (1984), in *Dits et Écrits*, vol. 4, no. 340, pp. 578–585 (p. 579); English translation by William Smock, "Preface to the *History of Sexuality*, volume II," in *The Essential Works of Foucault, 1954–1984*, vol. 1, *Ethics, Subjectivity and Truth*, ed. Paul Robinow (New York: New Press, 1997), pp. 199–205 (p. 200).
110. Foucault, "Archéologie d'une passion" (1983), in *Dits et Écrits*, vol. 4, no. 343, pp. 601–610, p. 608; English translation by Charles Ruas, "An Interview with Michel Foucault," in *Death and the Labyrinth: The World of Raymond Roussel*, by M. Foucault (New York: Continuum, 1986), p. 177.
111. Foucault, "An Interview with Michel Foucault," p. 176.
112. Foucault, *Maladie mentale et personnalité*, p. 111.
113. L. Binswanger, "Über Ideenflucht," *Schweizer Archiv für Neurologie und Psychiatrie* 27, no. 2 (1932): 203–217; 28, nos. 1–2 (1932): 18–26, 183–202; 29, no. 1 (1932): 193ff.; 30, no. 1 (1933): 68–85; published in one volume in Zürich by Orel Füssli in 1933 (reprinted in New York by Garland in 1980); *Ausgewählte Werke*, vol. 1, *Formen mißglückten Daseins*, ed. Max Herzog (Heidelberg: Asanger, 1992).
114. Binswanger, *Ausgewählte Vorträge und Aufsätze*, vol. 1, *Zur phänomenologischen Anthropologie* (Bern: Francke, 1947); vol. 2, *Zur Problematik*

der psychiatrischen Forschung und zum Problem der Psychiatrie (Bern: Francke, 1955).
115. Pfullingen: Neske, 1957.
116. Zürich: Niehans.
117. Binswanger, *Henrik Ibsen und das Problem der Selbstrealisation in der Kunst* (Heidelberg: L. Schneider, 1949).
118. H. C. Rümke, "Signification de la phénoménologie dans l'étude clinique des délirants," in *Congrès international de psychiatrie. Paris, 1950*, vol. 1, *Psychopathologie générale: Psychopathologie des délires* (Paris: Hermann, 1950), pp. 126–173, p. 131.
119. Paul Guiraud, "Pathogénie et étiologie des délires," in *Psychiatrie générale* (Paris: Librairie Le François, 1950), pp. 576–581.
120. Henri Ellenberger, "Analyse existentielle," in *Encyclopédie médico-chirurgicale: Traité de psychiatrie*, ed. Henri Ey (Paris: Éditions techniques, 1955), p. 1.
121. A. Hesnard and R. Laforgue, "Avant-propos," *L'Évolution psychiatrique* 1 (1925): 7–9, p. 8.
122. Hesnard and Laforgue, p. 7.
123. E. Minkowski, "La genèse de la notion de schizophrénie et ses caractères essentiels: Une page d'histoire contemporaine de la psychiatrie," *L'Évolution psychiatrique* 1 (1925): 193–236.
124. L. Binswanger, "La conception de l'homme, chez Freud, à la lumière de l'anthropologie philosophique" (1936), French translation by Hans Pollnow, *L'Évolution psychiatrique* 10, no. 1 (1938): 3–34.
125. During his studies in medicine and philosophy in Munich and Heidelberg, Pollnow attended the courses of Karl Jaspers, whose work he also translated in the 1930s. In 1938, he translated Karl Jaspers's book *Descartes et la philosophie* (Paris: Alcan, 1938). Deported by the Nazis in 1943, he died in the Mauthausen concentration camp.
126. E. Minkowski, "Étude psychologique et analyse phénoménologique d'un cas de mélancolie schizophrénique," *Journal de Psychologie Normale et Pathologique* 20 (1923): 543–558, p. 543.
127. L. Binswanger, "Über Phänomenologie," *Zeitschrift für die gesamte Neurologie und Psychiatrie* 82 (1923): 10–45.
128. Cf. E. Minkowski, "Les notions bleulériennes: voie d'accès aux analyses phénoménologiques et existentielles," *Annales Médico-Psychologiques*

15, no. 2 (1957): 833–844 (reprinted in *Au de-là du rationalisme morbide* [Paris: L'Harmattan, 1997], pp. 141–151 [p. 141]).
129. L. Binswanger, review of Eugène Minkowski, *La Schizophrénie: Psychopathologie des schizoïdes et des schizophrènes* (Paris, 1927), *Schweizer Archiv für Neurologie und Psychiatrie* 22 (1928): 158–163.
130. E. Minkowski, *La Schizophrénie: Psychopathologie des schizoïdes et des schizophrènes*, new ed. (Paris: Desclée de Brouwer, 1953), p. 237.
131. See on this topic Peter Widmer, "Lacan in der Schweiz," in *Lacan und das Deutsche: Die Rückkehr der Psychoanalyse über den Rhein*, ed. Jutta Prasse and Claus-Dieter Rath (Freiburg: Kore, 1994), pp. 242–258.
132. Letter from H. Maldiney to R. Kuhn dated June 26, 1953, in H. Maldiney and R. Kuhn, *Rencontre / Begegnung: Au péril d'exister, Briefwechsel / Correspondance, Français / Deutsch, 1953–2004*, ed. Liselotte Rutishauser and Robert Christe (Würzburg: Königshausen und Neumann, 2017), p. 26.
133. J.-P. Sartre, *L'Être et le néant: Essai d'ontologie phénoménologique*, Bibliothèque des idées (Paris: Gallimard, 1943); English translation by Hazel E. Barnes, *Being and Nothingness* (New York: Philosophical Library, 1956), pt. 4, chap. 2, §1, "Existential Psychoanalysis."
134. On Sartre's reception of existential analysis, see Alain Flajoliet, "Sartre's Phenomenological Anthropology Between Psychoanalysis and 'Daseinsanalysis,'" *Sartre Studies International* 16, no. 1 (2010): 40–59.
135. Merleau-Ponty, *Phenomenology of Perception*, pt. 1, chap. 5, "The Body in its Sexual Being." Merleau-Ponty refers to the following works by Binswanger: "Über Psychotherapie" (1935); "Traum und Existenz" (1930); "Über Ideenflucht" (1932–1933); "Das Raumprobleme in der Psychopathologie" (1933).
136. Letter dated December 9, 1950 (quoted by Max Herzog, *Weltenwürfe: Ludwig Binswangers phänomenologische Psychologie* [Berlin: De Gruyter, 1994], pp. 116–117). In general, on the French reception of phenomenology within the domain of psychopathology, see Herbert Spiegelberg, *Phenomenology in Psychology and Psychiatry: A Historical Introduction*, Northwestern University Studies in Phenomenology and Existential Philosophy (Evanston IL: Northwestern University

1. ARCHIVES AND INTELLECTUAL NETWORKS ᙏ 231

Press, 1972); and Bernard Waldenfels, *Phänomenologie in Frankreich* (Frankfurt: Suhrkamp, 1983).
137. See the letter from L. Binswanger to G. Bachelard dated October 5, 1950 ("Correspondance Gaston Bachelard-Ludwig Binswanger, 1948–1955," trans. and ed. Elisabetta Basso and Emmanuel Delille, *Revue germanique internationale*, no. 30 (2019): 183–208, 195.
138. Cf. the session summaries in *Premier Congrès mondial de psychiatrie, Paris, 1950*, vol. 1, *Psychopathologie générale*, published by Henri Ey, P. Marty, and Jean-Joseph Dublineau, Actualités scientifiques et industrielles (Paris: Hermann, 1952), pp. 381–384.
139. L. Binswanger, "La *Daseinsanalyse* en psychiatrie," French translation by Michel Gourevitch, *L'Encéphale* 40, no. 1 (1951): 108–113. Jacqueline Verdeaux collaborated with Binswanger on revising this paper in French.
140. Binswanger, pp. 108–109.
141. Merleau-Ponty, *Phenomenology of Perception*, "Preface," p. vii.
142. L. Binswanger, *Le rêve et l'existence*, French translation by Jacqueline Verdeaux, introduction and notes by Michel Foucault, Textes et études anthropologiques (Paris: Desclée de Brouwer, 1954), footnote, p. 131.
143. Letter dated "Thursday." Authorized by Foucault's family.
144. M. Foucault, *Phénoménologie et psychologie, 1953–1954*, ed. Philippe Sabot, Cours et travaux de Michel Foucault avant le Collège de France, ed. François Ewald (Hautes Études), (Paris: Seuil/Gallimard/EHESS, 2021), p. 207. See on this topic Ph. Sabot, "The 'World' of Michel Foucault: Phenomenology, Psychology, Ontology in the 1950s," in *Theory, Culture, and Society* (forthcoming).
145. See Georges Gusdorf, "Georges Daumézon, l'homme," in *Regard, accueil et présence: Mélanges en l'honneur de Georges Daumézon, trente-deux études de psychiatrie et de psychopathologie* (Toulouse: Privat, 1980), pp. 43–58 (p. 49).
146. In 1938 Georges Daumézon was named director of the psychotherapeutic establishment at Fleury-les-Aubrais, where he remained until 1951. Physician in the psychiatric hospitals of the Seine beginning in 1951, he directed a unit in the Maison Blanche psychiatric hospital in Neuilly-sur-Marne for a year and a half before becoming, in 1952, head of medicine at the Sainte-Anne psychiatric hospital, then at

Henri-Rousselle. After World War II, he headed a professional union of psychiatrists, the Syndicat des Médecins des hôpitaux psychiatriques, whose first members were Paul Sivadon, Paul Bernard, Jean Lauzier, Louis Le Guillant, Lucien Bonnafé, Xavier Abély, and Henri Ey. The team also founded a new journal, *Information psychiatrique*.

147. Gusdorf, "Georges Daumézon, l'homme," p. 48.
148. G. Bachelard, *La terre et les rêveries du repos* (Paris: José Corti, 1948), p. 76.
149. Letter dated January 9, 1955 ("Correspondance Gaston Bachelard-Ludwig Binswanger, 1948–1955," p. 207).
150. Gaston Bachelard, "De la nature du rationalisme," *Bulletin de la Société Française de Philosophie*, session of March 25, 1950, reproduced in G. Bachelard, *L'Engagement rationaliste* (Paris: PUF, 1972), pp. 45–87, p. 47.
151. Gaston Bachelard, *La Poétique de l'espace* (Paris: PUF, 1957) ; English translation by Maria Jolas, *The Poetics of Space* (Boston: Beacon, 1994).
152. Gaston Bachelard, *L'Eau et les rêves: Essai sur l'imagination de la matière* (Paris: José Corti, 1942).
153. Gaston Bachelard, *L'Air et les songes: Essai sur l'imagination du Mouvement* (Paris: José Corti, 1943); English translation by Edith R. Farrell and C. Frederick Farrell, *Air and Dreams: An Essay on the Imagination of Movement* (Dallas: Dallas Institute, 1988).
154. Ludwig Binswanger, "Der Fall Ellen West: Eine anthropologisch-klinische Studie," *Schweizer Archiv für Neurologie und Psychiatrie* 53 (1944): 255–727; 54 (1944): 69–117, 330–360; 55 (1945): 16–40; reprinted in *Schizophrenie*, study no. 2: 57–188; English translation by Werner M. Mendel and Joseph Lyons, "The Case of Ellen West," in *Existence—a New Dimension in Psychiatry and Psychology*, ed. Rollo May, Ernest Angel and Henri F. Ellenberger (New York: Basic, 1958), pp. 237–364 (p. 322).
155. Ludwig Binswanger, "Über die daseinsanalytische Forschungsrichtung in der Psychiatrie," *Schweizer Archiv für Psychiatrie und Neurologie* 57 (1946): 209–235; reprinted in *Ausgewählte Vorträge und Aufsätze*, vol. 1, *Zur phänomenologischen Anthropologie* (Bern: Francke, 1947), pp. 190–217, and in *Ausgewählte Werke*, vol. 3, *Vorträge und Aufsätze*, ed. Max Herzog (Heidelberg: Asanger, 1994), pp. 231–257; English translation

1. ARCHIVES AND INTELLECTUAL NETWORKS ◦ 233

by Ernest Angel, "The Existential Analysis School of Thought," in *Existence*, pp. 191–213 (p. 211).
156. Foucault, "Dream, Imagination and Existence," p. 70.
157. Simone de Beauvoir, *La Force de l'âge*, Soleil 49 (Paris: Gallimard, 1960), p. 614; English translation by Peter Green, *The Prime of Life* (New York: Penguin, 1962), p. 537. On the distance that nonetheless separates existential psychoanalysis from Bachelard's perspective, see Emmanuel de Saint Aubert, *Du lien des êtres aux éléments de l'être: Merleau-Ponty au tournant des années 1945–1951*, Bibliothèque d'histoire de la philosophie: Temps modernes (Paris: Vrin, 2004), chap. 3, §1, "Une étrange 'psychanalyse existentielle'"; and Pierre Rodrigo, "Sartre et Bachelard: Variations autour de l'imagination bachelardienne," *Cahiers Gaston Bachelard*, no. 8 (2006): 51–64. On the dialogue between Bachelard and Sartre, see also Grégory Cormann, "Sartre à Venise, l'homme qui allait vers le froid: Sur *La Reine Albemarle ou le dernier touriste* (1951–1952)," *Les Temps Modernes*, no. 679 (2014): 73–107.
158. Letter from Bachelard to Kuhn dated December 28, 1947. See "La correspondence Gaston Bachelard et Roland Kuhn," ed. Elisabetta Basso, with a postscript by Charles Alunni, *Revue de synthèse* 137, nos. 1–2 (2016): 177–189, p. 183.
159. "La Correspondence Gaston Bachelard et Roland Kuhn," pp. 182–183: "The second book on the earth and the reveries of repose is barely started.... For this second book I would need some more precise information on the *choc noir*. Mme Verdeaux has told me about a book by Dr. Hans Binder: *Die Hell-Dunkeldeutung im Rorschachschen Versuch* [*Die Helldunkeldeutungen im psychodiagnostischen Experiment von Rorschach* (Zurich: Füssli, 1932)]. Where can I procure this work[?]." In his response of January 7, 1948, Kuhn answers: "It is true that there is a book by Binder on all of these questions, but it is completely out of print and impossible to find even in Switzerland. If you really want it, I am certain that Mme Verdeaux will be able to get it for you to read. Two years ago she brought back one of the last Swiss copies, which is currently either in her possession or in that of Mr. Ombredane" (p. 186).
160. Letter of April 15, 1948, in "Correspondance Gaston Bachelard—Ludwig Binswanger (1948–1955)," p. 188.

161. Letter of January 26, 1948, "Correspondance Gaston Bachelard—Ludwig Binswanger (1948–1955)," p. 184.
162. Binswanger, "The Existential Analysis School of Thought," p. 212.
163. Gaston Bachelard, *La terre et les rêveries du repos*, p. 76.
164. L. Binswanger, "Dream and Existence," *Review of Existential Psychology and Psychiatry*, special issue, ed. Keith Hoeller, vol. 19, no. 1 (1986): 81–105, p. 81 (translation partly modified).
165. Binswanger, "Der Fall Suzanne Urban," *Schweizer Archiv für Neurologie und Psychiatrie* 69 (1952): 36–77; 70 (1952): 1–32; 71 (1952): 57–96; reprinted in *Schizophrenie* (Pfullingen: Neske, 1957), study no. 5, pp. 359–470 (1952), p. 7.
166. Binswanger, "Dream and Existence," p. 81.
167. See on this topic Jérôme Lamy, "De la psychologie des images à l'ontologie poétique: Vers une Métaphysique de l'imagination avec Bachelard," in *L'Histoire du concept d'imagination en France (de 1918 à nos jours)*, ed. Riccardo Barontini and Julien Lamy, Rencontres: Série Littéraire des XXe et XXIe siècles 34 (Paris: Classiques Garnier, 2019), pp. 79–96.
168. Binswanger, "The Existential Analysis School of Thought," p. 212n37. Binswanger mentions on this topic, in addition to *L'Air et les songes*, *L'Eau et les rêves*, *La Psychanalyse du feu* (Paris: Gallimard, 1938); and *Lautréamont* (Paris: José Corti, 1940).
169. "La correspondance Gaston Bachelard et Roland Kuhn," p. 183.
170. Letter of April 27, 1954, in "La correspondance Michel Foucault—Ludwig Binswanger," p. 195.
171. Staatsarchiv Thurgau, StATG 9'40, 2.3/2 StATG 9'40. I thank the Kuhn family as well as Liselotte Rutishauser, Roland Kuhn's former secretary at Münsterlingen, for having brought this document to my attention.
172. As we shall see, the use of the word *test* in English to describe Rorschach's procedure is misleading. See N. Akavia, *Subjectivity in Motion: Life, Art, and Movement in the Work of Hermann Rorschach*, Routledge Monographs in Mental Health (New York: Routledge, 2013).
173. See on this subject J.-F. Bert and E. Basso, "Foucault, Rorschach et les tests projectifs," in Bert and Basso, *Foucault à Münsterlingen*, p. 69–76. Foucault's notes bear the following titles: "Rorschach et les épileptiques," "Les processus psychologiques dans le Rorschach," "Formule

discriminative entre schizophrénie et psychose organique." The authors and works he cites include manuals by Ewald Bohm (*Lehrbuch der Rorschach-Psychodiagnostik: für Psychologen, Ärzte und Pädagogen* [Bern: Huber, 1951]) and by David Rapaport (*Diagnostic Psychological Testing: The Theory, Statistical Evaluation, and Diagnostic Application of a Battery of Tests* [Chicago: Year Book Publishers, 1945–1946]), as well as various articles from the *Revue de psychologie appliquée* (BnF, Fonds Michel Foucault, Box 44b, call number NAF 28730, and Box 2, call number NAF 28803).

174. Binswanger, "The Existential Analysis School of Thought," p. 212.
175. Bachelard, *La Terre et les rêveries du repos*, p. 76.
176. Ellenberger, "Analyse existentielle," p. 4.
177. Ellenberger, p. 4.
178. Ellenberger, p. 4.
179. Ellenberger, p. 4. We should note that, in 1954, Ellenberger also wrote the first study dedicated to H. Rorschach's biography: "The Life and Work of Hermann Rorschach (1884–1922)," *Bulletin of the Menninger Clinic* 18:173–219.
180. L. Binswanger, "Studien zu Schizophrenie Problem: Zweite Studie: Der Fall Jürg Zünd," *Schweizer Archiv für Neurologie und Psychiatrie* 56 (1946): 191–220; 58 (1947): 1–43; 59 (1947): 21–36 (reprinted in *Schizophrenie*, pp. 189–288).
181. M. Foucault, *Binswanger et l'analyse existentielle*, ed. Elisabetta Basso, Cours et travaux de Michel Foucault avant le Collège de France, ed. François Ewald (Hautes Études) (Paris: Seuil/Gallimard/EHESS, 2021), p. 140.
182. Hermann Rorschach, *Psychodiagnostik: Methodik und Ergebnisse eines wahrnehmungsdiagnostischen Experiments (Deutenlassen von Zufallsformen)* (Bern: Birker, 1932 [1921]).
183. Before becoming Head of Research at the Institute of Physiology of the University of Geneva, Marcel Monnier had trained in clinical and research establishments in Switzerland, the United States, and France, at the Salpêtrière Hospital. In 1941, he developed an EEG device with direct recording with the engineer Marc Marchand at the Institute of Physiology of the University of Geneva. It was the second electroencephalographic installation in Switzerland, after the Waldau psychiatric hospital in the Canton of Bern, where Roland Kuhn trained. See

Vincent Pidoux, "Expérimentation et clinique électroencéphalographiques entre physiologie, neurologie et psychiatrie (Suisse, 1935–1965)," *Revue d'histoire des sciences* 63, no. 2 (2010): 439–472.

184. M. Monnier, "Le test psychologique de Rorschach," *L'Encephale* 29, nos. 3–4 (1934): 189–199, 247–270, p. 189. Monnier also mentions a doctoral thesis, presented in the Faculty of Letters at the University of Paris in 1933 by a certain Pearce Bailey, which was published that year in Paris by the Librairie Lipschutz under the title *Études des types psychologiques au moyen des tests*, which also examined the Rorschach test.

185. Eugen Bleuler, "Der Rorschachsche Formdeutungsversuch bei Geschwistern," *Zeitschrift für die gesamte Neurologie und Psychiatrie* 118 (1928): 366–398.

186. M. Monnier, "Le test psychologique de Rorschach," p. 269.

187. Hermann Rorschach, *Psychodiagnostic, méthodes et résultats d'une expérience diagnostique de perception*, trans. from the 4th German edition (1941) and expanded with a critical introduction and index by André Ombredane and Augustine Landau, Bibliothèque scientifique internationale: Section Psychologie (Paris: PUF, 1947).

188. Daniel Lagache, "La rêverie imageante, conduite adaptative au test de Rorschach," *Bulletin d'orientation professionnelle*, December 1943, pp. 1–7; reprinted in *Bulletin du Groupement français du Rorschach* 9 (1957): 3–11; *Œuvres I, 1932–1946*, (Paris: PUF, 1977), pp. 401–412.

189. Françoise Minkowska (Franziska Brokman) had personally known Hermann Rorschach in Zurich at the turn of the century, as they had both been students of Eugen Bleuler. In 1915, when Eugène decided to enlist in the French army, the Minkowski spouses emigrated to Paris. Françoise could not practice medicine in France, but she continued to work as a psychologist and to publish. Her research focused particularly on schizophrenia and heredity, epilepsy, and, taking her reading of Jaspers's study of Strindberg and Van Gogh in the 1920s as a starting point, the work of Van Gogh (in 1933 she published "Van Gogh, les relations entre sa vie, sa maladie et son œuvre," *L'Évolution psychiatrique* 3 [1933]: 53–76). In 1945, during a trip to Zurich for the "Semaines Internationales de l'Enfance victime de la Guerre" (International Weeks for Child Victims of War), she visited an exhibition of drawings by children that had been organized for the event. When she

I. ARCHIVES AND INTELLECTUAL NETWORKS ⊰ 237

returned to Paris, she applied her experience from Switzerland, connecting it to the Rorschach test, to some children in a care home in Soulins, and then to Jewish orphans in the Parisian banlieue. She would then apply it to "normal" children, using it to follow their development over several years. See on this topic Eugène Minkowski, "Eröffnungsansprache und allgemeiner Lebenslauf anlässlich der Gedenkfeier zum 70. Geburtstag von Hermann Rorschach," *Rorschachiana*, Mitteilung der IGROF, suppl. *Zeitschrift für diagnostische Psychologie und Persönlichkeitsforschung* 3, no. 3 (1955): 271–279.

190. Françoise Minkowska, *Le Rorschach, à la recherche du monde des formes*; introduction by Eugène Minkowski (Paris: Desclée de Brouwer, 1956). The volume appeared in the series edited by Henri Ey, the "Bibliothèque neuro-psychiatrique de langue française."

191. See on this topic Peter Galison, "Image of Self," in *Things That Talk: Object Lessons from Art and Science*, ed. Lorraine Daston (New York: Zone, 2004), pp. 257–296.

192. Cf. Akavia, *Subjectivity in Motion*.

193. As for experimental psychology and psychotechnics, it was especially studies by Franziska Baumgarten-Tramer (1883–1970) that attracted French researchers' attention in the 1930s and 1940s. A psychologist originally from Poland, after having defended her doctoral thesis in Zurich on the subject of Maine de Biran's theory of knowledge, Franziska Baumgarten devoted many works to psychotechnics, *Arbeitswissenschaft*, and clinical psychological tests. A large number of these works were translated into French between 1931 and 1952.

194. On this topic, see especially Andrée Yanacopoulo, *Henri F. Ellenberger: une vie* (Montréal: Liber, 2009); and Emmanuel Delille, "Henri Ellenberger in Schaffhausen, 1943–1953: Ellenbergers 'Geschichte der dynamischen Psychiatrie' als Exilliteratur," in *125 Jahre Psychiatrische Klinik Breitenau Schaffhausen 1891–2016*, ed. Jörg Püschel (Zürich: Chronos Verlag, 2018), pp. 235–257.

195. As a young psychiatrist, Kuhn had had a machine installed in 1939 at the Waldau university psychiatric clinic; in the same year, he moved to the Münsterlingen asylum. See on this topic his various autobiographical sketches: "Roland Kuhn," in *Psychiatrie in Selbstdarstellungen*, ed. Ludwig J. Pongratz (Bern: Huber, 1977), pp. 219–257 (p. 223); "Esquisse d'une autobiographie," in *Écrits sur l'analyse*

existentielle, texts assembled and introduced by Jean-Claude Marceau, preface by Mareike Wolf-Fédida, Psychanalyse et civilisations. Série Trouvailles et retrouvailles (Paris: L'Harmattan, 2007), pp. 41–54 (pp. 46–47); "Geschichte und Entwicklung der psychiatrischen Klinik," in *150 Jahre Münsterlingen*, ed. Jürg Ammann and Karl Studer (Weinfelden: Druck Mühlemann, 1990), pp. 99–125.

196. Cf. Bernard Gueguen, "Hommage à Georges Verdeaux," *Neurophysiologie clinique* 34 (2004): 301–302.

197. BnF, Fonds Michel Foucault, Box 44a-b, call number NAF 28730.

198. Marcel Monnier, ed., *L'Organisation des fonctions psychiques* (Neuchâtel: Éditions du Griffon, 1951).

199. BnF, Fonds Michel Foucault, Box 44a, call number NAF 28730.

200. For an overview of the psychology training offered at the University of Paris at the turn of the 1950s, see Anne Ancelin-Schützenberger, "Aperçus sur les études de psychologie," *Bulletin du groupe d'études de psychologie de l'Université de Paris* 4, nos. 1–2 (1950): 1–2. Cf. Gautier Dassonneville, "Foucault auditeur: Les études de philosophie et de psychologie à Paris, 1946–1953," http://eman-archives.org/Foucault-fiches/exhibits/show/foucault-auditeur-les-ann——. es-.

201. On this topic, among the more recent biographical studies, we might cite Iris Blum and Peter Witschi, eds., *Olga und Hermann Rorschach: Ein ungewöhnliches Psychiater-Ehepaar* (Herisau: Appenzeller Verlag, 2008); Damion Searls, *The Inkblots: Hermann Rorschach, His Iconic Test and the Power of Seeing* (New York: Crown, 2017).

202. Roland Kuhn, "Zur ästhetischen Dimension daseinsanalytischer Erfahrung," in *Psychiatrie mit Zukunft: Beiträge zur Geschichte, Gegenwart, Zukunft der wissenschaftlichen und praktischen Seelenheilkunde* (Basel: Schwabe, 2004), pp. 62–90. On this topic, see also Gerhard Dammann, "Roland Kuhns phänomenologische und daseinsanalytische Arbeiten zu Ästhetik und künstlerischem Schaffen," in *Auf der Seeseite der Kunst: Werke aus der Psychiatrischen Klinik Münsterlingen, 1894–1960*, ed. Katrin Luchsinger, Gerhard Dammann, Monika Jagfeld, and André Salathé (Zürich: Chronos, 2015), p. 37–52.

203. Roland Kuhn, *Der Rorschachsche Formdeutversuch in der Psychiatrie* (Basel: Karger, 1940); *Über Maskendeutungen im Rorschachschen Versuch* (Basel, Karger, 1944), 2nd ed., 1954; "Über Rorschach's Psychologische

Grundlagen des Formdeutversuches," *Schweizer Archiv für Neurologie und Psychiatrie* 53, no. 1 (1944): 29–47.

204. Some of these drawings are currently conserved in the State Archives of the Canton of Thurgau in Frauenfeld (Staatsarchiv Thurgau). A selection of images was reproduced in Gerhard Dammann, "Roland Kuhns phänomenologische und daseinsanalytische Arbeiten zu Ästhetik und künstlerischem Schaffen," in Katrin Luchsinger et al., *Auf der Seeseite der Kunst*, pp. 37–52.
205. Letter of January 6, 1986: see Henri Maldiney and R. Kuhn, *Rencontre—Begegnung*, p. 494.
206. R. Kuhn, "Über die Bedeutung vom Grenzen im Wahn," *Monatsschrift für Psychiatrie und Neurologie* 124, nos. 4–6 (1952): 354–383 (BnF, Fonds Michel Foucault, Box 42b, folder 1, call number NAF 28730).
207. R. Kuhn, "Esquisse d'une autobiographie," in *Écrits sur l'analyse existentielle*, texts assembled and introduced by Jean-Claude Marceau, preface by Mareike Wolf-Fédida (Paris: L'Harmattan, 2007), pp. 41–54.
208. Kuhn, p. 47.
209. L. Binswanger, "Bemerkungen zu Hermann Rorschachs Psychodiagnostik," *Internationale Zeitschrift für ärztliche Psychoanalyse* 9 (1923): 512–523, p. 513. Binswanger and Rorschach knew each other personally. From their scientific exchange, a few letters remain: Hermann Rorschach, *Briefwechsel*, ed. Christian Müller and Rita Signer (Berne: Hans Huber, 2004).
210. See on this topic Akavia, *Subjectivity in Motion*, p. 129.
211. Binswanger, "Bemerkungen," p. 513.
212. Binswanger, p. 519.
213. P. Galison, "Image of Self"; Akavia, *Subjectivity in Motion*.
214. The correspondence between Kuhn and Ombredane is conserved in the Roland Kuhn Archives, Staatsarchiv Thurgau, Frauenfeld. I wish to thank Regula Kuhn and Liselotte Rutishauser for having brought this document to my attention.
215. Ruth Bochner and Florence Halpern, *The Clinical Application of the Rorschach Test* (New York: Grune and Stratton, 1942); French translation, *L'Application clinique du test de Rorschach*, with a foreword on terminology and symbols to be used in the French language by André Ombredane and Nella Canivet (Paris: PUF, 1948).

216. See Nina Rausch de Traubenberg, "Les cinquante années de publications du 'Groupement français du Rorschach' devenu 'Société du Rorschach et des méthodes projectives de langue française,'" *Psychologie clinique et projective* 9, no. 1 (2003): 9–17.
217. Binswanger, *Henrik Ibsen*, p. 41.
218. Kuhn, *Phénoménologie du masque: À travers le test de Rorschach*, French translation by Jacqueline Verdeaux, Bibliothèque neuro-psychiatrique de langue française (Paris: Desclée de Brouwer, 1957); newly revised and corrected edition, Épi-intelligence du corps, 1992, p. 30.
219. Kuhn, p. 31.
220. Kuhn, p. 54.
221. Kuhn, p. 196.
222. G. Bachelard, "Préface," in Kuhn, *Phénoménologie du masque*, p. 17.
223. L. Binswanger, *Einführung in die Probleme der allgemeinen Psychologie* (Berlin: Springer, 1922), p. 297.
224. Bachelard, "Préface," p. 17.
225. Georges Buraud, *Les Masques* (Paris: Éditions du Seuil, 1948). Quoted by Bachelard, "Préface," p. 17.
226. Jean Starobinski, "Des taches et des masques," *Critiques* 14, nos. 135–136 (1958): 793–804, p. 804. See also, on this topic, Aldo Trucchio, "Jean Starobinski, lecteur de Bachelard au début des années 1950," *Bulletin du Cercle d'études internationales Jean Starobinski* 6 (2013): 8–16.
227. Archives du Caphés, Fonds Georges Canguilhem (CAN 1080).
228. M. Foucault, "L'eau et la folie" (1963), in *Dits et écrits*, vol. 1, no. 16, pp. 268–272 (p. 268).
229. Foucault, p. 269.
230. *Les fous, la fête*

> *La tradition de la fête des fous*
> *Masques et blasphèmes*
> *Le bouffon*
> *L'ivresse du langage*
> *Quelques ex. de délire maniaque.* (BnF, Fonds Michel Foucault, Box 91, cahier no. 2, call number 28730).

231. See Roland Kuhn, "Geschichte und Entwicklung der psychiatrischen Klinik," in Ammann and Studer, *150 Jahre Münsterlingen*, pp. 99–125.

I. ARCHIVES AND INTELLECTUAL NETWORKS ◌ 241

232. Cf. Luchsinger et al., *Auf der Seeseite der Kunst*.
233. See Jacques Schotte, *Vers l'anthropopsychiatrie: un parcours*, Hermann Psychanalyse (Paris: Hermann, 2008).
234. See Heinrich G. Müldner, "Einleitung," in *Münsterlinger Kolloquien*, vol. 4, by Roland Kuhn (Würzburg: Königshausen and Neumann, 2014), pp. 9–21.
235. The correspondence between Verdeaux and Binswanger is conserved in the Binswanger Archives at the University of Tübingen, in Germany. Cf. also the letter from Jacqueline Verdeaux dated February 3, 1954: "We will arrive, if everything goes well, in Münsterlingen on Sunday night around 5 or 6 o'clock; we will phone you as soon as we arrive. In the end Foucault will accompany us, but it was only today that he learned that he could go and he thanks you very much in advance for your hospitality" (Universitätsarchiv Tübingen, 443/58).
236. Letter of January 6, 1954 (Universitätsarchiv Tübingen, 443/58).
237. This is a lecture he had given in 1934 to medical students in Amsterdam and Groningen: "Über Psychotherapie (Möglichkeit und Tatsächlichkeit psychotherapeutischer Wirkung)," *Der Nervenarzt* 8 (1935): 113–121, 180–189 (reprinted in *Ausgewählte Vorträge und Aufsätze*, vol. 1, pp. 132–158).
238. L. Binswanger, "Lebensfunktion und innere Lebensgeschichte," *Monatsschrift für Psychiatrie und Neurologie* 68 (1928): 52–79 (later in *Ausgewählte Vorträge und Aufsätze*, vol. 1, pp. 50–73).
239. L. Binswanger, "Geschehnis und Erlebnis (zur gleichnamigen Schrift von E. Straus, 1930)," *Monatsschrift für Psychiatrie und Neurologie* 80 (1931): 243–273 (reprinted in *Ausgewählte Vorträge und Aufsätze*, vol. 2, pp. 147–173).
240. L. Binswanger, *Introduction à l'analyse existentielle*, trans. and glossary by Jacqueline Verdeaux and Roland Kuhn, preface by Roland Kuhn and Henri Maldiney (Paris: Éditions de Minuit, 1971).
241. Universitätsarchiv Tübingen, 443/58.
242. Letter of June 24, 1954 (Universitätsarchiv Tübingen, 443/58).
243. In a letter that J. Verdeaux addressed to Binswanger on July 31, 1954, for example, she writes: "My husband must return to Paris on September 1, therefore Foucault is going to meet us somewhere along the way and we will come together to you because he really wants to come see you and talk with you" (Universitätsarchiv Tübingen, 443/60). See

also the letter of August 14, 1954: "I am very much looking forward to seeing you again soon; Foucault is working on a text on delusion, and I often encourage him to speak about it with you, because he is very reserved" (Universitätsarchiv Tübingen, 443/60); and of May 12, 1956: "May I ask you a favor? I believe that your book would enormously interest Foucault, who would be delighted to receive it; here is his address . . ." (Universitätsarchiv Tübingen, 443/61,3).

244. Universitätsarchiv Tübingen, 443/58.
245. The letter belongs to the Verdeaux family. I wish to thank Bruno Verdeaux who granted me access to it.
246. Cf. the postcard that Jacqueline Verdeaux sent Binswanger on January 2, 1954, from the Swiss Alps, where she was vacationing: "I have now begun to work for you and hope to send you the fruit of my late nights in a few weeks" (Universitätsarchiv Tübingen, 443/58).
247. Letter of February 3, 1954 (Universitätsarchiv Tübingen, 443/58).
248. Letter of February 3, 1954: "This translation is certainly very imperfect; its only quality is to have been made with all of my affection. And if I found it difficult, this text was really a joy for the spirit."
249. This information was provided by Liselotte Rutishauser.
250. We know about this trip through the letters that Jacqueline Verdeaux sent to Binswanger in order to organize the meeting: "I received your card this morning and, if you go to Brissago, that would be very convenient for me and I could see you there more easily; in this case I will not go to Münsterlingen because it would be too tiring. We must leave on Friday September 10 and my travel itinerary will very much depend on where you are. When you have received this letter, could you send me a simple telegram saying 'Wengen' or 'Brissago'; I will then go to one or the other place to meet you with Foucault around September 13" (letter of September 7, 1954, Universitätsarchiv Tübingen, 443/60). In her next letter, Verdeaux thanks Binswanger for the telegram he had sent her from Brissago: "If we arrive at a decent time, I will telephone; otherwise I will call you Wednesday morning because, before going to Brissago, I would like to show Foucault Villa Favorita. I hope there will be room for us in some hotel in Brissago starting on Wednesday evening" (letter of September 11, 1954, Universitätsarchiv Tübingen, 443/60).

I. ARCHIVES AND INTELLECTUAL NETWORKS ∞ 243

251. Letter from Ludwig Binswanger to Jacqueline Verdeaux of June 2, 1954 (Universitätsarchiv Tübingen, 443/58).
252. Letter from Jacqueline Verdeaux to Ludwig Binswanger, June 24, 1954 (Universitätsarchiv Tübingen, 443/58). Cf. also the letter of July 31, 1954: "I will of course send you, in a few days, the manuscript of the first part of Suzanne Urban and I ask you to be very tough" (Universitätsarchiv Tübingen, 443/60).
253. Letter of June 28, 1954 (Universitätsarchiv Tübingen, 443/58).
254. Cf. the letter from Foucault to Binswanger of April 27, 1954 (Universitätsarchiv Tübingen, 443/57, 1).
255. Universitätsarchiv Tübingen, 443/60.
256. Cf. Roland Kuhn's letters to Georges Verdeaux on December 14, 1955 (belonging to the Kuhn family) and to Ludwig Binswanger on 10 September 10, 1956 (Universitätsarchiv Tübingen, 443/20).
257. L. Binswanger, "Préface à la traduction française," *Le Cas Suzanne Urban: étude sur la schizophrénie*, Bibliothèque neuro-psychiatrique de langue française (Paris: Desclée de Brouwer), p. 11.
258. "La correspondance entre Michel Foucault et Ludwig Binswanger, 1954–1956," p. 188.
259. Binswanger is referring here to his *Wandlungen in der Auffassung und Deutung des Traumes von den Griechen bis zur Gegenwart* (Berlin: Springer, 1928).
260. After having read the *Wandlungen*, which Binswanger had sent him in 1928, Freud wrote to him: "I was unhappy to learn that I had omitted so many precious references in my review of the literature on dreams. They had not been mentioned to me, and for that matter, already at the time, it was difficult for me to study so many authors instead of attaching myself to the object. Apparently it is not in my nature to be a scholar, and I can admire your industriousness without envy" (letter of April 2, 1928, in Sigmund Freud and Ludwig Binswanger, *Briefwechsel: 1908–1938*, ed. and intro. Gerhard Fichtner [Frankfurt: Fischer, 1992], letter 164 F).
261. Bert and Basso, *Foucault à Münsterlingen*, p. 186.
262. Bert and Basso, p. 193.
263. See the virtual exhibition presented by Elisabetta Basso in the public platform FFL-Eman: "Les dossiers sur la psychopathologie

existentielle," http://eman-archives.org/Foucault-fiches/exhibits/show/binswanger-analyse-existentiel/les-dossiers-sur-la-psychopath.

2. THE BINSWANGER DOSSIER

1. On this topic, see my essay "'Le rêve comme argument': les enjeux épistémologiques à l'origine du projet existentiel de Ludwig Binswanger," *Archives de Philosophie* 73, no. 4: (2009) 655–686.
2. L. Binswanger, "Psychoanalyse und klinische Psychiatrie," *Internationale Zeitschrift für ärztliche Psychoanalyse* 7 (1920): 137–165; then in *Ausgewählte Vorträge und Aufsätze*, vol. 2, *Zur Problematik der psychiatrischen Forschung und zum Problem der Psychiatrie* (Bern: Francke, 1955), pp. 40–66 (p. 52).
3. L. Binswanger, "Über Phänomenologie" (1923), in *Ausgewählte Werke*, vol. 3, *Vorträge und Aufsätze*, ed. Max Herzog (Heidelberg: Asanger, 1993), pp. 35–69.
4. L. Binswanger, "Lebensfunktion und innere Lebensgeschichte" (1928), in *Ausgewählte Werke*, vol. 3, *Vorträge und Aufsätze*, pp. 71–94 (p. 94).
5. Binswanger, p. 87.
6. Jacques Lacan, "Au-delà du 'Principe de réalité,'" (1936), in *Écrits* (Paris: Les Éditions du Seuil, 1966, 1999), vol. 1; English translation by Bruce Fink, in collaboration with Heloïse Fink and Russel Grigg, "Beyond the 'Reality Principle,'" in *Écrits: The First Complete Edition in English* (New York: Norton, 2006), pp. 65–66.
7. Michel Foucault, *Maladie mentale et personnalité*, Initiation philosophique 12 (Paris: PUF, 1954), p. 37.
8. BnF, Fonds Michel Foucault, Box 46, folder 4, "Introduction générale."
9. Foucault, *Maladie mentale et personnalité*, chap. 3, pp. 48–51.
10. Foucault, "La psychologie de 1850 à 1950" (1957), in *Dits et écrits, 1954–1988*, ed. Daniel Defert and François Ewald, with the collaboration of Jacques Lagrange, Bibliothèque des sciences humaines (Paris: Gallimard, 1994), vol. 1, no. 2, pp. 120–137 (p. 128).
11. M. Foucault, "Dream, Imagination and Existence: An Introduction to Ludwig Binswanger's 'Dream and Existence,'" in *Dream and Existence*, by Michel Foucault and Ludwig Binswanger, special issue of *Review of Existential Psychology and Psychiatry*, ed. Keith Hoeller, vol. 19, no. 1 (1985): 29–78, p. 34.

12. M. Foucault, "Un manuscrit de Michel Foucault sur la psychanalyse," ed. Elisabetta Basso, *Astérion*, no. 21 (2019), http://journals.openedition.org.inshs.bib.cnrs.fr/asterion/4410.
13. Merleau-Ponty, *Phénoménologie de la perception*, Bibliothèque des idées (1945; Paris: Gallimard, 1976); English translation by Colin Smith, *Phenomenology of Perception* (London: Routledge and Kegan Paul, 1962), p. 166.
14. Merleau-Ponty, pp. 157–158.
15. Georges Politzer, *Critique des fondements de la psychologie: la psychologie et la psychanalyse* (Paris: Rieder, 1928); English translation by Maurice Apprey, *Critique of the Foundations of Psychology: The Psychology of Psychoanalysis* (Pittsburg, PA: Duquesne University Press, 1994), p. 97: "But after doing this justice to Freud there is no reason to hide the fact that his theoretical works . . . are incompatible with the concrete psychology of which he is said to be the founder."
16. There are numerous direct references to the project of "concrete psychology" in Lacan's *Thesis*, and Politzer is explicitly cited in his "Presentation on Psychical Causality," in *Écrits*, pp. 123–158 (p. 131): "It was, as I know, with such misgivings that Politzer, the great thinker, decided not to provide the theoretical expression with which he would have left his indelible mark, in order to devote himself to an activity that was to take him away from us definitively. When, following in his footsteps, we demand that concrete psychology be established as a science, let us not lose sight of the fact that we are still only at the stage of formal pleas" (in French, "Propos sur la causalité psychique," 1946, in *Écrits*, pp. 150–192).
17. Lacan, "Beyond the 'Reality Principle,'" p. 73. On this subject, see also "Presentation on Psychical Causality," p. 154: "The appearance of Freud's Oedipus complex marked a conceptual watershed, insofar as it contained the promise of a true psychology."
18. Jacques Lacan, *De la psychose paranoïaque dans ses rapports avec la personnalité* (Paris: Le François, 1932; Éditions du Seuil, 1975), pp. 319–320.
19. Lacan, pp. 319–320. Lacan therefore maintained that the systematized contents of delusion "immediately," "manifestly" express, "with a startlingly clear symbolism, one or several of the subject's essential vital conflicts" (p. 346).

20. Jacques Lacan, "Le problème du style et la conception psychiatrique des formes paranoïaques de l'expérience," in *De la psychose paranoïaque dans ses rapports avec la personnalité*, Le Champ freudien (Paris: Le François, 1932; Seuil, 1975), p. 387.
21. Eugène Minkowski, "Psychiatrie et métaphysique: À la recherche de l'humain et du vécu," *Revue de Métaphysique et de Morale* 52 (1947): 333–358, p. 347. This article had been solicited from Minkowski by Georges Gusdorf, who belonged to the journal's editorial board (with A. R. Aron, G. Bachelard, R. Bayer, J. Hyppolite, A. Koyré, M. Merleau-Ponty, and J. Wahl).
22. Eugène Minkowski, "Le contact humain," *Revue de Métaphysique et de Morale* 55, no. 2 (1950): 113–127, p. 126.
23. Foucault, "La psychologie de 1850 à 1950," p. 129.
24. Foucault, p. 128.
25. Foucault, "La recherche scientifique et la psychologie" (1957), in *Dits et écrits*, ed. Daniel Defert and François Ewald, with Jacques Lagrange, Bibliothèque des sciences humaines (Paris: Gallimard, 1994), vol. 1, no. 3, p. 157. If Politzer is mentioned only very rarely in Foucault's published works, in contrast his name often appears in Foucault's notes and manuscripts from the 1950s (BnF, Fonds Michel Foucault, Box 46, folder 4, call number NAF 28730): cf. the manuscript fragments titled, respectively, "La magie—le fait social total"; "Freud et la psychologie de la genèse"; "Un manuscrit de Michel Foucault sur la psychanalyse."
26. Georges Politzer, *Critique of the Foundations of Psychology*, chap. 3, "The Theoretical Frame of Psychoanalysis and the Survival of Abstraction," and chap. 4, "The Hypothesis of the Unconscious and Concrete Psychology."
27. Foucault, "Dream, Imagination and Existence," p. 36.
28. Merleau-Ponty, *Phénoménologie de la perception*, Bibliothèque des idées (1945; Paris: Gallimard, 1976); English translation by Colin Smith, *Phenomenology of Perception* (London: Routledge and Kegan Paul, 1962), p. 166.
29. Maurice Merleau-Ponty, *Les Sciences de l'homme et la phénoménologie* (Paris: Tournier et Constans, 1953), pp. 6 and 21.
30. Foucault, "Dream, Imagination and Existence," p. 71.

31. Cf. in particular Eugène Minkowski, *Vers une cosmologie: Fragments philosophiques*, Philosophie de l'esprit (Paris: Montaigne, 1936), pp. 48–49.
32. Lacan, "Le problème du style," p. 387.
33. Foucault, "Dream, Imagination and Existence," pp. 71–72.
34. Foucault, p. 72.
35. Merleau-Ponty, *Phenomenology of Perception*, p. 161.
36. Ludwig Binswanger, "Der Fall Suzanne Urban," *Schweizer Archiv für Neurologie und Psychiatrie* 69 (1952): 36–77; vol. 70 (1952): 1–32; vol. 71 (1952): 57–96, (1952): p. 7 (reprinted in *Schizophrenie* [Pfullingen: Neske, 1957], study no. 5, pp. 359–470).
37. Cf. Minkowski, *Vers une cosmologie*, p. 256.
38. Foucault, "Dream, Imagination and Existence," p. 32.
39. Foucault, p. 32.
40. Foucault, p. 35.
41. Foucault, pp. 37–38.
42. Foucault, p. 41.
43. Foucault, p. 42.
44. Foucault, p. 42.
45. Letter of April 27, 1954, in *Foucault à Münsterlingen: À l'origine de l'Histoire de la folie. Avec des photographies de Jacqueline Verdeaux*, ed. Jean-François Bert and Elisabetta Basso, L'histoire et ses représentations 10 (Paris: Éditions de l'EHESS, 2015), p. 183.
46. Cf. the letter from Binswanger to Foucault dated May 6, 1954, in Bert and Basso, *Foucault à Münsterlingen*, p. 185.
47. L. Binswanger, "Über Ideenflucht," *Schweizer Archiv für Neurologie und Psychiatrie* 27, no. 2 (1932): 203–217; 28, nos. 1–2 (1932): 18–26, 183–202; 29, no. 1 (1932), 193ff.; 30, no. 1 (1933), 68–85; published in one volume in Zürich by Orel Füssli in 1933 (reprinted in New York by Garland in 1980); *Ausgewählte Werke*, vol. 1, *Formen mißglückten Daseins*, ed. Max Herzog (Heidelberg: Asanger, 1992), p. 104.
48. Foucault, "Dream, Imagination and Existence," pp. 32–33.
49. Foucault, p. 33.
50. BnF, Fonds Michel Foucault, Box 46, folders 1 to 3 (call number NAF 28730). See M. Foucault, *La question anthropologique. Cours. 1954–1955*, ed. Arianna Sforzini, Cours et travaux de Michel Foucault avant le

Collège de France, ed. François Ewald (Hautes Études) (Paris: Seuil/Gallimard/EHESS, 2022), and *Phénoménologie et psychologie, 1953–1954,* ed. Philippe Sabot, Hautes Études (Paris: Seuil/Gallimard/EHESS, 2021).

51. Cf. "Travaux et publications des professeurs en 1952–1953," *Annales de l'université de Lille: Rapport annuel du Conseil de l'université (1952–1953)* (Lille, G. Sautai, 1954); quoted in D. Eribon, *Michel Foucault: 1926–1984* (Paris: Flammarion, 1989), 3rd published in 2011 (Champs: biographie 847); English translation by Betsy Wing, *Michel Foucault* (Cambridge, MA: Harvard University Press, 1991), p. 63. See also P. Sabot, "Entre psychologie et philosophie: Foucault à Lille, 1952–1955," in Bert and Basso, *Foucault à Münsterlingen*, pp. 105–120 (p. 109).
52. M. Foucault, "Dream, Imagination and Existence," p. 31.
53. Letter from M. Foucault to L. Binswanger of 27 April 1954, in Bert and Basso, *Foucault à Münsterlingen*, p. 183.
54. M. Foucault, *Binswanger et l'analyse existentielle*, ed. Elisabetta Basso, Hautes Études (Paris: Seuil/Gallimard/EHESS 2021), p. 167.
55. Foucault, "Dream, Imagination and Existence," p. 33.
56. According to the British neurologist John Hughlings Jackson (1835–1911), the nervous system's functioning was organized hierarchically in tiered functional levels. Each level controlled those below, from the most voluntary to the most automatic. The functions of the lower levels were freed when the higher levels of control failed. This model was applied in the field of neuropsychiatry by Henri Ey and Julien Rouart beginning in the 1930s, and then systematized in Henry Ey's theory of "organo-dynamism." See Jacqueline Carroy, "Jackson et la psychopathologie: évolution et évolutionnisme," in *Les évolutions: phylogenèse de l'individuation*, ed. Pierre Fédida and Daniel Widlöcher, Colloques de la Revue internationale de psychopathologie (Paris: PUF, 1994), pp. 151–172; and Emmanuel Delille, "L'organo-dynamisme d'Henri Ey: l'oubli d'une théorie de la conscience considéré dans ses relations avec l'analyse existentielle," *L'Homme et la société* 167-168-169 (2008): 203–219.
57. Foucault, *Maladie mentale et personnalité*, p. 33n1.
58. BnF, Fonds Michel Foucault, Box 4, NAF 28803.
59. Foucault, *Maladie mentale et personnalité*, p. 35.

60. Foucault, *Binswanger et l'analyse existentielle*, p. 18.
61. BnF, Fonds Michel Foucault, Box 46, folder 4, "Introduction générale."
62. Foucault, "Dream, Imagination and Existence," p. 34.
63. Foucault, *Binswanger et l'analyse existentielle*, p. 20: "The phenomenological essence is grasped on the deployed horizon of the possible, rather than in the instantaneous hollow of a real sensation."
64. Foucault, p. 21.
65. Foucault, p. 17: "The 'vital' is never more than a reductive hint relative to the lived experience, and discriminative relative to the morbid. If it reconciles man with himself, it does so by reducing him to less than himself, and by opposing him irreducibly to the pathological forms of his behaviour: in this twofold manner, the theory of life alienates the reflection on man."
66. Foucault, p. 23.
67. Foucault, p. 23.
68. Foucault, p. 23.
69. Foucault, p. 27.
70. Foucault, p. 27.
71. Foucault, p. 27.
72. Foucault, p. 27.
73. Foucault, p. 29.
74. Foucault, p. 30.
75. In chapters 1 and 3 of his *Allgemeine Psychopathologie* [*General Psychopathology*] (2nd ed. 1920 [1913]), on the topic of, respectively, "the subjective phenomena of psychic life" and "the meaningful connections of psychic life," Jaspers distinguishes between a static understanding of phenomena, whose goal is to define, describe, and order psychic states, and a genetic understanding of psychic events, which includes "affective interpenetration" (*Einfühlung*), and "the understanding of psychic relations" or "filiation of psychic states." According to Jaspers, these two types of understanding, which together make up "subjective psychology," are founded on a type of understanding pertaining to evidence and are thus totally distinct from objective or physiological psychology (*Leistungspsychologie*), which is founded on an inductive type of understanding whose goal is to establish causal links between psychic facts. In his manuscript, Foucault cites the second German edition of

Allgemeine Psychopathologie (1920), as well as the French translation of the third edition (1923), which appeared in 1928 (new ed., 1933).

76. Foucault, *Binswanger et l'analyse existentielle*, p. 35.
77. Foucault, p. 35.
78. Foucault, "La recherche scientifique et la psychologie," p. 152.
79. Foucault, p. 152.
80. Foucault, pp. 152–153.
81. This manuscript belongs to a series of preparatory notes for the article "La recherche scientifique et la psychologie." The manuscript is unfortunately incomplete and fragmentary (BnF, Fonds Michel Foucault, Box 4, call number NAF 28083).
82. BnF, Fonds Michel Foucault, Boîte 4, cote NAF 28083.
83. Foucault, *Binswanger et l'analyse existentielle*, p. 139.
84. R. Kuhn, "Henry Dunant vu par le psychiatre," in *De l'utopie à la réalité*, ed. Roger Durand, with the collaboration of Jean-Daniel Candaux (Genève: Société Henry Dunant, 1988), pp. 111–136.
85. Voir R. Kuhn, "Zum Problem der ganzheitlichen Betrachtung in der Medizin," *Schweizerisches Medizinisches Jahrbuch* (1957): 53–63.
86. L. Binswanger, "Der Fall Ellen West: Eine anthropologisch-klinische Studie," *Schweizer Archiv für Neurologie und Psychiatrie* 53 (1944): 255–727; 54 (1944): 69–117, 330–360; 55 (1945): 16–40; English translation by Werner M. Mendel and Joseph Lyons, "The Case of Ellen West," in *Existence: A New Dimension in Psychiatry and Psychology*, ed. Rollo May, Ernest Angel, and Henri F. Ellenberger (New York: Basic, 1958), pp. 237–364; "Studien zum Schizophrenienproblem: Der Fall Lola Voss," *Schweizer Archiv für Neurologie und Psychiatrie* 63 (1949): 29–97; "Der Fall Jürg Zünd," *Schweizer Archiv für Neurologie und Psychiatrie* 56 (1946): 191–220; 58 (1947): 1–43; 59 (1947): 21–36. These studies were later reprinted in L. Binswanger, *Schizophrenie* (Pfullingen: Neske, 1957).
87. See R. Kuhn, "Über die Bedeutung vom Grenzen im Wahn," *Monatsschrift für Psychiatrie und Neurologie* 124, nos. 4–6 (1952): 354–383; Kuhn, "Daseinsanalyse eines Falles von Schizophrenie," *Monatsschrift für Psychiatrie und Neurologie* 112 (1946): 233–257; Kuhn, "Mordversuch eines depressiven Fetischisten und Sodomisten an einer Dirne," *Monatsschrift für Psychiatrie und Neurologie* 116, nos. 1-2-3

(1948): 66–151; English translation by Ernest Angel, "The Attempted Murder of a Prostitute," in May, Angel, and Ellenberger, *Existence*, pp. 365–425; Kuhn, "Daseinsanalyse im psychotherapeutischen Gespräch," *Schweizer Archiv für Neurologie und Psychiatrie* 67, no. 1 (1951): 52–60.

88. M. Boss, *Sinn und Gehalt der sexuellen Perversionen: ein daseinanalytischer Beitrag zur Psychopathologie des Phänomens der Liebe* (Bern: Huber, 1947).
89. Letter dated April 27, 1954. See Bert and Basso, *Foucault à Münsterlingen*, p. 183.
90. Foucault, *Binswanger et l'analyse existentielle*, pp. 55–56.
91. Foucault, p. 139.
92. Foucault, p. 140.
93. Foucault, p. 95.
94. Foucault, p. 65.
95. J.-P. Sartre, *Baudelaire*, Les Essais 24 (Paris: Gallimard, 1947); English translation by Martin Turnell, *Baudelaire* (Norfolk, CT: New Directions, 1950); Sartre, *Saint Genet comédien et martyr* (Paris: Gallimard, 1952); English translation by Bernard Frechtman, *Saint Genet: Actor and Martyr* (Minneapolis: University of Minnesota Press, 2012).
96. K. Jaspers, *Nietzsche: An Introduction to the Understanding of His Philosophical Activity*, trans. Charles F. Wallraff and Frederick J. Schmitz (Baltimore: Johns Hopkins University Press, 1997). See in particular, in book 1, the various paragraphs that Jaspers devotes to illness. Among Foucault's work notes, one page is titled "La maladie et Nietzsche" (BnF, Fonds Michel Foucault, Box 33A, folder 1, call number NAF 28730).
97. Sartre, *Baudelaire*, p. 81.
98. BnF, Fonds Foucault, Box 46, folder 4, NAF 28730, 6 unnumbered recto-verso pages.
99. Foucault, "Dream, Imagination and Existence," p. 58.
100. Foucault, p. 58.
101. Foucault, p. 33.
102. Foucault, *Binswanger et l'analyse existentielle*, p. 142.
103. Foucault, p. 142.
104. Foucault, p. 141.
105. Foucault, p. 142.

106. Foucault, p. 144.
107. Foucault, *Mental Illness and Psychology* (Berkeley: University of California Press, 1987), pp. 84–85.
108. Foucault, "Dream, Imagination and Existence," p. 33 (translation modified).
109. Foucault, *Binswanger et l'analyse existentielle*, p. 144.
110. Foucault, p. 143.
111. Foucault, "Dream, Imagination and Existence," p. 33.
112. Foucault, p. 33.
113. Foucault, *Binswanger et l'analyse existentielle*, p. 166.
114. Foucault, p. 132.
115. BnF, Fonds Michel Foucault, Box 38, folder 1.
116. See especially Henri F. Ellenberger, "La psychiatrie suisse," *L'Évolution psychiatrique* 17, no. 2 (1952): 374–377.
117. R. Kuhn, "L. Binswanger, *Grundformen und Erkenntnis menschlichen Daseins*," *Schweizer Archiv für Neurologie und Psychiatrie* 51 (1943): 288–291.
118. BnF, Fonds Michel Foucault, Box 42b, folder 1.
119. Foucault, *Binswanger et l'analyse existentielle*, p. 148.
120. Foucault, p. 166.
121. Foucault, p. 149.
122. Foucault, p. 149–150.
123. Foucault, p. 149.
124. Foucault, p. 166.
125. BnF, Fonds Michel Foucault, Box 42b, folder 1, call number NAF 28730.
126. Karl Friedrich Scheid, "Existenziale Analytik und Psychopathologie," *Der Nervenarzt* 5, no. 12 (1932): 617–625.
127. Renato De Rosa, "Existenzphilosophische Richtungen in der modernen Psychopathologie," *Der Nervenarzt* 23, no. 7 (1952): 256–261.
128. Hans Cornelius Rümke, "Signification de la phénoménologie dans l'étude clinique des délirants," in *Congrès international de psychiatrie: Paris, 1950*, vol. 1, *Psychopathologie générale: Psychopathologie des délires* (Paris: Hermann, 1950), pp. 126–173 (pp. 134–135).
129. "Éditorial: Le Congrès international de psychiatrie et la crise de la psychiatrie contemporaine," *La Raison: Cahiers de psychopathologie scientifique* 2 (1951): p. 7.

130. Foucault, *Binswanger et l'analyse existentielle*, p. 166.
131. Foucault, p. 167.
132. Foucault, p. 166.
133. Foucault, p. 167.
134. Foucault, p. 167.
135. Letter dated April 27, 1954, see Bert and Basso, *Foucault à Münsterlingen*, p. 183.
136. Foucault, "Introduction générale," note 4.
137. Foucault, note 5.
138. Foucault, "Dream, Imagination and Existence," p. 31.
139. Foucault, p. 31.
140. Foucault, "Introduction générale," note 5.
141. Foucault, note 5.
142. Foucault, note 5.
143. M. Foucault, "L'agressivité, l'angoisse et la magie," BnF, Fonds Michel Foucault, Box 46, folder 4, (call number NAF 28730), sheet no. 1.
144. Foucault, sheet no. 1.
145. See Foucault, sheet no. 2: "This is Sartre's conception of the for-itself and of nihilation; it is, according to Merleau-Ponty, the idea of a prereflexive cogito that is rooted in a world that is itself preobjective, 'pregiven'; it is the conception, by E. Weil, of a dialectical subject that carries with its Logos the pure origin of the logic of History and of absolute freedom."
146. Foucault, sheets nos. 2–3.
147. Foucault, sheet no. 12.
148. Manuscript titled "Introduction" (BnF, Fonds Michel Foucault, Box 46, folder 4, call number NAF 28730), notes 2–4.
149. Foucault, sheet no. 3.
150. Foucault, sheet no. 4.
151. Letters from J. Verdeaux to L. Binswanger dated July 1 and September 2, 1954 (Binswanger Archives, Universitätsarchiv Tübingen, call number 443/60).
152. From Foucault's correspondence with the publisher Desclée de Brouwer, we learn that the philosopher had already completed the first part of his translation at the end of 1954 (BNF, Fonds Michel Foucault, Box 5, folder 1, call number NAF 28803).

153. Philippe Artières and Jean-François Bert, *Un succès philosophique: L'*Histoire de la folie à l'âge classique *de Michel Foucault* (Caen: Presses universitaires de Caen-IMEC Éd., 2011), pp. 40–47.
154. Letter from M. Foucault to J. Verdeaux of December 29, 1956 (Family Verdeaux's private archive).
155. This letter is quoted by Philippe Sabot, "The 'World' of Michel Foucault. Phenomenology, psychology, ontology in the 1950s," *Theory, Culture and Society* (forthcoming).
156. M. Foucault, "Philosophie et psychologie" (1965), in *Dits et Ecrits*, vol. 1, no. 30, pp. 438–448 (p. 448); English translation by Robert Hurley, "Philosophy and Psychology," in *Essential Works of Foucault, 1954–1984*, vol. 2, *Aesthetics, Method and Epistemology*, ed. James D. Faubion (New York: New Press, 1998), pp. 249–259 (p. 259).
157. Foucault, p. 259.
158. M. Foucault, "Préface à l'*Histoire de la sexualité*" (1984), in *Dits et Écrits*, vol. 4, no. 340; English translation by William Smock, "Preface to the *History of Sexuality*, volume II," in *The Essential Works of Foucault, 1954–1984*, vol. 1, *Ethics, Subjectivity and Truth*, ed. Paul Rabinow (New York: New Press, 1997), pp. 199–205 (p. 200).
159. Foucault, "Notice historique" (1964), in *Dits et Écrits*, vol. 1, no. 19, pp. 288–293 (p. 293, n. 1).
160. Foucault, "Dream, Imagination and Existence," p. 31.
161. Foucault, p. 31.
162. BNF, Fonds Michel Foucault, Box 41, folder 2 (call number NAF 28730).
163. BNF, Fonds Michel Foucault, Box 37 (call number NAF 28730).
164. Foucault's archives at BnF revealed a twenty-five-page reading note concerning Wilhelm Keller's work *Vom Wesen des Menschen* (Basel: Verlag für Recht und Gesellschaft, 1943) (BNF, Box 37, folder 2).
165. In two reading notes included in the folder on Scheler, titled, respectively, "Actes et fonctions" and "Équivoques de la distinction: actes-fonctions," Foucault mentions the book *Der Formalismus in der Ethik und die materiale Wertethik: Neuer Versuch der Grundlegung eines ethischen Personalismus* (Halle-sur-Saale: Niemeyer, 1927). On this topic, Foucault analyzes the distinction between acts and functions on the basis of Jules Vuillemin's reading of it in his study *L'Être et le Travail:*

2. THE BINSWANGER DOSSIER ⊗ 255

les conditions dialectiques de la psychologie et de la sociologie, Bibliothèque de philosophie contemporaine: Psychologie et sociologie (Paris: PUF, 1949). Foucault invokes in particular Scheler's studies: *Die Idole der Selbsterkenntnis* (in *Abhandlungen und Aufsätze*, vol. 2 [Leipzig: Verlag der Weissen Bücher, 1915], p. 3–168); "Zur Idee des Menschen" (1914, in *Vom Umsturz der Werte: Abhandlungen und Aufsätze*, vol. 1 (Leipzig: Neue Geist, 1919), pp. 271–312); and "Idealismus - Realismus" (*Philosophischer Anzeiger* 2 (1928): 255–324).

166. See *La question anthropologique. Cours. 1954–1955*, ed. Arianna Sforzini, Hautes Études (Paris: Seuil/Gallimard/EHESS, 2022); BnF, Box 46, folder 1, call number NAF 28730; and "Problèmes de l'anthropologie," notes by Jacques Lagrange, IMEC, Fonds Michel Foucault, C.2.1/ FCL 2. A03-08.

167. In his reading notes, Foucault mentions Scheler in particular in relation to the phenomenon of shame developed in Binswanger's clinical case study of Ellen West, as well as in relation to the concept of space in psychopathology—more specifically, Binswanger's concept of *"gestimmte Raum"* ("tuned" space) (BnF, Box 38, folder 3, call number NAF 28730). Foucault also mentions Scheler in some of his reading notes on Hans Kunz: in a reading note about the article "Idee, Wesen und Wirklichkeit des Menschen: Bemerkungen zu einem Grundproblem der philosophischen Anthropologie" (*Studia Philosophica* 4, no. 147 [1944]: 147–169), he cites Scheler on the problem of sexuality in relation to the determination of the essence of man (BnF, Box 42b, folder 1). In another series of notes held in the same box, Foucault summarizes Kunz's article "Die anthropologische Betrachtungsweise in der Psychopathologie" (*Zeitschrift für die gesamte Neurologie und Psychiatrie* 172 [1941]: 145–180) and refers to Scheler's definition of anthropology set out in "Mensch und Geschichte" (*Neue Rundschau* 37 [1926], 449–476). Foucault also mentions Franz Fischer's article "Zeitstruktur und Schizophrenie," which quotes Scheler on the subject of his conception of time as "Tätigkeitsform des Geistes" ("form of activity of the mind").

168. M. Scheler, *Nature et Formes de la sympathie: Contribution à l'étude des lois de la vie émotionnelle* was translated in 1928 by Marcel Lefebvre, Bibliothèque scientifique (Paris: Payot 1928); *L'Homme du ressentiment*

was published in 1933 (Paris: Gallimard, Les Essais 9]); the first three titles mentioned in the summary drawn up by Foucault were translated by Pierre Klossowski in 1936, in *Le Sens de la souffrance, suivi de deux autres essais*, in the series "Philosophie de l'esprit" directed by René Le Senne and Louis Lavelle (Paris: Aubier-Montaigne, 1936). *Le Saint, le Génie, le Héros* was published in 1944 (trans. Émile Marmy [Fribourg: Egloff, 1944]), while *La Situation de l'homme dans le monde* and *La Pudeur* had just appeared, in 1951 and 1952 respectively (trans. Maurice Dupuy [Paris: Aubier, 1951, 1952). On the French reading of Max Scheler's work, see Olivier Agard, "Max Scheler entre la France et l'Allemagne," *Revue germanique internationale*, no. 11 (2013): 15–34.

169. BnF, Fonds Michel Foucault, Box 37, folder 2, call number NAF 28730.
170. Foucault, *La question anthropologique. Cours. 1954–1955*.
171. Foucault, "La recherche scientifique et la psychologie," p. 152.
172. Foucault, *Binswanger et l'analyse existentielle*, p. 35.
173. Foucault, *La question anthropologique. Cours. 1954–1955*, p. 24.
174. Foucault, p. 50.
175. Foucault, p. 59.
176. Foucault, p. 41.
177. Foucault, p. 30.
178. Foucault, p. 33.
179. Foucault, p. 63.
180. Foucault, "Philosophy and Psychology," p. 257.
181. Foucault, *La question anthropologique. Cours. 1954–1955*, p. 128.
182. Foucault, p. 121.
183. Foucault, p. 131.
184. Foucault, p. 131.
185. On this topic, see Luca Paltrinieri, "A priori storico, archeologia, antropologia: suggestioni kantiane nel pensiero di Michel Foucault," *Studi kantiani* 20 (2007): 73–97. See also Béatrice Han-Pile, *Foucault's Critical Project: Between the Transcendental and the Historical* (Stanford: Stanford University Press, 2002).
186. Foucault, *Binswanger et l'analyse existentielle*, p. 35.
187. Foucault, p. 26.
188. Foucault, p. 27.
189. Foucault, p. 27.

2. THE BINSWANGER DOSSIER ⌘ 257

190. Foucault, p. 35.
191. Foucault, p. 35.
192. Foucault, *La question anthropologique. Cours. 1954–1955*, p. 17.
193. Foucault, *Binswanger et l'analyse existentielle*, p. 65.
194. Foucault, p. 144.
195. Foucault, *Maladie mentale et personnalité*, p. 54.
196. Foucault, "Dream, Imagination and Existence," p. 32.
197. Foucault, p. 32.
198. Foucault, p. 32.
199. Foucault, *Binswanger et l'analyse existentielle*, p. 143.
200. Foucault, "Dream, Imagination and Existence," p. 32.
201. Foucault, p. 32.
202. This reading note concerns Hans Kunz's essay "Die anthropologische Betrachtungsweise in der Psychopathologie" (BnF, Fonds Michel Foucault, Box 42b, folder 1, call number NAF 28730).
203. Foucault, *Binswanger et l'analyse existentielle*, p. 166.
204. Foucault, "L'agressivité, l'angoisse et la magie," sheet no. 12.
205. Foucault, sheet no. 9.
206. BnF, Fonds Michel Foucault, Box 3, folder 3, call number NAF 28803.
207. Foucault, "L'agressivité, l'angoisse et la magie," sheet nos. 2–3.
208. Foucault, sheet no. 11.
209. Cf. Foucault, *Introduction to Kant's* Anthropology, trans. Roberto Nigro and Kate Briggs, ed. Roberto Nigro (Los Angeles: Semiotext[e], 2008), p. 123.
210. Foucault, p. 124.
211. Foucault, *La question anthropologique. Cours. 1954–1955*, p. 168.
212. Foucault, p. 179.
213. Foucault, p. 166.
214. Foucault, p. 63.
215. Foucault, *Introduction to Kant's* Anthropology, p. 121.
216. Foucault, "Dream, Imagination and Existence," p. 32. From this point of view, we agree with B. Han, who maintains that "the possibility of establishing a specific relation between the empirical and the transcendental is precisely what is picked out by (existential) anthropology in the 'Introduction to Binswanger's *Dream and Existence*'" ("Phenomenology and Anthropology in Foucault's Introduction to Binswanger's

Dream and Existence: A Mirror Image of *The Order Of Things?*," *History and Theory* 55, no. 4 [2016]: 7–22," note 8, p. 9).

3. ARCHAEOLOGICAL METHOD

1. This document is reproduced in part in Philippe Artières and Jean-François Bert, *Un succès philosophique:* L'Histoire de la folie à l'âge classique *de Michel Foucault* (Caen: Presses universitaires de Caen-IMEC, 2011), pp. 94–95.
2. P. Artières and J.-F. Bert, "Porter le livre chez les historiens: histoire et psychologie," in *Un succès philosophique*, pp. 135–149.
3. M. Foucault, "Préface à l'*Histoire de la sexualité*" (1984), in *Dits et Écrits*, vol. 4, no. 340; English translation by William Smock, "Preface to the History of Sexuality, volume II," in *The Essential Works of Foucault, 1954–1984*, vol. 1, *Ethics, Subjectivity and Truth*, ed. Paul Rabinow (New York: New Press, 1997), p. 200.
4. Michel Foucault, *Mental Illness and Psychology*, English translation by Alan Sheridan (Berkeley: University of California Press, 1987), p. 85.
5. Foucault, p. 85.
6. Foucault, p. 56.
7. See on this topic the work of the Italian philosopher Enzo Melandri, *La linea e il circolo: Studio logico-filosofico sull'analogia* (Bologna: Il Mulino, 1968; Macerata: Quodlibet [Quaderni Quodlibet 18], 2004), p. 67.
8. M. Foucault, "Préface," in *Folie et Déraison* (Paris: Plon, 1961); reprinted in *Dits et Écrits, 1954–1988*, ed. Daniel Defert and François Ewald, with the collaboration of Jacques Lagrange (Paris: Gallimard, 1994), vol. 1, no. 4, pp. 159–167; English translation by Jonathan Murphy and Jean Khalfa, "Preface to the 1961 Edition," in *History of Madness*, ed. Jean Khalfa (London: Routledge, 2006), pp. xxvii–xxxvi (p. xxvii).
9. Foucault, *Mental Illness and Psychology*, p. 74.
10. G. Canguilhem, "Rapport sur le manuscrit déposé par M. Foucault," in *Œuvres complètes*, vol. 4, *Résistance, philosophie biologique et histoire des sciences 1940–1965* (Paris: Vrin, 2015), pp. 913–918 (p. 918). English translation by Ann Hobart, "Report from Mr. Canguilhem on the Manuscript Filed by Mr. Michel Foucault, Director of the Institut Français of Hamburg, in Order to Obtain Permission to Print His

Principal Thesis for the Doctor of Letters," *Critical Inquiry* 21, no. 2 (1995): 277–281, p. 281.
11. Pierre Macherey, "Aux sources de l'*Histoire de la folie*. Une rectification et ses limites," *Critique*, no. 471–472 (1986): 753–774, p. 770.
12. Foucault, *Introduction to Kant's* Anthropology, trans. Roberto Nigro and Kate Briggs, ed. Roberto Nigro (Los Angeles: Semiotext[e], 2008), p. 116.
13. M. Foucault, "Philosophie et psychologie" (1965), in *Dits et Ecrits*, vol. 1, no. 30, pp. 438–448 (p. 448); English translation by Robert Hurley, "Philosophy and Psychology," in *Essential Works of Foucault, 1954–1984*, vol. 2, *Aesthetics, Method and Epistemology*, ed. James D. Faubion (New York: New Press, 1998), pp. 249–259 (p. 250).
14. Foucault, *Les mots et les choses: Une archéologie des sciences humaines*, Bibliothèque des sciences humaines (Paris: Gallimard, 1966), p. 13; English translation, *The Order of Things: An Archaeology of the Human Sciences* (New York: Routledge, 2002), p. xxiii.
15. Georges Lanteri-Laura, "Le voyage dans l'anti-psychiatrie anglaise," *L'Évolution psychiatrique* 61, no. 3 (1996): 621–633, p. 623. Todd May makes a similar observation with regard to Foucault's career itself, in the context of locating a common thread between the early writings on phenomenology and the later works. According to May, what remains continuous throughout Foucault's career is an underlying nonreductive approach to the questions: "What are we? What might we be?" See May, "Foucault's Relation to Phenomenology," in *The Cambridge Companion to Foucault*, ed. Gary Gutting, 2nd ed., Cambridge Companions to Philosophy (Cambridge: Cambridge University Press, 2006), pp. 284–311 (pp. 307–308): "As Foucault's thought matures, the character of what is 'heavy and oppressive' changes. But what is at issue—who we are, who we might be—remains the same. In the end, Foucault leaves phenomenology, but the spirit of phenomenology does not leave him." See also Gérard Lebrun, "Note sur la phénoménologie dans *Les Mots et les Choses*," in *Michel Foucault philosophe: Rencontre International, Paris 9–11 janvier 1988*, Des Travaux (Paris: Éditions du Seuil, 1989), pp. 33–52. According to Lebrun, Foucault shares with Husserl's phenomenology the neutral position of the philosopher with regard to the knowledge whose presuppositions he intends to unmask.

16. Henri Maldiney, "Psychose et présence" (1976), in *Penser l'homme et la folie: À la lumière de l'analyse existentielle et de l'analyse du destin*, 3rd ed., Collection Krisis (Grenoble: Jérôme Millon, 1991, 2007), pp. 5–82 (p. 9).
17. We might think, for instance, of Laing's main work's subtitle: *An Existential Study in Sanity and Madness* (London: Tavistock, 1960), or the book series within which Laing and Cooper's *Reason and Violence* appeared in 1964: "Studies in Existential Analysis and Phenomenology." One might also mention the Italian psychiatrist Franco Basaglia, who linked existential psychiatry and Foucault's work; see his works from 1953 to 1968: *Scritti*, ed. Franca Ongaro Basaglia, vol. 1, *Dalla psichiatria fenomenologica all'esperienza di Gorizia* (Torino: Einaudi, 1981–1982).
18. M. Foucault, "Dream, Imagination and Existence," in *Dream and Existence*, by Michel Foucault and Ludwig Binswanger, special issue of *Review of Existential Psychology and Psychiatry*, ed. Keith Hoeller, vol. 19, no. 1 (1985): 29–78, p. 32.
19. M. Foucault, *Remarks on Marx: Conversation with Duccio Trombadori*, trans. R. James Goldstein and James Cascaito (New York: Semiotext[e], 1991), p. 72. Translation modified.
20. Foucault, "Preface to the *History of Sexuality* Volume II," p. 200. The italics are mine.
21. M. Foucault, *The Birth of the Clinic: An Archaeology of Medical Perception* (London: Tavistock, 1973), p. xv. The italics are mine.
22. See Karl Jaspers, "Kausale und 'verständliche' Zusammenhänge zwischen Schicksal und Psychose bei der Dementia praecox (Schizophrenie)," *Zeitschrift für die gesamte Neurologie und Psychiatrie* 14 (1913): 158–263; also in *Gesamtausgabe*, vol. 1-3, *Gesammelte Schriften über Psychopathologie*, ed. Chantal Marazia, with the collaboration of Dirk Fonfara (Basel: Schwabe, 2019), pp. 383–479.
23. Cf. Ludwig Binswanger's reply to Jaspers: *"Bemerkungen* zu der Arbeit Jaspers' 'Kausale und *verständliche* Zusammenhänge zwischen Schicksal und Psychose bei der Dementia praecox (Schizophrenie),'" *Internationale Zeitschrift für ärztliche Psychoanalyse* 1 (1913): 383–390.
24. Ludwig Binswanger, "Erfahren, Verstehen, Deuten in der Psychoanalyse," *Imago* 12, nos. 2–3 (1926): 223–237, see p. 229 (in *Ausgewählte*

Werke, vol. 3, *Vorträge und Aufsätze*, ed. Max Herzog [Heidelberg: Asanger, 1993], 3–16, p. 9).
25. Binswanger, p. 233 (*Ausgewählte Werke*, 3:12).
26. L. Binswanger, "Welche Aufgaben ergeben sich für die Psychiatrie aus den Fortschritten der neueren Psychologie?," *Zeitschrift für die gesamte Neurologie und Psychiatrie* 91, nos. 3–5 (1924): 402–436 (in *Ausgewählte Vorträge und Aufsätze*, vol. 2, *Zur Problematik der psychiatrischen Forschung und zum Problem der Psychiatrie* [Bern: Francke, 1955], pp. 111–146).
27. See Binswanger, "Erfahren, Verstehen, Deuten in der Psychoanalyse," p. 235 (*Ausgewählte Werke*, 3:13).
28. L. Binswanger, "Lebensfunktion und innere Lebensgeschichte," *Monatsschrift für Psychiatrie und Neurologie* 68 (1928): 52–79, p. 64; in *Ausgewählte Werke*, 3:71–94. Translations from Binswanger's works are mine, unless otherwise noted.
29. L. Binswanger, "Über Phänomenologie," *Zeitschrift für die gesamte Neurologie und Psychiatrie* 82 (1923): 10–45, p. 34; in *Ausgewählte Werke*, 3:57.
30. See in particular L. Binswanger, *Wandlungen in der Auffassung und Deutung des Traumes von den Griechen bis zur Gegenwart* (Berlin: Springer, 1928).
31. Binswanger, "Über Phänomenologie," p. 57.
32. L. Binswanger, "Über Ideenflucht," *Schweizer Archiv für Neurologie und Psychiatrie* 27, no. 2 (1932): 203–217; 28, nos. 1–2 (1932): 18–26, 183–202; 29, no. 1 (1932): 193ff.; 30, no. 1 (1933): 68–85; published in one volume in Zürich by Orel Füssli in 1933 (reprinted in New York by Garland in 1980); *Ausgewählte Werke*, vol. 1, *Formen mißglückten Daseins*, ed. Max Herzog (Heidelberg: Asanger, 1992), p. 132.
33. According to Heidegger, the "analytic" of the ontological (*existential*) structures of *Dasein* ("being-there") was only the preliminary condition for approaching the question of Being (*Seinsfrage*); that is the problem of the "*Fundamentalontologie*." In fact, Heidegger's "*Daseinsanalytik*" was grounded on what he called the "ontological difference" between *Being* and the ontic beings as "beings-at-hand" (*Vorhandensein*). This analytic should therefore not be confused with an "ontic" analysis and understanding of "man," like the analysis

offered by anthropology, psychology, or psychiatry. This is why Heidegger would later criticize Binswanger's project of *Daseinsanalyse*, in particular during the philosophical seminars he gave between 1959 and 1969 in Zurich before an audience of psychiatrists. M. Heidegger, *Zollikon Seminars: Protocols, Conversations, Letters*, ed. Medard Boss, trans. with notes and afterword by Franz Mayr and Richard Askay (Evanston, IL: Northwestern University Press, 2001).

34. L. Binswanger, "Über die daseinsanalytische Forschungsrichtung in der Psychiatrie," *Schweizer Archiv für Psychiatrie und Neurologie* 57 (1946): 209–235 (in his *Ausgewählte Werke*, 3:231–257); English translation by Ernest Angel, "The Existential Analysis School of Thought," in *Existence: A New Dimension in Psychiatry and Psychology*, ed. Rollo May, Ernest Angel, and Henri F. Ellenberger (New York: Basic, 1958), pp. 191–212 (p. 201).
35. Binswanger, "Über Ideenflucht," p. 104.
36. Binswanger, "The Existential Analysis School of Thought," p. 201.
37. L. Binswanger, *Drei Formen missglückten Daseins* (Tübingen: Niemeyer, 1956); *Ausgewählte Werke*, 1:411.
38. Binswanger, p. 398.
39. Binswanger, "Über Ideenflucht," p. 104. For a historical and theoretical account of the role of Kurt Goldstein's epistemological insights in the context of the medical sciences and clinical practice of his time, see Anne Harrington, *Reenchanted Science: Holism in German Culture from Wilhelm II to Hitler* (Princeton: Princeton University Press, 1996), especially chap. 5, "The Self-Actualizing Brain and the Biology of Existential Choice," pp. 140–174.
40. Binswanger, "The Existential Analysis School of Thought," p. 199.
41. L. Binswanger, "Über Ideenflucht," p. 209.
42. L. Binswanger "Review of E. Minkowski, *La Schizophrénie*," *Schweizer Archiv für Neurologie und Psychiatrie* 22 (1928): 158–163, p. 161.
43. M. Foucault, *Maladie mentale et personnalité*, Initiation philosophique (Paris: PUF, 1954), p. 54.
44. Binswanger, *Wandlungen in der Auffassung*, p. 108.
45. Foucault, "Dream, Imagination and Existence," p. 58.
46. Foucault, pp. 58–59. The italics are mine.
47. Cf. Giorgio Agamben, *Signatura rerum: Sul metodo* (Turin: Bollati Boringhieri, 2008); English translation by Luca D'Isanto with Kevin

Attel, *The Signature of All Things* (New York: Zone, 2009), chap. 3, "Philosophical Archaeology," pp. 81–111 (p. 107).
48. Binswanger, *Wandlungen in der Auffassung*, p. 38.
49. I thank Daniel Defert for making this document available to me. Foucault devoted another, rather schematic reading note to the *Wandlungen*; it is conserved at the BnF, Fonds Michel Foucault, Box 38, folder 1.
50. Foucault, "Dream, Imagination and Existence," p. 33.
51. Foucault, p. 32.
52. Martin Heidegger, *Being and Time*, trans. by John Macquarrie and Edward Robinson (Oxford: Basic Blackwell, 1962), §4, p. 33.
53. Henri Ey, "Le développement 'mécaniciste' de la psychiatrie à l'abri du dualisme 'cartésien,'" in *Études psychiatriques*, vol. 1 (Paris: Desclée de Brouwer & Cie, 1948; 2nd ed. [Bibliothèque neuro-psychiatrique de langue française], 1952), p. 65.
54. G. Canguilhem, *La connaissance de la vie* (Paris: Hachette, 1952; Problèmes et controverses Paris: Vrin, 1965), p. 36; translated by Stefanos Geroulanos and Daniela Ginsburg, *Knowledge of Life* (New York: Fordham University Press, 2008), p. xx.
55. Daniel Lagache, "Le normal et le pathologique d'après Georges Canguilhem," *Bulletin de la Faculté des Lettres de Strasbourg* 24 (1946): 117–130, pp. 129–130.
56. Georges Canguilhem, "Note sur la situation faite en France à la philosophie biologique," *Revue de Métaphysique et de Morale* 52 (1947): 322–332 (in *Œuvres complètes*, 4:307–320). It is worth noting that this paper preceded a contribution by Eugène Minkowski: "Psychiatrie et métaphysique. À la recherche de l'humain et du vécu," pp. 333–358.
57. Canguilhem, "Note sur la situation faite," p. 327.
58. G. Canguilhem, *On the Normal and the Pathological*, trans. Carolyn R. Fawcett (Dordrecht: Reidel, 1978), p. 104; "The Living and Its Milieu" (1946–47), in *Knowledge of Life*, p. 98–120.
59. Foucault, "Introduction" to Canguilhem, *On the Normal and the Pathological*, pp. ix–xx. This text was revised by Foucault in 1984 and published as "Life: Experience and Science," trans. Robert Hurley, in *Essential Works of Foucault*, 2:465–478.
60. Maurice Merleau-Ponty, "Le métaphysique dans l'homme," *Revue de Métaphysique et de Morale* 52, nos. 3–4 (1947): 290–307; translated by

Hubert Dreyfus and Patricia Allen Dreyfus, "The Metaphysical in Man," in *Sense and Non-Sense* (Evanston, IL: Northwestern University Press, 1964), pp. 83–98 (p. 93).
61. Merleau-Ponty, p. 93.
62. Foucault, "Dream, Imagination and Existence," p. 32.
63. Merleau-Ponty, "The Metaphysical in Man," p. 93.
64. Merleau-Ponty, *The Structure of Behavior*, trans. Alden L. Fisher (Boston: Beacon, 1965), p. 123.
65. Merleau-Ponty, *Phénoménologie de la perception*, Bibliothèque des idées (1945; Paris: Gallimard, 1976); English translation by Colin Smith, *Phenomenology of Perception* (London: Routledge and Kegan Paul, 1962), p. 61.
66. On Foucault's translation, see Stuart Elden, "Foucault as Translator of Binswanger and von Weizsäcker," *Theory, Culture and Society* (First Published 2020), https://doi.org/10.1177/0263276420950459.
67. Kurt Goldstein, *Der Aufbau des Organismus: Einführung in die Biologie unter besonderer Berücksichtigung der Erfahrungen am kranken Menschen* (Haag: M. Nijhoff, 1934); French translation by E. Burckhardt and Jean Kuntz, *La structure de l'organisme: Introduction à la biologie à partir de la pathologie humaine* (Paris: Gallimard, 1951). This work was published in Bibliothèque de philosophie, the philosophical series edited by Sartre and Merleau-Ponty: English translation, *The Organism: A Holistic Approach to Biology Derived from Pathological Data in Man* (New York: Zone, 1995).
68. Frederik J. J. Buytendijk, *Attitudes et mouvements: étude fonctionnelle du mouvement humain*, trans. L. van Haecht, Textes et études anthropologiques (Paris: Desclée de Brouwer, 1957).
69. See Julia Gruevska, "Von der Tierphysiologie zur Psychologie des Menschen: Ein Einblick in Werk und Wirken Frederik Buytendijks," *Internationales Jahrbuch für Philosophische Anthropologie* 8, no. 1 (2018): 87–106.
70. Eugène Minkowski, *La Schizophrénie: Psychopathologie des schizoïdes et des schizophrènes*, new ed., Bibliothèque neuro-psychiatrique de langue française (1933; Paris: Desclée de Brouwer, 1953), p. 237.
71. It is precisely to this idea, as it appeared in the field of psychiatry, that Canguilhem refers in his *On the Normal and the Pathological*, chap. 1. On this topic he cites Lagache, Minkowski, and Henri Ey.

72. Cf. Erwin Straus, *Vom Sinn der Sinne: ein Beitrag zur Grundlegung der Psychologie* (Berlin: Springer, 1931, 2nd ed., 1956), note 1, p. 373.
73. Straus, p. 298. The text by Binswanger that Straus is referring to is *Grundformen und Erkenntnis menschlichen Daseins*.
74. Foucault, "Dream, Imagination and Existence," p. 32.
75. M. Foucault, *Binswanger et l'analyse existentielle*, ed. Elisabetta Basso, Cours et travaux de Michel Foucault avant le Collège de France, ed. François Ewald (Hautes Études) (Paris: Seuil/Gallimard/EHESS, 2021), p. 144.
76. Foucault, "Dream, Imagination and Existence," p. 31.
77. Foucault, p. 34.
78. Merleau-Ponty, *Phenomenology of Perception*, pp. vii–viii.
79. Foucault, "Dream, Imagination and Existence," pp. 57–58. The italics are mine.
80. Foucault, pp. 57–58.
81. See, in particular, Jean-François Courtine, "Foucault lecteur de Husserl. L'*a priori* historique et le quasi-transcendantal," *Giornale di metafisica* 29, no. 1 (2007): 211–232; Luca Paltrinieri, "Les aventures du transcendantal: Kant, Husserl, Foucault," *Lumières*, no. 16 (2010): 11–31; Wouter Goris, "L'a priori historique chez Husserl et Foucault (I): La pertinence philosophique d'un concept directeur de l'épistémologie historique, " *Philosophie* 123, no. 4 (2014): 3–27; (II), *Philosophie* 125, no. 2 (2015): 22–43.
82. See on this subject Hubert Dreyfus and Paul Rabinow's argument that Foucault's archaeology does not escape the "analytic of finitude" that characterizes post-Kantian philosophy. If, as Foucault asserts, it is true that any discourse that seeks to establish the foundation of its own possibility is subject to the laws of this "empirico-transcendental doublet," then Foucault's own discourse must also fall into the trap of this doublet. Hubert Dreyfus and Paul Rabinow, *Michel Foucault: Beyond Structuralism and Hermeneutics*, 2nd ed. (Chicago: University of Chicago Press, 1983), chap. 4, "The Methodological Failure of Archaeology," pp. 79–100. This argument is taken up by Béatrice Han-Pile, according to whom Foucauldian archaeology, by defining the historical *a priori* simultaneously as the set of rules that characterize a discursive practice and as the condition of reality of statements, repeats the

confusion between empirical and transcendental that it had the goal of unmasking. Han-Pile articulates her question in the following way: "The problem becomes whether or not, in this renewal of the critical question and in this historicizing reformulation of the transcendental theme, Foucault really succeeds in escaping the 'anthropological illusions' denounced by the *Commentary*." Béatrice Han-Pile, *Foucault's Critical Project: Between the Transcendental and the Historical* (Stanford: Stanford University Press, 2002), p. 46. See also B. Han, "L'a priori historique selon Michel Foucault: difficultés archéologiques," in *Lectures de Michel Foucault*, vol. 2, *Foucault et la philosophie*, ed. Emmanuel Da Silva, Theoria (Lyon: ENS Éditions, 2003), pp. 23–38.
83. Han-Pile, *Foucault's Critical Project*, p. 36.
84. See on this topic Umberto Eco, *La struttura assente*, Nuovi saggi italiani 1 (Milano: Bompiani, 1968), pp. 346–350; Eco underscores that insofar as *The Order of Things* presents itself as a condemnation of modern man's misguided pretension to determine the transcendental foundation of knowledge, it makes no sense to expect Foucault to define a status—whether transcendental, ontological, or gnoseological—for the epistemological "grids" that he uncovers and uses.
85. The connection I am drawing between existential analysis and Foucault's archaeological method does not, however, consist in the idea advanced by Gary Gutting that starting with *History of Madness* Foucault was "envisaging some sort of historical application of existential analysis," namely, "trying to develop a way of extending the techniques of existential analysis to understand how people of past historical periods constituted the world of their experience." Gutting, *Michel Foucault's Archaeology of Scientific Reason*, Modern European Philosophy (Cambridge: Cambridge University Press, 1989), p. 68–69.
86. M. Foucault, *Archaeology of Knowledge*, trans. A. M. Sheridan Smith (London: Routledge, 2002), p. 144.
87. Foucault, *The Birth of the Clinic*, p. xix.
88. M. Foucault, "Structuralism and Post-Structuralism" (1983), trans. J. Harding, in *The Essential Works of Foucault, 1954–1984*, ed. Paul Rabinow, vol. 2, *Aesthetics, Method, and Epistemology*, pp. 433–458.
89. Foucault, *Archaeology of Knowledge*, p. 143.
90. Foucault, *The Order of Things*, p. 155. The italics are mine.

91. Georges Canguilhem, "Galilée: la signification de l'œuvre et la leçon de l'homme" (1964), in *Études d'histoire et de philosophie des sciences*, Problèmes et controverses (Paris: Vrin, 1968), pp. 37–50.
92. Foucault, "La recherche scientifique et la psychologie" (1957), in *Dits et écrits*, ed. Daniel Defert and François Ewald, with Jacques Lagrange (Paris: Gallimard, 1994), vol. 1, no. 3, pp. 137–138.
93. Foucault, p. 138.
94. Foucault, *The Order of Things*, p. 207.
95. Cf. Jocelyn Benoist, "Sur l'état présent de la phénoménologie," in *L'Idée de phénoménologie*, Le grenier à sel (Paris: Beauchesne, 2001), pp. 1–43.
96. Foucault, *The Birth of the Clinic*, p. x. The italics are mine.
97. Gaston Bachelard, *The Formation of the Scientific Mind: Contribution to a Psychoanalysis of Objective Knowledge*, trans. M. McAllester Jones (Manchester: Clinamen, 2001).
98. Foucault, *The Birth of the Clinic*, p. x.
99. Foucault, p. xi.
100. Foucault, p. xv.
101. Foucault, p. xi.
102. Foucault, p. xxi.
103. Foucault, *Archaeology of Knowledge*, p. 24.
104. Foucault, p. 147. The italics are mine.
105. Foucault, p. 147.
106. See, for example, Foucault, "Qui êtes-vous, professeur Foucault?" (1967), in *Dits et écrits*, vol. 1, no. 50, pp. 601–623 (p. 606); English translation by Lucille Cairns, "Who Are You, Professor Foucault?," in *Religion and Culture*, ed. Jeremy R. Carrette (Manchester: Manchester University Press, 1999), pp. 87–103 (p. 91).
107. Foucault, "Who Are You, Professor Foucault?," p. 97.
108. Foucault, *The Order of Things*, p. xvi.
109. Foucault, p. xviii.
110. Foucault, p. xvii. Translation modified to reflect the original French.
111. Foucault, p. xviii.
112. Foucault, p. xvi.
113. Foucault, p. xxi.
114. Foucault, p. xvii.
115. Foucault, p. xviii.

116. Foucault, p. xix.
117. Foucault, p. xxi.
118. Foucault, p. xxi.
119. Foucault, p. xxi.
120. Foucault, p. 299. The italics are mine.
121. Foucault, p. xxi.
122. Foucault, p. 240.
123. Foucault, p. xxi.
124. Foucault, p. xx.
125. Foucault, p. 53.
126. Foucault, p. 275.
127. L. Binswanger, *"Manieriertheit,"* in *Drei Formen missglückten Daseins* (Tübingen: Niemeyer, 1956); in *Ausgewählte Werke*, 1:360.
128. Foucault, *The Order of Things*, p. xx.
129. Foucault, p. xx.
130. Foucault, p. xix.
131. See A. Gelb et K. Goldstein, "Über Farbennamenamnesie," *Psychologische Forschungen* 11 (1924): 1127–1186. Goldstein returns to this example in a chapter of his book *Human Nature in the Light of Psychopathology* (Cambridge, MA: Harvard University Press, 1940), pp. 69–84. Foucault cites these two studies in a folder concerning Goldstein (BnF, Fonds Michel Foucault, Box 44b, folder 3, call number NAF 28730).
132. See chap. 1 of the present work.
133. Foucault, *The Order of Things*, p. xx.
134. Foucault, p. xx.
135. Foucault, *The Birth of the Clinic*, p. xi.
136. Foucault, p. x.
137. Foucault, *The Order of Things*, p. xxii.
138. Foucault, p. xxiii.
139. See M. Heidegger, *Sein und Zeit* (Halle: Niemeyer Verlag, 1927); *Gesamtausgabe* [GA], vol. 2, ed. F.-W. von Herrmann (Frankfurt am Main: Klostermann, 1977), §11 (GA, p. 70).
140. M. Foucault, *The Order of Discourse* (1971), in *Untying the Text: A Post-Structuralist Reader*, ed. Robert Young (Boston: Routledge and Kegan Paul, 1981), pp. 48–78 (p. 76).

141. Foucault, *Archaeology of Knowledge*, 143.
142. Foucault, p. 201.
143. Foucault, p. 224.
144. Foucault, *The Order of Things*, p. xix.
145. Foucault, p. 172.
146. M. Foucault, "Entretien avec Madeleine Chapsal" (1966), in *Dits et écrits*, vol. 1, no. 37, pp. 513–518 (p. 518).
147. See Foucault, "Foreword to the English Edition," in *The Order of Things*, pp. ix–xiv (p. xi).
148. Foucault, *The Order of Things*, p. 299.
149. In the English translation of *The Order of Things*, this term is translated as "arrangement," although in French it signifies *disposition* in the sense of an *attitude*. In what follows, while following the existing English translation, I will replace "arrangement" with "disposition."
150. Foucault, pp. 60, 149, 172, 330, 373, 394, 422.
151. Foucault, pp. 39, 171, 182, 235, 280, 285, 372.
152. Foucault, pp. 172, 285.
153. Minkowski, *La schizophrénie*; see in particular chapter 1, "Schizoïdie et syntonie." See also Minkowski, "Les notions bleulériennes: voie d'accès aux analyses phénoménologiques et existentielles," in *Annales Médico-Psychologiques* 15, no. 2 (1957): 833–844; reprinted in *Au de-là du rationalisme morbide* (Paris: L'Harmattan, 1997), pp. 141–151.
154. Minkowski, *La schizophrénie*, p. 45.
155. Foucault, *Archaeology of Knowledge*, p. 33.
156. G. Canguilhem, "Mort de l'homme ou épuisement du cogito?," *Critique*, no. 242 (1967): 599–618, p. 618; English translation by Catherine Porter, "The Death of Man, or Exhaustion of the Cogito?," in Gutting, *The Cambridge Companion to Foucault*, pp. 74–94 (p. 94).
157. Foucault, *Archaeology of Knowledge*, pp. 144, 145, 146, 215.
158. Foucault, p. 8.
159. Foucault, p. 45.
160. Foucault, p. 146.
161. Foucault, p. 204. The italics are mine.
162. M. Foucault, "Who Are You, Professor Foucault?," p. 102: "We have to resign ourselves to taking, faced with mankind, a position similar to the one taken towards the end of the eighteenth century with regard

to other living species, when it was realised that they do not function for someone—neither for themselves, nor for man, nor for God—but that they quite simply function. . . . Species do not function for themselves, nor for man, nor for the greater glory of God; they confine themselves to functioning."

163. M. Foucault, "Qu'est-ce qu'un auteur?" (1969), in *Dits et écrits*, vol. 1, no. 69, p. 791; English translation, "What Is an Author?," in *The Art of Art History: A Critical Ontology*, ed. Donald Preziosi, 2nd ed. (New York: Oxford University Press, 2009), pp. 321–333, 535–537 (p. 321). The translation has been modified in part; the italics are mine.

164. M. Foucault, "Les problèmes de la culture: Un débat Foucault-Preti" (1972), in *Dits et écrits*, ed. Daniel Defert and François Ewald, with Jacques Lagrange, Bibliothèque des sciences humaines (Paris: Gallimard, 1994), vol. 2, no. 109, p. 373; English translation by Jared Becker and James Cascaito, "An Historian of Culture," in *Foucault Live: Interviews, 1961–1984*, ed. S. Lotringer (New York: Semiotext[e], 1996), pp. 73–88 (p. 78). The italics are mine.

165. Foucault, *The Order of Things*, p. 331.

166. Foucault, *Archaeology of Knowledge*, p. 144.

167. Foucault, p. 161.

168. Foucault, p. 143.

169. Voir E. Minkowski, "Psychopathologie et psychologie," *Revue Philosophique de la France et de l'Étranger* 79 (1954): 200–217, p. 201.

170. Binswanger, "Über Ideenflucht," pp. 33–34.

171. Foucault, *Binswanger et l'analyse existentielle*, p. 56.

172. Foucault, *The Order of Things*, p. 376. The italics are mine.

173. Foucault, pp. 182–183. The italics are mine.

174. Cf. Michel Salanskis, "Les deux triades de Canguilhem-Foucault," in *Le concept, le sujet, la science: Cavaillès, Canguilhem, Foucault*, ed. Pierre Cassou-Noguès and Pascale Gillot, Problèmes et controverses (Paris: Vrin, 2009), p. 247.

175. For all of these biographical details, the reference is Didier Eribon, *Michel Foucault, 1926–1984* (Paris: Flammarion, 1989, 3rd published in 2011 [Champs: biographie 847]; English translation by Betsy Wing, *Michel Foucault* (Cambridge, MA: Harvard University Press, 1991), p. 41ff.

3. ARCHAEOLOGICAL METHOD ○R 271

176. Eribon, pp. 70–71.
177. Jean Hyppolite, *Figures de la pensée philosophique*, Epiméthée 47 (Paris: PUF, 1971; Quadrige, 1991), pt. 2, pp. 885–886.
178. On the importance of the phenomenological school of psychiatry in Lacan's earliest writings, see Henning Schmidgen, "'Fortunes diverses.' L'œuvre de jeunesse de Jacques Lacan et la phénoménologie," *Psychanalyse à l'université* 19, no. 76 (1994): 111–134. The literature on this topic is quite slim and has focused primarily on Lacan's citation of Jaspers; see in particular François Leguil, "Lacan avec et contre Jaspers," *Ornicar?*, 15, no. 48 (1989): 5–23, but also Jean-Claude Gens, "La réception de Jaspers dans la philosophie et la psychiatrie françaises: La première réception," *Le Cercle herméneutique*, nos. 8–9 (2007): 187–198. See also Jorge Baños Orellana, *Jacques Marie Lacan 1901–1932, Bildungsroman*, trans. from Spanish by Annick Allaigre, notes by Viviane Dubol (Paris: EPEL, 2018). Yet other worthwhile avenues of inquiry remain: for example, one might distinguish between the various approaches that characterized the French reception of German-language phenomenological psychiatry as early as the 1920s, and take Ludwig Binswanger's approach into consideration. On this topic, it must be noted that the "Presentation on Psychical Causality" still claims to adhere to the "phenomenological method," while presenting a frankly polemical position with regard to Jaspers's refusal of the notion of "psychic causality." It is therefore necessary to illuminate the distance that separates Jaspers's phenomenological approach from Binswanger's, in order to show how Lacan's critique of the former is nonetheless compatible with Binswanger's perspective. Indeed, as I showed earlier, in 1933 Lacan does not hesitate to explicitly manifest his appreciation of Binswanger's phenomenological approach: cf. "Le problème du style et la conception psychiatrique des formes paranoïaques de l'expérience," in *De la psychose paranoïaque dans ses rapports avec la personnalité*, (Paris: Le François, 1932; Seuil [Le Champ freudien], 1975).
179. Foucault, "Dream, Imagination and Existence," pp. 37–38.
180. Foucault, *History of Madness*, p. 510.
181. Foucault, p. 511.
182. Foucault, p. 339.

183. Foucault, p. 339.
184. Jacques Derrida, "'Être juste avec Freud': L'histoire de la folie à l'âge de la psychanalyse," in *Penser la folie: Essais sur Michel Foucault*, ed. Élisabeth Roudinesco, Débats (Paris: Galilée, 1992), p. 148; English translation by Pascale-Anne Brault and Michael Naas, "'To Do Justice to Freud': The History of Madness in the Age of Psychoanalysis," *Critical Inquiry* 20, no. 2 (1994): 227–266, p. 233.
185. Jacques Lacan, *De la psychose paranoïaque dans ses rapports avec la personnalité* (Paris: Le François, 1932; Seuil [Le Champ freudien], 1975), p. 15.
186. Jacques Lacan, "Compte rendu de E. Minkowski, *Le temps vécu*," *Recherches Philosophiques* 5 (1935–36): 424–431, p. 428.
187. Lacan, *De la psychose paranoïaque*, p. 248: "It is the merit of this new discipline that is psychoanalysis to have taught us to know these laws." This critique was particularly addressed to Jaspers, but also to Minkowski, whose phenomeno-structural approach excluded the "ideo-affective" account of disorders analyzed by psychoanalysis.
188. Jacques Lacan, "La chose freudienne ou Sens du retour à Freud en psychanalyse" (1956), in *Écrits*, pt. 1, p. 421; Engl. trans. "The Freudian Thing, or the Meaning of the Return to Freud in Psychoanalysis," in *Écrits, The First Complete Edition in English* (New York: Norton, 2006), pp. 334–363 (p. 353).
189. See Jacques Lacan, "Situation de la psychanalyse et formation du psychanalyste en 1956" (1956), in *Écrits* (Paris: Éditions du Seuil [Le Champ freudien], 1966; [Points. Essais], 1999), pt. 1, p. 469; English translation by Bruce Fink, in collaboration with Heloïse Fink and Russel Grigg, "The Situation of Psychoanalysis and the Training of Psychoanalysts in 1956," in *Écrits*, pp. 384–411 (p. 394).
190. Jacques Lacan, *Le séminaire*, book 3, *Les psychoses* (1955–56), ed. Jacques-Alain Miller (Paris: Éditions du Seuil, 1981), p. 163; English translation with notes by Russel Grigg, *The Psychoses: The Seminars of Jacques Lacan*, ed. Jacques-Alain Miller, book 3, *1955–1956* (London: Routledge, 1993), p. 143.
191. Lacan, p. 166.
192. Lacan, p. 183.
193. Testimonies differ on this point. According to Maurice Pinguet, "already in 1953, [Foucault] had read a lot of Freud. Each week he went

3. ARCHAEOLOGICAL METHOD ○ 273

to the Hôpital Sainte-Anne to audit the seminar that a stranger, Doctor Lacan, whom he infinitely admired, had just begun" (Pinguet, "Les années d'apprentissage," *Le Débat* 41, no. 4 [1986]: 122–131, p. 125). Didier Eribon, on the other hand, recalls the interviews with Duccio Trombadori, in which Foucault seems to say that he did not attend Lacan's seminars. David Macey, in his biography of Foucault, mentions Didier Anzieu, who had begun his analysis with Lacan in 1949 and purportedly took Lacan's course with Foucault (Macey, *The Lives of Michel Foucault: A Biography* [London: Verso, 2019], p. 36). Macey also cites an interview with Jacqueline Verdeaux, according to whom Foucault's knowledge of Lacan was derived from his lectures at ENS and some of the seminars he gave at Sainte-Anne starting in 1953 (p. 69).

194. According to Foucault, medical semiology operated, at the beginning of the nineteenth century, according to a grammatical model, in which there was a "fundamental isomorphism of the structure of the disease and of the verbal form that circumscribes it" (*The Birth of the Clinic*, p. 95). Consequently, the elements of the clinic —i.e., the symptoms—had a linguistic nature; in other words, the symptom would have the dual nature of the linguistic sign. Foucault was thus drawing links between medical and linguistic semiology. In his book *L'éclipse du symptôme: L'observation clinique en psychiatrie 1800–1950*, Steeves Demazeux argues very persuasively that during this period Foucault borrowed this model from Saussurian linguistics via the influence of Lacan's ideas (Demazeux, *L'éclipse du symptôme: L'observation clinique en psychiatrie, 1800–1950*, Philosophie, anthropologie, psychologie [Paris: Ithaque, 2019], pp. 81–82). It is in this context that we must also understand Foucault's interest in writers, such as Jean-Pierre Brisset or Raymond Roussel, who had a particular relationship to the materiality of the text.

195. M. Foucault, "La folie, l'absence d'œuvre" (1964); English translation by Peter Stastny and Deniz Sengel, "Madness, the Absence of a Work," in *Michel Foucault and His Interlocutors*, ed. Arnold I. Davidson (Chicago: University of Chicago Press, 1997), pp. 97–104 (p. 102). The latter italics are mine.

196. Foucault, p. 102.

197. Foucault, p. 102.

198. Michel Foucault, "La pensée du dehors" (1966), in *Dits et écrits*, vol. 1, no. 38, pp. 518–539 (p. 521); English translation by Brian Massumi,

"The Thought of the Outside," in Faubion, *Essential Works of Foucault, 1954–1984*, vol. 2, *Aesthetics, Method and Epistemology*, p. 149: the French term *béance* has been translated as "abyss."

199. Michel Foucault, *Raymond Roussel*, Le chemin (Paris: Gallimard, 1963), p. 210; English translation by Charles Ruas, *Death and the Labyrinth: The World of Raymond Roussel* (London: Continuum, 1986), p. 169. Translation partly modified.
200. Foucault, "The Thought of the Outside," p. 149.
201. Derrida, "'To Do Justice to Freud,'" p. 233.
202. Foucault, *Death and the Labyrinth*, p. 166.
203. Foucault, p. 168.
204. Foucault, p. 169.
205. Lacan, *The Psychoses*, p. 33.
206. Lacan, p. 7.
207. Lacan, p. 33.
208. Foucault, *Death and the Labyrinth*, p. 55.
209. Foucault, p. 88.
210. Foucault, p. 54.
211. Foucault, p. 59.
212. Foucault, p. 55.
213. Foucault, p. 53.
214. Lacan, *The Psychoses*, p. 6.
215. Lacan, p. 8.
216. Lacan, p. 10.
217. Lacan, p. 7.
218. Foucault, *Death and the Labyrinth*, p. 72. The italics are mine.
219. Binswanger, "Dream and Existence," p. 91.
220. Binswanger, p. 92.
221. Minkowski, *La schizophrénie*, p. 237.
222. Foucault, *Death and the Labyrinth*, p. 84.
223. Foucault, p. 78.
224. Foucault, p. 168. The structural "unity" that Foucault uses as an example in this context is that of anxiety. This is the same structure that he had chosen for his presentation of existential psychiatry in *Maladie mentale et personnalité*.
225. Foucault, p. 67.
226. Foucault, p. 107.

227. Foucault, p. 166.
228. Foucault, p. 72.
229. Foucault, "Philosophy and Psychology," pp. 252–253.
230. Foucault, p. 253.
231. Lacan, *The Psychoses*, p. 10.
232. Foucault, "Philosophy and Psychology," p. 254.
233. Michel Foucault, "Nietzsche, Freud, Marx" (1967), in *Dits et écrits*, vol. 1, no. 46, pp. 564–579; English translation by Jon Anderson and Gary Hentzi, "Nietzsche, Freud, Marx," in Faubion, *Essential Works of Foucault, 1954–1984*, vol. 2, *Aesthetics, Method and Epistemology*, pp. 269–278 (pp. 274–275).
234. Foucault, p. 274.
235. Foucault, p. 275.
236. Lacan, *The Psychoses*, p. 6.
237. Foucault, *The Order of Things*, p. 369.
238. Foucault, p. 369.
239. Foucault, p. 369.
240. Foucault, p. 421.
241. Foucault, p. 410.
242. Michel Foucault, "Lacan, le 'libérateur' de la psychanalyse" (1981), in *Dits et écrits*, vol. 4, no. 299, pp. 204–205, p. 205.

CONCLUSION

1. E. Basso, *Michel Foucault e la Daseinsanalyse: Un'indagine metodologica*, La scala e l'album (Milano: Mimesis, 2007).
2. M. Foucault, *Les mots et les choses: Une archéologie des sciences humaines*, Bibliothèque des sciences humaines (Paris: Gallimard, 1966); English translation, *The Order of Things: An Archaeology of the Human Sciences* (New York: Routledge, 2002), p. 155.
3. B. Han-Pile, "Phenomenology and Anthropology in Foucault's 'Introduction to Binswanger's *Dream And Existence*': A Mirror Image of *The Order Of Things?*," *History and Theory* 55, no. 4 (2016): 7–22, p. 13.
4. Han-Pile, p. 22.
5. A. Fontana, "Introduzione," in *Nascita della clinica*, trans. A. Fontana, Einaudi paperbacks 5 (Torino: Einaudi, 1969), pp. vii–xxxv, p. xviii.

6. C. Sini, *Semiotica e filosofia: Segno e linguaggio in Peirce, Nietzsche, Heidegger e Foucault*, Saggi 175 (Bologna: Il Mulino, 1978), p. 181.
7. Han-Pile, "Phenomenology and Anthropology," p. 9.
8. G. Canguilhem, *On the Normal and the Pathological*, English translation by Carolyn R. Fawcett, with editorial collaboration of Robert S. Cohen (Dordrecht: Riedel, 1978), p. 7 (translation modified).
9. On this topic, see especially Judith Revel, "Sur l'Introduction à Binswanger (1954)," in *Michel Foucault: Lire l'œuvre*, ed. Luce Giard (Grenoble: Jérôme Millon, 1992), pp. 51–56.
10. M. Foucault, "Dream, Imagination and Existence," in *Dream and Existence*, by Michel Foucault and Ludwig Binswanger, special issue of *Review of Existential Psychology and Psychiatry*, ed. Keith Hoeller, vol. 19, no. 1 (1985): 29–78, p. 31.
11. Merleau-Ponty, *Phénoménologie de la perception*, Bibliothèque des idées (1945; Paris: Gallimard, 1976); English translation by Colin Smith, *Phenomenology of Perception* (London: Routledge and Kegan Paul, 1962), p. 60.
12. M. Foucault, *Archaeology of Knowledge*, English translation by A. M. Sheridan Smith (London: Routledge, 2002), p. 143.
13. Georges Lanteri-Laura, *La psychiatrie phénoménologique: fondements philosophiques*, Bibliothèque de psychiatrie (Paris: PUF, 1963), p. 158.

BIBLIOGRAPHY

WORKS BY MICHEL FOUCAULT

"Introduction," in Ludwig Binswanger, *Le rêve et l'existence*, French translation by Jacqueline Verdeaux, Paris: Desclée de Brouwer, Textes et études anthropologiques, 1954, pp. 9–128; reprinted in *Dits et écrits, 1954–1988*, edited by Daniel Defert and François Ewald, with the collaboration of Jacques Lagrange, Paris: Gallimard, Bibliothèque des sciences humaines, 1994, vol. 1, no. 1, pp. 65–118; English translation by Forrest Williams, "Dream, Imagination and Existence," in Michel Foucault and Ludwig Binswanger, *Dream and Existence*, special issue of *Review of Existential Psychology and Psychiatry*, edited by Keith Hoeller, vol. 19, no. 1 (1985): 29–78.

Maladie mentale et personnalité, Paris: PUF, Initiation philosophique, 1954.

"La psychologie de 1850 à 1950" (1957), in *Dits et écrits, 1954–1988*, edited by Daniel Defert and François Ewald, with the collaboration of Jacques Lagrange, Paris: Gallimard, Bibliothèque des sciences humaines, 1994, vol. 1, no. 2, pp. 120–137.

"La recherche scientifique et la psychologie" (1957), in *Dits et écrits, 1954–1988*, edited by Daniel Defert and François Ewald, with the collaboration of Jacques Lagrange, Paris: Gallimard, Bibliothèque des sciences humaines, 1994, vol. 1, no. 3, pp. 137–158.

Folie et déraison: Histoire de la folie à l'âge classique, Paris: Plon, Civilisations d'hier et d'aujourd'hui, 1961.

"Préface," in *Folie et Déraison*, Paris: Plon, Civilisations d'hier et d'aujourd'hui, 1961; reprinted in *Dits et Écrits, 1954–1988*, edited by Daniel Defert and

François Ewald, with the collaboration of Jacques Lagrange, Paris: Gallimard, Bibliothèque des sciences humaines, 1994, vol. 1, no. 4, pp. 159–167; English translation by Jonathan Murphy and Jean Khalfa, "Preface to the 1961 Edition," in *History of Madness*, edited by Jean Khalfa, London: Routledge, 2006, pp. xxvii–xxxvi.

Maladie mentale et psychologie, Paris: PUF, Initiation philosophique, 1962; English translation by Alan Sheridan, *Mental Illness and Psychology*, Berkeley: University of California Press, 1987.

"L'eau et la folie" (1963), in *Dits et écrits, 1954–1988*, edited by Daniel Defert and François Ewald, with the collaboration of Jacques Lagrange, Paris: Gallimard, Bibliothèque des sciences humaines, 1994, vol. 1, no. 16, pp. 268–272.

Naissance de la clinique: Une archéologie du regard médical, Paris, PUF, Galien 1, 1963; 2nd ed. 1972; English translation by A. M. Sheridan, *The Birth of the Clinic: An Archaeology of Medical Perception*, London: Tavistock, 1973.

Raymond Roussel, Paris: Gallimard, Le chemin, 1963; English translation by Charles Ruas, *Death and the Labyrinth: The World of Raymond Roussel*, London: Continuum, 1986.

"La folie, l'absence d'œuvre" (1964), in *Dits et écrits, 1954–1988*, edited by Daniel Defert and François Ewald, with the collaboration of Jacques Lagrange, Paris: Gallimard, Bibliothèque des sciences humaines, 1994, vol. 1, no. 25, pp. 412–420; English translation by Peter Stastny and Deniz Sengel, "Madness, the Absence of a Work," in Arnold I. Davidson, ed., *Michel Foucault and His Interlocutors*, Chicago: University of Chicago Press, 1997, pp. 97–104.

"Notice historique" (1964), in *Dits et écrits, 1954–1988*, edited by Daniel Defert and François Ewald, with the collaboration of Jacques Lagrange, Paris: Gallimard, Bibliothèque des sciences humaines, 1994, vol. 1, no. 19, pp. 288–293.

"Philosophie et psychologie" (1965), *Dits et écrits, 1954–1988*, edited by Daniel Defert and François Ewald, with the collaboration of Jacques Lagrange, Paris: Gallimard, Bibliothèque des sciences humaines, 1994, vol. 1, no. 30, pp. 438–448; English translation by Robert Hurley, "Philosophy and Psychology," in *Essential Works of Foucault, 1954–1984*, vol. 2, *Aesthetics, Method and Epistemology*, edited by James D. Faubion, New York: New Press, 1998, pp. 249–259.

Les mots et les choses: Une archéologie des sciences humaines, Paris: Gallimard, Bibliothèque des sciences humaines, 1966; English translation *The Order of Things: An Archaeology of the Human Sciences*, New York: Routledge, 2002.

"La pensée du dehors" (1966), in *Dits et écrits, 1954–1988*, edited by Daniel Defert and François Ewald, with the collaboration of Jacques Lagrange, Paris: Gallimard, Bibliothèque des sciences humaines, 1994, vol. 1, no. 38, pp. 518–539; English translation by Brian Massumi, "The Thought of the Outside," in *Essential Works of Foucault, 1954–1984*, vol. 2, *Aesthetics, Method and Epistemology*, edited by James D. Faubion, New York: New Press, 1998, pp. 147–169.

"Entretien avec Madeleine Chapsal" (1966), in *Dits et écrits, 1954–1988*, edited by Daniel Defert and François Ewald, with the collaboration of Jacques Lagrange, Paris: Gallimard, Bibliothèque des sciences humaines, 1994, vol. 1, no. 37, pp. 513–518.

"Qui êtes-vous, professeur Foucault?" (1967), in *Dits et écrits, 1954–1988*, edited by Daniel Defert and François Ewald, with the collaboration of Jacques Lagrange, Paris: Gallimard, Bibliothèque des sciences humaines, 1994, vol. 1, no. 50, pp. 601–623; English translation by Lucille Cairns, "Who Are You, Professor Foucault?," in *Religion and Culture*, edited by Jeremy R. Carrette, Manchester: Manchester University Press, 1999, pp. 87–103.

"Nietzsche, Freud, Marx" (1967), in *Dits et écrits, 1954–1988*, edited by Daniel Defert and François Ewald, with the collaboration of Jacques Lagrange, Paris: Gallimard, Bibliothèque des sciences humaines, 1994, vol. 1, no. 46, pp. 569–570; English translation by Jon Anderson and Gary Hentzi, "Nietzsche, Freud, Marx," in *Aesthetics, Method, and Epistemology*, edited by James D. Faubion, New York: New Press, 1998, pp. 269–278.

L'Archéologie du savoir. Paris: Gallimard, Bibliothèque des sciences humaines, 1969; English translation by A. M. Sheridan Smith, *Archaeology of Knowledge*, London: Routledge, 2002.

Qu'est-ce qu'un auteur?" (1969), in *Dits et écrits, 1954–1988*, edited by Daniel Defert and François Ewald, with the collaboration of Jacques Lagrange, Paris: Gallimard, Bibliothèque des sciences humaines, 1994, vol. 1, no. 69, pp. 789–821. English translation, "What Is an Author?," in Donald

Preziosi, ed., *The Art of Art History: A Critical Ontology*, 2nd ed., New York: Oxford University Press, 2009, pp. 321–333, 535–537.

L'Ordre du discours. Paris: Gallimard, 1971; English translation by Ian McLeod, *The Order of Discourse*, in Robert Young, ed., *Untying the Text: A Post-Structuralist Reader*, Boston: Routledge and Kegan Paul, 1981, pp. 48–78.

"Les problèmes de la culture: Un débat Foucault-Preti" (1972), in *Dits et écrits, 1954–1988*, edited by Daniel Defert and François Ewald, with the collaboration of Jacques Lagrange, Paris: Gallimard, Bibliothèque des sciences humaines, 1994, vol. 2, no. 109, pp. 369–380; English translation by Jared Becker and James Cascaito, "An Historian of Culture," in *Foucault Live: Interviews, 1961–1984*, edited by Silvère Lotringer, New York: Semiotext(e), 1996, pp. 73–88.

"Entretien avec Michel Foucault" (1980), in *Dits et écrits, 1954–1988*, edited by Daniel Defert and François Ewald, with the collaboration of Jacques Lagrange, Paris: Gallimard, Bibliothèque des sciences humaines, 1994, vol. 4, no. 281, pp. 41–95; English translation by R. James Goldstein and James Cascaito, *Remarks on Marx: Conversation with Duccio Trombadori*, New York: Semiotext(e), 1991.

"Lacan, le 'libérateur' de la psychanalyse" (1981), in *Dits et écrits, 1954–1988*, edited by Daniel Defert and François Ewald, with the collaboration of Jacques Lagrange, Paris: Gallimard, Bibliothèque des sciences humaines, 1994, vol. 4, no. 299, pp. 204–205.

"Archéologie d'une passion" (1983), in *Dits et écrits, 1954–1988*, edited by Daniel Defert and François Ewald, with the collaboration of Jacques Lagrange, Paris: Gallimard, Bibliothèque des sciences humaines, 1994, vol. 4, no. 343, pp. 601–610; English translations by Charles Ruas, "An interview with Michel Foucault," in M. Foucault, *Death and the Labyrinth: The World of Raymond Roussel*, New York: Continuum, 1986.

"Structuralisme et postructuralisme" (1983), in *Dits et écrits, 1954–1988*, edited by Daniel Defert and François Ewald, with the collaboration of Jacques Lagrange, Paris: Gallimard, Bibliothèque des sciences humaines, 1994, vol. 4, no. 330, pp. 431–462; English translation by Jeremy Harding "Structuralism and Post-Structuralism," in *The Essential Works of Foucault, 1954–1984*, vol. 2, *Aesthetics, Method, and Epistemology*, edited by. James D. Faubion, New York: New Press, 1998, pp. 433–458.

"Préface à l'*Histoire de la sexualité*" (1984), in *Dits et écrits, 1954–1988*, edited by Daniel Defert and François Ewald, with the collaboration of Jacques

Lagrange, Paris: Gallimard, Bibliothèque des sciences humaines, 1994, vol. 4, no. 340, pp. 578–585, English translation by William Smock, "Preface to the *History of Sexuality*, vol. II," in *The Essential Works of Foucault, 1954–1984*, vol. 1, *Ethics, Subjectivity and Truth*, edited by Paul Rabinow, New York: New Press, 1997, pp. 199–205.

"Le retour de la morale" (1984), in *Dits et écrits, 1954–1988*, edited by Daniel Defert and François Ewald, with the collaboration of Jacques Lagrange, Paris: Gallimard, Bibliothèque des sciences humaines, 1994, vol. 4, no. 354, pp. 698–708; English translation by John Johnston, "The Return of Morality," in *Foucault Live: Interviews 1961–1984*, New York: Semiotext(e), 1996, pp. 465–473.

"La vie: l'expérience et la science" (1985), in *Dits et écrits, 1954–1988*, edited by Daniel Defert and François Ewald, with the collaboration of Jacques Lagrange, Paris: Gallimard, Bibliothèque des sciences humaines, 1994, vol. 4, no. 361, pp. 763–776; English translation by Robert Hurley, "Life: Experience and Science," in *Essential Works of Foucault, 1954–1984*, vol. 2, *Aesthetics, Method, and Epistemology*, edited by James D. Faubion, New York: New Press, 1998, pp. 465–478.

Introduction to Kant's Anthropology, translated by Roberto Nigro and Kate Briggs, edited with an afterword and critical notes by Roberto Nigro, Los Angeles: Semiotext(e), 2008.

Mal faire, dire vrai: Fonction de l'aveu en justice, edited by Fabienne Brion and Bernard E. Harcourt, Louvain: Presses universitaires de Louvain, 2012.

"Considérations sur le marxisme, la phénoménologie et le pouvoir: Entretien avec Colin Gordon et Paul Patton," edited by Alain Beaulieu, *Cités* 52, no. 4 (2012): 101–126; English version "Considerations on Marxism, Phenomenology and Power: Interview with Michel Foucault," *Foucault Studies* 14 (2012): 98–114.

"Une histoire de la manière dont les choses font problème: Entretien de Michel Foucault avec André Berten (7 mai 1981)," *Culture et Conflits*, nos. 94, 95, 96 (2014): 99–109.

"Pratiques de soi," in Didier Fassin and Samuel Lézé, eds., *La question morale: Une anthropologie critique*, Paris: PUF, 2014, pp. 65–73.

Michel Foucault and Ludwig Binswanger, "La correspondance entre Michel Foucault et Ludwig Binswanger," edited by Elisabetta Basso, in Jean-François Bert and Elisabetta Basso eds., *Foucault à Münsterlingen: À l'origine de l'Histoire de la folie*. Avec des photographies de Jacqueline Verdeaux, Paris: Éditions EHESS, L'histoire et ses représentations 10, 2015, pp. 175–195.

"Introduction à *L'Archéologie du savoir*," edited and introduction by Martin Rueff, *Les Études philosophiques* 153, no. 3 (2015): 327–352.

"La littérature et la folie: Une conférence inédite de Michel Foucault," *Critique*, vol. 12, no. 835 (2016): 965–981.

"La magie—le fait social total," edited by Jean-François Bert, *Zilsel* 2, no. 2 (2017): 305–326.

"Un manuscrit de Michel Foucault sur la psychanalyse," edited by Elisabetta Basso, *Astérion*, no. 21 (2019), https://journals.openedition.org/asterion/4410.

L'origine de l'herméneutique de soi: Conférences prononcées à Dartmouth College, 1980, edited by Henri-Paul Fruchaud and Daniele Lorenzini, introduction and critical apparatus by Laura Cremonesi, Arnold I. Davidson, Orazio Irrera, Daniele Lorenzini, and Martina Tazzioli. Paris: Vrin, Philosophie du présent: Foucault inédit, 2013; English translation by Graham Burchell, *About the Beginning of the Hermeneutics of the Self: Lectures at Dartmouth College, 1980*, Chicago: University of Chicago Press, 2016.

Œuvres, edited by Frédéric Gros, Paris: Gallimard, Bibliothèque de la Pléiade, 2015.

Qu'est-ce que la critique?, suivi de *La culture de soi*, edited by Henri-Paul Fruchaud and Daniele Lorenzini, introduction and critical apparatus by Daniele Lorenzini and Arnold I. Davidson, Paris: Vrin, Philosophie du présent: Foucault inédit, 2015.

Discours et vérité, précédé de *La parrêsia*, introduction and critical apparatus by Henri-Paul Fruchaud and Daniele Lorenzini, introduction by Frédéric Gros, Paris: Vrin, Philosophie du présent: Foucault inédit, 2016.

Dire vrai sur soi-même Conférences prononcées à l'Université Victoria de Toronto, 1982, edited, introduction, and critical apparatus by Henri-Paul Fruchaud and Daniele Lorenzini, Paris: Vrin, Philosophie du présent: Foucault inédit, 2017.

Folie, langage, littérature, edited by Henri-Paul Fruchaud, Daniele Lorenzini, and Judith Revel, introduction by Judith Revel, Paris: Vrin, Philosophie du présent: Foucault inédit, 2019.

La sexualité: Cours donné à l'Université de Clermont-Ferrand, 1964; suivi de *Le discours de la sexualité: Cours donné à l'Université de Vincennes, 1969*, edited by Claude-Olivier Doron, Paris: Seuil/Gallimard/EHESS, Cours et travaux de Michel Foucault avant le Collège de France, edited by François Ewald, Hautes Études, 2018; English translation by Graham Burchell, *Sexuality: The 1964 Clermont-Ferrand and 1969 Vincennes Lectures*, foreword by Bernard E. Harcourt, Foucault's Early Lectures and Manuscripts, New York: Columbia University Press, 2021.

Les aveux de la chair, edited by Frédéric Gros, Paris: Gallimard, Bibliothèque des histoires, 2018; English translation by Robert Hurley, *Confessions of the Flesh*, London: Penguin Random House, 2021.

Binswanger et l'analyse existentielle, edited by Elisabetta Basso, Paris: Seuil/Gallimard/EHESS, Cours et travaux de Michel Foucault avant le Collège de France, edited by François Ewald, Hautes Études, 2021.

Phénoménologie et psychologie. 1953–1954, edited by Philippe Sabot, Paris: Seuil/Gallimard/EHESS, Cours et travaux de Michel Foucault avant le Collège de France, edited by François Ewald, Hautes Études, 2021.

La question anthropologique. Cours. 1954–1955, edited by Arianna Sforzini, Paris: Seuil/Gallimard/EHESS, Cours et travaux de Michel Foucault avant le Collège de France, edited by François Ewald, Hautes Études, 2022.

PRIMARY LITERATURE

Ancelin-Schützenberger, Anne. "Aperçus sur les études de psychologie." *Bulletin du groupe d'études de psychologie de l'Université de Paris* 4, nos. 1–2 (1950): 1–2.

Anon. "Éditorial: Le Congrès international de psychiatrie et la crise de la psychiatrie contemporaine." *La Raison. Cahiers de psychopathologie scientifique* 2 (1951): 7.

Bachelard, Gaston. *L'Air et les songes: Essai sur l'imagination du mouvement*. Paris: José Corti, 1943; English translation by Edith R. Farrell and C. Frederick Farrell, *Air and Dreams: An Essay on the Imagination of Movement*. Dallas: Dallas Institute, 1988.

——. "De la nature du rationalisme." *Bulletin de la Société Française de Philosophie*, session of March 25, 1950; reproduced in G. Bachelard, *L'Engagement rationaliste*, pp. 45–87. Paris: PUF, 1972.

---. *L'Eau et les rêves: Essai sur l'imagination de la matière*. Paris: José Corti, 1942.

---. *La Formation de l'esprit scientifique: Contribution à une psychanalyse de la connaissance objective*. Paris: Vrin, 1938; English translation by Mary McAllester Jones, *The Formation of the Scientific Mind: Contribution to a Psychoanalysis of Objective Knowledge*. Manchester: Clinamen, 2001.

---. *Lautréamont*. Paris: José Corti, 1940.

---. *La Poétique de l'espace*. Paris: PUF, Bibliothèque de philosophie contemporaine: Logique et philosophie des sciences, 1957; English translation by Maria Jolas, *The Poetics of Space*. Boston: Beacon, 1994.

---. "Préface." In Roland Kuhn, *La Phénoménologie du masque: À travers le test de Rorschach*, pp. 7–14. Paris: Desclée de Brouwer, Bibliothèque neuropsychiatrique de langue française, 1957; newly revised and corrected edition, 1992, pp. 15–24.

---. *La Psychanalyse du feu*. Paris: Gallimard, 1938.

---. *La Terre et les rêveries du repos*. Paris: José Corti, 1948.

Bachelard, Gaston, and Ludwig Binswanger. "Correspondance Gaston Bachelard-Ludwig Binswanger, 1948–1955," French translation and edited by Elisabetta Basso and Emmanuel Delille, *Revue germanique internationale*, no. 30 (2019): 183–208.

Bachelard, Gaston, and Roland Kuhn. "La correspondance Gaston Bachelard et Roland Kuhn," edited by Elisabetta Basso, with a postscript by Charles Alunni, *Revue de synthèse* 137, nos. 1–2 (2016): 177–189.

Bailey, Pearce. *Études des types psychologiques au moyen des tests*. Paris: Librairie Lipschutz, 1933.

Baños Orellana, Jorge. *Jacques Marie Lacan, 1901–1932. Bildungsroman*, trans. from Spanish by Annick Allaigre, notes by Viviane Dubol. Paris: EPEL, 2018.

Basaglia, Franco. *Scritti*. Vol. 1, *Dalla psichiatria fenomenologica all'esperienza di Gorizia*. Edited by Franca Ongaro Basaglia. Turin: Einaudi, Einaudi paperbacks 128, 1981–1982.

Beauvoir, Simone de. *La Force de l'âge*. Paris: Gallimard, Soleil 49, 1960; English translation by Peter Green, *The Prime of Life*. New York: Harper and Row, 1962.

Béguin, Albert, ed. *Misère de la psychiatrie. Esprit* 197, no. 12 (1952).

Binder, Hans. *Die Helldunkeldeutungen im psychodiagnostischen Experiment von Rorschach*. Zurich: Füssli, 1932.

Binswanger, Ludwig. *Ausgewählte Vorträge und Aufsätze*, vol. 1, *Zur phänomenologischen Anthropologie*. Bern: Francke, 1947; vol. 2: *Zur Problematik der psychiatrischen Forschung und zum Problem der Psychiatrie*. Bern: Francke, 1955.

———. "Bemerkungen zu der Arbeit Jaspers' 'Kausale und verständliche Zusammenhänge zwischen Schicksal und Psychose bei der Dementia praecox (Schizophrenie),'" *Internationale Zeitschrift für ärztliche Psychoanalyse* 1 (1913): 383–390.

———. "Bemerkungen zu Hermann Rorschachs Psychodiagnostik." *Internationale Zeitschrift für ärztliche Psychoanalyse* 9 (1923): 512–523.

———. "La conception de l'homme, chez Freud, à la lumière de l'anthropologie philosophique" (1936), French translation by Hans Pollnow, *L'Évolution psychiatrique* 10, no. 1 (1938): 3–34.

———. "La *Daseinsanalyse* en psychiatrie." French translation by Michel Gourevitch. *L'Encéphale* 40, no. 1 (1951): 108–113.

———. *Drei Formen missglückten Daseins*. Tübingen: Niemeyer, 1956.

———. *Einführung in die Probleme der allgemeinen Psychologie*. Berlin: Springer, 1922.

———. "Erfahren, Verstehen, Deuten in der Psychoanalyse." *Imago* 12, nos. 2–3 (1926): 223–237; in *Ausgewählte Werke*, vol. 3, *Vorträge und Aufsätze*, edited by Max Herzog, pp. 3–16. Heidelberg: Asanger, 1993.

———. "Der Fall Ellen West: Eine anthropologisch-klinische Studie." *Schweizer Archiv für Neurologie und Psychiatrie* 53 (1944): 255–727; 54 (1944): 69–117, 330–360; 55 (1945): 16–40; reprinted in *Schizophrenie*, Zweite Studie, pp. 57–188; English translation by Werner M. Mendel and Joseph Lyons, "The Case of Ellen West," in *Existence—a New Dimension in Psychiatry and Psychology*, edited by Rollo May, Ernest Angel, and Henri F. Ellenberger, pp. 237–364. New York: Basic, 1958.

———. "Geschehnis und Erlebnis (zur gleichnamigen Schrift von E. Straus, 1930)." *Monatsschrift für Psychiatrie und Neurologie* 80 (1931): 243–273; in *Ausgewählte Vorträge und Aufsätze*, vol. 2, *Zur Problematik der psychiatrischen Forschung und zum Problem der Psychiatrie*, pp. 147–173. Bern: Francke, 1955.

———. *Grundformen und Erkenntnis menschlichen Daseins*. Zürich: Niehans, 1942.

———. *Henrik Ibsen und das Problem der Selbstrealisation in der Kunst*. Heidelberg: L. Schneider, 1949.

———. *Introduction à l'analyse existentielle*. Paris: Éditions de Minuit, Arguments 50, 1971, translation and glossary by Jacqueline Verdeaux and Roland Kuhn, preface by Roland Kuhn and Henri Maldiney.

———. "Lebensfunktion und innere Lebensgeschichte." *Monatsschrift für Psychiatrie und Neurologie* 68 (1928): 52–79; in *Ausgewählte Vorträge und Aufsätze*, vol. 1, *Zur phänomenologischen Anthropologie*. Bern: Francke, 1947, pp. 50–73; in *Ausgewählte Werke*, vol. 3, *Vorträge und Aufsätze*, edited by Max Herzog, pp. 71–94. Heidelberg: Asanger, 1993.

———. "Préface à la traduction française." In *Le Cas Suzanne Urban: Étude sur la schizophrénie*, pp. 7–11. Paris: Desclée de Brouwer, Bibliothèque neuro-psychiatrique de langue française, 1957.

———. "Psychoanalyse und klinische Psychiatrie." *Internationale Zeitschrift für ärztliche Psychoanalyse* 7 (1920): 137–165; in *Ausgewählte Vorträge und Aufsätze*, vol. 2, *Zur Problematik der psychiatrischen Forschung und zum Problem der Psychiatrie*, pp. 40–66. Bern: Francke, 1955.

———. "Das Raumproblem in der Psychopathologie." *Zeitschrift für die gesamte Neurologie und Psychiatrie* 145 (1933): 598–647; in *Ausgewählte Vorträge und Aufsätze*, vol. 2, *Zur Problematik der psychiatrischen Forschung und zum Problem der Psychiatrie*, pp. 174–225. Bern: Francke, 1955.

———. Review of Eugène Minkowski, *La Schizophrénie: Psychopathologie des schizoïdes et des schizophrènes*, Paris, 1927. *Schweizer Archiv für Neurologie und Psychiatrie* 22 (1928): 158–163.

———. *Schizophrenie*. Pfullingen: G. Neske, 1957.

———. "Studien zum Schizophrenienproblem: Der Fall Lola Voss." *Schweizer Archiv für Neurologie und Psychiatrie* 63 (1949): 29–97.

———. "Studien zum Schizophrenieproblem: Der Fall Suzanne Urban." *Schweizer Archiv für Neurologie und Psychiatrie* 69 (1952): 36–77; 70 (1952): 1–32; vol. 71 (1952): 57–96; reprinted in *Schizophrenie*, study no. 5, pp. 359–470. Pfullingen: Neske, 1957; French translation by Jacqueline Verdeaux, *Le Cas Suzanne Urban: Étude sur la schizophrénie*. Paris: Desclée de Brouwer, Bibliothèque neuro-psychiatrique de langue française, 1957.

———. "Studien zu Schizophrenie Problem, study no. 2: Der Fall Jürg Zünd." *Schweizer Archiv für Neurologie und Psychiatrie* 56 (1946): 191–220; vol. 58 (1947): 1–43; 59 (1947): 21–36; reprinted in *Schizophrenie*, pp. 189–288. Pfullingen: G. Neske, 1957.

———. "Traum und Existenz." *Neue Schweizer Rundschau* 23 (1930): 673–685, 766–779; Zürich: H. Girsberger, 1930; French translation by Jacqueline

Verdeaux, *Le rêve et l'existence*, introduction and notes by Michel Foucault. Paris: Desclée de Brouwer, Textes et études anthropologiques, 1954; English translation by Jacob Needleman, "Dream and Existence," *Review of Existential Psychology and Psychiatry*, special issue edited by Keith Hoeller, vol. 19, no. 1 (1986): 81–105.

———. "Über die daseinsanalytische Forschungsrichtung in der Psychiatrie." *Schweizer Archiv für Psychiatrie und Neurologie* 57 (1946): 209–235; reprinted in *Ausgewählte Vorträge und Aufsätze*, vol. 1, *Zur phänomenologischen Anthropologie*, pp. 190–217. Bern: Francke, 1947, and in *Ausgewählte Werke*, vol. 3, *Vorträge und Aufsätze*, edited by Max Herzog, pp. 231–257. Heidelberg: Asanger, 1994; translation by Ernest Angel, "The Existential Analysis School of Thought," in *Existence—A New Dimension in Psychiatry and Psychology*, edited by Rollo May, Ernest Angel, and Henri F. Ellenberger, pp. 191–213. New York: Basic, 1958.

———. "Über Ideenflucht." *Schweizer Archiv für Neurologie und Psychiatrie* 27, no. 2 (1932): 203–217; 28, nos. 1–2 (1932): 18–26, 183–202; 29, no. 1 (1932): 193ff.; 30, no. 1 (1933): 68–85; Zürich: Orel Füssli, 1933 (reprinted, New York: Garland, 1980); in *Ausgewählte Werke*, vol. 1, *Formen mißglückten Daseins*, edited by Max Herzog. Heidelberg: Asanger, 1992.

———. "Über Phänomenologie." *Zeitschrift für die gesamte Neurologie und Psychiatrie* 82 (1923): 10–45; in *Ausgewählte Werke*, vol. 3, *Vorträge und Aufsätze*, edited by Max Herzog, pp. 35–69. Heidelberg: Asanger, 1993.

———. "Über Psychotherapie (Möglichkeit und Tatsächlichkeit psychotherapeutischer Wirkung)." *Der Nervenarzt* 8 (1935): 113–121, 180–189; in *Ausgewählte Vorträge und Aufsätze*, vol. 1, *Zur phänomenologischen Anthropologie*, pp. 132–158. Bern: Francke, 1947.

———. *Wandlungen in der Auffassung und Deutung des Traumes von den Griechen bis zur Gegenwart*. Berlin: Springer, 1928.

———. "Welche Aufgaben ergeben sich für die Psychiatrie aus den Fortschritten der neueren Psychologie?" *Zeitschrift für die gesamte Neurologie und Psychiatrie* 91, nos. 3–5 (1924): 402–436; in *Ausgewählte Vorträge und Aufsätze*, vol. 2, *Zur Problematik der psychiatrischen Forschung und zum Problem der Psychiatrie*, pp. 111–146. Bern: Francke, 1955.

Bleuler, Eugen. "Der Rorschach'sche Formdeutungsversuch bei Geschwistern." *Zeitschrift für die gesamte Neurologie und Psychiatrie* 118 (1928): 366–398.

Bochner, Ruth, and Halpern, Florence. *The Clinical Application of the Rorschach Test*. New York: Grune and Stratton, 1942; French translation *L'Application clinique du test de Rorschach*, with a foreword on terminology and symbols to be used in the French language by André Ombredane et Nella Canivet. Paris: PUF, Bibliothèque scientifique internationale. Section Psychologie 2, 1948.

Bohm, Ewald. *Lehrbuch der Rorschach-Psychodiagnostik: für Psychologen, Ärzte und Pädagogen*. Bern: Huber, 1951.

Boss, Medard. *Sinn und Gehalt der sexuellen Perversionen: ein daseinanalytischer Beitrag zur Psychopathologie des Phänomens der Liebe*. Bern: Huber, 1947.

Buraud, Georges. *Les Masques*. Paris: Éditions du Seuil, Pierres vives, 1948.

Canguilhem, Georges. *La connaissance de la vie*. Paris: Hachette, 1952; 2nd ed. Paris: Vrin, Problèmes et controverses, 1965; English translation by Stefanos Geroulanos and Daniela Ginsburg, *Knowledge of Life*. New York: Fordham University Press, 2008.

——. *Essai sur quelques problèmes concernant le normal et le pathologique*. Clermont-Ferrand: La Montagne, 1943; 2nd ed., Paris: Les Belles Lettres, Publications de la Faculté des lettres de l'Université de Strasbourg 100, 1950; English translation by Carolyn R. Fawcett, *On the Normal and the Pathological*, with editorial collaboration of Robert S. Cohen. Dordrecht: Riedel, 1978.

——. "Galilée: la signification de l'œuvre et la leçon de l'homme" (1964), in *Études d'histoire et de philosophie des sciences*, pp. 37–50. Paris: Vrin, Problèmes et controverses, 1968.

——. "Mort de l'homme ou épuisement du cogito?" *Critique*, no. 242 (1967): 599–618; English translation by Catherine Porter, "The Death of Man, or Exhaustion of the Cogito?," in *The Cambridge Companion to Foucault*, edited by Gary Gutting, pp. 74–94. Cambridge: Cambridge University Press, 2005.

——. "Note sur la situation faite en France à la philosophie biologique." *Revue de Métaphysique et de Morale* 52 (1947): 322–332; *Œuvres complètes*, vol. 4, *Résistance, philosophie biologique et histoire des sciences*, edited by Camille Limoges, pp. 307–320. Paris: Vrin, Bibliothèque des textes philosophiques, 2015.

——. "Report from Mr. Canguilhem on the Manuscript Filed by Mr. Michel Foucault, Director of the Institut Français of Hamburg, in Order to

Obtain Permission to Print His Principal Thesis for the Doctor of Letters," English translation by Ann Hobart, *Critical Inquiry* 21, no. 2 (1995): 277–281.

———. "Qu'est-ce que la psychologie?" *Revue de métaphysique et de morale* 63, no. 1 (1958): 12–25; reprinted in *Études d'histoire et philosophie des sciences* (1968), 7th ed., pp. 365–381. Paris: Vrin, Problèmes et controverses, 1994; English translation by David M. Peña-Guzmán, "What Is Psychology?," *Foucault Studies*, no. 21 (2016): 200–213.

De Rosa, Renato. "Existenzphilosophische Richtungen in der modernen Psychopathologie." *Der Nervenarzt* 23, no. 7 (1952): 256–261.

Ellenberger, Henri F. "Analyse existentielle." In *Encyclopédie médico-chirurgicale. Traité de psychiatrie*, edited by Henri Ey. Paris: Éditions techniques, 1955.

———. "The Life and Work of Hermann Rorschach (1884–1922)." *Bulletin of the Menninger Clinic* 18 (1954): 173–219.

———. "La psychiatrie suisse I–VII." *L'Évolution psychiatrique* (1951–1953), vol. 16, no. 2: 321–354; vol. 16, no. 4: 619–644; vol. 17, no. 1: 139–158; vol. 17, no. 2: 369–379; vol. 17, no. 3: 593–606; vol. 18, no. 2: 299–318; vol. 18, no. 4: 719–751; *La psychiatrie suisse*. Aurillac: Poirier-Bottreau, 1954.

Ey, Henri, P. Marty, and Jean-Joseph Dublineau, eds. *Premier Congrès mondial de psychiatrie, Paris, 1950*, vol. 1, *Psychopathologie générale*. Paris: Hermann, Actualités scientifiques et industrielles, 1952.

Fischer, Franz. "Zeitstruktur und Schizophrenie." *Zeitschrift für die gesamte Neurologie und Psychiatrie* 121, no. 1 (1929): 544–574.

Freud, Sigmund, and Ludwig Binswanger. *Briefwechsel: 1908–1938*. Edited and introduction by Gerhard Fichtner. Frankfurt: Fischer, 1992.

Gebsattel, Viktor Emil von. "Störungen des Werdens und des Zeiterlebens im Rahmen psychiatrischer Erkrankungen." In *Gegenwartsprobleme der psychiatrisch-neurologischen Forschung: Vorträge auf dem Internationalen Fortbildungskurs*, edited by Christel Heinrich Roggenbau, pp. 54–71. Stuttgart: Enke, 1939.

———. "Über Fetischismus." *Der Nervenarzt* 2, no. 1 (1929): 8–20.

———. "Die Welt des Zwangskranken." *Monatsschrift für Psychiatrie und Neurologie* 99 (1938): 10–74.

———. "Zur Frage der Depersonalisation: Ein Beitrag zur Theorie der Melancholie." *Der Nervenarzt* 10, no. 4 (1937): 169–178; 10, no. 5 (1937): 248–257.

———. "Zur Psychopathologie der Phobien. I. Teil: Die psychasthenische Phobie." *Der Nervenarzt* 8, no. 7 (1935): 337–346; no. 8 (1935): 398–408.

Gelb, Adhemar, and Kurt Goldstein. "Über Farbennamenamnesie." *Psychologische Forschungen* 11 (1924): 1127–1186.

Goldstein, Kurt. *Der Aufbau des Organismus: Einführung in die Biologie unter besonderer Berücksichtigung der Erfahrungen am kranken Menschen*. Haag: M. Nijhoff, 1934; French translation by E. Burckhardt and Jean Kuntz, *La structure de l'organisme: Introduction à la biologie à partir de la pathologie humaine*. Paris: Gallimard, Bibliothèque de philosophie, 1951; English translation *The Organism: A Holistic Approach to Biology Derived from Pathological Data in Man*, with a foreword by Oliver Sacks. New York: Zone, 1995.

———. *Human Nature in the Light of Psychopathology*. Cambridge, MA: Harvard University Press, 1940.

Guiraud, Paul. "Pathogénie et étiologie des délires." In *Psychiatrie générale*, pp. 576–581. Paris: Librairie Le François, 1950.

Gusdorf, Georges. "Georges Daumézon, l'homme." In *Regard, accueil et présence: Mélanges en l'honneur de Georges Daumézon, trente-deux études de psychiatrie et de psychopathologie*, pp. 43–58. Toulouse: Privat, 1980.

Häberlin, Paul. *Briefwechsel, 1908–1960*. Edited by Jeannine Luczak. Basel: Schwabe, 1997.

———. *Der Charakter*. Basel: Kober, 1925.

———. "Der Gegenstand der Psychiatrie." *Schweizer Archiv für Neurologie und Psychiatrie* 60, nos. 1–2 (1947): 132–144.

———. *Der Gegenstand der Psychologie: Eine Einführung in das Wesen der Empirischen Wissenschaft*. Berlin: Springer, 1921.

———. *Der Mensch: Eine philosophische Anthropologie*. Zürich: Schweizer Spiegel, 1941.

Heidegger, Martin. *Kant und das Problem der Metaphysik* (1929). Frankfurt: Klostermann, 1951; introduction and French translation by Alphonse De Waelhens and Walter Biemel, *Kant et le problème de la métaphysique*. Paris: Gallimard, Bibliothèque de philosophie, 1953.

———. "Lettre sur l'humanisme" (1947); French translation by Roger Munier, *Cahiers du Sud*, no. 319 (1953): 385–406; and no. 320 (1953): 68–88; reprinted in *Lettre sur l'humanisme*. Paris: Éditions Montaigne, 1957.

———. *Sein und Zeit*. Halle: Niemeyer, 1927; *Gesamtausgabe* [GA], vol. 2, edited by Friedrich-Wilhelm von Herrmann. Frankfurt: Klostermann,

1977; English translation by John Macquarrie and Edward Robinson, *Being and Time*. Oxford: Blackwell, 1962.

———. "Der Spruch des Anaximander." In *Holzwege*, pp. 296–343. Frankfurt: Klostermann, 1950.

———. *Zollikoner Seminare: Protokolle—Gespräche—Briefe*, edited by Medard Boss, Frankfurt: Klostermann, 1987; *Gesamtausgabe* [GA], vol. 89, English translation with notes and afterword by Franz Mayr and Richard Askay, *Zollikon Seminars: Protocols, Conversations, Letters*, Evanston, IL: Northwestern University Press, 2001.

Herzog, Max. *Weltenwürfe: Ludwig Binswangers phänomenologische Psychologie*. Berlin: De Gruyter, 1994.

Hesnard, Angelo. *L'Univers morbide de la faute*. Paris: PUF, Bibliothèque de psychanalyse et de psychologie clinique, 1949.

Hesnard, Angelo, and René Laforgue. "Avant-propos." *L'Évolution psychiatrique* 1 (1925): 7–9.

Hyppolite, Jean. *Figures de la pensée philosophique: Écrits, 1931–1968*. Paris: PUF, Epiméthée 47, 1971, Quadrige 131, 1991.

Jaspers, Karl. *Allgemeine Psychopathologie: Für Studierende, Ärzte und Psychologen* (1913), 3rd ed. Berlin: Springer, 1923; French translation by Alfred Kastler and Jean Mendousse, *Psychopathologie générale*. Paris: Félix Alcan, 1928, new ed. 1933.

———. *Descartes und die Philosophie*. Berlin: de Gruyter, 1937; French translation by Hans Pollnow. *Descartes et la philosophie*. Paris: Alcan, 1938.

———. "Kausale und 'verständliche' Zusammenhänge zwischen Schicksal und Psychose bei der Dementia praecox (Schizophrenie)." *Zeitschrift für die gesamte Neurologie und Psychiatrie* 14 (1913): 158–263; *Gesamtausgabe*, 1:3, *Gesammelte Schriften über Psychopathologie*, edited by Chantal Marazia, with the collaboration of Dirk Fonfara, pp. 383–479. Basel: Schwabe, 2019.

———. *Nietzsche: Einführung in das Verständnis seines Philosophierens*. Berlin: De Gruyter, 1936; French translation by Henri Niel, *Nietzsche: Introduction à sa philosophie*, letter-preface by Jean Wahl. Paris: Gallimard, Collection Philosophie, 1950; English translation by Charles F. Wallraff and Frederick J. Schmitz, *Nietzsche: An Introduction to the Understanding of His Philosophical Activity*. Baltimore: Johns Hopkins University Press, 1997.

———. *Strindberg und van Gogh: Versuch einer pathographischen Analyse unter vergleichender Heranziehung von Swedenborg und Hölderlin*. Leipzig:

Bircher, 1922; French translation by Hélène Naef, *Strindberg et Van Gogh, Swedenborg, Hölderlin. Étude psychiatrique comparative*, preceded by a study by Maurice Blanchot. Paris: Éditions de Minuit, 1953.

Keller, Wilhelm. *Vom Wesen des Menschen*. Basel: Verlag für Recht und Gesellschaft, 1943.

Kuhn, Roland. "Daseinsanalyse eines Falles von Schizophrenie." *Monatsschrift für Psychiatrie und Neurologie* 112 (1946): 233–257.

———. "Esquisse d'une autobiographie." In *Écrits sur l'analyse existentielle*, texts assembled and introduced by Jean-Claude Marceau, preface by Mareike Wolf-Fédida, pp. 41–54. Paris: L'Harmattan, Psychanalyse et civilisations: Série Trouvailles et retrouvailles, 2007.

———. "Geschichte und Entwicklung der psychiatrischen Klinik." In *150 Jahre Münsterlingen*, edited by Jürg Ammann and Karl Studer, pp. 99–125. Weinfelden: Druck Mühlemann, 1990.

———. "Henry Dunant vu par le psychiatre." In *De l'utopie à la réalité*, edited by Roger Durand, with the collaboration of Jean-Daniel Candaux, pp. 111–136. Geneva: Société Henry Dunant, 1988.

———. "Mordversuch eines depressiven Fetischisten und Sodomisten an einer Dirne." *Monatsschrift für Psychiatrie und Neurologie* 116, nos. 1-2-3 (1948): 66–151; English translation by Ernest Angel, "The Attempted Murder of a Prostitute," in *Existence—a New Dimension in Psychiatry and Psychology*, edited by Rollo May, Ernest Angel, and Henri F. Ellenberger, pp. 365–425. New York: Basic, 1958.

———. Review of "L. Binswanger, Grundformen und Erkenntnis menschlichen Daseins." *Schweizer Archiv für Neurologie und Psychiatrie* 51 (1943): 288–291.

———. "Roland Kuhn." In *Psychiatrie in Selbstdarstellungen*, edited by Ludwig J. Pongratz, pp. 219–257. Bern: Huber, 1977.

———. *Der Rorschachsche Formdeutversuch in der Psychiatrie*. Basel: Karger, 1940.

———. "Über die Bedeutung vom Grenzen im Wahn." *Monatsschrift für Psychiatrie und Neurologie* 124, nos. 4–6 (1952): 354–383.

———. *Über Maskendeutungen im Rorschachschen Versuch*. Basel: Karger, 1944; 2nd ed. 1954; French translation by Jacqueline Verdeaux, *Phénoménologie du masque: À travers le test de Rorschach*. Paris: Desclée de Brouwer, Bibliothèque neuro-psychiatrique de langue française, 1957; newly revised and corrected edition, Épi-intelligence du corps, 1992.

———. "Über Rorschach's Psychologie und die psychologische Grundlagen des Formdeutversuches." *Schweizer Archiv für Neurologie und Psychiatrie* 53, no.1 (1944): 29–47.

———. "Zum Problem der ganzheitlichen Betrachtung in der Medizin." *Schweizerisches Medizinisches Jahrbuch* 29 (1957): 53–63.

———. "Zur ästhetischen Dimension daseinsanalytischer Erfahrung." In *Psychiatrie mit Zukunft: Beiträge zur Geschichte, Gegenwart, Zukunft der wissenschaftlichen und praktischen Seelenheilkunde*, pp. 62–90. Basel: Schwabe, 2004.

Kunz, Hans. *Die anthropologische Bedeutung der Phantasie*. Basel: Verlag für Recht und Gesellschaft, 1946.

———. "Die anthropologische Betrachtungsweise in der Psychopathologie." *Zeitschrift für die gesamte Neurologie und Psychiatrie* 172 (1941): 145–180.

———. "Idee, Wesen und Wirklichkeit des Menschen: Bemerkungen zu einem Grundproblem der philosophischen Anthropologie." *Studia Philosophica* 4, no. 147 (1944): 147–169.

———. "Die Psychoanalyse als Symptom einer Wandlung im Selbstverständnis des Menschen." *Zentralblatt für Psychotherapie und ihre Grenzgebiete* 4 (1931): 280–302.

Lacan, Jacques. "Au-delà du 'Principe de réalité'" (1936). In *Écrits*, 1:72–91. Paris: Éditions du Seuil, Le Champ freudien, 1966, Points: Essais, 1999; English translation by Bruce Fink, in collaboration with Heloïse Fink and Russel Grigg, "Beyond the 'Reality Principle.'" In *Écrits: The First Complete Edition in English*, pp. 58–74. New York: Norton, 2006.

———. "La chose freudienne ou Sens du retour à Freud en psychanalyse" (1956). In *Écrits*, 1:398–433. Paris: Éditions du Seuil, Le Champ freudien, 1966; Points: Essais, 1999; English translation by Bruce Fink, in collaboration with Heloïse Fink and Russel Grigg, "The Freudian Thing, or the Meaning of the Return to Freud in Psychoanalysis." In *Écrits: The First Complete Edition in English*, pp. 334–363. New York: Norton, 2006.

———. *De la psychose paranoïaque dans ses rapports avec la personnalité*. Paris: Le François, 1932; Éditions du Seuil, Le Champ freudien, 1975.

———. "Le problème du style et la conception psychiatrique des formes paranoïaques de l'expérience." *Minotaure*, nos. 1, 2 (1933). In *De la psychose paranoïaque dans ses rapports avec la personnalité* (suivi de) *Premiers écrits sur la paranoïa*, pp. 383–388. Paris: Éditions du Seuil, Le Champ freudien, 1975; English translation by Jon Anderson, "The Problem of

Style and the Psychiatric Conception of Paranoiac Forms of Experience." *Critical Texts* 5, no. 3 (1988): 4–6.

———. "Propos sur la causalité psychique" (1946). In *Écrits*, 1:150–192. Paris: Éditions du Seuil, Le Champ freudien, 1966, Points: Essais, 1999; English translation by Bruce Fink, in collaboration with Heloïse Fink and Russel Grigg, "Presentation on Psychical Causality." In *Écrits: The First Complete Edition in English*, pp. 123–158. New York: Norton, 2006.

———. Review of Minkowski's *Le temps vécu*, in *Recherches Philosophiques*, no. 5 (1935–36): 424–431.

———. *Le Séminaire*. Book 3, *Les psychoses* (1955–56). Edited by Jacques-Alain Miller. Paris: Éditions du Seuil, 1981; English translation with notes by Russel Grigg, *The Psychoses: The Seminars of Jacques Lacan*, book 3, 1955–1956. Edited by Jacques-Alain Miller. London: Routledge, 1993.

———. "Situation de la psychanalyse et formation du psychanalyste en 1956" (1956). In *Écrits*, 1:457–489. Paris: Éditions du Seuil, Le Champ freudien, 1966, Points: Essais, 1999; English translation by Bruce Fink, in collaboration with Heloïse Fink and Russel Grigg, "The Situation of Psychoanalysis and the Training of Psychoanalysts in 1956." In *Écrits: The First Complete Edition in English*, pp. 384–411. New York: Norton, 2006.

Lagache, Daniel. "Le normal et le pathologique d'après Georges Canguilhem." *Revue de Métaphysique et de Morale* 51, no. 4 (1946): 355–370.

———. "La rêverie imageante, conduite adaptative au test de Rorschach." *Bulletin d'orientation professionnelle* (December 1943): 1–7; reprinted in *Bulletin du Groupement français du Rorschach* 9 (1957): 3–11; *Œuvres 1, 1932–1946*, pp. 401–412. Paris: PUF, 1977.

Laing, Ronald D. *The Divided Self: An Existential Study in Sanity and Madness*. London: Tavistock, 1960.

Laing, Ronald D., and David Cooper. *Reason and Violence: A Decade of Sartre's Philosophy, 1950–1960*. London: Tavistock, 1964. 2nd edition published in 1971.

Maldiney, Henri. "Psychose et présence" (1976). In *Penser l'homme et la folie: À la lumière de l'analyse existentielle et de l'analyse du destin*, pp. 5–82. Grenoble: Jérôme Millon, Collection Krisis, 1991. 3rd edition published in 2007.

Maldiney, Henri, and Roland Kuhn. *Rencontre / Begegnung: Au péril d'exister, Briefwechsel / Correspondance, Français / Deutsch, 1953–2004*. Edited by

Liselotte Rutishauser and Robert Christe. Würzburg: Königshausen und Neumann, 2017.

Merleau-Ponty, Maurice. *Merleau-Ponty à la Sorbonne: Résumé de cours, 1949–1952*. Grenoble: Cynara, 1988.

———. "Le métaphysique dans l'homme." *Revue de Métaphysique et de Morale* 52, nos. 3–4 (1947): 290–307; English translation by Hubert Dreyfus and Patricia Allen Dreyfus, "The Metaphysical in Man." In *Sense and Non-Sense*, pp. 83–98. Evanston, IL: Northwestern University Press, 1964.

———. *Phénoménologie de la perception*. Paris: Gallimard, Bibliothèque des idées, 1945; English translation by Colin Smith, *Phenomenology of Perception*. London: Routledge and Kegan Paul, 1962.

———. *Les Sciences de l'homme et la phénoménologie*. Paris: Tournier et Constans, 1953.

———. *La Structure du comportement*. Paris, PUF, Bibliothèque de philosophie contemporaine, 1942; English translation by Alden L. Fisher. *The Structure of Behavior*. Boston: Beacon, 1963.

Minkowska, Françoise. *Le Rorschach: À la recherche du monde des formes*. Introduction by Eugène Minkowski. Paris: Desclée de Brouwer, Bibliothèque neuro-psychiatrique de langue française, 1956. New edition published in Paris by l'Harmattan, 2003.

———. "Van Gogh, les relations entre sa vie, sa maladie et son œuvre." *L'Évolution psychiatrique* 3 (1933): 53–76.

Minkowski, Eugène. "À la recherche de la norme en psychopathologie." *L'Évolution Psychiatrique* 9, no. 1 (1938): 67–91.

———. "Le contact humain." *Revue de Métaphysique et de Morale* 55, no. 2 (1950): 113–127.

———. "Eröffnungsansprache und allgemeiner Lebenslauf anlässlich der Gedenkfeier zum 70. Geburtstag von Hermann Rorschach." *Rorschachiana*, Mitteilung der IGROF, suppl. *Zeitschrift für diagnostische Psychologie und Persönlichkeitsforschung* 3, no. 3 (1955): 271–279.

———. "Étude psychologique et analyse phénoménologique d'un cas de mélancolie schizophrénique." *Journal de Psychologie Normale et Pathologique* 20 (1923): 543–558.

———. "La genèse de la notion de schizophrénie et ses caractères essentiels: Une page d'histoire contemporaine de la psychiatrie." *L'Évolution psychiatrique* 1 (1925): 193–236.

———. "Les notions bleulériennes: voie d'accès aux analyses phénoménologiques et existentielles." *Annales Médico-Psychologiques* 15, no. 2 (1957): 833–844; reprinted in *Au de-là du rationalisme morbide*, pp. 141–151. Paris: L'Harmattan, Psychanalyse et civilisations: Série Trouvailles et retrouvailles, 1997.

———. "Psychiatrie et métaphysique: À la recherche de l'humain et du vécu." *Revue de Métaphysique et de Morale* 52 (1947): 333–358.

———. "Psychopathologie et psychologie." *Revue Philosophique de la France et de l'Étranger* 79 (1954): 200–217.

———. *La Schizophrénie: Psychopathologie des schizoïdes et des schizophrènes* (1927), new ed. 1933; Paris: Desclée de Brouwer, Bibliothèque neuropsychiatrique de langue française, 1953.

———. *Vers une cosmologie: Fragments philosophiques*. Paris: Montaigne, Philosophie de l'esprit, 1936.

Monnier, Marcel, ed. *L'Organisation des fonctions psychiques*. Neuchâtel: Éditions du Griffon, 1951.

———. "Le test psychologique de Rorschach." *L'Encephale* 29, nos. 3–4 (1934): 189–199, 247–270.

Mounier, Emmanuel. *Traité du caractère*. Paris: Éditions du Seuil, Collection Esprit, 1946. New edition (Collection Esprit: La Condition humaine) published in 1955.

Ombredane, André. *L'Aphasie et l'élaboration de la pensée explicite*. Paris: PUF, Bibliothèque de philosophie contemporaine, 1951.

———. *Études de psychologie médicale*. Vol. 1, *Perception et langage*. Rio de Janeiro: Atlantica Editora, 1944.

Politzer, Georges. *Critique des fondements de la psychologie: La psychologie et la psychanalyse*. Paris: Rieder, La collection de l'esprit 4, 1928; English translation by Maurice Apprey. *Critique of the Foundations of Psychology: The Psychology of Psychoanalysis*. Pittsburg, PA: Duquesne University Press, 1994.

———. "Où va la psychologie concrète?" *Revue de Psychologie Concrète*, no. 2 (1929): 199. In *Écrits*, edited by Jacques Debouzy, 2:137–188. Paris: Éditions sociales, 1969.

Rapaport, David. *Diagnostic Psychological Testing: The Theory, Statistical Evaluation, and Diagnostic Application of a Battery of Tests*. Chicago: Year Book, 1945–1946.

Rorschach, Hermann. *Briefwechsel*. Edited by Christian Müller and Rita Signer. Berne: Hans Huber, 2004.

———. *Psychodiagnostic, méthodes et résultats d'une expérience diagnostique de perception*. Translation from the 4th German edition (1941) and expanded with a critical introduction and index by André Ombredane and Augustine Landau. Paris: PUF, Bibliothèque scientifique internationale: Section Psychologie, 1947.

———. *Psychodiagnostik: Methodik und Ergebnisse eines wahrnehmungsdiagnostischen Experiments (Deutenlassen von Zufallsformen)*. Bern: Birker, 1921. 2nd edition published in 1932.

Rümke, Hans Cornelius. "Signification de la phénoménologie dans l'étude clinique des délirants." In *Congrès international de psychiatrie: Paris, 1950*, vol. 1, *Psychopathologie générale: Psychopathologie des délires*, pp. 126–173. Paris: Hermann, 1950.

Sartre, Jean-Paul. *Baudelaire*. Paris: Gallimard, Les Essais 24, 1947; English translation by Martin Turnell, *Baudelaire*. Norfolk, CT: New Directions, 1950.

———. *L'Être et le néant: Essai d'ontologie phénoménologique*. Paris: Gallimard, Bibliothèque des idées, 1943; English translation by Hazel E. Barnes. *Being and Nothingness*. New York: Philosophical Library, 1956.

———. *Saint Genet comédien et martyr*. Paris: Gallimard, 1952; English translation by Bernard Frechtman. *Saint Genet: Actor and Martyr*. Minneapolis: University of Minnesota Press, 2012.

Scheid, Karl Friedrich. "Existenziale Analytik und Psychopathologie." *Der Nervenarzt* 5, no. 12 (1932): 617–625.

Scheler, Max. *Der Formalismus in der Ethik und die materiale Wertethik: Neuer Versuch der Grundlegung eines ethischen Personalismus*. Halle-sur-Saale: Niemeyer, 1927.

———. *L'Homme du ressentiment*. Paris: Gallimard, Les Essais 9, 1933.

———. "Idealismus-Realismus." *Philosophischer Anzeiger* 2 (1928): 255–324.

———. *Die Idole der Selbsterkenntnis*. In *Abhandlungen und Aufsätze*, vol. 2, pp. 3–168. Leipzig: Verlag der Weissen Bücher, 1915.

———. "Mensch und Geschichte." *Neue Rundschau* 37 (1926): 449–476.

———. *Nature et Formes de la sympathie: Contribution à l'étude des lois de la vie émotionnelle*. French translation by Marcel Lefebvre. Paris: Payot, Bibliothèque scientifique, 1928.

———. *La Pudeur*. French translation by Maurice Dupuy. Paris: Aubier, Philosophie de l'esprit, 1952.

———. *Le Saint, le Génie, le Héros*. French translation by Émile Marmy. Fribourg: Egloff, 1944.

———. *Le Sens de la souffrance, suivi de deux autres essais*. French translation by Pierre Klossowski. Paris: Aubier-Montaigne, Philosophie de l'esprit, 1936.

———. *La Situation de l'homme dans le monde*. French translation by Maurice Dupuy. Paris: Aubier, Philosophie de l'esprit, 1951.

———. "Zur Idee des Menschen" (1914). In *Vom Umsturz der Werte: Abhandlungen und Aufsätze*, vol. 1, pp. 271–312. Leipzig: Neue Geist, 1919.

Schotte, Jacques. *Vers l'anthropopsychiatrie: Un parcours*. Paris: Hermann, Hermann Psychanalyse, 2008.

Starobinski, Jean. "Des taches et des masques." *Critiques* 14, nos. 135–136 (1958): 793–804.

Storch, Alfred. *Das archaisch-primitive Erleben und Denken der Schizophrenen: Entwicklungspsychologisch-klinische Untersuchungen zum Schizophrenieproblem*. Berlin: Springer, 1922.

———. "Die Daseinsfrage der Schizophrenen." *Schweizer Archiv für Neurologie und Psychiatrie* 59, no. 1 (1947): 330–385.

———. "Existenzphilosophisch Richtungen in der modernen Psychopathologie: Erwiderung zu R. De Rosa." *Der Nervenarzt* 23 (1952): 421–423.

———. "Die Psychoanalyse und die menschlichen Existenzprobleme." *Schweizer Archiv für Neurologie und Psychiatrie* 44 (1939): 102–118.

———. "Tod und Erneuerung in der schizophrenen Daseins-Umwandlung." *Archiv für Psychiatrie und Neurologie* 181 (1948): 275–293.

———. "Die Welt der beginnenden Schizophrenie und die archaische Welt: Ein existential-analytischer Versuch." *Zeitschrift für die gesamte Neurologie und Psychiatrie* 127, no. 1 (1930): 799–810.

Storch, Alfred, and Caspar Kulenkampff. "Zum Verständnis des Weltuntergangs der Schizophrenen." *Der Nervenartz* 21, no. 3 (1950): 102–108.

Straus, Erwin. "Die aufrechte Haltung: Eine anthropologische Studie." *Monatsschrift für Psychiatrie und Neurologie* 117, nos. 4–6 (1949): 367–379.

———. "Ein Beitrag zur Pathologie der Zwangserscheinungen." *Monatsschrift für Psychiatrie und Neurologie* 98, no. 2 (1938): 61–81.

———. "Die Formen des Räumlichen: Ihre Bedeutung für die Motorik und die Wahrnehmung." *Der Nervenarzt* 3, no. 11 (1930): 633–656.

———. *Geschehnis und Erlebnis: Zugleich eine historiologische Deutung des psychischen Traumas und Renten-Neurose*. Berlin: Springer, 1930.

———. *Vom Sinn der Sinne: Ein Beitrag zur Grundlegung der Psychologie*. Berlin: J. Springer, 1935; 2nd edition published in Berlin by Springer, 1956.

———. "Das Zeiterlebnis in der endogenen Depression und in der psychopatischen Verstimmung." *Monatsschrift für Psychiatrie und Neurologie* 68 (1928): 126–140.

Vuillemin, Jules. *L'Être et le travail: Les conditions dialectiques de la psychologie et de la sociologie*. Paris: PUF, Bibliothèque de philosophie contemporaine: Psychologie et sociologie, 1949.

———. "Nietzsche aujourd'hui." *Les Temps modernes* 6, no. 67 (1951): 1921–1954.

SECONDARY LITERATURE

Agamben, Giorgio. *Signatura rerum: Sul metodo*. Turin: Bollati Boringhieri, 2008; English translation by Luca D'Isanto with Kevin Attel, *The Signature of All Things*. New York: Zone, 2009, chap. 3, "Philosophical Archaeology," pp. 81–111.

Agard, Olivier. "Max Scheler entre la France et l'Allemagne." *Revue germanique internationale*, no. 11 (2013): 15–34.

Akavia, Naamah. *Subjectivity in Motion: Life, Art, and Movement in the Work of Hermann Rorschach*. New York: Routledge, Routledge Monographs in Mental Health, 2013.

Artières, Philippe, and Jean-François Bert. *Un succès philosophique: L'Histoire de la folie à l'âge classique de Michel Foucault*. Caen: Presses universitaires de Caen-IMEC Éd., 2011.

Artières, Philippe, Jean-François Bert, Frédéric Gros, and Judith Revel, eds. *Michel Foucault:* Paris: L'Herne, Cahiers de l'Herne 95, 2011.

Artières, Philippe, Jean-François Bert, Judith Revel, Mathieu Potte-Bonneville, and Pascal Michon. "Dans l'atelier Foucault." In *Les Lieux de savoir II: Les mains de l'intellect*, edited by Christian Jacob, pp. 944–962. Paris: Albin Michel, 2011.

Basso, Elisabetta. *Michel Foucault e la Daseinsanalyse: Un'indagine metodologica*. Milan: Mimesis, La scala e l'album, 2007.

———. "'Le rêve comme argument': les enjeux épistémologiques à l'origine du projet existentiel de Ludwig Binswanger." *Archives de Philosophie* 73, no. 4 (2010): 655–686.

Basso, Elisabetta, and Laurent Dartigues, eds. *Michel Foucault à l'épreuve de la psychiatrie et de la psychanalyse, Astérion: Philosophie, histoire des idées, pensée politique*, vol. 21, no. 2 (2019). https://journals.openedition.org/asterion/4074.

Basso, Elisabetta, Arianna Sforzini, Vincent Ventresque, and Carolina Verlengia. "Présentation du Fonds: présentation scientifique." http://eman-archives.org/Foucault-fiches/prsentation-du-fonds.

Benoist, Jocelyn. "Sur l'état présent de la phénoménologie." In *L'idée de phénoménologie*, pp. 1–43. Paris: Beauchesne, Le grenier à sel, 2001.

Bert, Jean-François, and Elisabetta Basso, eds. *Foucault à Münsterlingen: À l'origine de l'Histoire de la folie*. Avec des photographies de Jacqueline Verdeaux. Paris: Éditions EHESS, L'histoire et ses représentations 10, 2015.

———. "Foucault, Rorschach et les tests projectifs." In *Foucault à Münsterlingen: À l'origine de l'Histoire de la folie*. Avec des photographies de Jacqueline Verdeaux. pp. 69–76. Paris: Éditions EHESS, L'histoire et ses représentations 10, 2015.

Bert, Jean-François, and Jérôme Lamy. "Michel Foucault 'inédit.'" *Cahiers d'histoire: Revue d'histoire critique*, no. 140 (2018): 149–164.

Bianco, Giuseppe, ed. *Georges Politzer, le concret et sa signification: Psychologie, philosophie et politique*. Paris: Hermann, Hermann philosophie, 2016.

Blum, Iris, and Peter Witschi, eds. *Olga und Hermann Rorschach: Ein ungewöhnliches Psychiater-Ehepaar*. Herisau: Appenzeller Verlag, 2008.

Braunstein, Jean-François. "Bachelard, Canguilhem, Foucault. Le 'style français' en épistémologie." In *Les philosophes et la science*, edited by Pierre Wagner, pp. 920–963. Paris: Gallimard, Folio: Essais 408, 2002.

———. "Foucault, Canguilhem et l'histoire des sciences humaines." *Archives de philosophie* 79, no. 1 (2016): 13–26.

Brückner, Burkhart, Lukas Iwer, and Samuel Thoma. "Die Existenz, Abwesenheit und Macht des Wahnsinns: Eine kritische Übersicht zu Michel Foucaults Arbeiten zur Geschichte und Philosophie der Psychiatrie."

NMT Zeitschrift für Geschichte der Wissenschaften, Technik und Medizin 25 (2017): 69–98.

Buytendijk, Frederik J. J. *Attitudes et mouvements: Étude fonctionnelle du mouvement humain*. French translation by L. van Haecht. Paris: Desclée de Brouwer, Textes et études anthropologiques, 1957.

Carroy, Jacqueline. "Jackson et la psychopathologie: Évolution et évolutionnisme." In *Les Évolutions: Phylogenèse de l'individuation*, edited by Pierre Fédida and Daniel Widlöcher, pp. 151–172. Paris: PUF, Colloques de la Revue internationale de psychopathologie, 1994.

Coffin, Jean-Christophe. "'Misery' and 'Revolution': The Organization of French Psychiatry, 1900–1980." In *Psychiatric Cultures Compared: Psychiatry and Mental Health Care in the Twentieth Century: Comparisons and Approaches*, edited by Marijke Gijswijt-Hofstra et al., pp. 225–247. Amsterdam: Amsterdam University Press, 2006.

Cormann, Grégory. "Sartre à Venise, l'homme qui allait vers le froid. Sur *La Reine Albemarle ou le dernier touriste* (1951–1952)." *Les Temps Modernes*, no. 679 (2014): 73–107.

Courtine, Jean-François. "Foucault lecteur de Husserl: L'*a priori* historique et le quasi-transcendantal." *Giornale di metafisica* 29, no. 1 (2007): 211–232.

Dammann, Gerhard. "Roland Kuhns phänomenologische und daseinsanalytische Arbeiten zu Ästhetik und künstlerischem Schaffen." In *Auf der Seeseite der Kunst: Werke aus der Psychiatrischen Klinik Münsterlingen, 1894–1960*, edited by Katrin Luchsinger, Gerhard Dammann, Monika Jagfeld, and André Salathé, pp. 37–52. Zürich: Chronos, 2015.

Dassonneville, Gautier. "Foucault auditeur: Les études de philosophie et de psychologie à Paris, 1946–1953." http://eman-archives.org/Foucault-fiches/exhibits/show/foucault-auditeur-les-ann———. es-.

Defert, Daniel. "Chronologie (1926–1967)." In *Œuvres*, vol. 1, by Michel Foucault, edited by Frédéric Gros, pp. xxxv–liv. Paris: Gallimard, Bibliothèque de la Pléiade, 2015.

———. "'Je crois au temps. . . .': Daniel Defert légataire des manuscrits de Michel Foucault." Interview with Guillaume Bellon. *Recto/Verso*, no. 1 (2007): 1–7.

Delille, Emmanuel. "Henri Ellenberger in Schaffhausen, 1943–1953: Ellenbergers 'Geschichte der dynamischen Psychiatrie' als Exilliteratur." In

125 Jahre Psychiatrische Klinik Breitenau Schaffhausen 1891–2016, edited by Jörg Püschel, pp. 235–257. Zürich: Chronos Verlag, 2018.

———. "L'organo-dynamisme d'Henri Ey: l'oubli d'une théorie de la conscience considéré dans ses relations avec l'analyse existentielle." *L'Homme et la société* 167–168–169 (2008): 203–219.

———. *Réseaux savants et enjeux classificatoires dans l'Encyclopédie médico-chirurgicale (1947–1977): L'exemple de la notion de psychose.* PhD diss., Contemporary History, École des Hautes Études en Sciences Sociales (Paris), December 6, 2008.

Del Vento, Christian, and Jean-Louis Fournel. "L'édition des cours et les 'pistes' de Michel Foucault." *Laboratoire italien*, no. 7 (2007). http://journals.openedition.org.inshs.bib.cnrs.fr/laboratoireitalien/144.

Demazeux, Steeves. *L'Éclipse du symptôme: L'observation clinique en psychiatrie, 1800–1950.* Paris: Ithaque, Philosophie, anthropologie, psychologie, 2019.

Derrida, Jacques. "'Être juste avec Freud': L'histoire de la folie à l'âge de la psychanalyse." In *Penser la folie: Essais sur Michel Foucault*, edited by Élisabeth Roudinesco. Paris: Galilée, Débats, 1992; English translation by Pascale-Anne Brault and Michael Naas, "'To Do Justice to Freud': The History of Madness in the Age of Psychoanalysis." *Critical Inquiry* 20, no. 2 (1994): 227–266.

Dreyfus, Hubert, and Paul Rabinow. *Michel Foucault: Beyond Structuralism and Hermeneutics.* 2nd ed. Chicago: University of Chicago Press, 1983.

Eco, Umberto. *La struttura assente.* Milan: Bompiani, Nuovi saggi italiani 1, 1968.

Elden, Stuart. "Afterword: Afterlives." In *The Lives of Michel Foucault: A Biography*, by David Macey, pp. 481–491. London: Verso, 2019.

———. *The Early Foucault.* Cambridge: Polity, 2021.

———. "Foucault as Translator of Binswanger and von Weizsäcker." *Theory, Culture and Society* (First Published 2020). https://doi.org/10.1177/0263276420950459.

Elden, Stuart, Orazio Irrera, and Daniele Lorenzini, eds. "Foucault Before the Collège de France." *Theory, Culture and Society* (2020): www.theoryculturesociety.org/blog/special-issue-foucault-before-the-college-de-france.

Eribon, Didier. *Michel Foucault: 1926–1984.* Paris: Flammarion, 1989. 3rd edition published in 2011, Champs: biographie 847; English translation by

Betsy Wing, *Michel Foucault*. Cambridge: MA, Harvard University Press, 1991.
———. *Michel Foucault et ses contemporains*. Paris: Fayard, 1994.
Ey, Henri. "Le développement 'mécaniciste' de la psychiatrie à l'abri du dualisme 'cartésien.'" In *Études psychiatriques*, vol. 1. Paris: Desclée de Brouwer et Cie, 1948; 2nd edition published in 1952.
———. "Introduction aux débats." In "La conception idéologique de 'L'Histoire de la folie' de Michel Foucault." Annual conference of *Évolution psychiatrique*, December 6–7, 1969, *L'Évolution Psychiatrique* 36, no. 2 (1971): 225–226.
———. "*Rêve et existence*. (En hommage à E. Minkowski. Réflexions sur une Étude de L. Binswanger)." *L'Évolution Psychiatrique* 21, no. 1 (1956): 109–118.
Flajoliet, Alain. "Sartre's Phenomenological Anthropology Between Psychoanalysis and 'Daseinsanalysis.'" *Sartre Studies International* 16, no. 1 (2010): 40–59.
Fontana, Alessandro. "Introduzione." In *Nascita della clinica*, by Michel Foucault, pp. vii–xxxv. Italian translation by A. Fontana. Turin: Einaudi, Einaudi paperbacks 5, 1969.
Galison, Peter. "Image of Self." In *Things That Talk*: *Object Lessons from Art and Science*, edited by Lorraine Daston, pp. 257–296. New York: Zone, 2004.
Gens, Jean-Claude. "La réception de Jaspers dans la philosophie et la psychiatrie françaises: La première réception." *Le Cercle herméneutique*, nos. 8–9 (2007): 187–198.
Germain, Marie-Odile. "Michel Foucault de retour à la BnF." *Chroniques de la Bibliothèque nationale de France*, no. 70 (2014): 26–27.
Goris, Wouter. "L'a priori historique chez Husserl et Foucault (I): La pertinence philosophique d'un concept directeur de l'épistémologie historique." *Philosophie* 123, no. 4 (2014): 3–27; (II) *Philosophie* 125, no. 2 (2015): 22–43.
Gruevska, Julia. "Von der Tierphysiologie zur Psychologie des Menschen: Ein Einblick in Werk und Wirken Frederik Buytendijks." *Internationales Jahrbuch für Philosophische Anthropologie* 8, no. 1 (2018): 87–106.
Gueguen, Bernard. "Hommage à Georges Verdeaux." *Neurophysiologie clinique* 34, no. 6 (2004): 301–302.

Gutting, Gary. *Michel Foucault's Archaeology of Scientific Reason*. Cambridge: Cambridge University Press, Modern European philosophy, 1989.

Han-Pile, Béatrice. "L'a priori historique selon Michel Foucault: difficultés archéologiques." In *Lectures de Michel Foucault*, vol. 2, *Foucault et la philosophie*, edited by Emmanuel Da Silva, pp. 23–38. Lyon: ENS Éditions, Theoria, 2003.

———. *Foucault's Critical Project: Between the Transcendental and the Historical*. Stanford: Stanford University Press, 2002.

———. "Phenomenology and Anthropology in Foucault's 'Introduction to Binswanger's *Dream And Existence*': A Mirror Image of *The Order Of Things*?" *History and Theory* 55, no. 4 (2016): 7–22.

Harrington, Anne. *Reenchanted Science: Holism in German Culture from Wilhelm II to Hitler*. Princeton: Princeton University Press, 1996.

Joranger, Line. "Individual Perception and Cultural Development. Foucault's 1954 Approach to Mental Illness and Its History." *History of Psychology* 19, no. 1 (2016): 40–51.

Kisker, Karl Peter. "Antipsychiatrie (AP)." In *Psychiatrie der Gegenwart. Forschung und Praxis*, vol. 1, t. 1, *Grundlagen und Methoden der Psychiatrie*, edited by Karl Peter Kisker, Joachim-Ernst Meyer, Christian Müller, and Erik Strömgren, pp. 811–825, §F, "Theorien," 2: "Philosophische Züflüsse." Berlin: Springer, 1960; 2nd edition published in 1979.

———. *Dialogik der Verrücktheit: Ein Versuch an den Grenzen der Anthropologie*. Den Haag: Martinus Nijhoff, 1970.

Lamy, Jérôme. "De la psychologie des images à l'ontologie poétique: Vers une Métaphysique de l'imagination avec Bachelard." In *L'Histoire du concept d'imagination en France (de 1918 à nos jours)*, edited by Riccardo Barontini and Julien Lamy, pp. 79–96. Paris: Classiques Garnier, Rencontres: Série Littérature des XXe et XXIe siècles 34, 2019.

Lanteri-Laura, Georges. *La psychiatrie phénoménologique: Fondements philosophiques*. Paris: PUF, Bibliothèque de psychiatrie, 1963.

———. "Le Voyage dans l'anti-psychiatrie anglaise." *L'Évolution psychiatrique* 61, no. 3 (1996): 621–633.

Le Blanc, Guillaume. "Se moquer de la phénoménologie, est-ce encore faire de la phénoménologie?" *Les Études philosophiques* 106, no. 3 (2013): 373–381.

Le Bras, Laurence. "Les fiches de lecture de Michel Foucault." *Le Blog Gallica*. https://gallica.bnf.fr/blog/18112020/les-fiches-de-lecture-de-michel-foucault?mode=desktop.

Lebrun, Gérard. "Note sur la phénoménologie dans *Les Mots et les Choses*." In *Michel Foucault philosophe: Rencontre International, Paris 9–11 janvier 1988*, pp. 33–52. Paris: Éditions du Seuil, Des Travaux, 1989.

Leguil, François. "Lacan avec et contre Jaspers." *Ornicar?* 15, no. 48 (1989): 5–23.

Macey, David. *The Lives of Michel Foucault: A Biography*. London: Verso, 2019.

Macherey, Pierre. "Aux sources de l'*Histoire de la folie*: Une rectification et ses limites." *Critique*, nos. 471–472 (1986): 753–774.

Massot, Marie-Laure, Arianna Sforzini, and Vincent Ventresque. "Transcribing Foucault's handwriting with Transkribus." *Journal of Data Mining and Digital Humanities*. Episciences.org. https://jdmdh.episciences.org/5218.

May, Todd. "Foucault's Relation to Phenomenology." In *The Cambridge Companion to Foucault*, edited by Gary Gutting, 2nd ed., pp. 284–311. Cambridge: Cambridge University Press, Cambridge Companions to Philosophy, 2006.

Melandri, Enzo. *La linea e il circolo: Studio logico-filosofico sull'analogia*. Bologna: Il Mulino, 1968; Macerata: Quodlibet, Quaderni Quodlibet 18, 2004.

Monod, Jean-Claude, ed. *Foucault et la phénoménologie. Les Études philosophiques* 106, no. 3 (2013).

———. "Présentation." *Les Études philosophiques* 106, no. 3 (2013): 311–315.

Moreno Pestaña, José Luis. *En devenant Foucault: Sociogenèse d'un grand philosophe*. French translation by Philippe Hunt. Broissieux: Éditions du Croquant, Collection Champ social, 2006.

Müldner, Heinrich G. "Einleitung." In *Münsterlinger Kolloquien*, vol. 4, by Roland Kuhn, pp. 9–21. Würzburg: Königshausen and Neumann, 2014.

Paltrinieri, Luca. "A priori storico, archeologia, antropologia: suggestioni kantiane nel pensiero di Michel Foucault." *Studi kantiani* 20 (2007): 73–97.

———. "Les aventures du transcendantal: Kant, Husserl, Foucault." *Lumières*, no. 16 (2010): 11–31.

———. "De quelques sources de *Maladie mentale et personnalité*. Réflexologie pavlovienne et critique sociale." In *Foucault à Münsterlingen: À l'origine de l'Histoire de la folie*, edited by Jean-François Bert and Elisabetta Basso,

Avec des photographies de Jacqueline Verdeaux, pp. 197–219. Paris: Éditions EHESS, L'histoire et ses représentations 10, 2015.

Piaget, Jean. *Sagesse et illusions de la philosophie.* Paris: PUF, 1965; English translation by Wolfe Mays, *Insights and Illusions of Philosophy.* New York: World, 1971.

Pidoux, Vincent. "Expérimentation et clinique électroencéphalographiques entre physiologie, neurologie et psychiatrie (Suisse, 1935–1965)." *Revue d'histoire des sciences* 63, no. 2 (2010): 439–472.

Pinguet, Maurice. "Les années d'apprentissage." *Le Débat* 41, no. 4 (1986): 122–131.

Pinto, Louis. "Foucault avant Foucault: psychologie et sciences de l'homme." In *Lire les sciences sociales*, vol. 3, edited by Gérard Mauger and Louis Pinto, pp. 116–122. Paris: Hermès Sciences, 1994–1996.

Pitts, Walter, and Warren S. McCulloch. "How We Know Universals: The Perception of Auditory and Visual Forms." *Bulletin of Mathematical Biophysics*, no. 9 (1947): 127–147.

Rausch de Traubenberg, Nina. "Les cinquante années de publications du 'Groupement français du Rorschach' devenu 'Société du Rorschach et des méthodes projectives de langue française.'" *Psychologie clinique et projective* 9, no. 1 (2003): 9–17.

Revel, Judith. "Sur l'Introduction à Binswanger (1954)." In *Michel Foucault: Lire l'œuvre*, edited by Luce Giard, pp. 51–56. Grenoble: Jérôme Millon, 1992.

Rodrigo, Pierre. "Sartre et Bachelard: Variations autour de l'imagination bachelardienne." *Cahiers Gaston Bachelard*, no. 8 (2006): 51–64.

Rogove, John. "La phénoménologie manquée de Foucault: Husserl et le contre-modèle de l'anthropologisme kantien." *Philosophie* 123, no. 4 (2014): 58–67.

Sabot, Philippe. "Archives: Vivre et enseigner à Lille." In *Foucault à Münsterlingen: À l'origine de l'Histoire de la folie*, edited by Jean-François Bert and Elisabetta Basso. Avec des photographies de Jacqueline Verdeaux. pp. 121–123. Paris: Éditions EHESS, L'histoire et ses représentations 10, 2015.

———. "L'expérience, le savoir et l'histoire dans les premiers écrits de Michel Foucault." *Archives de Philosophie* 69, no. 2 (2006): 285–303.

———. "The 'World' of Michel Foucault: Phenomenology, Psychology, Ontology in the 1950s." *Theory, Culture and Society* (forthcoming).

Saint Aubert, Emmanuel de. *Du lien des êtres aux éléments de l'être: Merleau-Ponty au tournant des années 1945–1951*. Paris: Vrin, Bibliothèque d'histoire de la philosophie: Temps modernes, 2004.

Salanskis, Michel. "Les deux triades de Canguilhem-Foucault." In *Le concept, le sujet, la science. Cavaillès, Canguilhem, Foucault*, edited by Pierre Cassou-Noguès and Pascale Gillot, pp. 237–270. Paris: Vrin, Problèmes et controverses, 2009.

Schmidgen, Henning. "'Fortunes diverses': L'œuvre de jeunesse de Jacques Lacan et la phénoménologie." *Psychanalyse à l'université* 19, no. 76 (1994): 111–134.

Searls, Damion. *The Inkblots: Hermann Rorschach, His Iconic Test and the Power of Seeing*. New York: Crown, 2017.

Sforzini, Arianna. "Michel Foucault numérique: Les archives à l'épreuve des nouvelles archéologies du savoir." *Implications philosophiques*. www.implications-philosophiques.org/michel-foucault-numerique/.

Sheridan, Alan. *Michel Foucault: The Will to Truth*. London: Tavistock, 1980.

Sini, Carlo. *Semiotica e filosofia: Segno e linguaggio in Peirce, Nietzsche, Heidegger e Foucault*. Bologna: Il Mulino, Saggi 175, 1978.

Smyth, Bryan. "Foucault and Binswanger: Beyond the Dream." *Philosophy Today*, no. 55, suppl. (2011): 92–101.

Spiegelberg, Herbert. *Phenomenology in Psychology and Psychiatry: A Historical Introduction*. Evanston, IL: Northwestern University Press, Northwestern University Studies in Phenomenology and Existential Philosophy, 1972.

Trucchio, Aldo. "Jean Starobinski, lecteur de Bachelard au début des années 1950." *Bulletin du Cercle d'études internationales Jean Starobinski* 6 (2013): 8–16.

Verdeaux, Bruno. "'Nous étions un peu plus qu'un et un peu moins que deux': Jacqueline et Georges Verdeaux." In *Foucault à Münsterlingen: À l'origine de l'Histoire de la folie* edited by Jean-François Bert and Elisabetta Basso, Avec des photographies de Jacqueline Verdeaux. pp. 270–272 Paris: Éditions EHESS, L'histoire et ses représentations 10, 2015.

Yanacopoulo, Andrée. *Henri F. Ellenberger: Une vie*. Montreal: Liber, 2009.

Widmer, Peter. "Lacan in der Schweiz." In *Lacan und das Deutsche: Die Rückkehr der Psychoanalyse über den Rhein*, edited by Jutta Prasse and Claus-Dieter Rath, pp. 242–258. Freiburg: Kore, 1994.

Wyrsch, Jakob. *Die Person des Schizophrenen: Studien zur Klinik, Psychologie, Daseinsweise.* Bern: Haupt, 1949; French translation by Jacqueline Verdeaux, *La personne du schizophrène: Étude clinique, psychologique et anthropophénoménologique.* Paris: PUF, Bibliothèque de psychiatrie, 1956.

INDEX

Abély, Xavier, 231n146
Abraham, Karl, 82
abstraction, 17, 58, 86, 108, 177, 246n26
act, biological, 148, 173
adaptation, 84, 173
aesthetics, 118, 127, 254n156, 259n13, 266n88, 274n198, 275n233, 278, 279, 280, 281
affectivity, 40
Agamben, Giorgio, 213n16, 262n47, 289
Agard, Olivier, 256n168, 299
Ajuriaguerra, Julian de, 182
Akavia, Naamah, 55, 234n172, 237n192, 239n210, 239n213, 299
alienation, 24–25, 102, 182
Allaigre, Annick, 271n178, 284
Allen Dreyfus, Patricia, 264n60, 295
alterity, 167–168, 185
Althusser, Louis, 15, 23, 24, 41, 182
Alunni, Charles, 233n158, 284
Ammann, Jürg, 238n195, 240n231, 292

analytic, of *Dasein*, *Daseinsanalytik*, 68, 93, 104, 113, 144–145, 148, 157, 203, 261n33; of finitude in Foucault, 199, 265n82
Ancelin-Schützenberger, Anne, 238n200
Anderson, Jon, 227n103, 275n233, 279, 293
Angel, Ernest, 232n154, 232n155, 250n86, 251n87, 262n34, 285, 287, 292
anthropology, 5, 23, 30, 46, 47, 57, 67, 93, 96, 116–119, 121–134, 139–140, 156, 180, 182, 186, 196, 198, 202, 204, 205, 214n16, 255n167, 257n216, 262n33, 275n3, 276n7, 304; clinical, 135; cultural, 22; existential, 98, 109, 116–117, 129, 137, 157, 199, 201, 257n216; of the imagination, 47, 93; Kant's, 5, 121–122, 128, 125–126, 133, 135, 140, 257n209, 257n215, 259n12, 281; medical, 148; phenomenological, 3–4, 8, 34, 81, 111, 122–123,

anthropology (*continued*)
  125–126, 131, 138–139, 230n134, 303; philosophical, 5, 7, 11, 22, 29, 30, 35, 37, 82, 121–122, 125, 127, 134, 139; scientific, 50
anthropometry, 133
antipsychiatry, 141
anxiety, *angoisse*, 20, 75, 84, 107, 118, 150, 169, 225n57, 253n243, 257n204, 257n207, 274n224
Anzieu, Didier, 273n193
aphasia, 147, 168–169, 219n4
Apprey, Maurice, 225n59, 245n15, 296
a priori, cognition, 131; concrete, 135, 138, 155; empirical, 151; existential, of existence, xii, 130, 150–152, 161, 193; historical, xi–xiii, 9, 140–141, 158–164, 170, 172, 176, 178, 199, 201, 204–205, 256n185, 265–266nn81–82, 301, 303, 304, 305; phenomenological, 142; of the species, 154. *See also* structure
archaeology, ix, xi, xiii, 1, 8, 9, 13, 121, 139, 141–142, 158–164, 166–167, 170, 172–176, 180, 183, 190, 192, 196, 198–199, 201, 203, 213n16, 259n14, 260n21, 263n47, 265n82, 266nn85–86, 266n89, 267n103, 269n141, 269n155, 269n157, 270n166, 275n2, 276n12, 278, 279, 299, 304
Aron, A. R., 246n21
Aron, Jean-Paul, 19, 20, 121, 220n8, 221n22

Artières, Philippe, 218nn41–42, 254n53, 258nn1–2, 299
Askay, Richard, 266n33, 291
associationism, 26
asylum, 25, 61, 62, 182, 184, 237n195
atopia, 169
Attel, Kevin, 213n16
automatism, 103

Bachelard, Gaston, 23, 42, 43–49, 57–59, 163, 215n28, 231n137, 232nn148–153, 233nn157–160, 234n161, 234n163, 234n167, 234n169, 235n175, 240n222, 240nn224–226, 246n21, 267n97, 283–284, 300, 304, 306, 307
Baños Orellana, Jorge, 271n178, 284
Barnes, Hazel E., 230n133, 297
Barontini, Riccardo, 234n167, 304
Basaglia, Franco, 260n17, 284
Basso, Elisabetta, x–xv, 211, 214n21, 215n22, 217n35, 218n41, 218n44, 220n5, 220n8, 221n22, 222nn28–29, 224n52, 231n137, 233n158, 234n173, 235n181, 243nn261–263, 245n12, 247nn45–46, 248n51, 248nn53–54, 251n89, 253n135, 265n75, 275n1, 282, 283, 284, 299, 300, 305, 306, 307
Bastide, Georges, 23
Baudelaire, Charles, 107, 251, 297
Baudouin, Alphonse, 52
Baumgarten-Tramer, Franziska, 237n193
Bayer, Raymond, 246n21

Bayle, Pierre, 20
béance (gaping, abyss), 189, 194, 274n198
Beaulieu, Alain, 218n41, 222n33, 281
Beauvoir, Simone de, 43, 233n157, 284
Becker, Jared, 270n164, 280
Béguin, Albert, 25, 225n55, 284
behavior, 17, 19, 53, 57, 77, 87, 100, 108, 112, 140, 145–148, 151, 154, 156, 171, 173, 178, 264n64, 295
behaviorism, 24
Being, *être*, 40, 111, 144; *Seinslehre* (doctrine of B.), 113, 230n133, 261n33, 263n52, 291, 297
being, *étant*, 113; 135; being-at-hand, 261n33; being-man, *Menschsein*, 50, 178, 198; mode, manner, way of, x, 91, 109, 147, 161, 164, 166, 170–172, 177, 178; sense of, 126. *See also Dasein*
Bellon, Guillaume, 217n32, 301
Benoist, Jocelyn, 267n95, 300
Berg, Hendrik van den, 48
Bergson, Henri, 19
Bernard, Paul, 231n146
Bert, Jean-François, 214n21, 215n22, 216n31, 218nn41–42, 220n5, 220n8, 221n22, 222n28, 224n52, 234n173, 243nn261–262, 247nn45–46, 248n51, 248n53, 251n89, 253n135, 254n153, 258nn1–2, 282, 299, 300, 305, 306, 307
Berten, André, 218n41, 281

Bewegungsvollzug (movement completion), 74
Bewusstseinsgestalt (configuration of the consciousness), 168
Bianco, Giuseppe, 225n60, 300
Biemel, Walter, 23, 223n44, 290
Bilz, Rudolf, 77
Binder, Hans, 233n159, 284
Binswanger, Ludwig (the elder), 61
Blanchot, Maurice, 224n49, 292
Bleuler, Eugen, 29, 35, 37, 50, 82, 236n185, 236n189, 287
Blum, Iris, 238n201, 300
Bochner, Ruth, 56, 239n215, 288
Bohm, Ewald, 235n173, 288
Bollnow, Otto Friedrich, 123
Bonnafé, Lucien, 25, 235n146
Bopp, Franz, 198
Borges, Jorge Luis, 165–169
Boss, Medard, 39, 77, 105, 251n88, 262n33, 288, 291
Bouman, L., 149
Brault, Pascale-Anne, 292n184, 302
Braunstein, Jean-François, 10, 215n28, 221n16, 300
Brecht, Franz Josef, 124
Briggs, Kate, 257n209, 259n12, 281
Brion, Fabienne, 216n31, 281
Brisset, Jean-Pierre, 273n194
Brokman, Franziska, 51, 236n189, 237n190, 295. *See also* Minkowska, Françoise
Brückner, Burkhart, 214n16, 300
Buffon, Georges-Louis, 175
Buraud, Georges, 59, 240n225, 288

Burchell, Graham, 217n37, 282, 283
Burckhardt, E., 264n67, 290
Buytendijk, Frederik J. J., 2, 21, 48, 155, 156, 264nn68–69, 301, 303

Cabanis, Pierre Jean Georges, 16
Cairns, Lucille, 267n106, 279
Candaux, Jean-Daniel, 250n84, 292
Canguilhem, Georges, 18, 20, 27, 29, 47, 59–60, 120, 138, 153, 154, 161, 174, 201, 215, 221nn15–16, 225n64, 226n71, 240n227, 258n10, 263nn54–59, 264n71, 267n91, 269n156, 270n174, 276n8, 288, 294, 300, 307
Canivet, Nella, 239n215, 288
care, 9, 212n1, 225n56, 237n189, 301
Carrette, Jeremy R., 267n106, 279
Carroy, Jacqueline, 248n56, 301
Cascaito, James, 260n19, 270n164, 280
Cassou-Noguès, Pierre, 270n174, 307
catamnèse (catamnesis), 75
causality, 15, 88, 160, 178, 183, 186, 245nn16–17, 271n178, 294
Chapoutier, Fernand, 17
Chapsal, Madeleine, 269n146, 279
Christe, Robert, 230n132, 295
classification: clinical, 2, 138; psychiatric, 147, 149
clinic, xiii, 27, 38, 56, 160, 162–163, 169, 188, 199, 216n30, 260n21, 266n87, 267n96, 267n98, 268n135, 268n137, 273n194, 275n5; *clinica*, 278, 303

clinical case, 7, 29, 31, 36, 43, 44–45, 49, 53, 85, 90, 97, 105, 120, 130, 150, 155, 167, 168, 203, 255n167
Coffin, Jean-Christophe, 225n56, 301
cogito, 253n145, 269n156, 288
Cohen, Robert S., 276n8, 288
Communist Party (French), 19, 24
complex, 87, 88, 97, 245n17
comprehension, *compréhension*, 72, 102; static and genetic in Jaspers, 72, 102
concrete, xiii, 26–28, 34, 39–40, 56, 67, 68, 81, 86–87, 89, 93, 100, 102, 107, 108, 111, 115, 117, 119, 120, 123, 129, 130, 132, 135, 137, 138, 152, 154, 155, 157, 158, 167, 175, 186, 228n105, 245nn15–16, 246n26, 296
conditioning, *conditionnement*, 17, 73
conflict, 24–25, 87–88, 245n19
consciousness, 39, 40, 52, 68, 90, 99–101, 103, 134, 153, 154, 157, 189, 195; configuration of (*Bewusstseinsgestalt*), 168
connaissance (knowledge), 74, 124, 162–163, 200, 263n54, 284, 288
constitution (phenomenology), 68, 101, 103, 129; psychological, 107
contradiction, 84, 126
Cooper, David, 141, 260n17, 294
Cormann, Grégory, 233n157, 301
cosmology, 46
"counter-science," 195
Courtine, Jean-François, 265n81, 301
culpabilité (culpability), 75

INDEX ☙ 313

culture, 20, 51, 164, 167, 179, 189, 216, 217n38, 218n41, 218n43, 225n56, 231n144, 254n155, 262n39, 264n66, 267n106, 270n164, 279, 280, 281, 282, 301, 302, 304, 306
Cuvier, Georges, 198
cybernetics, 22

Dammann, Gerhard, 238n202, 239n204, 301
Dartigues, Laurent, 222n29, 300
Darwin, Charles, 99
Dasein (being-in-the-world), 36, 39–40, 44, 45, 70, 71, 73, 91, 93, 97, 106, 110–111, 129, 130, 131, 132, 133, 144, 146, 148, 152, 155, 170, 204, 205, 228n113, 247n47, 252n117, 261nn32–33, 262n37, 265n73, 268n127, 285, 287, 292, 298
Daseinsanalyse, Daseinsanalysis, xi, xiii–xiv, 29, 31, 36, 38, 39, 45, 46–49, 56–57, 63, 67–68, 71, 73–77, 94, 96–97, 103–105, 107–117, 119–120, 122, 125, 139, 157, 160, 175, 177, 180, 203, 230n134, 231n139, 250–251n87, 262n33, 275n1, 285, 292, 299, 303. *See also* existential analysis
Da Silva, Emmanuel, 266n82, 304
Dassonneville, Gautier, 217n39, 238n200, 301
Daston, Lorraine, 237n191, 303
Daumézon, Georges, 25, 42, 182, 231nn145–146, 232n147, 290
Davidson, Arnold I., 10, 216n31, 273n195, 278, 282

death, of man, 133, 269n156, 288; of God, 133
Defert, Daniel, xv, 9, 208, 212n5, 213n9, 213n13, 217n32, 219n3, 220n13, 224n45, 244n10, 246n25, 258n8, 263n49, 267n92, 270n164, 277, 278, 279, 280, 281, 301
Delay, Jean, 2, 16, 53, 114
Delille, Emmanuel, 212n7, 231n137, 237n194, 248n56, 284, 301
delusion, *délire, Wahn*, 22, 54, 61, 75, 76, 77, 88, 113, 223n38, 229nn118–119, 239n206, 240n230, 242n243, 245n19, 250n87, 252n128, 290, 292, 297; *Eifersuchtwahn* (jealousy delusion), 72
Del Vento, Christian, 217n32, 302
Demazeux, Steeves, 273n194, 302
De Rosa, Renato, 32, 113, 252n127, 289, 298
Derrida, Jacques, 185, 189, 272n184, 274n201, 302
Descartes, René, 11, 126, 229n125, 291
destiny, 107–108, 116, 128
diagnosis, xiii, 1, 54, 140, 164
dialectic, *dialectique*, 79, 84, 86, 89, 199, 255n165
Dilthey, Wilhelm, 128
D'Isanto, Luca, 213n16, 262n47, 299
discursive practice, 175–176, 265n82
disposition, 57, 112, 148, 160, 172–174, 269n149
Doron, Claude-Olivier, 217n37, 283
drama, dramatic, dramatization, 59, 83, 85–89, 150

dream, *rêve*, *Traum*, xi, xv, 1, 3, 5, 6, 7, 29, 34, 38, 39, 40, 41, 43, 45, 46, 47, 57–59, 62–67, 70, 76, 81, 82, 85–87, 89, 91–94, 96, 98, 100, 105, 107, 109, 114–117, 122, 123, 127, 131, 135, 144, 150–152, 155, 158, 183–185, 191, 197–199, 202, 205, 212n5–6, 213n16, 214n16, 228n106, 230n135, 231n142, 232nn152–153, 233n156, 234n164, 234n166, 234n168, 243n259, 244n1, 244n11, 246n27, 246n30, 247n33, 247n38, 247n48, 248n52, 248n55, 249n62, 251n99, 252n108, 252n111, 253n138, 254n160, 257nn196–198, 257n200, 257–258n216, 260n18, 261n30, 262n45, 263n50, 264n62, 265n74, 265nn76–77, 265nn79–80, 271n179, 274n219–220, 275n3, 276n10, 277, 283, 284, 286–287, 300, 303, 304, 307
Dreyfus, Hubert, 216n29, 264n60, 265n82, 295, 302
Dublineau, Jean-Joseph, 231n138, 289
Dubol, Viviane, 271n178, 284
Dumas, Georges, 17, 219n4
Dumézil, Georges, 21
Dunant, Henry, 250n84, 292
Dupuy, Maurice, 256n168, 298
Durand, Roger, 250n84, 292

Eco, Umberto, 266n84, 302
eidetic, 99, 100, 101
Einfühlung (affective interpenetration), 249n75

Eitingon, Max, 82
Elden, Stuart, 214n16, 216n31, 217n38, 264n66, 302
electroencephalogram (EEG), 16, 51–53, 235n183
electroencephalography, x, 50, 52–53, 220n5
Eliasberg, Wladimir, 149
Ellenberger, Henri F., 36, 49, 51, 110, 229n120, 232n154, 235n176–79, 237n194, 250n86, 251n87, 252n116, 262n34, 285, 287, 289, 292, 301, 307
epilepsy, 236n189
épiphénoménisme (epiphenomenalism), 74
episteme, ix, 167, 179
epistemology, 162, 200, 254n156, 259n13, 266n88, 274n198, 275n233, 278, 279, 280, 281; historical, 164; naturalist, 84, 101
Eribon, Didier, 215n23, 222n25–27, 223n36, 224n46, 248n51, 270n75, 271n76, 273n193, 302
Erklären versus *Verstehen* (explaining versus understanding), 186
Erlebnistypen, types of lived experience, 55
Eros, 84
essence, 26, 28, 30, 40, 45, 76, 83, 100, 101, 112, 116, 118–119, 128–130, 132, 134, 145–146, 180, 249n63, 255n167
ethics, 81, 228n109, 254n158, 258n3, 281
event, 33, 63, 177, 179, 249n75

evidence, 101, 145, 154, 163, 249n75; self-evidence, 166, 170
evolution, 84, 85, 88, 99, 100, 109, 179, 248, 301
evolutionism, 99, 248, 301
Ewald, François, 208, 212n5, 213n9, 213n13, 217nn34–37, 220n13, 224n45, 231n144, 235n181, 244n10, 246n25, 248n50, 258n8, 265n75, 267n92, 270n164, 277–281, 283
existence, *existence, Existenz*, xi, xiv, xv, 3, 5, 6, 7, 32, 34, 38, 39–40, 41, 43, 44, 47, 63, 64, 66, 71, 72, 81, 82, 85–86, 89–91, 93, 94, 96–98, 100, 103, 105–109, 111–112, 114–116, 117, 122, 123, 130, 131–132, 135, 146, 150–152, 154–155, 157, 159, 168, 171, 176, 178, 183, 184, 185; *a priori* of, xii, 130, 148, 150–152, 158, 161, 193, 197, 198, 199, 204, 205, 212nn5–6, 214n16, 228n106, 231n142, 232n154, 233nn155–156, 234n164, 234n166, 244n11, 246n27, 246n30, 247nn33–34, 247nn38–44, 247n48, 248n52, 248n55, 249n62, 250n86, 251n87, 251nn99–101, 252n108, 252nn111–112, 253nn138–139, 254n160, 257nn196–198, 257nn200–201, 257–258n116, 260n18, 262n34, 262nn45–46, 263nn50–51, 264n62, 265n74, 265nn76–77, 265nn79–80, 271n179, 274nn219–220, 275n3, 276n10, 277, 285, 287, 292, 303, 304; form,
mode of, 58, 109, 130, 133, 142, 148, 158, 173, 192
existential analysis, *analyse existentielle*, xi–xiv, 5, 7, 9, 11, 24, 33–40, 43–44, 47–50, 53, 56, 58, 68, 70, 81, 82, 85, 91, 93–94, 96–97, 99–100, 104–115, 120, 122, 125, 129–132, 137, 141–142, 147–149, 152, 156, 159–160, 164, 171, 173, 175, 177–178, 180–181, 191, 196–198, 202–205, 211n5, 217n35, 229n120, 230n134, 232n155, 233n155, 233n157, 234n162, 234n168, 235n174, 235nn176–179, 235n181, 239n207, 241n240, 248n54, 248n56, 249n60, 249n63, 250nn76–77, 250n83, 251nn90–94, 251nn102–105, 252nn109–110, 252nn113–114, 252nn119–124, 253nn130–134, 256n172, 256n186, 257nn193–194, 257n199, 257n203, 260nn16–17, 262n34, 262n36, 262n40, 265n75, 266n85, 270n171, 283, 286, 287, 289, 292, 294, 302. See also Daseinsanalyse, Daseinsanalysis
Existentialism, 40–42, 107
Existenzerhellung (existential illumination), 71, 123
experience, *expérience*, ix, xi–xiii, 3, 9, 21, 31, 34, 46, 55, 56, 87, 93, 97, 100, 103, 104, 106, 118, 127, 129, 132, 137, 138, 140, 145–146, 151, 154–155, 158, 159–160, 163, 171, 174, 189, 191, 194, 199, 202, 213n16, 227n103, 236n187,

experience (*continued*)
237n189, 246n20, 263n59, 266n85, 271n178, 281, 293, 294, 297, 306; of dreaming, 89, 97, 114; form, style of, xiv, 21, 24, 54, 114, 121, 142, 143, 149–150, 152, 169, 170–172, 193, 204, 205; clinical, 157; life, 54, 100; limit, 202; lived, xii, 33, 53, 55, 57, 63, 90, 98–101, 125, 130, 143, 144, 177, 227n103, 249n65; natural, 146; pathological, 81, 101–103, 106, 111, 116, 129, 130–31, 147, 151, 172, 204; principle of in Salanskis, 180; sense-experience, 127; of time, 31, 33; transcendental constitution of, 68; of the world, x, 156

expression, *expression*, 21, 30, 45, 47, 53, 57, 72, 89–92, 94, 97, 105, 114–115, 120, 184

Ey, Henri, 1, 25, 36, 98, 152, 212n3, 212nn6–7, 229n120, 231n138, 232n246, 237n190, 248n56, 263n53, 264n71, 289, 303

facticity, 40–41, 67–68, 146, 148
Faktische (factual), 74
fantasy, *Phantasie*, 30
Farrell, C. Frederick, 232n153, 283
Farrell, Edith R., 232n153, 283
Fassin, Didier, 218n41, 281
Faubion, James D., 254n156, 259n13, 274n198, 275n233, 278, 279, 280, 281
Faverge, Jean-Marie, 17
Fawcett, Carolyn R., 263n58, 276n8, 288

Fédida, Pierre, 248n56, 301
fétichiste, 79
Feuchtwanger, Erich, 149
Feuerbach, Ludwig, 128, 133
FFL-Eman, 13, 217n39, 243n263
Fichtner, Gerhard, 243n260, 289
finitude, 126–128, 140, 199, 265n82
Fink, Bruce, 225n62, 244n6, 272n189, 293, 294
Fink, Eugen, 72
Fink, Heloïse, 225n62, 244n6, 272n189, 293, 294
Fischer, Franz, 77, 255n167, 289
Fisher, Alden L., 264n64, 295
Fishgold, Herman, 52
Flajoliet, Alain, 230n134, 303
Fleck, Ludwik, 215n28
flight of ideas, *Ideenflucht*, 36, 74–75, 147, 149, 177, 178, 227n103, 228n113, 230n135, 247n47, 261n32, 262n35, 262n39, 262n41, 270n170, 287
Fonfara, Dirk, 260n22, 291
Fontana, Alessandro, 199, 207, 275n5, 303
foreclosure in Lacan, 190
for-itself (Sartre), 253n145
Fournel, Jean-Louis, 217n32, 302
Fraisse, Paul, 57
Frank, Simon, 39
Frechtman, Bernard, 251n95, 297
freedom, 107–8, 148, 151, 177, 253n145
Freud, Sigmund, xi, 16, 20, 35, 37, 67, 70, 82, 83–89, 92, 98, 99–101, 143–144, 151, 184–188, 191, 193–194, 222n30, 229n124, 232n155, 243n260, 245n15, 245n17,

246n25, 272n184, 272n288, 272n193, 274n201, 275n233, 279, 285, 289, 293, 302
Fruchaud, Paul-Henri, 208, 216n31, 282, 283
future, 107, 112, 148, 150–151, 158–159

Gadamer, Hans-Georg, 30
Galilei, Galileo, 126
Galison, Peter, 55, 237n191, 239n213, 303
Gastaut, Henri, 52
Gebsattel, Viktor Emil von, 29, 30–31, 32, 48, 57, 62, 73, 289
Geist (spirit), 74, 255n167; in Dilthey, 128
Gelb, Adhémar, 149, 268n131, 290
genealogy, ix; of logic in Husserl, 116; in Foucault, 121
genesis, 88, 99–101, 103, 109, 129, 174; psychology of, 20, 85; of significations, 20, 99–100
Genet, Jean, 107, 251n95, 297
Gens, Jean-Claude, 271n178, 303
Germain, Marie-Odile, 214n19, 303
Geroulanos, Stefanos, 263n54, 288
Gestalt theory, 16, 74, 154
Gestaltauffassung (conceiving of the form), 149
Gestimmtheit (disposition, mood), 44
Giard, Luce, 276n9, 306
Gijswijt-Hofstra, Marijke, 225n56, 301
Gillot, Pascale, 270n174, 307
Ginsburg, Daniela, 263n54, 288
God, 126, 133, 270n162
Goldstein, James, 260n19, 280

Goldstein, Kurt, 28, 62, 99, 111–12, 147, 149, 151, 153, 155–56, 168, 262n39, 264n67, 268n131, 290
Gordon, Colin, 218n41, 222n33, 281
Goris, Wouter, 265n81, 303
Gouhier, Henri, 20
Gourevitch, Michel, 231n139, 285
Green, Peter, 233n157, 284
Grigg, Russel, 225n62, 244n6, 272nn189–190, 293, 294
Gros, Frédéric, 214n18, 216n31, 217n33, 218n41, 219n3, 282, 283, 299, 301
Gruevska, Julia, 264n69, 303
Grünbaum, Abraham A., 149
Gueguen, Bernard, 220n5, 238n196, 303
Guillaume, Paul, 17
Guiraud, Paul, 36, 42, 229n119, 290
Gusdorf, Georges, 42, 48, 182, 231n145, 232n147, 246n21, 290
Gutting, Gary, 259n15, 266n85, 269n156, 288, 304, 305

Häberlin, Paul, 29, 30, 69, 79, 124, 226n73, 290
Haecht, Louis van, 264n68, 301
hallucination, 22, 74, 79, 223n38
Halpern, Florence, 56, 239n215, 288
Han-Pile, Béatrice, 159, 198–200, 214, 216n29, 256n185, 265–266n82, 266n83, 275nn3–4, 276n7, 304
Harding, Jeremy, 266n88, 280
Harrington, Anne, 262n39, 304
Head, Henry, 147
health, 38, 58, 147, 225n56, 234n172, 299, 301

Hegel, Georg Wilhelm Friedrich, 11, 22, 128, 198
Heidegger, Martin, x, xi, 22, 34, 40, 65, 68, 104, 109, 111, 116, 123, 131, 144–146, 148, 149, 152, 153, 157, 170, 197, 203, 204, 223nn42–44, 261–262n33, 263n52, 268n139, 276n6, 290, 307
Hentzi, Gary, 275n233, 279
heredity, 50, 236n189
hermeneutics, 216n29, 265n82, 302; Freud's, psychoanalytic, 91, 184, 188; psychiatric, 174; of the self in Foucault, 216n31, 282; of the subject in Foucault, 196
Herrmann, Friedrich-Wilhelm von, 268n139, 290
Herzog, Max, 228n113, 230n136, 232n155, 244n3, 247n47, 261n24, 261n32, 285, 286, 287, 291
Hesnard, Angelo, 35, 37, 228n107, 229nn121–122, 291
historicity, 24, 121, 160, 163, 169, 170, 176, 205
history, xiii–xiv, 2, 3, 5, 8, 15, 17, 18, 35, 37, 48, 51, 84, 88, 99, 107, 116, 131, 137, 138, 142, 144, 150–152, 159–162, 175, 200–201, 205, 253n145; affective, 27; of ideas, 172; individual, 84, 137; life, 83, 137, 161, 177; literary, 144; natural, 179; patient's, 54, 81, 99; social, 35; versus eternity, 115
Hobart, Ann, 258n10, 289
Hoeller, Keith, 212n5, 228n106, 234n164, 244n11, 260n18, 276n10, 277, 287

Hölderlin, Friedrich, 224n49, 291–292
homo natura, 70
homosexuel (homosexual), 79
Horkheimer, Max, 124
Horst, Lammert van der, 37
Hunt, Philippe, 213n15, 305
Hurley, Robert, 217n33, 254n156, 259n13, 263n59, 278, 281, 283
Husserl, Edmund, x, xi, 8, 16, 19, 21, 34, 37, 85, 92, 99, 100, 101, 104, 107–108, 116, 121, 129, 144, 145, 146, 149, 159, 197, 203, 215n29, 221n18, 221n21, 222n30, 222n33, 259n15, 265n81, 301, 303, 305, 306
Hyppolite, Jean, 182, 220n11, 246n21, 271n177, 291

idealism, *Idealismus*, 255n165, 297; genetic, 116; neo-Kantian, 99
illness, *maladie*, 20, 24, 28, 58, 81, 85, 90, 98–99, 102, 104, 106–108, 111–112, 116, 143, 174, 178, 188, 190, 193, 251n96; mental, psychiatric, xii, xiii, xiv, 1, 2, 3, 23, 24, 25–26, 28, 31, 49, 94, 102, 104, 108–109, 113, 137–139, 142, 156, 173, 201, 213nn10–12, 214n16, 252n107, 258nn4–6, 258n9, 278, 304
image, 46, 67, 88–92, 133, 150, 183, 185, 189, 191, 192, 214n16, 234n167, 237n191, 239n213, 258n216, 275n3, 303, 304; of the world, 58
imagination, *imagination*, ix, 43–44, 46–47, 59, 67, 72, 90, 93,

127, 199, 212n5, 228n106,
232nn152–153, 233nn156–157,
234n167, 244n11, 246n27, 246n30,
247n33, 247n38, 247n48, 248n52,
248n55, 249n62, 251n99, 252n108,
252n111, 253n138, 254n160,
257nn196–198, 257nn200–201,
257n216, 260n18, 262nn45–46,
263nn50–51, 264n62, 265n74,
265nn76–77, 265n79, 271n179,
276n10, 277, 283, 284, 304, 306;
anthropology of, 47, 93; creative,
46; imaginative process, poetic,
42, 90; psychology of, 49
Imipramine, 62
immanence, *immanence*, 73, 115, 153,
162, 205; principle of in Benoist,
162, 180, 204
individuality, 86
information theory, 16–17
instant, 70
instinct, 40, 109, 144
intelligence, 66, 220
interpretation, *interprétation*,
Interpretation, 7, 21, 22, 33, 54,
57–58, 72, 73, 76, 77, 86–88, 97,
120, 194, 199; of dreams, 57–58,
85–86, 89, 150, 191
intersubjectivity, 91, 97, 106, 110
Irrera, Orazio, 216n31, 217n38, 282,
302
Iwer, Lukas, 214n16, 300

Jackson, John Hughlings, 99, 147,
248n56, 301
Jagfeld, Monika, 238n202, 301
Janet, Pierre, 17, 97

Jaspers, Karl, 23, 29, 30, 33, 70,
71–72, 99, 102, 107, 123, 141, 143,
186, 224, 227n101, 229n125,
236n189, 249n75, 251n96,
260nn22–23, 271n178, 272n187,
285, 291, 303, 305
Johnston, John, 224n45, 281
Jolas, Maria, 232n151, 284
Joranger, Line, 214n16, 304
Jung, Carl Gustav, xi, 29, 83

Kant, Immanuel, 5, 23, 121–23, 125,
126, 128, 133, 140, 197, 198,
223n44, 257n209, 257n215,
259n12, 265n81, 281, 290, 305
Kastler, Alfred, 227n101, 291
Keller, Wilhelm, 124, 254n164, 292
Khalfa, Jean, 213n9, 258n8, 278
Kisker, Karl Peter, 1, 2, 212nn1–2,
213n8, 304
Klossowski, Pierre, 256n168, 298
Koffka, Kurt, 149
Köhler, Wolfgang, 149
Kojève, Alexandre, 38
Koyré, Alexandre, 246n21
knowledge, 9, 12, 13, 26, 36, 52,
55–56, 87, 91, 101, 104, 119, 129,
132, 135, 140, 141, 142, 144–145,
154, 156, 157, 159, 160–162, 164,
166, 170–175, 179–180, 181, 190,
198, 201, 202, 203, 205, 208,
237n193, 259n15, 263n54, 263n58,
266n84; anthropological, 67;
archaeology of, xi, xiii, 8, 9, 160,
161, 174, 266n86, 266n89,
267n103–105, 269nn141–143,
269n155, 269nn157–161,

knowledge (*continued*)
270nn166–168, 276n12, 279, 288; as *connaissance*, *Erkennen*, 163, 200; mode of knowledge versus world of objects to be known, scientific, 162; psychoanalysis of, 163, 172, 267n97, 284; as *savoir*, 163, 171, 175–176, 179, 200–201, 204

Kraepelin, Emil, 30, 34, 35

Kuhn, Regule, 208

Kuhn, Roland, 2, 6, 7, 29, 38, 41, 43–44, 46, 47, 49, 51, 53–54, 56–59, 62–66, 69, 76, 104, 105, 110, 120, 156, 208, 215n26, 220n6, 230n132, 233nn158–159, 234n169, 234n171, 235n183, 237n195, 238nn202–203, 239nn205–208, 239n214, 240nn218–222, 240n231, 241n234, 241n240, 243n256, 250nn84–85, 250–251nn87, 252n117, 284, 286, 292, 294, 305

Kulenkampff, Caspar, 32, 77, 298

Kuntz, Jean, 264n67, 290

Kunz, Hans, 29, 30, 48, 72, 77, 123, 131, 255n167, 257n202, 293

Küppers, Egon, 70

Lacan, Jacques, 27–28, 34, 38, 56, 84, 86, 87, 89, 90, 181–183, 185–187, 189–194, 196, 225nn61–63, 226nn65–66, 227n103, 230n131, 244n6, 245nn16–19, 246n20, 247n32, 271n78, 272nn185–192, 273nn193–194, 274nn205–207, 274nn214–217, 275n231, 275n236, 275n242, 280, 284, 293–294, 305, 307

Lacroix, Jean, 23–24, 224n51

Laforgue, René, 37, 229nn121–122, 291

Lagache, Daniel, 17, 18, 27, 35, 51, 52, 56, 153, 225n64, 236n188, 263n55, 264n71, 294

Lagrange, Jacques, 212n5, 213n9, 213n13, 220n13, 224n45, 244n10, 246n25, 255n166, 258n8, 267n92, 270n164, 277–281

Laing, Ronald D., 141, 260n17, 294

La Mettrie, Julien Offray de, 15

Lamy, Jérôme, 216, 234n167, 300, 304

Landau, Augustine, 236n187, 297

Landsberg, Paul Ludwig, 123

language, 21, 22, 46, 55, 61, 92, 114, 115, 163, 168–169, 179, 180, 183–85, 187–195

Lantéri-Laura, Georges, 141, 206, 259n15, 276n13, 304

Lauzier, Jean, 25, 231n146

Lavelle, Louis, 256n168

law (in biology, philosophy, psychology), 9, 92, 143, 156, 159, 166, 173–174, 176, 183, 186–188, 192–193, 204–205, 265n82, 272n187

Leben (life) in Dilthey, 128

Le Blanc, Guillaume, 214n16, 304

Le Bras, Laurence, 219n45, 304

Lebrun, Gérard, 216n29, 259n15, 305

Lefebvre, Marcel, 255n168, 297

Leguil, François, 271n178, 305

Le Guillant, Louis, 25, 232n146

Leibniz, Gottfried Wilhelm, 15
Le Senne, René, 256n168
Lézé, Samuel, 218n41, 281
liberation, 45, 150
liberty, *liberté*, 73, 119
libido, 87, 88
lifeworld, *Lebenswelt*, 101–102, 129, 165
linguistics, 186, 193, 273n194
Litt, Theodor, 124
lived body, 39
logic, 45, 116, 222n33, 253n145
Lorenzini, Daniele, 10, 216n31, 217n38, 282–283, 302
Lotringer, Sylvère, 270n164, 280
love, *amour*, 68, 110–111, 115, 132
Löwith, Karl, 30, 48
Luchsinger, Katrin, 238n202, 239n204, 241n232, 301
Luczak, Jeannine, 226n73, 290
Lyons, Joseph, 232n154, 250n86, 285

Macey, David, 216n31, 220n7, 273n193, 302, 305
Macherey, Pierre, 139, 259n11, 305
Macquarrie, John, 263n52, 291
madness, xii, xiii, 1–5, 15, 25, 42, 59, 61, 64, 94, 125, 137–139, 141, 180, 182–185, 187–190, 194, 196, 202, 213n9, 258n8, 260n17, 266n85, 271n180, 272n184, 273n195, 278, 294, 302
Maine de Biran, François-Pierre, 19, 237n193
Maldiney, Henri, 38, 48, 53, 62, 141, 230n132, 239n205, 241n240, 260n16, 286, 294

Malebranche, Nicolas, 19, 20
Marazia, Chantal, 260n22, 291
Marceau, Jean-Claude, 238n195, 239n207, 292
Marmy, Émile, 256n168, 298
Marty, P., 231n138, 289
Marx, Karl, 128, 175, 194, 260n19, 275n233, 279, 280
Marxism, 35, 160, 218n41, 222–223n33, 281
mask, *masque*, *Mask*, 7, 57–59, 61, 64, 99, 120, 215n26, 238n203, 292
Massot, Marie-Laure, 207, 219n46, 305
Massumi, Brian, 273n198, 279
materialism, x, xiv, 34, 35, 120, 169
May, Rollo, 232n254, 250n86, 251n87, 262n34, 285, 287, 292
May, Todd, 259n15, 305
Mayr, Franz, 262n33, 291
Mays, Wolfe, 221n14, 306
McAllester Jones, Mary, 267n97, 284
McCulloch, Warren S., 220n10, 306
McLeod, Ian, 280
medicine, 27–28, 30, 51, 54, 62, 104, 163, 168, 201–202, 229n125, 231n146, 236n189; global (*Ganzheitsmedizin*), 105; mental, psychiatric, 61; organic, 28
Melandri, Enzo, 258n7, 305
Mendel, Werner M., 232n154, 250n86, 285
Mendousse, Jean, 227n101, 291
Menschsein, being-human, 50, 111, 113, 198

Merleau-Ponty, Maurice, 7, 16, 18, 19, 21, 26, 28, 38–42, 47, 48, 57, 85–86, 89–91, 104, 117, 154–158, 204, 221n17–21, 230n135, 231n141, 233n157, 245nn13–14, 246n21, 246nn28–29, 247n35, 253n145, 263n60, 264nn61–65, 264n67, 265n78, 276n11, 295, 307
metaphor, 43, 45–46, 90–91, 163, 164, 165, 167, 171
metaphysics, 23, 89, 90, 114, 126
method, methodology, *méthode*, *Methode*, *Methodik*, ix–xiv, 4, 5, 8, 12, 26, 27, 36, 37, 49, 50, 55, 58, 72, 74, 83, 84, 87, 88, 93, 97, 100, 114, 135, 140–142, 144, 149, 157, 160, 164, 179, 180, 183, 186, 196, 199, 200–206, 212n2, 235n182, 236n187, 240n216, 254n156, 259n13, 266n85, 266n88, 271n178, 274n198, 275n233, 278, 279, 280, 281, 297, 304, 306
Meyer, Joachim-Ernst, 212n2, 304
Michon, Pascal, 218n42, 299
Michotte, Albert, 149
Miller, Jacques-Alain, 272n190, 294
Minkowska, Françoise, 51, 236n189, 237n190, 295
Minkowski, Eugène, 2, 21, 29, 32, 34, 37–39, 48, 51, 56, 57, 79, 88–91, 141, 149, 155–156, 173, 176, 186, 192, 212n6, 228nn103–104, 229n123, 229n126, 229n128, 230nn129–130, 236–237n189, 237n190, 246nn21–22, 247n31, 247n37, 262n42, 263n56, 264nn70–71, 269nn153–154, 270n169, 272nn186–187, 274n221, 286, 294, 295, 303
Monakow, Constantin von, 147
Monnier, Marcel, 50, 52, 235n183, 236n184, 236n186, 238n198, 296
Monod, Jean-Claude, 213n16, 215n29, 305
Moreno Pestaña, José Luis, 3, 213n15, 305
Morfaux, Louis-Marie, 222n32
Mounier, Emmanuel, 26, 225n60, 296
Müldner, Heinrich G., 241n234, 305
Müller, Christian, 212n2, 239n209, 297, 304
Munier, Roger, 23, 223n43, 290
Murphy, Jonathan, 213n9, 258n8, 278
myth, mythology, 26, 61, 85, 86, 88, 89, 127, 189, 191

Naas, Michael, 272n184, 302
Naef, Hélène, 224n49, 292
Narrenschiff (ship of fools), 61
naturalism, 100, 104
Needleman, Jacob, 212n5, 287
neo-Jacksonism, 98
neurology, *Neurologie*, 31, 38, 70, 72, 73, 76, 77, 148, 205, 215n25, 220n4, 226n76, 226n80, 226n85, 226n89, 227nn90–92, 227n96, 227nn99–100, 228n113, 229n127, 230n129, 232n154, 232n155, 234n165, 235n180, 236n183, 236n185, 239n203, 239n206, 241n238, 241n239, 247n36, 247n47, 250n86, 250–251n87, 252n117, 255n167, 260n22, 261n26,

261n28, 261n29, 261n32, 262n34, 262n42, 285, 286, 287, 289, 290, 291, 292, 293, 298, 299, 306
neurosis, 33, 85
Niel, Henri, 224n48, 291
Nietzsche, Friedrich W., 11, 22, 23, 107, 134, 164, 194, 224nn47–49, 251n96, 275n233, 276n6, 279, 291, 299, 307
Nigro, Roberto, 257n209, 259n12, 281
nihilation (Sartre), 253n145
norm, *norme*, 108, 112, 145–148, 150, 154–55, 174–176, 178, 204, 228n104, 295
normal, *normal*, 16, 27, 29, 72, 76, 106, 112, 153, 173, 182, 201, 203, 225n64, 226n71, 229n126, 237n189, 263n55, 263n58, 263n59, 264n71, 276n8, 288, 294, 295
normativity, 112, 145–146; self-normativity, 145, 148, 153, 155–156, 171, 174–176, 192, 204
Nunberg, Herman, 83

objectivity, 40, 55, 118–119, 128, 153, 161–163
Ombredane, André, 16–17, 56, 168, 219n4, 220n4, 220n11, 233n159, 236n187, 239nn214–215, 288, 296, 297
Ongaro Basaglia, Franca, 260n17, 284
ontology, 39, 67, 93, 96, 111, 113, 122, 148, 156, 231n144, 254n155, 270n163, 280, 306
order, xi, xiii, 11, 91, 122, 125, 128, 139, 140, 142, 161, 162, 164–170, 172, 174, 175–176, 178–179, 183, 190, 195, 198, 211n1, 214n16, 258n216, 259n14, 266n84, 266n90, 267n94, 267–68nn108–126, 268nn128–130, 268nn133–134, 268nn137–138, 268n140, 269nn144–145, 269nn147–152, 270n165, 270nn172–173, 275nn237–241, 275nn2–3, 279, 280, 304; *mise en ordre* (putting into order), 170; symbolic (Lacan), 186–187
organism, *organisme*, *Organismus*, 112, 153, 155, 175, 264n67, 290
organo-dynamism, 36, 248n56, 302
origin, 25, 102, 108, 110, 128, 134, 135, 139, 174, 253n145; truth-origin, 163; *Ursprung*, 113
Other, versus Same in Foucault's *The Order of Things*, 165–166

Paltrinieri, Luca, 224n52, 256n185, 265n81, 305
paranoia, 90, 293
past, 84, 107, 112, 150–51
pathology, 28, 33, 52, 85, 105, 182, 220
Patton, Paul, 218n41, 222n33, 281
Pavlov, Ivan Petrovič, 25, 35
pedagogy, 29, 50
Peña-Guzmán, David M., 221n15, 289
perception, 16, 17, 19, 22, 33, 40, 49, 58, 74, 76, 85, 92, 117, 154, 156, 161, 163, 166, 214n16, 220n4, 220n10, 221n19, 230n135, 231n141, 236n187, 245n13, 246n28, 247n35, 260n21, 264n65, 265n78, 276n11, 278, 295, 296, 297, 304, 306

person, science of, 226n66
personalism, *Personalismus*, 192, 254n165, 297
personality, *personnalité*, xii, 3, 4, 5, 17, 20, 23, 24, 25, 27, 28, 34, 35, 52, 53, 83, 84, 98, 99, 120, 125, 131, 138, 149, 182, 186, 211n4, 213n11, 224n52, 225n53, 225n55, 225nn61–62, 226nn67–70, 227n103, 228n112, 244n7, 244n9, 245n18, 246n20, 248n57, 248n59, 257n195, 262n43, 271n178, 272n185, 274nn224–226, 275nn227–228, 277, 293, 305
personology, 17
Philosophieren (philosophizing), 71, 224n48, 291
phobie (phobia), 31, 73, 290
physiology, *physiologie*, 26, 148, 235n183, 236n183, 306
Piaget, Jean, 18, 221n14, 306
Pidoux, Vincent, 236n183, 306
Piéron, Henri, 17, 57
Pinel, Philippe, 35, 196
Pinguet, Maurice, 224n45, 272–273n193, 306
Pinto, Louis, 214n20, 306
Pitts, Walter, 220n10, 306
Plessner, Helmuth, 48, 124, 149
Polin, Raymond, 20
Politzer, Georges, 26, 34–35, 39, 47, 56, 86–89, 225nn59–60, 228n105, 245nn15–16, 246nn25–26, 296, 300
Pollnow, Hans, 37, 70, 229nn124–125, 285, 291

Pongratz, Ludwig J., 237n195, 292
Porter, Catherine, 269n156, 288
positivism, 117
positivity, 103, 119, 140, 164, 172
Potte-Bonneville, Mathieu, 218n42, 299
Prasse, Jutta, 230n131, 307
presence, *présence*, 40, 59, 90, 101, 105, 169, 192, 231n145, 260n16, 290, 294; presence-in-the-world, 130–131
Preti, Giulio, 170n164, 280
Preziosi, Donald, 270n163, 280
projective technique, 17
psyche, 43, 83, 84, 86, 144, 145
psychiatry, *psychiatrie*, *Psychiatrie*, xii, xiv, 1, 3, 4, 7, 8, 17, 25, 27, 29, 31–32, 34, 35–41, 48, 49, 50, 52, 62, 70–73, 76–77, 82–84, 96, 98, 104, 108, 110, 113–114, 138, 141–143, 145, 147, 153, 156, 173, 181–183, 185, 192, 202, 211n1, 212nn1–2, 214n16, 215n24, 215n25, 215n27, 222n29, 225nn55–56, 226n76, 226n80, 226n85, 226n89, 227nn90–92, 227n96, 227nn99–100, 228n113, 229n114, 229nn118–120, 229n123, 229n127, 230n129, 230n136, 231nn138–139, 231n145, 232nn154–155, 234n165, 235n180, 236n183, 236n185, 237nn194–195, 238–239nn202–203, 239n206, 241nn238–239, 244n2, 246n21, 247n36, 247n47, 250–251nn86–87, 252nn116–117, 252n129, 255n167,

260n22, 261n26, 261n28, 261n32, 262nn33–34, 262n42, 263n53, 263n56, 264n71, 271n178, 273n194, 276n13, 283–287, 289–293, 295–304, 306–308; anthropological, 183; clinical, 53, 83, 177, 244n2; existential, x, xiv, 28, 34, 61, 137, 138, 141, 156, 167–168, 171–172, 183, 192–193, 197, 201, 212n5, 228n106, 234n164, 244n11, 260nn17–18, 274n224, 276n10, 277, 287; medical, 31; phenomenological, 48, 142, 172, 183, 197, 201, 271n178; positivist, 84; social, *Sozialpsychiatrie*, 1, 212n1
psychoanalysis, *psychanalyse*, *Psychoanalyse*, xi, 1, 20–21, 24, 30, 31, 32, 36, 50, 72, 73, 75, 81–83, 85–89, 91–92, 97–98, 105, 122, 143, 163, 181–189, 191–193, 195, 203n131, 218n41, 222n29, 225n59, 226n66, 228n107, 232n155, 234n168, 238n195, 239n209, 241n233, 244n2, 245n12, 245n15, 246nn25–26, 260nn23–24, 261n27, 271n178, 272n184, 272nn187–189, 275n242, 280, 282, 284–286, 291–294, 296, 298, 300, 302–303, 307; of elements (Bachelard), 42; existential (Sartre), 39, 43, 230nn133–134, 233n157; Lacanian, 185, 189, 293–294; of objective knowledge (Bachelard), 172, 200, 267n97, 284

psychogenesis, 98, 192–193
psychologism, 104
psychology, *psychologie*, *Psychologie*, x, xi, xii, 3, 5, 8, 11, 15–20, 22, 24, 26–29, 30, 32–35, 41, 46, 48–50, 52–53, 55, 58, 68, 72, 74, 76, 79, 81–89, 96, 98, 100–101, 103–104, 109, 116–120, 125, 129, 131, 133–134, 137–139, 143, 149, 152–153, 156, 161–163, 182–183, 200–202, 204, 213n10, 213nn12–13, 214n16, 214n20, 215n24, 215n27, 217n36, 218n39, 219–220n4, 220n13, 221nn15–17, 221n21, 225nn59–60, 226n66, 227n95, 229n126, 230n136, 231n144, 232n154, 235n173, 236n187, 237n189, 240n223, 244n10, 245n15, 245n17, 246nn23–26, 248nn50–51, 250nn78–81, 250n86, 252n107, 254–255nn155–156, 256n171, 256n180, 258n2, 258n4, 258n9, 259n13, 261n26, 262nn33–34, 264n69, 265n72, 267nn92–93, 270n169, 273n194, 275nn229–230, 275n232, 277, 278, 283, 285, 287–290, 292, 295–297, 299–304, 306–308; animal, 22; ascensional (Bachelard), 48; child, 18, 37, 219n4; clinical, 35, 228n107, 240n216, 291, 306; concrete (Politzer), 26, 228n105, 245nn15–16, 296; ego, 186; eidetic, 101; empirical, 38;

psychology (*continued*)
evolutionary, 24, 84, 99;
existential, 4, 212n5, 228n106, 234n164, 244n11, 260n18, 276n10, 287; experimental, 15, 18, 49–51, 219n4, 237n193, 238n200; of expression, 57; Freudian, 87; of genesis, 20, 85, 246n25; of the image/imagination, 49, 92, 183, 185, 234n167, 304; of language, 92, 185; medical, 30, 31, 70; pathological, 53; phenomenological, 7, 48, 99–100, 118, 230n136, 291; physiological (*Leistungspsychologie*), 249n75; scientific, 18; social, 22; structural, 152; subjective (Jaspers), 249n75; *understanding* (*verstehende Psychologie*) (Jaspers), 143; work, 51
psychometrics, 50
psychophysics, 22
psychosis, 27, 34, 87–88, 90, 149, 178, 181, 185–187, 190, 192–196, 227n103, 272nn190–192, 274nn205–207, 274nn214–217, 275n231, 275n236, 294
psychosurgery, 53
psychotechnics, *psychotechnique*, 51, 219n4, 237n193
psychotherapy, *Psychoterapie*, 30, 31, 63, 70, 76, 226n82, 230n135, 241n237, 287, 293
Püschel, Jörg, 237n194, 302

Rabinow, Paul, 211n10, 216n29, 254n158, 258n3, 265n82, 266n88, 281, 302
Rapaport, David, 235n173, 296
Rath, Claus-Dieter, 230n131, 307
reaction, 28, 53, 98, 227n103
reason, *raison*, 3, 24, 59, 88, 108, 127, 145, 155, 180, 181, 188, 202, 204, 260n17, 266n85, 294, 304
reduction, 119, 121; phenomenological, 117
reflexology, 22, 34, 148, 173
regime (Nazi), 30
regularity, 55, 135, 176
Remond, Antoine, 52
Revel, Judith, 216n31, 218nn41–42, 276n9, 283, 299, 306
revery, *rêverie*, 42, 44–45, 49, 232n148, 233n159, 234n163, 235n175, 236n188, 284, 294
Ribot, Théodule-Armand, 17
Ricardo, David, 198
Ricoeur, Paul, 22, 23
Riklin, Franz, 82
Ritter, Joachim, 124
Robinson, Edward, 263n52, 291
Rodrigo, Pierre, 233n157, 306
Roggenbau, Christel Heinrich, 226n87, 289
Rogove, John, 215n29, 306
Rorschach, Hermann, 7, 16, 47–51, 53–59, 61, 120, 156, 215n26, 233n159, 234nn172–173, 235n173, 235n179, 235n182, 236nn184–189, 237nn189–190, 238n201, 238n203, 239n209, 239n215, 240n216,

INDEX 327

240n218, 284, 285, 287, 288, 289, 292–297, 299, 300, 306, 307
Rouart, Julien, 98, 248n56
Roudinesco, Élisabeth, 272n184, 302
Rousseau, Jean-Jacques, 22, 223n38
Roussel, Raymond, 190–193, 228n110, 273n194, 274n199, 278, 280
Ruas, Charles, 228n110, 274n199, 278, 280
Rueff, Martin, 218n41, 282
rule, 92, 147, 155, 160, 175–176, 265n82
Rutishauser, Liselotte, 208, 230n132, 234n171, 239n214, 242n249, 295
Rümke, Henricus Cornelius, 36, 39, 113, 229n118, 252n128, 297

Sabot, Philippe, 213n16, 217n36, 222n28, 231n144, 248nn50–51, 254n155, 283, 306
Saint Aubert, Emmanuel de, 233n157, 307
Salanskis, Michel, 270n174, 307
Salathé, André, 238n202, 301
Sartre, Jean-Paul, 7, 26, 38–41, 47, 68, 107, 116, 230nn133–134, 233n157, 251n95, 251n97, 253n145, 264n67, 294, 297, 301, 303, 306
Schamphänomen (phenomenon of shame), 76
Scheid, Karl Friedrich, 113, 252n126, 297
Scheler, Max, 22, 28, 107, 116, 124, 254–255n165, 255–256nn167–68, 297, 299

Schilder, Paul Ferdinand, 149
schizophrenia, *schizophrénie*, *Schizophrenie*, 31–32, 36–38, 76, 77, 106, 149, 156, 173, 192, 215n25, 229n123, 230nn129–130, 232n154, 234n165, 235n173, 235n180, 236n189, 243n257, 247n36, 250nn86–87, 255n167, 260nn22–23, 262n42, 264n70, 269nn153–154, 274n221, 285, 286, 289, 291, 292, 295, 296, 298
Schmidgen, Henning, 28, 226n66, 271n178, 307
Schmitz, Frederick J., 251n96, 291
Schotte, Jacques, 62, 241n233, 298
science, *science*, *Wissenschaft*, 2, 13, 15, 19, 21, 27, 29, 37, 52, 56, 59–60, 74, 79, 84, 88, 91, 98, 100, 103, 104, 113, 119, 128, 131, 140, 142, 144, 145, 149, 153, 156, 157, 161–162, 170, 175, 179, 186, 195, 201, 204, 208, 213n7, 214n16, 237n193, 214n20, 215n28, 219n2, 221n15, 221n16, 226n66, 236n183, 237n191, 245n16, 258n10, 262n39, 263n59, 267n91, 270n174, 281, 284, 288, 289, 290, 301, 302, 303, 304, 306, 307; human, xi, 19, 20, 22, 84, 89, 99, 115, 118–121, 125, 132–134, 139, 149, 157, 178, 195–196, 212n5, 214n20, 221n13, 221n18–19, 224n45, 244n10, 246n25, 246n29, 259n14, 270n164, 275n2, 277, 278, 279, 280, 281, 295, 300, 306
Searls, Damion, 238n201, 307

Seinslehre (doctrine of Being), 113
Selbstwerden (self-becoming), 71
semiology, 273n194
Sengel, Deniz, 273n195, 278
sensation, *Empfinden*, 73–74, 249n63
sense, *Sinn*, 32–33, 45, 77, 91, 124, 126, 147, 149, 157, 191, 227n95, 251n88, 264n60, 265n72, 288, 295, 299; direction (*Bedeutungsrichtung*), 39, 45, 57, 93, 114, 150; embodied, 90; sense-connections (*Sinnzusammenhänge*), 143; sense-experience, 127
sexuality, ix, x, xiii–xiv, 9, 10, 11, 85–86, 121, 137, 142, 202, 211n10, 211n11, 217n37, 228n109, 254n158, 255n167, 258n3, 260n20, 281, 283
Sforzini, Arianna, 217n34, 218n44, 219n46, 247n50, 255n166, 300, 305, 307
Sheridan Smith, Alan M., 213n10, 213n14, 258n4, 266n86, 276n12, 278, 279, 307
sign, 89, 91, 167, 184, 193–194, 273n194
Signer, Rita, 239n209, 297
signification, genesis, theory of, 91, 183
signifier, 187, 189
Simon, Gérard, 15, 219n2, 224n50
singularity, 143, 146–147
Sini, Carlo, 199, 276n6, 307
Sivadon, Paul, 231n146

Smith, Colin, 221n19, 245n13, 246n28, 264n65, 276n11, 295
Smock, William, 228n109, 254n158, 258n3, 281
Smyth, Bryan, 213n16, 307
society, 24–25, 37, 52, 212n1, 217n38, 231n144, 254n155, 264n66, 302, 306
sociology, 22, 118
soul, 40, 134
space, *espace*, *Raum*, x, 33, 42, 59, 74, 76–77, 79, 92, 97, 104, 106–107, 128, 129, 160, 162, 167–170, 194, 199, 232n151, 284; *espace vécu* (lived space), 79; familiar (*vertrauter Raum*), 48; *gestimmter Raum* (tuned space), 255n167
spatiality, *spatialité*, *Räumlichen*, 33, 69, 77, 106, 299
species, 154, 175, 270n162
speculation, 26, 110, 114–115, 119, 130–132, 142, 144, 152, 203, 205
speech, 91, 183, 187–188, 190; disorders, 220
Spiegelberg, Herbert, 215n27, 230n136, 307
spirit, 11, 46, 55, 100, 128, 144, 242n248, 259n15
Starobinski, Jean, 59, 240n226, 298, 307
Stastny, Peter, 273n195, 278
statement, *énoncé*, 161, 170, 174, 176, 265n82
Sternberger, Dolf, 123
Storch, Alfred, 29, 31, 73, 298

Straus, Erwin, 29, 32–33, 48, 57, 73, 77, 157, 241n239, 265n72–73, 285, 298
Strindberg, Johan August, 224n49, 236n189, 291–292
Strömgren, Erik, 212n2, 304
structure, xi–xii, 2, 19, 29, 46, 53, 58, 74, 87, 92, 93, 97, 101, 105–106, 108–110, 114, 130, 132, 140–141, 143, 145–152, 154–156, 158, 160–164, 170–171, 172–175, 176, 178, 183, 184, 187, 193, 204, 227n103, 261n33, 264n64, 264n67, 273n194, 290, 295
Studer, Karl, 238n195, 240n231, 292
style, ix, 8, 97–98, 103, 106, 112, 130, 193, 200, 204, 215n28, 227n103, 246n20, 247n32, 271n178, 293, 294, 300
subject, 16, 27, 35, 59, 85, 89, 99, 150, 175, 189–190, 192, 195–196; transcendental, 175, 198, 245n19, 253n145
subjectivity, 138, 153, 192, 228n109, 234n172, 237n192, 239n210, 239n213, 254n158, 258n3, 281, 299; transcendental, 104
Swedenborg, Emanuel, 224n49, 291–292
symbol, 56, 87, 90–92, 105, 188, 239n215, 288
symbolism, 87, 89, 91, 97, 105, 245n19
symptom, *symptôme*, *Symptom*, 30, 91, 99, 273n194, 293, 302; hysterical, 194
synesthésie (synesthesia), 73

system, 49, 85, 141–142, 166, 170–172, 174–177, 179. *See also* knowledge
Szilasi, Wilhelm, 65, 74, 77

taxonomy, 165, 167, 169, 179
Tazzioli, Martina, 216n31, 282
temporality, *temporalité*, 70, 106, 151
test, 48–50, 55, 234n172, 235n173, 284, 296; painting, 53; projective, 234n173, 300; psychometric, 49; Rorschach (psychodiagnostic) inkblot, 7, 16, 48–51, 53–59, 120–121, 156, 215n26, 236n184, 236n186, 236n188, 237n189, 237n193, 238n201, 239n215, 240n218, 284, 288, 292, 294, 296, 307; tachiscopic, 16
Thanatos, 84
theology, 119, 133
Thiel, Matthias, 124
Thoma, Samuel, 214n16, 300
time, *temps*, *Zeit*, 23, 31, 33, 73–75, 77, 79, 92, 97, 106–107, 144, 151, 159, 166, 167, 217, 223, 228n103, 265n167, 263n52, 268n139, 272n186, 290, 291, 294, 299, 301
Tosquelles, François, 25
totality, 28, 104, 112–113, 119, 126, 170, 197, 227n103
Trân Duc Thao, 22
transcendence, 46, 68, 115, 170, 192
transcendental, 11, 128, 141, 175, 178, 198–199, 216n29, 256n185, 257n216, 266n82, 266n84, 304

Traubenberg, Nina Rausch de, 240n216, 306
trauma, 33, 151, 227n98, 299
Trombadori, Duccio, 260n19, 273n193, 280
Trucchio, Aldo, 240n226, 307
true saying (*dire vrai*) and being in the true (*dans le vrai*), in Canguilhem, 161
truth, x, 2–3, 88, 92, 104, 107–108, 126–128, 134, 138–139, 162–163, 178, 189, 196, 202, 213n14, 228n109, 254n158, 258n3, 281, 307
Turnell, Martin, 251n95, 297

Übermensch, 133
unconscious, *inconscient*, 20, 40, 89, 103, 105, 107, 187, 193, 195, 246n46
understanding, xii, xiv, 5, 7, 8, 12, 26, 28, 32, 34, 40, 46, 49, 54–56, 85, 87, 102–104, 108, 116, 127, 129, 147, 178, 182–183, 185–87, 190–191, 249n75, 251n96, 261n33, 291; self-understanding, 30; static (Jaspers), 249n75; genetic (Jaspers), 249n75. *See also* psychology
Unheimlich (uncanny), 55
Unheimlichkeit (uncanniness), 75
universality, 143, 154
unreason, 3, 61, 64, 184–185, 190, 192

Van Gogh, Vincent, 224n49, 236n189, 291–292, 295

Ventresque, Vincent, 207, 218n44, 219n46, 300, 305
Verdeaux, Bruno, 208, 220n5, 242n245, 307
Verdeaux, Georges, 6, 16, 36, 43, 49, 51–53, 56, 62, 66, 69, 220nn5–6, 238n196, 242n245, 243n256, 254n154, 303, 307
Verdeaux, Jacqueline, xv, 6, 16, 22, 34, 41, 43–44, 49, 51–53, 56–57, 62–66, 69, 120, 212n5, 215n21, 215nn24–26, 220n5, 223n37, 231n139, 233n159, 240n218, 241n235, 241n240, 241n243, 242nn245–246, 242n250, 243n251–252, 247n45, 253n151, 254n154, 273n193, 277, 282, 286–287, 292, 300, 306, 307, 308
Verdinglichung (reification), 73
Verlengia, Carolina, 218n44, 300
Verstehen (understanding), 186, 260n24, 261n27, 285. *See also Erklären*
Volland, Erich, 123
Vorhandensein (beings-at-hand), 261n33
Vuillemin, Jules, 20, 23, 224n49, 254n165, 299

Waelhens, Alphonse de, 23, 223n44, 290
Wagner, Pierre, 215n28, 300
Wahl, Jean, 39, 224n48, 246n21, 291
Waldenfels, Bernard, 230n136
Wallon, Henri, 24, 35, 57, 219n4
Wallraff, Charles F., 251n96, 291

INDEX ◎ 331

Walter, Grey, 52
Weber, Arnold, 51
Weisheit (wisdom), 41
Weizsäcker, Viktor von, 2, 48, 120, 147–148, 151–152, 155, 156–157, 173, 264n66, 302
Wertheimer, Max, 149
Wetzel, René, 214n21
Widlöcher, Daniel, 248n56, 301
Widmer, Peter, 230n131, 307
will, 134, 213n14, 307
Williams, Forrest, 212n5, 277
Wing, Betsy, 215n23, 222n25, 248n51, 270n175, 303
Witschi, Peter, 238n201, 300
Wolf-Fédida, Mareike, 238n195, 239n207, 292
world, *monde*, *Welt*, x, xii, 22, 28, 31, 32, 40, 42, 45–46, 49, 58, 62, 73, 79, 85, 90, 92, 101–103, 105–107, 121, 125, 126–131, 133–134, 138, 146, 153–156, 162–167, 169–171, 173–174, 177–178, 192, 205, 227n103, 228n110, 231n144, 237n190, 253n145, 254n155, 256n168, 266n85, 274n199, 278, 280, 289, 295, 298, 306; back-world, *arrière-monde*, 178; common, environing, *Umwelt*, 45; imaginary, 92, 183; individual, own (*eigene Welt*), self-world (*Eigenwelt*), personal, 44, 45, 53, 167, 172, 174; intentional, 83, 135; interhuman, *Mitwelt*, 45; *Weltanschauung*, *Weltansicht* (worldview), 72, 124; *Weltorientierung* (orientation in the world), 69, 71; *Weltuntergang* (end of the world), 298; world-design, 44, 146; world-project (*Weltentwurf*), xiii, 93, 97, 106, 230n136, 138, 145–146, 148, 156, 163, 192, 291. *See also Dasein* (being-in-the-world); lifeworld
Wyrsch, Jakob, 7, 39, 57, 77, 120, 215n24, 308

Yanacopoulo, Andrée, 237n194, 307
Young, Robert, 268n140, 280

Zulliger, Hans, 51
Zutt, Jürg, 77

GPSR Authorized Representative: Easy Access System Europe, Mustamäe tee 50, 10621 Tallinn, Estonia, gpsr.requests@easproject.com

www.ingramcontent.com/pod-product-compliance
Lightning Source LLC
Chambersburg PA
CBHW022029290426
44109CB00014B/801